MW01156766

War and Society in Afghanistan

War and Society
in
Afghanistan

*From the Mughals to
the Americans, 1500–2013*

KAUSHIK ROY

OXFORD
UNIVERSITY PRESS

OXFORD
UNIVERSITY PRESS

Oxford University Press is a department of the University of Oxford.
It furthers the University's objective of excellence in research, scholarship,
and education by publishing worldwide. Oxford is a registered trademark of
Oxford University Press in the UK and in certain other countries

Published in India by
Oxford University Press
YMCA Library Building, 1 Jai Singh Road, New Delhi 110001, India

© Oxford University Press 2015

The moral rights of the author have been asserted

First Edition published in 2015

All rights reserved. No part of this publication may be reproduced, stored in
a retrieval system, or transmitted, in any form or by any means, without the
prior permission in writing of Oxford University Press, or as expressly permitted
by law, by licence, or under terms agreed with the appropriate reprographics
rights organization. Enquiries concerning reproduction outside the scope of the
above should be sent to the Rights Department, Oxford University Press, at the
address above

You must not circulate this work in any other form
and you must impose this same condition on any acquirer

ISBN-13: 978-0-19-809910-9
ISBN-10: 0-19-809910-X

Typeset in ITC Giovanni Std 9.5/13
by SPEX Infotech, Puducherry, India 605 005
Printed in India by G.H. Prints Pvt Ltd, New Delhi 110 020

For Suhrita again

CONTENTS

MAPS

PREFACE

This monograph has been partly possible due to the moral and material support provided by the Centre for the Study of Civil War (CSCW), Peace Research Institute Oslo (PRIO), Norway, in 2011. Special thanks to the Norwegian Ministry of Defence, which funded a project of Professor Scott Gates (I was also a member of this project) in 2012. The conference held at Oslo (organized by Professor Scott Gates and myself) in February 2012 on the nature of counter-insurgency in Afghanistan enriched my thinking regarding the dynamics of warfare on the rugged land. The Norwegian Ministry of Defence's funding of the project under Professor Scott Gates and others on Future Warfare in 2013 has also partly aided work on this monograph. It goes without saying that the excellent library facilities of PRIO has been of great help to me. At PRIO, two individuals deserve special mention: Professor Scott Gates and the present director, Professor Kristian Berg Harpviken, without whose help the monograph could not have seen the light of the day. A portion of Chapter 5 has been published in an issue of *International Area Studies Review* (Vol. 15, No. 3, September 2012). Oxford University Press, New Delhi, deserves praise for taking interest in the Afghanistan project. Special thanks to my undergraduate students at Jadavpur University, who, during the first half of 2011 and of 2013, had to 'bear' the series of lectures on insurgency and counter-insurgency in Afghanistan as part of their course. I am indebted to my PhD student Moumita for collecting some sources on my behalf. Without a stable domestic base, a successful counter-insurgency campaign cannot be waged. Similarly, without a stable domestic front, I cannot write a book. Hence, special thanks to my wife for keeping the 'home front' stable. This book is slated to be published when the Americans are pulling out of Afghanistan and international interest once again is declining as regards this 'unfortunate' country. And for the future, it might have disastrous consequences as it had been the case in the past. Here lies the importance of this volume.

Kaushik Roy
Kolkata, 2014

ABBREVIATIONS

ADG	Adjutant-General
AFV	Armoured Fighting Vehicle
ANA	Afghan National Army
ANLF	Afghanistan National Liberation Front
ANP	Afghan National Police
ANSF	Afghan National Security Forces
APC	Armoured Personnel Carrier
BL	British Library, London
BLR	Breech Loading Rifled Gun
BMP	Boyevaya Mashina Pekhoty/Amphibious Infantry Fighting Vehicle
BTR	Bronyetransportyer/Armoured Personnel Carrier
CAS	Close Air Support
CENTCOM	Central Command
CIA	Central Intelligence Agency
CJTF	Combined Joint Task Force
COIN	Counter Insurgency
COSC	Chiefs of Staff Committee

CP	Cabinet Papers
DFID	Department for International Development
EIC	East India Company
FATA	Federally Administered Tribal Areas in Pakistan
FCO	Foreign and Commonwealth Office
FSP	Foreign Secret Proceedings
4GW	Fourth Generation Warfare
GID	General Intelligence Directorate
GOI	Government of India
GPS	Global Positioning System
GRU	Glavnoye Razvedyvatel'noye Upravleniye (Military Secret Service of the USSR)
GWOT	Global War on Terror
HD	Home Department
HUMINT	Human Intelligence
IOR	India Office Records, British Library
IRF	Immediate Response Force
ISAF	International Security Assistance Force in Afghanistan
ISI	Inter-Services Intelligence
IUA	Islamic Union for the Liberation of Afghanistan
IUAM	Islamic Unity of Afghan Mujahideen
JSS	*Journal of Strategic Studies*
KGB	Komitet gosudarstvennoy bezopasnosti/State Secret Bureau of the USSR
KIA	Killed in Action
KP	Khyber Pakhtunkhwa, new name of Pakistan's North-West Frontier Province
LOC	Line of Communication
MD	Military Department
ML	Muzzle Loader
MR	Military Revolution

MTR	Military Technical Revolution
MVD	Soviet Ministry of Internal Affairs
NAI	National Archives of India
NATO	North Atlantic Treaty Organization
NCO	Non-Commissioned Officer
NIFA	National Islamic Front of Afghanistan
NIR	Native (Indian) Infantry Regiment
NMML	Nehru Memorial Museum and Library
NWFP	North-West Frontier Province
OEF	Operation Enduring Freedom
Offg.	Officiating
OODA	Observe, Orient, Decide, and Act
PDPA	The People's Democratic Party of Afghanistan, that is, the Communist Party of Afghanistan
PFF	Punjab Frontier Force
PGM	Precision-Guided Munition
PIF	Punjab Irregular Force
PRO	Public Records Office, London. Now known as The National Archives (TNA)
PRT	Provincial Reconstruction Team
QF	Quick Firing
QMG	Quarter-Master General
RA	Royal Artillery
RAF	Royal Air Force
RBL	Rifled Breech Loader
RDF	Rapid Deployment Force
RE	Royal Engineer
RFA	Royal Field Artillery
RHA	Royal Horse Artillery
RMA	Revolution in Military Affairs
RML	Rifled Muzzle Loader

SALT	Strategic Arms Limitation Treaty
Secy.	Secretary
SIGINT	Signal Intelligence
SOF	Special Operation Force, that is, elite units of the US armed forces who specialize in conducting irregular operations
SSG	Special Services Group
UAV	Unmanned Aerial Vehicle
UKTF	United Kingdom Task Force
UN	United Nations
VCO	Viceroy's Commissioned Officer, also known as 'Native' Officers
WIA	Wounded in Action
ZSU 23-4	Zenitnaya Samokhodnaya Ustanovka 23-4/Self-propelled air defence weapon system. It fires four 23-mm machine guns simultaneously

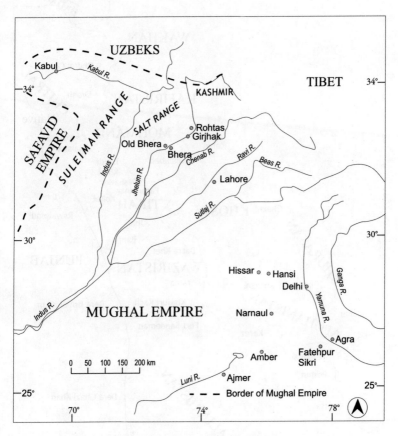

Map 1 Mughal North-West Frontier

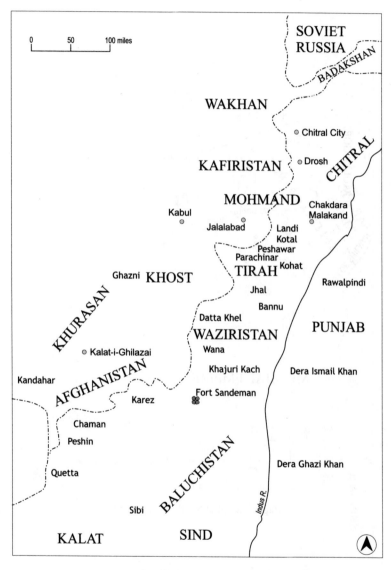

Map 2 British India's North-West Frontier, c. 1900

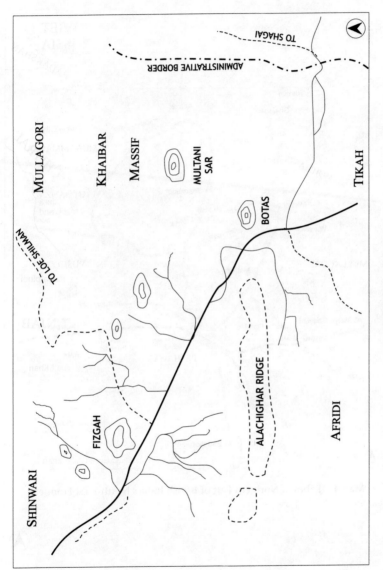

Map 3   Khaibar Pass

Map 4 Tribes of Northern Part of British India's North-West Frontier

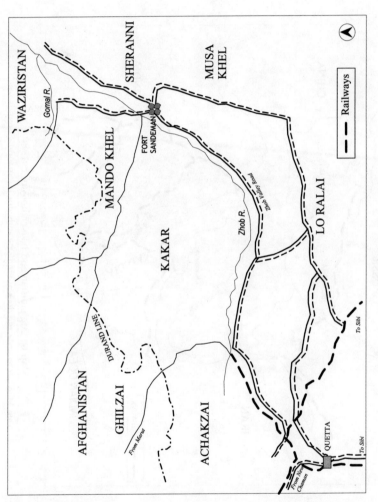

Map 5 Zhob Valley

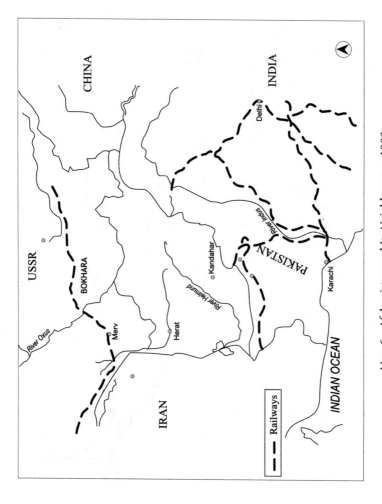

Map 6 Afghanistan and Its Neighbours, c. 1980

Note: Map not to scale and does not indicate authentic international boundaries.

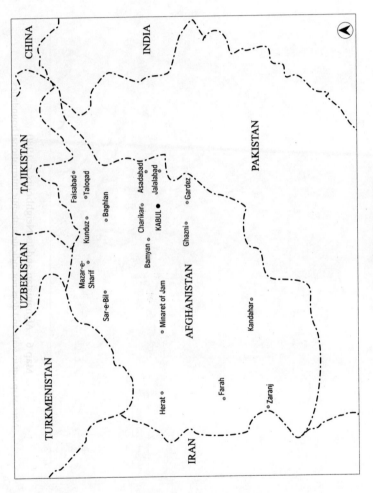

Map 7 Afghanistan 2000

Note: Map not to scale and does not indicate authentic international boundaries.

INTRODUCTION

AFTER OPERATION ENDURING FREEDOM (OEF), publications regarding the insurgency in Afghanistan have proliferated. Most of the books and articles focus on the recent developments. Some of them trace the lineages of the present fragmentation of Afghanistan back to the Soviet invasion of the 1980s.[1] A few scholars go back to the triple British invasions of Afghanistan.[2] Some have even attempted to show that the Afghans from the dawn of civilization have proved to be tough opponents.[3] David Loyn's and Paddy Docherty's narratives attempt to provide a clinical perspective by the 'men from the spot'. Both had travelled around Afghanistan and tried to cull out the specific features of warfare in Afghanistan. Moreover, Loyn's and Docherty's monographs somewhat forcibly try to assert what the British and Americans at present can learn from Afghan military history. On the other hand, several historical works do not strictly follow a utilitarian perspective. T.A. Heathcote, Edgar O'Ballance, and Stephen Tanner, despite following a historical perspective, do not use archival sources in a critical manner.

In contrast, this volume attempts to understand the formation and breakdown of the state and its effect on society in Afghanistan due to the dynamics of warfare on a *longue durée*. Our journey starts from the pre-modern era. This is because great power rivalries, attempts at empire

2 WAR AND SOCIETY IN AFGHANISTAN

building, and in reaction to it, internal rebellions by the Afghans started long before the arrival of the British and Americans on the frontier of Afghanistan. This book tries to analyse why the Mughals, British, Soviets, and Americans won the conventional wars but were defeated in the unconventional wars in Afghanistan.

In this book, the term 'counter-insurgency' (hereafter COIN) comprises all sorts of non-conventional operations. So, COIN is equivalent to irregular war/unconventional war/'small war'/sub-conventional operations/low-intensity conflicts, and so on. Special emphasis is given to ecology, terrain, and logistics to explain sub-conventional operations and state building in Afghanistan. Though the focus remains on unconventional warfare, conventional warfare is not neglected totally. This is because throughout history, COIN and conventional warfare have been interrelated. Hence, attention will be given to conventional operations to show the linkages between the two forms of war. Politics and diplomacy, the two crucial components of COIN, remain in the background. The result is roughly a political and military narrative of Afghanistan's conventional and unconventional warfare for the last five centuries based on a synthesis of primary and secondary sources. An attempt is made here to contextualize the Afghan 'problem' as part of the wider struggle among the great powers for controlling the 'heart' of Eurasia. The Afghan response, that is, guerrilla war against the imperial powers with conventional military superiority, is also contextualized in the wider context of such a struggle led by other Eurasian tribes like the Basmachi and the Chechens against the Soviets/Russians. Further, unlike most of the present Western accounts of warfare in Afghanistan, this volume also delineates the role of regional powers like Iran (Persia of pre-modern era), Central Asia, and India (and after 1947, Pakistan) in shaping the contours of the Afghan struggle. Thus, this book does not deal merely with how the Afghans fought but also how the great powers fought in Afghanistan. Unlike most of the present publications, the objective is not to privilege the last 50 years over the last 500 years of Afghanistan's history.

Chapter 1 charts empire building, conventional military operations, and COIN in Afghanistan in the pre-modern era, that is, under the Mughals. The tripolar Mughal–Safavid–Uzbek rivalry and its effect on Afghanistan are brought under the scanner. Since Afghanistan is an economically deficit region, poppy cultivation, loot and plunder of the surrounding sedentary civilizations, along with military service was the mainstay for the male populace of the region. The Mughals failed to control the tribal *sirdars* at the local levels who sponsored insurgencies in the 'badlands' of present Pakistan. This in turn resulted in the Mughals launching regular annual expeditions against the tribal areas. The heavy Mughal cavalry columns were often ambushed along the narrow mountainous tracks by the nimble Afghans fighting from the mountain tops. Inter-state rivalry between Persia and Mughal India over Kandahar and decline of the Safavids resulted in a unified Afghan monarchy which became a threat to both the Safavid and Mughal empires. At this stage (i.e., during the 1750s), the Afghan threat escalated from sub-conventional to the conventional level.

Chapter 2 analyses regular and irregular warfare in Afghanistan under the British era. The dialectical relationship between social and political conditions within Afghanistan and turbulence in its foreign policy has been chalked out in detail. By the mid-nineteenth century, the previous tripolar struggle over Afghanistan was replaced by bipolar struggle between Russia and Britain. The complex interconnections between North-West Frontier defence against the Pathans/Pashtuns/ Pushtuns and power projection in Afghanistan in response to the Russian threat remain the focus of this chapter. The British doctrine of Small War partly developed in relation to operations in Afghanistan during the late nineteenth century. This doctrine gave birth to Britain's COIN doctrine of the twentieth century (which was used in Malaya, and so on). Just like the Mughals, the British realized that continuous instability in Afghanistan resulted in the Small Wars becoming hot wars, that is, the three Afghans Wars (1839–42, 1878–80, 1919). The Mughal *mansabdars* and the British generals during operations in Afghanistan from their bases in north-west India found out that more than 50 per cent of the units were tied up in guarding the long line of communications (LOCs). And the LOCs suffered from continuous harassing attacks from the Afghan *lashkars*. Both the British and the Mughal invading armies had to retreat because there was no permanent objective to capture and the land was too infertile to support a big invasion army. Since Afghanistan was not a state in the Westphalian model, the capture of the capital, Kabul, did not result in control over the territory of Afghanistan. And once the Afghan regular army was destroyed, innumerable war bands under the clan leaders emerged all along the countryside like a hydra-headed monster. During the 1919 Third Afghan War and the subsequent Waziristan Campaign, the British found out that light tanks and armoured cars were useless when the Afghans blocked the narrow roads in the valleys by rolling boulders. Rather, light infantry skilled in road-opening duties and escorting convoys were more important. Continuous pacification campaigns were conducted by the British in Waziristan to seal off the (present Pakistan) border with Afghanistan in order to prevent the local Pathans/Pushtuns in Waziristan from providing logistical support to the insurgents roaming in southern Afghanistan. It is to be noted that the Taliban–Al-Qaeda Pushtun personnel, even now, acquire logistical support from the Pushtuns of north Pakistan. And at present, Waziristan is witnessing a massive pacification campaign by the Pakistan army (due to US pressure) in order to prevent infiltration of the insurgents from southern Afghanistan into Pakistan and vice versa.

Chapter 3 deals with the Russian intervention in Afghanistan. This chapter focuses on the emergence of the fragile 'rentier state' in the post–World War II era. A political scientist, Barnett R. Rubin, introduced the concept of rentier state in an article published in 1992 and then elaborated it in a book published in 1995. In his paradigm, the roots of the rentier state could be traced back to the era after the Second Anglo-Afghan War (1878–80), when the Afghan ruling elites became dependent on subsidy from foreign countries for expanding the state apparatus. Due to flow of cash from a neighbouring strong power, the ruling elites had no incentive to bargain or enter into negotiations with the local elites within the country. The net result was expansion of the state apparatus but there was no concomitant representation by the citizens. Instead of taxation and representation, a patron–client relationship held the state together. Such a state was not accountable to its subjects. Hence, such a state, though superficially strong, was weak in reality. And once the foreign aid ceased, the state was bound to disintegrate. Rubin continues that during the latter half of the nineteenth century, state building in Afghanistan was dependent on subsidies from Britain. In the post–World War II era, the principal supplier of cash (as foreign aid and in return for purchase of natural gas) from abroad was the USSR. Till 1991, aid to Kabul constituted the largest item in the Soviet foreign aid budget. Once the USSR collapsed, without foreign aid, the Najibullah regime cracked.[4]

It is true that the Afghan state even under strong rulers in both the pre-modern and modern eras was like the Wizard of Oz: strong in appearance but weak in reality. Ahmad Shah Abdali had to depend on loot and plunder in India to sustain state building in Afghanistan. When his successors failed in raiding India for booties, as Chapter 1 shows, the Abdali polity cracked. Chapter 2 shows that powerful rulers like Amir Dost Muhammad and Amir Abd al Rahman Khan were not overtly dependent on British subsidy which amounted to little. Besides our analysis of archival documents, two books by Christine Noelle and Hasan Kakar,[5] which detail the internal conditions of Afghanistan under Dost Muhammad and Abd al Rahman Khan respectively, show no trace of a rentier state emerging in late nineteenth-century Afghanistan. However, Rubin's rentier state model applies well during the 1950–80 eras in Afghanistan. Even the Hamid Karzai government in the new millennium is dependent on financial aid from Western countries (especially the USA).

The structural weakness of state building in Afghanistan in the mid-twentieth century and the 'Afghan Revolution' in the 1970s leading to the Soviet invasion and its consequences are discussed in detail in Chapter 3. Whether *mujahideen* victory against the 'Godless Soviets' was inevitable and how far the USA was responsible for Soviet withdrawal from Afghanistan are the two principal issues analysed in the latter sections of this chapter. The USSR directly intervened in Afghanistan in 1979. A modern armoured heavy conventional army failed against the irregular opponents (at its peak, there were about 70,000 lightly armed mujahideens and, of them, 20,000 were fighting at any time), thus vindicating the British and Mughal experiences; for instance, the Battles of Zhawar (September 1985–April 1986) fought near the Pakistan–Afghanistan border. The mujahideens, in the complex centred around the caves, were supplied from Pakistan through Miran Shah. Even the Soviet air attacks on the caves with smart munitions did not prove that effective, just as British artillery attacks against the *sangar*s proved to be ineffective during the second decade of the twentieth century. The Soviet ground force attacked in the traditional World War I style. First heavy artillery opened up and then the infantry advanced. The mujahideen were tipped by the opening of artillery barrage that the Soviet ground attack was forthcoming. With the beginning of the artillery barrage, the mujahideen took cover in the caves and after the end of the artillery barrage, they opened up on the advancing Soviet infantry with machine guns and rocket launchers. Several MI-8 helicopters used for ferrying Spetsnaz troops were also lost during the course of the operation. Mughal heavy cavalry, British heavy field artillery, and Soviet Armoured Fighting Vehicles (AFVs) proved useless in the roadless and bridgeless Afghan terrain.

Between 1980 and 1985, the Soviets bombed the villages, and destroyed the granaries and the irrigation systems in order to eliminate the villagers' support for the mujahideen. This resulted in 7 million Afghans becoming refugees. Some of them migrated to Iran and most of them settled in north-west Pakistan. Many of these young male refugees later swelled the mujahideen ranks. Soviet firepower-heavy COIN operations (using fixed wing assault aircraft, helicopter gunships, and commandos) and forcible transfer of population (similar to the British technique used in Malaya against the Chinese immigrants) backfired as it alienated even the moderate Afghans. Lack of respect for Afghan culture and Islam and a rigid imposition of inflexible Marxist doctrine further made the scenario worse for the Soviets. The role of the USA in strengthening the mujahideen will be focused upon. For pricking the Bear, the Central Intelligence Agency (CIA) funded and equipped the *jihadis* with Stingers and other high-technology hand-held weapons. The Pushtunistan dispute which resulted in tension between Afghanistan and Pakistan over the Durand Line resulted in Pakistan supporting the Islamist political groups rather than the comparatively 'nationalist' elements within the Afghan mujahideen. The spread of *madrasa*s in Zia-ul-Haq's Pakistan (USA's 'all weather' ally) constituted the seedbed of the rise of the Al-Qaeda and the Taliban. This monograph argues that social and political conditions in present-day Af–Pak border are related with changing conditions within India over a *longue durée*. Sana Haroon shows that the rise of Deobandi Islam could be traced back to the United Provinces (present-day Uttar Pradesh) in India during mid-nineteenth century. 'Communal' hard-line Islamist groups strengthened their hold in North-West Frontier Province (NWFP) during late nineteenth and early twentieth centuries. And social and political developments in Pakistan after 1947 allowed the Deobandi *mullah*s to strengthen their control in the 'badlands' of Pakistan. Initially, the jihadis/mujahideens fought the 'Godless Soviets'. And after the retreat of Soviet Union from Afghanistan, they turned their attention against the capitalist West. The Deobandi mullahs and their *murid*s played an important role in the rise of the Taliban and now are supporting the neo-Taliban.[6]

Chapter 4 turns the focus on the Americans and the North Atlantic Treaty Organization (NATO) activities in Afghanistan. The effectiveness of British philosophy of 'minimum force' vis-à-vis 'brute force' approach of the Americans in COIN is assessed in the Afghan context. This chapter compares and contrasts the US peacekeeping activities in Afghanistan with that of Iraq. Iraq and Afghanistan, though dissimilar in many ways, are also similar to an extent. The United States is at present the world's sole superpower. With 2 million uniformed personnel in the military and a budget of half a trillion dollars per year (2007), the armed forces of the USA are the strongest on planet Earth.[7] The real problem for the USA in Afghanistan started after the end of OEF, which proved to be a hollow victory. Similarly, the full blast of insurgency hit US forces in Iraq after the regular forces of Saddam Hussein folded up during Operation Iraqi Freedom (or the Second Gulf War). In both Afghanistan and Iraq, a large number of US troops are engaged in a quagmire and a quick victory is not in sight. Intervention in another trouble spot (North Korea or Iran in the near future) would result in an overstretch of US capabilities. It seems that the US and its ally the NATO are in a lose–lose situation. The tribal structure is more powerful in Afghanistan while the reach of the state throughout history has been stronger in *Ajam* (Arabic name for Iraq). The Americans are still debating about how many troops are required for policing Afghanistan with 31 million people and Iraq with a populace of 27 million. Recently, the US pulled out troops from Iraq but the insurgency remains.

The last chapter is both prescriptive and descriptive in nature. Chapter 5 attempts to contextualize the nature of the ongoing war in Afghanistan in the context of recent debates regarding the changing character of war in the twenty-first century. The so-called Revolution in Military Affairs (RMA, especially centring around information technology which some pundits presumed started in the late 1980s) is of no use for fighting the insurgents in Afghanistan. Technology is no panacea for tackling the problems posed by the light-footed armed insurgents. Cruise missiles, smart weapons, and Black Hawk helicopters proved useless against the AK-47 of the Afghan jihadis just as Sniders and Vickers guns of the British proved useless against the *jezails* of Afghan jihadis in the late nineteenth century. Those who do not learn from history are bound to repeat the mistakes, which leads us to conclude that the US focus should be on human intelligence (HUMINT) and not on signal intelligence (SIGINT). Instead of armoured/motorized formations, air mobile brigade should be used for rapid transport of troops to quell disturbances in the inaccessible regions. The US–NATO, like the Russians, erroneously use ground attack helicopters and aircraft. This results in collateral damage and loss of legitimacy for the coalition forces. It is to be noted that Field Marshal Rawlinson (commander-in-chief, British India, from 1920 to 1925) did not allow the Royal Air Force (RAF) to bomb the Afghan and the Indus tribesmen. A successful COIN operation needs to be a 'just war'. Stability in Afghanistan requires holding the ground with a large infantry army. What is required is 'bite and hold' strategy with large ground forces. The US should use local Afghan armies for conducting close-quarter small-scale combat with Al-Qaeda and Taliban, and this requires 'hugging tactics'. Fighting from a distance with missiles remains ineffective. Like the British Indian infantry, the US–NATO troops require light ambush drill, picketing the mountaintops and sides of the hills. The US–NATO military planners would do well to read Charles Callwell's chapter on mountain war in his magnum opus titled *Small Wars* published in 1896.

Within the US military and the NATO at least some officers are tinkering with new ideas about how to win COIN operations and the ways to engage in nation-building tasks in the 'enemy' country. Douglas M. Macgregor (a retired American officer who wrote a book titled *Breaking the Phalanx*)[8] argues that the hierarchical structure of the US military forces need to be flattened to enable quick flow of information from top to bottom and vice versa, and this would allow the men on the spots to take quick decisions which would enable them to get inside the enemy's Observe, Orient, Decide, and Act (OODA) loop. Here, we are back at the American officer-turned-scholar John Boyd's OODA loop which was initially designed to implement rapid manoeuvre campaigns (involving air–land battles) based on *Auftragstaktik* (mission-oriented command system) against the Soviet forces in central Europe. Overall, the American and Canadian commanders are impressed with the retired British General Rupert Smith's concept as formulated in his book *The Utility of Force* (2007).[9] Several American officers are arguing that they need a new COIN doctrine which will focus not on the enemy (i.e., not to concentrate on the number of enemy soldiers killed) but on the common people of the regions dominated by insurgency. So, the focus is on a people-centric COIN, a concept somewhat similar to Rupert Smith's concept of fighting the 'war amongst the people'.

Increasing the level of US troops, as the Obama administration has proclaimed, will not be of much use for pacifying Afghanistan. Even with 30,000 of 'surge troops' (temporary US reinforcements in 2009), the US–NATO were not able to achieve much, as in 1986, the Soviets had greater number of soldiers compared to the US-led coalition. Still the Soviets failed. The US and the NATO needed to streamline their cumbersome command systems instead of merely increasing their numerical presence. A unified joint command both as regards civil and military affairs need to be set up in Afghanistan for the coalition and indigenous forces.

It is to be noted that the local Afghan forces played a vital role in ousting the Al-Qaeda and Taliban, especially from north Afghanistan during OEF. These forces should be equipped and trained by the US–NATO forces and officers from the NATO and US armies should learn the local vernaculars and function as trainers and officers. The British practised this technique and built up the combat-effective and loyal Indian army during the late nineteenth century. At present there is a debate whether to organize the Afghan National Army (ANA) as mixed units (various communities recruited from diverse regions were organized in companies of a particular regiment) or class units (comprising a particular community from a particular region constituting a regiment). The Soviet experiment with mixed units for the Afghan army failed miserably during the 1980s. Class units have better motivational strength. The British Indian army of the nineteenth century and the present Indian army with their mixed and class regiments could provide a model for the security managers associated with organizing the ANA. The Afghan security forces (war bands of the warlords) could function as paramilitaries. The British had a number of them like the Khaibar Rifles, Tochi Scouts, and so on, during the late nineteenth century. At present, the USA, instead of focusing primarily on equipping and training the Afghan National Police (ANP) and ANA, are crying for more military manpower from the NATO states. Due to lax discipline, inadequate training, and paucity of funds, the desertion rates from the ANP and the ANA are quite high and the combat effectiveness of the latter two organizations is extremely low.

Can we speak of a Western way of warfare, and is it failing in Afghanistan? Further, is Afghan resistance a part and parcel of asymmetric war or is there a specific 'Afghan way of warfare'? These are some of the issues discussed in the last chapter. Afghanistan is probably neither experiencing a New War nor can it be described as Fourth Generation Warfare (4GW).[10] Despite considerable technological change, the nature of the conflict in Afghanistan has exhibited a remarkable level of continuity from the Mughal to the recent era. In spite of advances in technology, physical geography, cultural characteristics, and historical factors restrict the degree to which 'rebel' activities can be suppressed by the state-sponsored pacification campaigns.

This volume takes a long sweep of about five centuries. The monograph is a synthesis of published works and archival research. While Chapter 1 depends mostly on the translated Persian histories and memoirs of the Mughal emperors and accounts written by the Mughal scholar officials, Chapter 2 is based on archival materials gathered from the British Library, Public Records Office, Kew, and the National Archives of India. In addition, Chapter 2 also utilizes official and quasi-official histories of campaigns, regimental histories, and memoirs of the British officers stationed in India. Chapters 3 and 4 depend on the autobiographies of those officers who participated in the war in Afghanistan and also on the official and semi-official documents, and newspaper and journal articles (many of them penned by the participants) which have been released in the public domain.

One problem with the sources is that most of them are generated not by the Afghans but by their enemies, that is, the big powers like Mughals, British, and the Americans who fought and are still fighting in Afghanistan for their own objectives. Abdulkader H. Sinno writes that the Chechens and the Afghans epitomize societies that preserve their clan and tribe-based acephalous social structure and oral culture. They come together temporarily under one regional and, at times, ethnic or nationwide banner to resist the invader. The large-scale *jihad*s that they had waged in history are engraved in societal consciousness through poetry and story telling.[11] But lack of written accounts from the Afghan side has made it difficult, if not impossible, to portray the Afghan side of the story in a balanced manner. Recently, a British historian has made a courageous attempt to portray the cultural ingredients of war making by the Afghans. However, lack of adequate sources generated by the Afghans somewhat mars his effort.[12] Now, let us turn the focus on early sixteenth-century Afghanistan.

NOTES

1. Abdulkader H. Sinno, *Organizations at War in Afghanistan and Beyond* (Ithaca/London: Cornell University Press, 2008); William Maley, *The Afghanistan Wars* (2002; reprint, London: Palgrave Macmillan, 2009); Larry P. Goodson, *Afghanistan's Endless War: State Failure, Regional Politics and the Rise of the Taliban* (Seattle/London: University of Washington Press, 2001).

2. See, for instance, T.A. Heathcote, *The Afghan Wars: 1839–1919* (1980, reprint, Gloucestershire: Spellmount, 2007); Edgar O'Ballance, *Afghan Wars: Battles in a Hostile Land 1839 to the Present* (2002; reprint, Karachi: Oxford University Press, 2003); David Loyn, *In Afghanistan: Two Hundred Years of British, Russian and American Occupation* (New York: Palgrave Macmillan, 2009); Victoria Schofield, *Afghan Frontier: At the Crossroads of Conflict* (2003; reprint, London: I.B. Tauris, 2010). To be fair to Schofield, she gives a sketchy account of Afghanistan's political and military history from the time of Alexander's invasion. Paddy Docherty in *The Khyber Pass: A History of Empire and Invasion* (London: Faber and Faber, 2007) portrays the historical importance of Khyber/Khaibar Pass. It is a lucid narrative lacking in analysis.

3. See, for instance, Stephen Tanner, *Afghanistan: A Military History from Alexander the Great to the Fall of the Taliban* (New York: Da Capo, 2002).

4. Barnett R. Rubin, 'Political Elites in Afghanistan: Rentier State Building, Rentier State Wrecking', *International Journal of Middle East Studies* 24, 1 (1992): 77–89; Rubin, *The Fragmentation of Afghanistan: State Formation and Collapse in the International System* (1995; reprint, New Haven/London: Yale University Press, 2002).

5. Christine Noelle, *State and Tribe in Nineteenth-Century Afghanistan: The Reign of Amir Dost Muhammad Khan (1826–1863)* (1997; reprint, London/New York: Routledge, 2008); M. Hassan Kakar, *A Political and Diplomatic History of Afghanistan: 1863–1901* (Leiden: Brill, 2006).

6. Sana Haroon, 'The Rise of Deobandi Islam in the North-West Frontier Province and its Implications in Colonial India and Pakistan 1914–1996', *Journal of Royal Asiatic Society*, Series 3, 18, 1 (2008): 47–70.

7. Peter W. Chiarelli and Stephen M. Smith, 'Learning from Our Modern Wars: The Imperatives of Preparing for a Dangerous Future', *Military Review* (Sept–Oct 2007): 2–15.

8. Douglas A. Macgregor, *Breaking the Phalanx: A New Design for Landpower in the 21st Century* (Westport, Connecticut/London: Praeger, 1997).

9. Rupert Smith, *The Utility of Force: The Art of War in the Modern World* (2005; reprint, London: Penguin, 2006).

10. Colonel Thomas X. Hammes, *The Sling and the Stone: On War in the 21st Century* (St Paul, MN: Zenith Press, 2006).

11. Sinno, *Organizations at War in Afghanistan and Beyond*, 85.

12. Rob Johnson, *The Afghan Way of War: Culture and Pragmatism, A Critical History* (London: Hurst & Co., 2011).

1

MUGHAL EMPIRE AND WARFARE IN AFGHANISTAN
1500–1810

AFGHANISTAN COMPRISES AN AREA OF about 250,000 square miles. The north and the east consist of mountain systems which emerge from the tablelands of Pamirs. Northern and southern parts of the Afghanistan were known in the medieval era as Kabulistan and Zabulistan.[1] The eastern fringe of the country is mountainous, especially in the north-east where the protruding Wakhan Corridor joins the Pamirs. Elevations frequently exceed 10,000 feet and forests appear at medium elevations. The Paropamisus extends eastwards from Herat and merges into the Hindu Kush north of Kabul. The Hindu Kush merges with the Pamirs and Karakoram ranges in the north-east. Central mountainous region, the Hindu Kush, forms an obstruction as regards communications across the centre of the country. The Hindu Kush Mountains descend from the Wakhan Corridor and bisect Afghanistan. These mountains average 14,769 to 19,692 feet in height in the zone around Kabul, with some peaks as high as 24,615 feet in the north-east. In the centre of the country, the Hindu Kush broadens out into the high Hazarajat Plateau which descends and disappears into the western deserts on the Persian (Iranian) border (Registan, Dasht-i-Margo, Dasht-i-Lut). The Turkoman Plain, characterized by sandy desert and scattered scrub grasses, dominates the northern edge of Afghanistan. The Herat–Farah lowlands in the west are part of the Iranian plateau and some regions of it are suitable for cultivation. South-western Afghanistan is mostly sandy desert.[2] Persia's (Iran) frontier lies west of Herat, from Zulfiqar in the north to Koh-i-Malik Siah in the south, spanning across a distance of about 400 miles.[3] The area north of Hindu Kush, known as Afghan Turkestan, is part of the Central Asian plains.

The Kabul River forms part of the Indus River system, whereas the dry western and south-western parts of Afghanistan geographically are a continuation of the Iranian Plateau.[4] Except the Kabul River, all the rivers of Afghanistan lie within the interior drainage basin of Central Eurasia. None of them reach the ocean. Most of the northern rivers even fail to reach the Amu drainage but provide water for irrigation for the cities from Tashqurghan to Maimana. The Helmand River and its tributaries end up in the desert marshes of Seistan near the Persian (Iran) border squeezed between Registan (Land of Sand) and the Dasht-i-Margo (Waterless Plain of Death). The Kabul River does connect with the Indus River just east of Peshawar (now in Pakistan), and descends rapidly through many deep gorges. Hence, it is not navigable but could be crossed by boats or inflated goatskins. In the absence of navigable rivers, the principal means of transport in Afghanistan till the twentieth century were the mules, camels, and pack horses.[5]

The origin of the Afghans is still debated. The Iranians, Greeks, and Scythians (Aryan stock) settled in Afghanistan between third and first century BCE. Nineteenth-century British scholar-officials of the Raj believed in the Armenian and Jewish origin of the Afghans.[6] H.W. Bellew, the Sanitary Commissioner of Punjab, in an article dated 1881 asserted that the Afghans were partly Israelites. The Afghans belonged to the 'lost tribes of Israel'. The Assyrian ruler Tiglath Pilesar captured many Israelites and they were settled in Ghor in around 700 BCE. The Israelites intermixed with the Arians (Bellew meant Aryans) who were the original inhabitants of Afghanistan. Bellew divided the Arians into eastern (Indian) Arian and western (Persian) Arian. The Persian Arians were Tajiks and inhabited western Afghanistan. The eastern Arians, who inhabited eastern Afghanistan, were later known as Pathans. They were very similar to the Kshatriyas (Rajputs) of India. In addition, in the mountainous fastness, lived the Turanian (Mongol) people. Further, intermixture occurred with the coming of the Scythians

(Sakas, Parthians, Huns, and so on) from north of the River Oxus (Amu Darya) into Afghanistan after the Common Era. The Scythians especially settled in Seistan and in the Kandahar region. Overall, in Bellew's format, the Mongols were in north Afghanistan, Arians in southern Afghanistan, and the Semitic people were sandwiched between them in central Afghanistan.[7]

Olaf Caroe, writing in the 1950s, divided the Afghans into Eastern and Western Afghans. Among the Western Afghans he includes the Saduzois (who ruled Afghanistan from 1747 to 1818) and the Muhammadzais (who reigned in Afghanistan from 1826 till the 1950s). And among the Eastern Afghans he includes the Shinwaris (around Khaibar), Mohmands, Daudzais, and Khalils (inhabiting the region around Peshawar), and the Yusufzais (Dir, Swat, and Buner region).[8] A somewhat similar division of the Pathans/Pushtuns/Pashtuns is followed by the modern anthropologist Thomas Barfield. In his estimate, the Pashtuns comprise some 40 per cent of Afghanistan's population. Barfield divides the Pashtuns into western Durrani Pashtuns and eastern Gilzai Pashtuns. While the Durrani Pashtuns are more hierarchical, the Gilzai Pashtuns, in his eyes, are more egalitarian in their tribal framework.[9]

Nirodbhusan Roy asserts that the Afghan 'race' sprang from the intermixture of Scythian and Jewish colonists. The tribes who inhabited eastern Afghanistan, especially the region west of the Indus River, were called Pathans by the nineteenth-century British officials. Now they are called Pashtuns/Pustuns. According to one tradition, the word Pathan is a corrupted version of Pahtan which was derived from the word Batan. The word means 'delivered', 'set free'.[10] The Pathans would prove it by repeatedly rising against all sort of foreign regimes throughout history.

One Muslim chronicler who wrote in around tenth century CE noted that Kabul was inhabited by the Buddhists, Jews, and the Muslims. The Arabs entered Afghanistan after seventh century CE. Islam accompanied the Arab force which under Qutaiba entered Afghanistan by the end of seventh century CE. Many of the Arabs were from Prophet's own family. The many groups of Pathans who claim to be Sayyids or Quraish probably have sprung from them. Conversion of the Afghans into Muslims was not complete even during twelfth century CE.[11] Most of the inhabitants from the medieval era have been

Muslims and the majority belongs to the Sunni faith. At present, about 85 per cent of Afghanistan's inhabitants are Sunnis and the rest 15 per cent are Shias and Ismailis.[12] Among the various tribes, the Durranis from Zamindwar and Ghor were dominant. Many of them settled in Derajat and Multan in India.[13] Most of the Afghans were intensely Islamic and generally maintained long beards.[14] Jos Gommans writes that the pre-modern Afghans had the triple identities of being shepherds, traders, and cavalrymen. The Afghans of Gilzai and Lodhi tribes participated in long-distance trade with Central Asia and India.[15] Wheat bread (*nan*) still remains the basic diet of the Afghans.[16] Till the nineteenth century, the Afghans were addicted to a local wine, referred to as 'grape juice'. It was purified in clay vats and then boiled and poured into goatskins. It was said to improve after two years, and one British officer declared during the early nineteenth century that it tasted like Madeira.[17]

BEGINNING OF MUGHAL INTERVENTION IN AFGHANISTAN: FROM BABUR TO HUMAYUN, 1504–56

The Mughal intervention in Afghanistan started with the Chaghtai Turkish warlord named Zahir-ud-din Muhammad Babur, the founder of the Mughal empire. In June 1494, Babur (b. 14 February 1483, d. 1530), at the tender age of eleven, became the ruler of Ferghana. Ferghana is an oasis between the deserts of Khiva and the Takla Makan, and now in Uzbekistan. On the east of Ferghana is Kasghar; Samarkhand is on its west; and the mountains of Badakshan are in the south.[18] Babur's motley force comprised 2,000 Mongol cavaliers. When Babur was nineteen, he captured Samarkhand.[19] In 1501, at the Battle of Sar-i-Pul, the Uzbek *sirdar* Shaibani Khan defeated Babur.[20] In 1502, Shaibani Khan could mobilize some 60,000 soldiers. His personal force comprised some 30,000 cavalry.[21] He was the most powerful man in Central Asia. After being unsuccessful to found a kingdom in Central Asia, in 1504, Babur decided to move into Afghanistan. Due to Shaibani Khan's depredations, many Badakshanis joined Babur's party.[22]

Babur provides description of Afghan defensive combat techniques: 'I first heard the word *sangar* after coming to Kabul where people describe fortifying themselves on a hill as making a sangar.'[23] At that time, Sayyid Ali Khan was the ruler of Kabul. He owed allegiance to Sultan Sikander Lodhi of Delhi (r. 1489–1517).[24] By September 1504, Babur had captured Kabul (the biggest city in Afghanistan) and made it the capital of his Afghan principality. Babur in his memoir describes Kabul as a multi-ethnic city where various languages like Arabi, Farsi, Turki, Hindi, Afghani, Lamghani, Pashai, Paraji, and so on, were spoken. Afghans, Turks, Mongols, Arabs, and Iranians—some of them peasants, others merchants who moved in armed caravans, and so on—populated Kabul.[25] Ghazni (at that time also known as Zabulistan) was captured in October 1504.[26] At that time, Herat was under the Timurid Sultan Husain Bauqara, and his sons controlled parts of Khorasan.[27] Herat is located at an elevation of 920 metres in an arid zone experiencing hot currents of air in the summer. The name of the city Herat is derived from the river Harirud which flows from the mountains to the Herat–Farah lowlands. Herat is mainly populated by the Persian-speaking populace.[28] In 1505, the fort of Khilat-i-Ghilzai, situated half-way between Ghazni and Kandahar, was captured by Babur. Babur's victory was due to his generalship as well as the technological advantage which his army enjoyed over the tribes of Afghanistan. While the Afghan tribes were mostly armed with bows, Babur's soldiers possessed firearms.[29] Babur's Kabul *vilayat* extended from Peshawar in the east, including Lamghan, up to Kohistan in the west comprising the mountainous region of Ghor. In the north, Babur's control extended up to the Hindu Kush Mountains including Andarab and Kunduz provinces and in the south up to Farmul, Bannu, Nanghar, and the Suleiman Mountains southeast of Kabul.[30] Eastern Afghanistan is the wettest part of the country and the only place where natural forests are found. The drier winds from Central Eurasia are blocked by the Hindu Kush and Pamir chains. The grape-growing region of Parwan is north of Kabul and the grain belt in the Logar Valley is south of Kabul.[31]

Babur mainly faced rural insurgencies. Afghanistan even today is a land of small villages. Approximately, 80 per cent of the population lives in the rural countryside. Village houses on the plains still are surrounded by 3- to 4-metre-high mud walls. Such fortified houses are known as *qala* houses.[32] Babur rewarded his loyal *begs* by distributing the villages to them. In 1506, Babur conducted a COIN campaign against the rebellious Hazaras. The Hazaras are actually a Central Asian Turkish group and inhabited the Hazara District east of the River Indus.

Their homeland is known as Hazarat, in the central region of Hindu Kush. There are Shia Muslims who engage in alpine subsistence agriculture and livestock breeding. Today the Hazaras, according to an estimate, make up some 15 per cent of Afghanistan's population. As punishment, he collected sheep and horses from them and about eighty Hazaras were executed. While coming back from the Hazara expedition, Babur collected revenue from Baran. A detachment under the joint command of Jahangir Mirza and Kasim Beg stormed the sangars at the hilltops which were defended by the rebellious Afghans.[33] Babur levied 400,000 *shahrukis* from Bhira on the left bank of the River Jhelum as the price for protection. Hindu Beg was assigned the revenues of this region for maintenance of the troops required for policing. The headmen of Bhira were assembled and Babur fixed the ransom as 1,000 shahrukis per head. Khushab on the right bank of Jhelum was assigned to Shah Hasan. Shah Hasan was ordered that he should assist Hindu Beg in maintaining law and order in this region.[34] Nevertheless, Babur did not tolerate his soldiery unnecessarily disturbing the Afghans. For instance, in February 1519, when it was reported to him that some of his soldiers without reason were robbing the people of Bhira, he ordered the ringleaders to be executed. And the other guilty soldiers had their noses slit and then marched throughout the camp and were discharged from the army.[35] Babur also followed marital alliance in order to co-opt potentially rebellious subjects within his realm. To give an example, Babur married the daughter of the Yusufzai sirdar in order to conciliate the Yusufzais. Actually, in 1519, Babur was contemplating an expedition against the Swatis and the Yusufzais. Then, Taus Khan, the younger brother of Shah Mansur (the chieftain of the Yusufzais) bought the latter's daughter and submitted to the Mughals.[36]

In June 1507, Shaibani Khan took Herat and posed a threat to both Persia and Babur's fledgling kingdom of Kabul.[37] The distance between Herat and Kabul as the crow flies is some 500 miles. Initially, Babur attempted to build up a power base in Kabul in order to defend Timurid power south of Amu Darya and then to build a state in Central Asia. By 1512, he failed to achieve these two goals and turned his attention in the eastern direction, that is, South Asia.[38] Since Afghanistan did not yield much revenue, the only way for Babur to ward off the threat to his kingdom of Kabul from Central Asia and Persia was either to launch plundering raids into Punjab and north India or to extend his rule to west and north India. In 1519, Babur raided Bajaur,[39] which later was to operate as the staging post for military operations in north-west India.

Afghanistan was important for the rulers of north India for the fact that this country was the transit point for India's horse trade. The climate of India was not suited for breeding high-quality war horses. And warfare in Central and South Asia put a high premium on good-quality horses. So, the horse merchants with about 10,000 horses annually moved through Kabul into north India. The horses were brought from Balkh and Turkestan and fattened in Kabul. The dry and sandy soil of the Central Asian arid zone generated high-quality Turkoman horses. This trade was highly lucrative for the merchants as they were able to make 300 per cent to 500 per cent profit.[40] Besides Kabul, another great horse market was Herat.[41] The rulers of India required a constant supply of horses not only to replace the war casualties but also because horses did not last long in the climate of India. Heat, dust, and heavy rainfall of Hindustan did not suit the Central Asian horses. Babur jotted in his memoirs: 'Sometimes it rains 10, 15 or 20 times a day; torrents pour down all at once.... The fault is that the air becomes very soft and damp.'[42] The ruler of Afghanistan by imposing taxes could raise the price of war horses in India. Worse, a hostile ruler of Afghanistan, by stopping the horse trade, could actually choke the supply of military horses to India and make the country militarily weak. In addition, till the British conquest of India, all the invasions of the subcontinent had taken place through Afghanistan. During the pre-British era, there were four roads between Kabul and India. One was through the Khyber Mountains. The Nur-Dara Mountains near the Safed Koh is in the neighbourhood of Khyber. After crossing the Khyber Pass near Jalalabad from Afghanistan, the first big city on India's side was Peshawar in west Punjab. And another road was by way of Bangash. The third was by way of Naghar in Baghzan, about 70 miles from Kabul. The fourth road was through Farmuli along the Urghun.[43] Hence, security of India demanded control over Afghanistan.

In 1525, Babur invaded India with 12,000 soldiers (Turks, Tajiks, and so on) from Afghanistan.[44] The Tajiks are non-tribal Persian-speaking Sunni Muslims, who at present constitute some 30 per cent of Afghanistan's population.[45] Babur's army comprised many Afghan soldiers, especially the Hazaras and the Baluchis.[46] The Baluch have their own language known as Baluchi. The Baluchis are mostly pastoral nomads in south Afghanistan.[47] Babur politically co-opted the potentially rebellious Hazaras by recruiting them in his army of invasion. The prospect of pillage and plunder of Hindustan had always attracted the Afghans and had prevented uprising against the central government by the 'unruly' tribes. Military recruitment for the Afghans was important because only 12 per cent of Afghanistan's land is arable even now.[48] As the next chapter will show, political co-option of potentially rebellious Pathans through military recruitment was also a technique followed by the British. Babur's eldest son Humayun recruited troops from Badakshan for the army which was preparing to invade Hindustan. The Badakshanis were experts in mounted archery.[49] While proceeding towards India, in January 1526, Babur took the fort of Bajaur with the aid of firearms.[50]

At that time, north India was under the Lodhi dynasty (1450–1526). The Lodhis were also Afghans who had migrated to India during the thirteenth century. From thirteenth century onwards, Afghans from Roh, Suleiman, and Ushtughar mountain ranges moved into India in search of military employment. Many of them settled in the Ganga–Jamuna doab and formed military outposts of the Muslim sultanates in north India. Roh is roughly the region from Bajaur to Siwi in Bhakkar and from Hasan Abdal to Kabul. Those Pathans who hailed from Roh (highlands) and settled in the western part of north India (Rohilkhand) were known as Rohillas.[51] As Babur moved into west Punjab, two Lodhi nobles, named Daulat Khan and Alam Khan, raised an army of about 30,000 from mostly mercenary Afghans. Thus, we see that the Afghans, not for the last time, were fighting on both sides for pay.[52] Daulat Khan, the Lodhi Governor of Punjab was at odds with Sultan Ibrahim Lodhi due to the latter's centralizing tendencies. In fact, Daulat Khan's son Dilawar Khan invited Babur to attack the Lodhi Sultanate.[53] Babur raised the money for the Indian campaign by plundering Peshawar and from the 10,000 gold *ashrafis* given to him by Daulat Khan. On 21 April 1526, in the First Battle of Panipat, Babur defeated and killed Sultan Ibrahim Lodhi of Delhi (r. 29 December 1517–21 April 1526). According to one estimate, while the Mughal army was 24,000 strong, Sultan Ibrahim commanded 50,000 men and 2,000 elephants. However, the Lodhi army was raked by internal dissensions.[54] To a great extent, Ibrahim's downfall was due to clan rivalries among the Afghans. The various Afghan clans like the Lodhis, Sahukhails, Nuhanis, and Sarwanis fought amongst each other.[55] After the battle, Babur captured Delhi and Agra and founded the Mughal empire in India.[56] Better equipments (crossbows in the hands of mounted archers, handheld firearms for the infantry, and mortars)[57] and Babur's generalship resulted in Mughal victories over the Lodhis. Not for the last time, a warlord from Afghanistan had established an empire over Hindustan. In 1526, Babur's empire included Kabul, Kandahar, Kunduz, Badakshan, and the Delhi–Agra region.[58]

Babur's position was anything but secure. He had written in his autobiography that while at his rear the Uzbek chieftains posed a threat, in the east, Bihar and Bengal remained under the Afghan sirdars. The Uzbeks controlled Turan, which means Uzbekistan, Tajikistan, and Kazakhstan.[59] Babur had solid reasons for feeling insecure. He commented that if the Uzbek sirdars united, they would be able to mobilize about 100,000 cavalry. Luckily, for Babur, the various Uzbek sirdars were busy fighting against each other. For instance, in October 1526, the Uzbek sirdar Ubaidullah Khan of Bokhara attacked Merv.[60] According to a Persian estimate, in 1528, the Uzbek Khanate had some 80,000 standing troops and some 40,000 auxiliaries. The Uzbek army also included the Mongols who were settled between the Volga River and Kasghar.[61] In 1539, the Uzbek Khan Ubaidullah died. In 1545, Abdul Aziz declared himself as an independent ruler against the successor of Uzbek Khan.[62]

Babur was succeeded by his eldest son Nasir-ud-din Humayun (b. 1508–d. 1556) in 1530. Humayun's brothers got parts of Babur's empire. The brothers were practically independent in their principalities but accepted the nominal sovereignty of Humayun. Mirza Kamran (d. 1557) obtained Kabul and Kandahar as his fief and Badakshan was given to Mirza Sulaiman. In 1535, when Humayun was busy annexing Gujarat, the Safavids threatened Kabul. Mirza Kamran marched from Lahore to Kabul and on 25 January 1536 defeated Sam Mirza, the brother of Shah Tahmasp, the Safavid monarch. Meanwhile, Humayun had to deal with the rising power of Sher Khan, the Afghan warlord of Bihar. Sher Khan belonged to the Afghan tribe named Sur. His grandfather was an Afghan horse dealer who settled in Bihar. At that critical juncture, Kamran, who commanded 20,000 cavalry and controlled the region between Kabul and Zamindawar (north-west of

Kandahar) in the north to Sirhind in the south, refused to come to Humayun's aid. On 17 May 1540, Sher Khan defeated Humayun at the Battle of Chausa. Humayun pursued by the Suri forces retreated to Agra and evacuated through Sirhind to Sind in 1541. In September 1541, Humayun marched into Thatta (Mughal name for Sind). However, he failed to take the Shewan Fort because the ruler of Thatta prevented any grain from reaching the besieging Mughal force by laying waste the surrounding countryside.[63] Meanwhile, Sher Khan proclaimed himself ruler of Hindustan and took the title of Sher Shah.[64]

In 1543, the fugitive Humayun reached Seistan, an eastern province of Persia, 300 miles in length and 160 miles in breadth. The modern capital is Doosah. The western part of Seistan consists of a vast arid plain. In 1544, Shah Tahmasp of Persia (r. 1524–76) granted an audience to Humayun and agreed to provide the latter with 14,000 Turcoman cavalry for recapturing Kabul.[65] Humayun's aim was to capture Kabul and use it as a launching pad to reconquer the lost Mughal dominion in Hindustan. With the Persian force, Humayun from Seistan marched towards Kandahar which was held by his rebellious brother Mirza Askari (1518–51). Kandahar was captured in 1545 and Bairam Khan, a noble loyal to Humayun, was put in charge of the fort. Then Humayun raised a force from the Afghans. In accordance with the deal struck between Shah Tahmasp and Humayun, Kandahar Fort was turned over to the Persians. Using a ruse, Humayun captured 1,700 horses from the Persian garrison during a night raid.[66]

Then, Humayun turned against his rebellious brothers for establishing his rule in Afghanistan. The Afghans joined both sides as mercenaries during the Mughal civil war in Afghanistan. Kamran laid siege to the fort of Zamindawar with the help of Khizr Khan, a Hazara chieftain. However, Kamran's attempt was foiled due to the vigorous action of Bairam Khan and the reinforcements sent by Humayun. The Hazaras then deserted Kamran. The Afghan mercenaries throughout history have displayed the tendency of deserting the losing side and joining the winner even in midst of a conflict. In 1545, Humayun marched towards Badakshan which was held by Mirza Sulaiman. However, Humayun fell ill at Shakhdan and the Mughal officials panicked and abandoned their posts in Badakshan.[67]

In 1546, during winter when snow was falling, Humayun marched towards Kabul with a cavalry force and the baggage was drawn by the camels. Jouher, the private secretary of Humayun, had written in his history: '... such a quantity of snow had fallen that the roads were quite blocked up; we were therefore obliged to ram the snow well down; after which the horses and camels were enabled to move on'.[68] In fact, Babur points out in his memoirs that snow made all but one of the passes of Hindu Kush impassable for four to five months during the winter. Before the construction of the Salang Tunnel in 1964 with Soviet aid, only the Shibar/Shibartu Pass could be crossed in winter for reaching Kabul from north Afghanistan. This pass was reached through Charikar and Ghorband Valley and led into Bamian. And after the snow started melting in April, the rivers in the narrow mountain valleys were flooded, which in turn prevented deployment of large forces for another two months. So, the months from May to October seemed to be best for conducting military operations in the Kabul region. But Babur warns in his memoir that Kabul could be reached from the western direction through the Herat–Kandahar road which was comparatively flat and easily traversed even during the winter.[69] At the vicinity of Kabul, Humayun's force was attacked by an Afghan mercenary named Sher Afghan (not to be confused with Sher Khan/Sher Shah Suri) and Khizr Khan Hazara, who were in the pay of Kamran. However, the Afghan mercenaries were defeated by Humayun.[70] In April 1547, after a siege of three months, Humayun was able to capture Kabul from his brother Mirza Kamran.[71] Kamran escaped to Ghakkar territory but the Ghakkar chieftain handed him over to Humayun due to promise of a large reward. Humayun later blinded Kamran.[72] Thus, we see that financial incentives sometimes overcame the frontier tribes' sense of hospitality to a fugitive who had taken refuge in their territory. So, the British colonial and Western post-colonial scholars portrayal of the Afghan tribes' value system being shaped by *melmastia* and *mehrmapalineh* (hospitality to guest),[73] can be categorized as contextual rather than static. Not all the tribes accepted Humayun's rule without a struggle. In 1548, one Mughal official named Ulugh Mirza was killed during an encounter with the Hazaras.[74] In 1553, Humayun captured Peshawar and ordered the construction of a fort in that place for pacification of the surrounding region.[75]

Sher Shah, the founder of the short-lived Suri empire, was aware that the Mughals might stage a comeback. He had formulated a strategy to prevent this. But he died suddenly in 1545 due to accidental explosion

of a mine during the Siege of Chanderi. Sher Shah's unworthy
successors failed to implement Sher Shah's defensive strategy. In Sher
Shah's own words:

> I wished to have depopulated the country of Roh, and to have transferred
> its inhabitants to the tract between the Nilab and Lahore, including the hills
> below Ninduna, as far as the Siwalik; that they might have been constantly
> on the alert for the arrival of the Mughals, and not allow anyone to pass
> from Kabul to Hind, and that they might also keep the zamindars of the hills
> under control and subjection. Another is to have entirely destroyed Lahore,
> that so large a city might not exist on the very road of an invader, where
> immediately after capturing it on his arrival, he could collect his supplies.[76]

Sher Shah's scheme of ethnic transplantation for checking both conventional threat of a foreign power and to suppress the unruly frontier
chieftains was novel in the medieval context.

In 1555, Humayun crossed into India and reached Sirhind. In
response, Sultan Sikander Suri (Sher Shah's successor) advanced with
an army of about 80,000 cavalry. Humayun's army had also recruited
some Uzbek freebooters. In the ensuing battle, a charge at the rear of the
Suri army resulted in its dissolution.[77] The Mughal victory at the Battle
of Machiwarra on the bank of Sutlej was possible due to the deployment of mounted archers. Since Humayun controlled Afghanistan, he,
unlike the Lodhis and the Suris, could recruit mounted archers.[78]

While Humayun was engaged in re-establishing the Mughal empire
in north India, one of his officers named Selim Khan built a fortress
with four strong forts at Mankot. Each fort was constructed on the top
of a hill. The forts were made with stone and mortar. The forts had
good supply of water and were very difficult to access. A garrison was
installed in this fortress to pacify the warlike Ghakkar tribe. In addition, this fortress was also designed to act as a refuge for the Mughal
army in case it met with a defeat in north India and had to retreat
to Afghanistan. After Humayun's death, Selim Khan from his base in
this fortress started plundering the environs of Lahore. However, he
soon died a natural death. The fortress came under control of the rebel
Sikander. Humayun's son Akbar sent the imperial army to capture the
fortress. The Mughals constructed redoubts and drew lines of circum-
vallation around the fort. However, the rebel garrison defended itself
with cannons and muskets.[79]

PACIFICATION AND CONSOLIDATION OF MUGHAL RULE IN AFGHANISTAN FROM AKBAR TO AURANGZEB: 1556–1707

Under Sher Shah, the Salt Range in north-west Punjab comprised the border of his empire and the North-West Frontier defence was centred around the Rohtas Fort. Rohtas was built on the highest part of a long ridge of hills. The wall was defended by several bastions and the road leading to the gateway was steep which, in turn, made the approach to the fort difficult. An Afghan tribe named Sarangazi inhabited the region around the Salt Range.[80] Under Mughal Emperor Akbar (b. 1542; r. 1556–1605), North-West Frontier defence centred around the Attock Fort which guarded the main ferry across the Indus. Akbar realized, writes M. Athar Ali, that Mughal India's 'scientific frontier' should run along the Kabul–Kandahar axis. So, Akbar shifted the principal defence line from the Indus to further north-west across the Hindu Kush Mountains.[81] Later, some of the hard-liners of British India also accepted the Kabul–Kandahar axis as the scientific frontier of India.

Akbar pre-empted the British in realizing that Sind constituted the crucial southern component of the 'scientific frontier'. The route from India to southern Afghanistan, that is, Kandahar, passed through Siwi and the Bolan Pass, which made Sind a strategic prize. Further, sulphur was available in Sind. And sulphur was required for the manufacture of gunpowder.[82] The Mughals had to deal with three clan groupings in Sind. The biggest of them was the Kalmati Baluch tribe. One section among them inhabited Siwistan and Lakhi and they maintained 20,000 cavalry. Another section of this tribe inhabited the Karah Hills near Kachh Gandawa and was able to mobilize about 4,000 cavalry. The Nahmardi who inhabited the territory from Sehwan to Kirthar Range had 3,000 cavalry and 7,000 infantry. And the Baluch Nazhari had about 1,000 cavalry.[83] In 1586, the Mughals invaded Sind. The Mughal commander Sadiq Khan defeated Jani Beg's force and then marched towards Sehwan and besieged the fort there. The garrison was well equipped with cannons and muskets. And the guns at the fort proved too much for the besieging Mughal army. Mughal mining techniques proved to be of no avail. The earthen parapet of the fort was quite high and the defenders constructed a new wall. So, Sadiq Khan was forced to retreat. Further, Mirza Jani Beg's war boats equipped with cannons and musketeers harassed Sadiq Khan's force which then retreated near Lakhi Hills. In 1590, another Mughal force under Khan-i-Khanan was sent to Sind. Meanwhile, Jani Beg had bolstered his army with the aid of Ottoman and Portuguese mercenaries. The Mughals made greater use of cannons to destroy Jani Beg's war boats.[84]

After Humayun's death, the state of affairs in Kabul fell into a chaos. Mirza Sulaiman, the ruler of Badakshan, his wife, Haram Bagum, and their son, Mirza Ibrahim, planned to occupy Kabul. Munim Khan, the Mughal noble was in charge of Kabul. When he learnt of the advance of the Badakshanis, he strengthened the bastions and the bulwarks of the fort. With cannons and muskets, the garrison fought the 10,000 Badakshanis. Meanwhile, the main Mughal army was engaged in the Delhi–Agra region against the Hindu General Hemu. Many Afghans fought on the side of Hemu. On 5 November 1556, at the Second Battle of Panipat, Hemu was defeated and Mughal rule became secure in north India. Before the main Mughal army in north India could redeploy in Afghanistan, the Mughal regional government in Kabul, without any substantial aid from the central government, was able to defeat the Badakshanis. Nevertheless, troubles continued in Afghanistan. Khan Zaman rebelled in Zamindawar. Khan Zaman's brother, Bahadur Khan, gathered an Afghan militia and tried to capture Kandahar which was Emperor Akbar's regent Bairam Khan's jagir. When Shah Muhammad (Bairam Khan's deputy), in charge of the Kandahar Fort, heard of the impending invasion by Bahadur Khan, the former realized that Akbar was not in a position to send help from India. In desperation, Shah Muhammad requested assistance from the ruler of Persia. This was an instance of weak Mughal centre encouraging Persian intervention in Afghanistan. This pattern would be repeated in early eighteenth century. The Shah of Persia sent 3,000 Turcoman cavalry gathered from Seistan, Farah, and Gurmsir under the command of Ali Yar Beg Afshar. Afshar's force defeated Bahadur Khan's Afghan auxiliaries. Shah Muhammad, however, did not hand over Kandahar to the Persians. Bahadur Khan submitted to Akbar and the latter transferred him to a jagir in Multan in order to prevent him from doing any further mischief in Afghanistan. In order to exert greater control over Kabul, Akbar decided to appoint his court official Munim Khan as the guardian of Mirza Hakim, who was Akbar's brother and ruled in a semi-autonomous manner.[85]

Due to Akbar's centralizing administrative measures and religious reforms, a big chunk of the Mughal nobility rebelled against him. Many rebellious nobles were Uzbeks. The Uzbeks were quite powerful in Balkh, Bokhara, Khorasan, and in Ferghana. Several immigrants from these regions had entered Akbar's service.[86] In 1563, Iskander Khan became the ruler of the Uzbek Khanate and in 1583, his son, Abdullah Khan, took over.[87] By early 1581, Akbar was able to crush the rebellion by the Mughal nobles against his authority. Akbar decided to measure sword with his brother Mirza Hakim, the ruler of Kabul. When Akbar was engaged against the rebels in north India, Hakim had invaded Punjab. Akbar marched through Ambala and Sirhind. When Akbar reached Payal beyond Sirhind, he heard the news that Hakim had evacuated Punjab. Akbar then crossed Sutlej and Beas rivers through a bridge of boats. He avoided the direct road through Lahore in order to keep near to the base of the hills. The River Ravi was crossed by a bridge of boats but when the army reached the River Chenab, boats were not easily available. A collection of ferry boats took about three days to transport the whole army. The Mughal army reached the Rohtas Fort which was held by Yusuf against Hakim. On arrival at the Indus, Akbar stopped for fifty days. This was necessary because construction of a bridge during the rainy season was impossible and a small force taking a defensive position on the opposite bank could have prevented the passage of the army across the flooded the Indus. Most of the imperial officials were unwilling to face the hardship and dangers of an invasion of Afghanistan. However, Akbar overruled them. He ordered a fort to be built at Attock. Kasim Khan (an engineer who constructed the Agra Fort) was left in charge of this fort with the order to subdue the refractory tribes in the surrounding region and to construct a bridge. On 12 July, Akbar finally crossed the Indus. On 1 August, when Prince Murad's advance guard was attacked by Hakim's force, the Rajput mansabdar Man Singh arrived with the main force and stabilized the situation. After making a halt at the junction of the rivers Kabul and Indus, the Mughals marched to Peshawar, which was evacuated and burnt by Hakim's officials. Prince Salim/Selim (later Emperor Jahangir) entered the Khyber Pass in advance of his father Akbar and marched to Ali Masjid and Jalalabad. On 3 August, the Mughals entered Kabul and Hakim fled to the hills. Hakim never submitted to Akbar. And Akbar knew that he could not remain in Kabul with a big army indefinitely.

Sooner or later, he had to go back to north India. Akbar was sure that as soon as he would cross the Indus with the main body of the Mughal army, Hakim would create problems in Kabul. Akbar tried to play off the Badakshanis against Hakim. Bakht-un-Nissa, the half sister of Akbar was the wife of Khwaja Hasan, the ruler of Badakshan. Akbar offered the province of Kabul to this lady. Then, the Mughal army left Kabul and Akbar reached Agra on 1 December 1581.[88] Though Hasan did not occupy Kabul, the very threat of the Badakshanis prevented Hakim from creating large-scale trouble for the Mughals.

The Hindu Kush separated the Mughal *suba* of Kabul from Balkh and Badakshan. Badakshan is on the bank of the River Oxus. On the east of Badakshan lies the Pamirs. In earlier times, the capital of the region was a city also named Badakshan. But in the late medieval era, Badakshan's capital was Faizabad. In general, the Mughals did not give overt importance to Badakshan because they considered the Oxus as not a good defensive barrier. Secondly, Badakshan was a mountainous country and its revenue was considered inadequate even for maintaining a high-ranking mansabdar.[89] In 1585, Abdullah Khan Uzbek conquered Badakshan and in the following year occupied Balkh. In response, Akbar strengthened Mughal rule in Kabul. By this time, Hakim had died and Akbar established direct administration over Kabul which was organized into a suba.

In response to the rising Uzbek threat, Akbar decided to strengthen Mughal control over the Indus tribes. Zain Khan was ordered to annex Swat and Bajaur. Bajaur was inhabited by some 30,000 Yusufzai households and Swat by some 40,000 Yusufzai families. At the bank of the Indus, Zain Khan attacked the Yusufzais and the Mughal *altamash* (advance guard) dispersed the tribesmen. To ensure permanent control over this region, Zain Khan constructed a fort named Jagdara in midst of the Yusufzai territory. When the Yusufzais realized that the Mughals were going to stay permanently in their region, they attacked the Mughals repeatedly. Yusufzai resistance was intense in the hills of Karagar and in the Buner region. Due to continuous fighting and for patrolling the mountainous country, Zain Khan requested reinforcements. Akbar sent Raja Birbal a Hindu mansabdar with a detachment and another force with Hakim Abul Fath. However, Birbal and Abul Fath failed to cooperate with each other. Personal dissension between these two Mughal commanders further hampered the Mughal COIN campaign. In 1586, the three Mughal commanders met at the Malakand Hills to hammer out a coherent strategy. Despite Zain Khan's attempt, cooperation was not forthcoming from the other two Mughal commanders. The three commanders marched towards Jagdara Fort. Zain Khan argued that he would have final say in the campaigns against the Yusufzais but Birbal and Fath disagreed. Zain Khan emphasized that while one strong Mughal detachment should occupy Jagdara, the other two detachments should launch mobile patrols for flushing out the insurgents. Zain Khan added that such a strategy would be time consuming. However, Birbal and Fath Khan disagreed. They asserted that proper strategy should not mean permanent control of the Yusufzai territory but destruction of the hostile force. Hence, the three detachments should advance and meet the Yusufzais in a decisive battle. And after destruction of the Yusufzais, Birbal and Fath Khan reasoned that they, with their contingents, should retire to Delhi. Zain Khan pointed out that for controlling the Yusufzais, permanent occupation of their homeland was necessary. Further, moving into the mountain defiles without proper reconnaissance might be dangerous. In the end, Birbal–Fath Khan's view prevailed. The whole army moved out from Jagdara and the right and left wings were under the command of Birbal and Fath Khan. On the first day of advance, the army covered five *kos* and halted at the village of Kandak. Next day, the army moved into the narrow defiles of the mountainous country and the right wing was left as rear guard. On the third day, the Yusufzais attacked. As the Mughal advance guard attacked the Yusufzias and drove them away, the tribesmen plundered the baggage animals of the Mughal force. Birbal and Fath Khan mistakenly believed that they have the Yusufzais on the run. So, the Mughal force moved another six kos to Khanpur. Zain Khan advised that the Mughal should not advance further into the mountainous country because of lack of water supply. Further, Zain Khan commented that due to absence of level plains, the Mughals would be unable to deploy their superior cavalry force against the Yusufzais. However, Birbal and Fath Khan disagreed and the following day, the Mughals penetrated further into the mountainous region. As the Mughals reached the Bulandari Mountains, the Yusufzais attacked from the hilltops. Zain Khan commanded the rear guard. Fighting continued till nightfall. Next morning, the Yusufzais attacked again and as the Mughal advance guard tried to clear the defile, it was repulsed. Then, the Afghans attacked from all sides with arrows and stones. In the narrow defiles, the Mughal force lost all order and the elephants, horses, and men all got mixed up. The Yusufzais, taking advantage of the terrain, launched nocturnal attacks and the Mughals panicked. In their attempt to retreat during the night, many Mughal cavaliers with their mounts fell off the precipice. The 8,000-strong Mughal detachment under Birbal was wiped out in the Swat defile. Zain Khan and Abul Fath were able to retreat with their contingents.[90] Lack of unity of command and failure to conduct a thorough reconnaissance of the terrain before advancing into narrow mountainous country held by the hostile tribesmen spelled doom for the Mughals.

Akbar was angry with Zain Khan and Abul Fath Khan for running away from the battlefield. The emperor appointed another Hindu mansabdar Raja Todar Mal. He implemented Zain Khan's strategy. Todar Mal constructed several forts and launched several detachments simultaneously to flush out the Yusufzais from their mountain fastness. Overall, Todar Mal was successful in crushing the Yusufzai insurgency.[91]

For Akbar, the principal danger across the North-West Frontier remained the conventional threat posed by the Uzbeks and to a lesser extent by the Safavids. In order to ensure the protection of the LoC between Lahore and Kabul, Akbar overlooked the tribal depredations and patched up a fragile peace with them.[92] In 1598, Abdullah Khan died and civil war broke out in Transoxiana (Central Asia). This gave an opportunity to Shah Abbas I of Safavid Persia (r. 1587–1629) to occupy Khorasan.[93] Its principal cities were Herat and Meshed/Mashad. Gurmsir, an Afghan district, formed the boundary between Kandahar and Khorasan. Gurmsir is located on both banks of the River Helmand and inhabited by pastoral tribes.[94] In an attempt to maintain good relations with Persia, in March 1603, Husain Beg was sent by the Mughal emperor as the Mughal ambassador to Persia.[95]

For maintaining secure military connections with Afghanistan, under Emperor Akbar, the Mughals constructed a highway along the Khyber Pass. Every spring, the stones were removed and the scrubs and the bushes were cleared. The road was made suitable for the bullock carts, which carried the baggage of the Mughal army.[96] Akbar's successors repeatedly tried to develop secure communications between India and Afghanistan.

Joannes De Laet, the Flemish geographer, philologist, and naturalist was born in Antwerp in 1593 and died at Leiden in 1649. In 1625, he was director of the Company of the West Indies. Later, he became one of the directors of the Dutch East India Company (EIC). In 1631, he published his observations on the Mughal Empire in Latin.[97] De Laet describes the internal security situation of Mughal North-West Frontier under Emperor Jahangir: 'The road from Lahore to Kabul is infested by Pathan brigands; and although the king has established 23 guard stations of troops at regular intervals, nonetheless travellers are frequently robbed by these brigands, who in the year 1611 actually attacked and looted the city of Kabul'.[98]

In general, the journey from Lahore (the important Mughal military outpost in western Punjab) to Kabul took about three months, because of the great detours which the travellers had to make in order to avoid the robber-infested regions and also due to lack of good tracks across the mountainous regions. However, the Mughal royal road from Lahore to Kabul, with guard posts constructed at regular intervals, reduced the time of the journey to 20–25 days. De Laet gives details about the Mughal road from Lahore to Kabul. The different stages along the road with corresponding distance are given in Table 1.1. The road from Lahore to Kabul was designed to strengthen Mughal control over central and northern Afghanistan. Another road was constructed from Lahore to Kandahar to secure Mughal domination over southern Afghanistan and especially to guard against any possible Persian incursion. The Mughals maintained about 12,000–15,000 cavalry in Kandahar. Kandahar Fort was protected on the west by a steep rugged mountain, and in the south and east by a strong wall. The details of the royal highway from Lahore to Kandahar as described by De Laet are given in Table 1.2. Construction of royal roads assisted the transfer of military assets from the core of the empire to the turbulent frontier not only to deal effectively with frontier uprisings but also to check external threats posed by the Uzbeks and the Persians. Road building and maintenance of internal peace also boosted up long-distance commerce. Large caravans from Kabul journeyed for two to three months to reach Kasghar. The chief trading centre was Yarkhand where large quantities of silk, musk, rhubarb from China were exported to Afghanistan.[99]

Table 1.1 Outposts in the Mughal Road from Lahore to Kabul

Outposts	Distance (in kos)	Remarks
Lahore to Kacha Sarai	10	
Kacha Sarai to Aminabad town where the River Ravi was crossed	8	
Aminabad to Chima the Gakhar city	12	
Chima Gakhar to Gujerat, a trading post	14	Not to be confused with the Mughal suba Gujarat bordering on the Arabian Sea in west India
Gujerat to the crossing of the River Chenab	7	
Crossing point at Chenab to Khawaspur	12	
Khawaspur to Rohtas-i-Khurd	15	A fort constructed on top of a mountain. Sher Shah Suri's frontier fort was still in operation under the Mughals
Rohtas-i-Khurd to Hatea	15	
Hatea to Pakka	4	
Pakka to Rawalpindi	14	
Rawalpindi to Hasan Abdal	4	
Hasan Abdal to Attock	15	A city on the Indus with a strong fort
Attock to Peshawar	36	
Peshawar to Ali Masjid	10	The path between Peshawar and Ali Masjid was extremely dangerous because here the tribal sirdars can effectively mobilize somewhere between 10,000 to 12,000 cavalry

Ali Masjid to Dakka	12
Dakka to Basawal	6
Basawal to Bariku	6
Bariku to Ali Boghan (on the River Kabul)	11
Ali Boghan to Jalalabad	14
Jalalabad to Charbourg Khurd	4
Charbourg Khurd to Nomle	14
Nomle through Gandamak to Surkhab Sarai	4
Surkhab Sarai to Jagdalak	8
Jagdalak to Abi Barik	8
Abi Barik to Dowabad	8
Dowabad to Butkhak	8
Butkhak to Bikrami	3
Bikrami to Kabul	3

Source: The Empire of the Great Mogul, De Laet's Description of India and Fragment of Indian History, translated by J.S. Hoyland and annotated by S.N. Banerjee (1928; reprint, New Delhi: Munshiram Manoharlal, 1974), 55–6.

Table 1.2   Outposts in the Mughal Road from Lahore to Kandahar

Mughal Posts	Distance (in kos)
Lahore to Chak Sunder, a small town	11
Chak Sunder to Naushera	15
Naushera to Mopalki Kamal Khan	8
Mopalki Kamal Khan to Qamal Chan	19
Qamal Chan to Harappa	16
Harappa to Chak Ali Shah	12
Chak Ali Shah to Tulamba	12
Tulamba to Siddhu Sarai	14
Siddhu Sarai to Khatti Churikabadai	15
Khatti Churikabadai to Multan (a big city situated 3 kos from the bank of the Indus)	12
Multan to the small village of Petto Ali	20
Petto Ali to Katzai Duki	72
Katzai Duki to Secota	14
Secota to the defiles of Khoja Amran Mountains	24
Khoja Amran Mountains to Peshingaon Fort	23
Peshingaon Fort to Kandahar	60

Source: *The Empire of the Great Mogul, De Laet's Description of India and Fragment of Indian History*, translated by J.S. Hoyland and annotated by S.N. Banerjee (1928; reprint, New Delhi: Munshiram Manoharlal, 1974), pp. 69–70.

After Akbar's death, his eldest son, Prince Salim, ascended the Mughal throne as Jahangir on 23 October 1605.[100] By May 1606, the Persians posed a threat to Kandahar. Jahangir jots in his memoirs:

> I had gathered from the reports of Shah Beg Khan, the Governor of Kandahar, that the *amir*s of the Qizilbash frontier were going to make a move owing to the corrupting influence of several men remaining from the army of the *mirza*s of that area who were always shaking the chain of contention and strife and writing letters encouraging [the Qizilbash] to take Kandahar.[101]

Actually, the death of Humayun and the rebellion of Jahangir's son Khusrau encouraged the Persians to make a move against Kandahar.[102] Khusrau fled from Agra and with his force appeared before Lahore. The Governor of Lahore refused to open the gates of the city to Khusrau.

The imperial force defeated and captured Khusrau while he was trying to cross the River Chenab. Meanwhile, the Safavid Empire was reviving. In 1603, Shah Abbas captured Tabriz and Erivan fell to him next year. Then, Abbas decided to grab Kandahar.[103] Jahangir tells us: 'The Governor of Farah, the *malik* of Seistan, and the *jagirdars* of that region attacked Kandahar with the assistance of Husayn Khan, the Governor of Herat. Thanks to his courage and bravery, Shah Beg Khan made a manly defence by fortifying and securing the fortress.'[104] Jahangir congratulated Shah Beg for not offering a pitched battle to the Persians in front of Kandahar. In his memoirs, Jahangir wrote that Shah Beg's decision to shut himself up in the Kandahar Fort and prepare the garrison for a siege was the right decision.[105] At the time of Persian Siege of Kandahar, the Mughal garrison was lucky because both the Mughal Emperor Jahangir and the Mughal court were located at Lahore. And, from Lahore, a relief force was easily dispatched to relieve the siege of Kandahar. Jahangir himself was aware of the good luck of the Mughals. He notes in his memoirs: 'By chance, the imperial forces, that had been sent after Khusrau from Agra were camped in Lahore, just then.'[106] The preparation of a relief army is described by the Emperor Jahangir:

> I immediately appointed a large contingent under the leadership of Mirza Ghazi, who was accompanied by a number of officers and servants of the court such as Qara Beg ... Tokhta Beg ... Khwaja Aqil was appointed as *bakshi* to this campaign. To cover expenses, forty-three thousand rupees were given to Qara Khan, and fifteen thousand rupees were given to Naqdi Beg and Qilich Beg, who accompanied Mirza Ghazi. I decided to stay in Lahore in order to settle this matter, and to visit Kabul.[107]

When the Persian force learnt that a Mughal relief force was marching towards Kandahar, they lifted the siege and retreated across the River Helmand, some fifty-six kos from Kandahar. The Mughal relief army entered Kandahar on 31 January 1607. In this siege, the regional army of Governor of Farah was involved and the Persian royal army did not take part. Jahangir came to believe that the Kandahar expedition was undertaken by the governors of Farah and Herat without any direct order from Shah Abbas I. In December 1607, the Mughal North-West Frontier defence was put in the hands of Mirza Ghazi, the commandant of the relief force. He was given charge of the subas of Thatta, Multan, and Kandahar.[108] In 1612, Shah Abbas made peace with the Ottoman

Turks and again turned his attention towards the Safavid Empire's Eastern Front. In 1620, a Persian army was sent to capture Kandahar. The main Mughal army at that time was then engaged in Deccan. Shah Jahan (Jahangir's son and the future Emperor) marched with reinforcements to Mandu. Within three weeks of the beginning of the siege, the Persians mined the walls of Kandahar Fort and were able to capture it. With the Persian occupation of Kandahar, the Gilzai and the Abdali tribes became subjects of the Safavid Empire. When these tribes complained to Shah Abbas I about their displeasure of being ruled directly by Persian royal officials, Shah Abbas I appointed *kalantars* (administrators) from the tribesmen in order to manage their internal affairs. However, the Abdalis revolted and were forced to migrate to the province of Herat. In 1625–6, Jahangir made his last visit to Kabul probably to strengthen Mughal defence in this crucial region. However, Jahangir's visit was marred by the rebellion of the Mughal General Mahabat Khan. Mahabat Khan's rebellion was suppressed and then Jahangir left Kabul for Lahore. In November 1627, while in Kashmir, Jahangir passed away.[109]

When the Russians occupied the Astrakhan Khanate in mid-sixteenth century, an Uzbek chief named Jan took refuge in Bokhara. He married the daughter of Iskander, the ruler of Bokhara. Iskander's son, Baki Muhammad, succeeded his maternal uncle, Abdullah II, as the Khan of Bokhara in 1599. He established his control over Samarkhand, Bokhara, Ferghana, Balkh, and Badakshan.[110] About twenty kos beyond Kabul was the town of Charikar and twenty kos further in the north was Ghorband. Under Jahangir, it was at the boundary of the Uzbek Empire whose capital was Samarkhand.[111] During the last years of Jahangir's reign, the northern frontier of the Mughal suba of Kabul was also threatened. Nazar Muhammad, son of Imam Kuli, launched a raid towards Kabul, and a second raid resulted in the capture of Bamian in 1629.[112]

In 1629, Shah Abbas died and his successor Shah Safi (r. 1629–42) after accession to the throne murdered most of his relations and the previous monarch's trusted generals and councillors. The Governor of Kandahar, Ali Mardan Khan, was ordered to report to Isfahan. Fearing for his life, in desperation, Ali Mardan Khan surrendered the fort to the Mughals. The Mughal relief army also defeated the Persian army which was sent from Isfahan to capture Ali Mardan Khan.[113]

With Kandahar coming back under Mughal control, Shah Jahan (b. 1592, d. 1666, r. 1628–58) turned his attention towards Afghanistan's northern frontier. In 1639, Shah Jahan visited Kabul with the express intention of teaching the Uzbeks a lesson. However, famine conditions in Kabul and the presence of Imam Kuli Khan with a strong force at Balkh discouraged the Mughal emperor's aggressive intention. In 1645, Shah Jahan prepared a plan for conquering Badakshan and Balkh by launching operations from Kabul. Not only the Mughals started assembling military contingents from various parts of India to Kabul but the imperial court itself moved to Kabul.[114] On 6 April 1645, Shah Jahan ordered Asalat Khan, the *mir bakshi*, to collect mansabdars, *ahadi*s, and musketeers in Kabul for the forthcoming campaign.[115] About the utilization of the Afghan mercenaries by the Mughals, Inayat Khan writes:

> He [Shah Jahan] moreover instructed the said Khan [Asalat Khan] to recruit a band of gallant and sturdy youths from amongst the Oymaqs, Chaghtais, and other tribes dwelling in the neighbourhoods of Kabul on the Badakshan frontier. With *Amir-ul Umara*'s concurrence, he was to recommend the worthiest for suitable mansabs and enlist the rest into the ranks of the ahadis.[116]

The *Amir-ul-Umara* and Asalat Khan were ordered to send a party to widen and level the road leading to Badakshan and also to construct bridges along the route of invasion. The emperor further informed them that reinforcements from Punjab would soon reach them. Meanwhile, the blind Imam Kuli was replaced by Nazar Muhammad. The latter's attempt to conquer Khiva resulted in an insurrection. Abdul Aziz, son of Nazar Muhammad who was sent to quell the rising, proclaimed himself the king of Bokhara. Nazar Muhammad fled to Balkh. During August 1645, Nazar Muhammad and his son Abd al-Aziz Khan, who held the possession of Samarkhand, Bokhara, and parts of Transoxiana, were fighting against each other. The civil war in Central Asia provided an opportunity to the Mughals to intervene in the region north of Afghanistan.[117] Actually, Nazar Muhammad sent an envoy to the Mughal durbar to plead Mughal support for his cause.[118]

The *Amir-ul Umara* dispatched Khalil Beg with 2,000 cavalry and 1,000 infantry to seize the Kahmard Fort. After capturing this fort, Khalil Beg returned with most of his force to Zuhak for collecting supplies and munitions of war. The detachment from Zuhak which was escorting the heavy baggage and military stores going towards

Fort Kahmard was attacked by the Uzbeks at Bamiyan. Before Khalil Beg could move with the reinforcements to aid the Zuhak detachment, the Uzbeks withdrew. Meanwhile, Abd al-Rahman and Tardi Ali with their Uzbek soldiers captured the Kahmard Fort from the Mughal garrison. Khalil Beg wrote to the Amir-ul Umara that no further reinforcements could be sent for assaulting the Kahmard Fort because the route between Zuhak and Kahmard was devoid of grass for the horses and provisions for the men due to frequent to-and-fro passage of the armies who pillaged and plundered the villages and fields along this route. Moreover, the tracks between the mountains were not only narrow but also very difficult to traverse. The local Afghan chieftains who had transferred their loyalty to the Mughals in response to the changing military balance advised the Amir-ul Umara that a full-scale invasion of Badakshan during the winter was not possible due to logistical problems. In response, the Amir-ul Umara sent a force of 10,000 cavalry towards Khinjan to conduct a reconnaissance with regards to the nature of terrain for conducting military operations after the winter. Asalat Khan led a force over the Hindu Kush in an expedition which lasted for sixteen days. He bought back many prisoners and also horses, camels, cattle, and sheep from the inhabitants in retaliation for their rebellious activities. Shah Jahan ordered the Amir-ul Umara to send masons, carpenters, and sappers in order to improve the road by Thul. He took up winter quarter at Peshawar and the Rajput contingent was stationed at Attock. While Rustam Khan guarded Rohtas, Qilij Khan with a detachment was stationed at Bhera.[119]

Raja Jagat Singh, a Mughal mansabdar, with 1,500 cavalry and 2,000 infantry, recruited from Rajasthan was deployed in Kabul. After they were financially recompensed from the Mughal treasury at Kabul, Jagat Singh's force crossed the Thul Pass and sent an advance guard under Bhao Singh to ravage Khost.[120] Khost is a district on the northern slope of the Hindu Kush between south and south-east of Kunduz and lies near the hill tracts which the British described as Kafiristan. It is in the west of Badakshan.[121] During November 1645, Jagat Singh advanced towards Sirab and Indarab. When the Uzbeks attacked, he built a series of stockades made of wood and successfully engaged in a defensive close-quarter battle. The Hazara infantry, allied with the Uzbek cavalry, was driven back by the matchlockmen in Jagat Singh's force. Then, 4,000 cavalry (2,000 Rajputs under Rajrup and 2,000 raised from the

Afghans in Kabul) attacked the Uzbek cavalry which, though numbered to 20,000, was driven back.[122] The Uzbeks were masters at mobile battles as their mounted archers practising Parthian tactics were just unbeatable since the time of Alexander. But in a static defensive battle, lacking hand-held firearms, the Uzbek cavalry was unable to defeat a well-armed adversary (especially infantry) taking advantage of the terrain and field fortifications.

In 1646, a 60,000-strong army with an artillery park was assembled under Prince Murad. The imperial objective was either to restore Nazar Muhammad as a tributary ruler in Balkh or to annex his kingdom to the Mughal empire. In July 1646, Murad and his commander, Mardan Khan, occupied Balkh. The Mughals got hold of Nazar Muhammad's treasury with Rs 12 million, but Nazar fled the city. Termez was taken and the Mughal cavalry pursued Nazar Muhammad to Shibarghan. Nazar Muhammad was defeated again and fled to Persia.[123] Within a month, Murad retreated from Balkh due to logistical difficulties and Shah Jahan ordered his *wazir* Sadullah Khan to reorganize the army for another invasion. In 1647, Prince Aurangzeb was appointed as the commander of the second imperial invading force and Shah Jahan himself moved towards Kabul to provide logistical support to the invading force. The Uzbeks under Abdul Aziz failed to stand against the musketeers and field artillery of the Mughals but the light Uzbek horse proved adept in skirmishing and ambushing, and harassing the lumbering Mughal columns. During the summer of 1647, the Mughals in Balkh opened negotiations with Abdul Aziz at Bokhara. The Mughal army could not live off the land in desolate countryside. The sparsely populated desolate countryside did not generate adequate surplus for sustaining the Mughal troops. There were no *banjara*s in Central Asia to supply the Mughal soldiers and their horses with grain and fodder. Nazar Muhammad reappeared in the scene with Persian reinforcements. In order to maintain a balance of power in Afghanistan, the Safavids at times supported the Mughals (Humayun) and, at others, when their interests demanded, they played the Turcomans (Nazar Muhammad) against the Mughals. The 'Great Game'—the tussle between the Safavids, Mughals, and Uzbeks to control Afghanistan is categorized as a sort of Great Game before the British–Russian Great Game started in early nineteenth century to dominate Central Asia in general and Afghanistan in particular—was going on at full spree. In October 1647, with the winter approaching, Prince Aurangzeb offered Balkh and the surrounding districts to Nazar Muhammad in return for nominal submission of the latter to the Mughal Emperor. As the Mughals retreated to Kabul over the snow-filled passes, the Uzbek cavalry took a heavy toll on them. Overall, the Mughal–Uzbek treaty resulted in the shifting of Mughal frontier some 50 miles north of Kabul. However, the Mughals had failed to capture Bokhara and Samarkhand. The two-year-long campaign caused the Mughal court an expenditure of some Rs 40 million (as per calculations in mid-seventeenth century).[124] To put this figure in context, the annual Mughal revenue in 1590 was some Rs 110 million. During mid-seventeenth century, the annual Mughal revenue doubled to Rs 220 million.[125]

As soon as the Mughal power projection in Central Asia failed, the Safavid threat in Afghanistan reappeared. Shah Safi died in 1642 and was succeeded by his son, then aged 10 years. The latter was crowned as Abbas II.[126] In 1648, Abbas II (r. 1642–66) advanced to Tus city (old name: Mashhad-i-Mukaddas) for capturing Kandahar. From the border of Khorasan, Shah Abbas recruited matchlock men and pioneers. Agents were sent to Farah, Seistan, and Herat for collecting grain to feed the army on its march. The Persians planned to attack in the winter when the Mughals would be unable to send reinforcements through Multan and Kabul to Kandahar. Nevertheless, the Mughal court appointed Prince Muhammad Aurangzeb *Bahadur* as the commander of the relief force which numbered to 50,000 cavalry and 10,000 infantry (including matchlock men and soldiers equipped with *bans*). Aurangzeb was ordered to proceed through the shortest route which was across Bangash-i-Bala, Bangash-i-Payin, Kabul, Ghazni, and then to Kandahar. Meanwhile, Abbas II marched from Herat to Tus, and then to Farah. After halting at the last mentioned place for some days, he then advanced towards Kandahar. The main body of the Persian army was under the Shah. He detached two contingents which comprised the Persian advanced guard. One detachment comprising 8,000 cavalry and some matchlock men under Mehrab Khan was ordered to besiege the fortress of Bust. Another detachment comprising some 6,000 Qizilbash cavalry under Saz Khan Balik was ordered to occupy Zamindawar.[127]

Daulat Khan, the Mughal commandant of Kandahar, took position in the interior of the fort. Besides depending on the Mughal garrison, he tried to strengthen his position by levying Afghan mercenaries from Kandahar. He stationed a party of imperial and locally raised matchlock men at the top of the Kambul Hill. Kakar Khan defended the towers with some matchlock men.[128] Mughal troops as well as local levies raised in Kandahar garrisoned the fortifications at Daulatabad and Mandavi. Kandahar Fort was surrounded by three hills. However, Chihal Zinah (forty steps), the towers on the top of the highest hill, constructed by Qilich/Kalich Khan were not guarded properly. From these towers, guns and matchlocks could be fired into the interiors of the forts of Daulatabad and Mandavi. The Qizilbash captured these towers and posted some matchlock men who opened a destructive fire on the garrisons of the two above-mentioned forts.[129] Meanwhile, a defeatist attitude spread among the Mughal mansabdars, ahadis, and the matchlock men. They argued that since no aid from India would reach them, if they stayed to fight the Persians then they would either be killed by the Qizilbash or become prisoners and would have to endure captivity for life. Daulat Khan failed to provide resolute leadership. As a result, most of the Mughal soldiers deserted the entrenchments. Hence, the Persians quite easily entered the Sher Haji. The siege of Kandahar, which lasted for fifty-four days, cost the Persians some 2,000 (including 600 Qizilbash) and about 400 men of the Mughal garrison dead. The Persian ruler with most of his cavalry left Kandahar due to lack of forage and grain. However, before leaving for Khorasan, the Shah appointed Mehrab Khan with 10,000 Qizilbash cavalry and matchlock men to garrison Kandahar. Dost Ali Uzbek was left with another detachment to garrison Bust.[130]

Prince Aurangzeb with the relief army reached Multan and then reached Kohat. At that place, he halted and sent agents to get information about the level of snow fall before advancing further. Khalil Beg was sent in advance to level the road and construct the bridges. He sent an intelligence report that the route through the hilly country of Kohistan was so deep with snow that it cannot be used for another one month. Aurangzeb then decided to advance through Peshawar by way of the rugged Sendh–Basta Pass and finally reached Kabul. From Kabul, he marched to Kandahar and fixed his headquarter half a kos from the fort. In 1649, when the Mughal siege of Kandahar Fort had dragged for three and a half months, the Mughal besieging army started suffering due to lack of grain and fodder. Due to absence of a siege train of battering guns and absence of skilled artillery men, the Mughals failed to capture the fort. Aurangzeb could not bring the heavy guns with him due to the difficult route through which he entered Kabul from Peshawar. When the winter approached, Aurangzeb decided to withdraw from Kandahar due to rising logistical difficulties.[131]

In 1651, Shah Jahan appointed Sadullah Khan and Aurangzeb with 50,000 cavalry and 10,000 infantry (including gunners, matchlock men, rocket men, and so on), respectively, and they were given orders to capture the forts of Kandahar, Bust, and Zamindawar. This time, Emperor Shah Jahan decided to fit out an artillery train with the relief army. Sadullah Khan was given eight heavy and twenty light guns. The latter threw projectiles which weighed between four to five pounds. In addition, 20 *hathnals* and 100 *shutarnals* were present. About 3,000 camels were employed for carrying lead, powder, and iron shots. When the siege had dragged for sixty-eight days, one Mughal gun named Fateh Lashkar by a lucky shot was able to kill the Persian Commandant of Artillery named Muhammad Beg. The Qizilbash sallied out of the Kandahar Fort and attacked the Mughal trenches. The Mughals prevailed and carried on the parallels and zig-zag trenches. The Mughals had with them seven breaching guns. They were able to destroy the parapets and bastions of the fort. Of these seven guns, the barrels of two cracked due to continuous firing. The gunners of the other five breaching guns were not skilled enough to fire the guns with effect. The imperial chronicler Inayat Khan in his account of the siege of Kandahar accepts Mughal technical inferiority in the sphere of siege guns and skilled gunners vis-à-vis the Safavids. Meanwhile, news reached Aurangzeb that the Uzbeks had reached the vicinity of Ghazni. Aurangzeb was afraid that his LOC with Kabul might be severed. So, he decided to retreat and raised the siege.[132]

Shah Jahan just could not accept the fact that the Mughals had lost Kandahar to the Safavids. In 1652, Aurangzeb's brother Prince Dara Shikoh (Shah Jahan's favourite son and designated successor) was given the subas of Kabul and Multan with the express order of recapturing Kandahar. A heavier siege train accompanied Dara. Two breaching guns were given to him which threw iron shots. The gunners of these two guns were under Kasim Khan. Another big gun which accompanied Dara threw shots, each of which weighed one cwt. About 30,000 cannon balls, 5,000 maunds of gunpowder, 2,500 maunds of lead, and 14,000 bans also accompanied Dara's army. In 1653, the Mughals under Rustam Khan were able to capture the Bust Fort. He dismantled the fort and joined the main army near Kandahar. However, Kandahar Fort still eluded the Mughals. The siege dragged on for five months. By this time, all lead, powder, and iron shots were expended. And due to the presence of a huge force in the environs of Kandahar for such a long time, supply of forage also grew scarce. As winter approached, Dara, like his brother Aurangzeb in 1651, decided to retreat.[133] The Mughal adventure in Kandahar was over. The three failed Mughal sieges of Kandahar (1649, 1652, and 1653) cost Rs 120 million or half of Mughal annual revenue.[134] The Mughals would not make any further attempt to recover Kandahar. British India would send its troops twice in the nineteenth century to occupy Kandahar temporarily.

Being a strategic province, the Mughals spent much blood and trea-sure for maintaining their rule in Afghanistan. The Khyber Pass was the gateway of India for any power marching into India from either Persia or Central Asia. Security of the Khyber Pass required control over Jagdalak and Kabul. Further, the Mughals imported Turki horse through Kabul. And the possession of Turki horse which was supe-rior to all types of horse breeds in India gave Mughals the superiority of cavalry in the subcontinent. And the cream of the Mughal army comprised cavalry. During late seventeenth century, the Mughals main-tained some 100,000 Turki horses.[135] Lastly, the Mughals also had a sentimental attachment towards Kabul where Babur first established his kingdom after being expelled from his ancestral Ferghana. From an economic point of view, the Mughals had to spend more than the revenue they derived from Afghanistan in maintaining their rule over this country. In fact, Kabul was one of the poorest subas of the Mughal empire. A revenue statement of Shah Jahan's reign shows that the provinces of Agra and Lahore yielded the greatest amount of revenue. Each of these provinces yielded 822,500,000 dams (currency used in Akbar's time) annually. In contrast, Kabul and Kashmir yielded only 250,000,000 dams annually. And the military expenditure was highest for maintaining Mughal rule in Afghanistan.[136] The suba of Kabul was divided into forty mahals (subdivision of suba). The rev-enue from Kabul amounted to 157,625,380 dams.[137] Most of the revenues from Afghanistan were derived from poppy cultivation. Like the scenario at present, even 500 years earlier, the principal prof-itable crop for the Afghan cultivators was poppy. However, unlike the present US–NATO-dominated Hamid Karzai government, the Mughals encouraged poppy cultivation for several reasons. Military campaigns were dependent on *majun* (opium). Both the Muslim (Turkish and Afghans) and Rajput troopers and the Hindu and Muslim mansabdars took opium during campaigning and especially before the beginning of battles. In fact, sometimes campaigns ceased due to inadequate supply of opium. The ladies of the royal harem were also heavily addicted to opium. Further, the Mughal aristocrats were addicted to a drink which was a mixture of water, opium, apricots, and plums.[138] So, poppies remained Afghanistan's principal exportable cash crop from medieval times till the rise of the Taliban.

In general, the Afghans hated Mughal overlordship. Indigenous Pashtun (not Afghan) patriotism was expressed by the Pathan warrior poet Khusal Khan (b. 1613) of the Khatak tribe.[139] In the 1660s and the 1670s, the Afghan tribes proved to be a problem for Emperor Aurangzeb (r. 1659–1707). The situation would have been far more dangerous for the Mughals had the Afghan uprising occurred simultaneously with the anticipated Persian invasion. Tarbiyat Khan, the Mughal envoy in Persia, reported negatively about Shah Abbas. The latter was reported to be preparing for war against the Mughals from Khorasan. Aurangzeb sent Prince Muhammad Muazzam and Maharaja Jaswant Singh to Kabul and himself decided to march to Punjab from Deccan. On 22 August 1666, the Persian monarch died while travelling from Farrukhabad to Isfahan. The danger of war with Persia being over, Aurangzeb ordered Muazzam to stop at Lahore.[140] The Afridis were concentrated around the Khyber Pass and threatened Mughal control in this region.[141]

In 1667, the Yusufzais, who inhabited the region of Swat and Bajaur Valley and the plains north of Peshawar, rebelled under Mulla Chalak. The latter appointed Bhagu as wazir of his new-fangled dominion. Bhagu with 5,000 clansmen crossed the Indus above Attock and invaded Pakhli. Pakhli is the plain lying east of the Pakhli River in the Hazara district and through this region ran the principal road from Punjab to Kashmir. Bhagu captured the Shadman Fort. Encouraged by the Mughal reverses, Yusufzai bands began to plunder western Peshawar and Attock districts.[142] Kamil Khan, the *faujdar* of Attock, was ordered to concentrate the contingents of all the jagirdars near Nilab and crush the rebellious tribesmen. Nilab was a town near the River Nilab (blue water), that is, the upper Indus. Amir Khan, the *subadar* of Kabul, sent Shamsher Khan with 5,000 men to cooperate with Kamil Khan. However, Kamil Khan did not wait for the reinforcements under Shamsher Khan but attacked the Yusufzais.[143] On 2 May 1667, Shamsher Khan crossed the Nilab River and came towards Attock. The Yusufzais retreated to the hills. On the same date, Aurangzeb sent Muhammad Amir Khan, the mir bakshi, with 9,000 cavalry to crush the Yusufzais. However, before the arrival of the imperial reinforcements, Shamsher Khan was able to defeat the rebellious tribe and took 300 of their maliks as prisoners.[144]

Muhammad Amin Khan, the subadar of Lahore, was appointed as subadar of Kabul. When the winter set in and there was heavy snow fall, all the roads in the Kabul region were blocked. To avoid the privation of facing the Kabul winter and also to maintain line of communications with India, that is, especially Punjab, Amin Khan put Kabul in charge of his *naib* (deputy) and left for the milder climate of Peshawar. While stationed in Peshawar, Amin Khan had to deal with the Afridi uprising in 1672. He sent a strong force against the Shipa Sept near Shahbazgarhi and the Bajaur tribes. Shahbazgarhi was plundered and 6,000 cattle were taken from the tribe as punishment. Looting the livestock of the rebellious tribesmen was a technique which the British also followed in the nineteenth century. During the Rabi (spring) season, Amin Khan started preparation for return to Kabul. Mirza Ali Beg, the faujdar of Jalalabad, was harsh towards the Pathans of his district. In retaliation, the Pathans blocked the road to Kabul to obstruct the journey of Amin Khan to Kabul. When the advance guard of Amin Khan reached Jamrud, about seven kos from Peshawar, news reached the Mughals that the Afghans had blocked the road further up. One lobby within the Mughal camp was for conciliating and negotiating with the Afghans. However, Amin Khan refused to treat with the rebellious Afghans and marched towards Jamrud. When the Mughals reached Ali Masjid, news reached that the Afghan attack was imminent. Amin Khan hastily prepared his artillery *morchas* (batteries) to meet the imminent attack. At the Tarta Pass (3,400 feet), the Afghans descended from the hillside in several waves and attacked Amin's camp. The imperial camp was cut off totally by the Afghans who surrounded it. Amin Khan made a mistake in not placing guards at the heights on both sides of the road. The Afghans cut off the water supply and the Mughals suffered from a shortage of drinking water. Amin Khan sent feelers to the Afghan camp. Negotiations and confrontation occurred simultaneously in case of Mughal COIN. The Afghan sirdars demanded not only restoration of their annual subsidies but also *inams* (special rewards). Amin Khan found the demand for extra subsidy humiliating and decided to attack the Afghans again.[145]

On 21 April 1672, the Afghans from the top of the hills equipped with bows, arrows, and muskets attacked the Mughals from all sides. Some veteran Mughal soldiers tried to climb up the hills to drive away the Afghans. However, the Mughals being caught in a disadvantageous lower position were defeated. Utter confusion prevailed in the Mughal camp. Pandemonium broke out in the Mughal column. Amin Khan's son Abdullah Khan died. Though Amin Khan was able to escape to Peshawar, about 10,000 Mughal soldiers became casualties. Further, 2 crore in cash and kind was looted from the Mughal camp. To cap it all, the Afghans were able to capture 20,000 men and women who were sold as slaves in Turan (Central Asia).[146] As a mark of imperial resentment, Amin Khan was transferred from the suba of Kabul. Then, Aurangzeb gave the task of preparing an army of retaliation to Muazzam Khan, the subadar of Lahore, and Mahabat Khan, a mansabdar, who was transferred from Deccan to the North-West Frontier. The Mughal army under their joint command marched to Peshawar and then established a camp as all the roads were blocked due to the winter snow fall. During the spring season, the Mughal army with an advance guard of 5,000 cavalry under Raja Mandhata moved into Jamrud. Aurangzeb decided to strengthen the army moving towards Kabul. Rajput mansabdar and the subadar of Gujarat, Maharaja Jaswant Singh, was assigned the province of Kabul and Shujat Khan with a strong park of artillery was appointed as the leader of his vanguard.[147] Shujat Khan made a mistake in advancing too rapidly and was thus separated from the main body under Jaswant Singh. Shujat Khan crossed Gandak and, while passing through the Kharapa Pass, was ambushed by the Afghans on 14 February 1674. In a daring night attack, the Afghans charged from the hilltops. The next morning, Shujat Khan's force was attacked again.[148]

When the news of the attack was bought to Jaswant, he decided to hurry. He immediately dispatched the artillery under two Rajput sirdars named Bachraj and Raghunath. A contingent of 200 cavalry was ordered to guard the artillery park and another contingent of 300 cavalry was ordered to attack the Afghans. The Afghans who had surrounded Shujat

Khan's camp were attacked suddenly and simultaneously from all sides and were defeated.[149] However, Shujat Khan died in this encounter.[150]

Hearing the news of continuous Afghan attacks on the imperial armies, Aurangzeb decided to intervene personally. On 7 April 1674, Aurangzeb, with another army and a strong park of artillery, started marching towards Kabul. On reaching Lahore, he stopped for twenty days in order to recruit more soldiers. Sarbuland Khan with 2,500 troopers and artillery was ordered to move along the foot of the hills. Meanwhile, Jaswant Singh came from Jamrud and paid his respects to Aurangzeb at Rawalpindi. In September 1674, Prince Akbar and Asad Khan were ordered to move quickly to Kabul through Kohat. Aurangzeb with the main army crossed the Indus at Attock. The news of the entry of Mughal emperor into Kabul created a flurry among the rulers of Persia (Safi II/Suleiman, r. 1666–94) and Turan, and they sent their ambassadors. Prince Muhammad Akbar was appointed as the subadar of Kabul.[151] On 14 June 1675, Mukarram Khan and Muhammad Yaqub were ordered to attack the Afghans at Khapash. The tribesmen's houses were plundered and many males were taken as prisoners. However, the imperial force was ambushed in a water-less and road-less rugged terrain. Mukarram Khan escaped to Izzat Khan, the *thanadar* of Bajaur. On 14 June 1675, Sarbuland Khan with 9,000 troopers was sent against the rebellious Afghans. The imperial troops plundered the Afghans and destroyed their homes. In an attempt to consolidate Mughal control over the recently subdued regions, Aghar Khan and Hazbar Khan were appointed as thanadars of Jalalabad and Jagdalak, respectively.[152]

The Mughals realized that the Afghan chieftains ruled on the sufferance of their followers. Their power over the tribes was nominal. So, instead of propping up the tribal sirdars with imperial support, by late seventeenth century, the Mughal policy was to deter the tribesmen from rebellion by 'showing the flag'. However, the British went to a great extent in supporting the authority of the tribal sirdars. The Mughals did not close the door to political concessions. The Mughal durbar allowed the Afridis, Shinwaris, Khattaks, and Yusufzais to levy toll on the trade caravans which passed between Lahore and Kabul. Further, Rs 600,000 annually was granted to the various tribes as political pension. Still, the financial package seemed inadequate. Occasionally, leaders emerged among the tribes who claimed princely or religious authority (mad *mullah*s of British era) and led rebellion against imperial authority.

Then, the Mughal army had to be used to crush the rebels. Mughal COIN techniques involved sending a military detachment to crush the uprising and then to establish *thanas* with garrisons in each of them in order to consolidate Mughal hold over this region and establish security in the erstwhile troubled zone. At least till the mid-seventeenth century, most Mughal outposts in Afghanistan were withdrawn during winters and the pacification process had to start anew in spring.[153] The Mughals sent mobile columns to suppress the rebellious Ghurids, Gilzai, and Yusufzai tribes. The rebellious tribesmen were expelled from their villages. The seats of the tribal sirdars were raided and thanas with strong garrisons were established there. Prince Shah Alam Bahadur was appointed as the subadar of Kabul and then Aurangzeb left for Agra.[154]

MUGHAL DECLINE AND AFGHAN REVIVAL: 1707–1810

By the beginning of the eighteenth century, the three Islamic empires of Central and Southern Asia (Safavids, Uzbeks, and Mughals) were declining. Decline of the Central Asian trade and reduction in agricultural productivity were key factors in the weakening of the landed agrarian bureaucratic Islamic empires of Asia. The Mughal empire was racked by agrarian crisis which in turn intensified faction fight among the mansabdars, resulting in the decline of the power of the Mughal durbar and rise of semi-autonomous subadars in the outlying regions of the empire.[155] Especially after the death of the last great Mughal emperor Aurangzeb, in 1707, the Mughal central government lost control over the outlying subas. During the late seventeenth century, the Uzbek Khanate was economically impoverished because large-scale movement of the caravans along the Great Silk Road had stopped.[156] Decline of Persia's silk export to the West weakened the financial foundations of the Safavid monarchy. In addition, unchecked debauchery by Shah Hossein (r. 1694–1726) and centrifugal tendencies of the Qizilbash chieftains further weakened the central government at Isfahan. In 1719, Asadullah Khan's 15,000 Afghans of Herat defeated a 30,000-strong Persian army under Saif Quli Khan.[157] In 1722, the Afghans invaded Persia which was then under the weak rule of Shah Hossein. On 8 March 1722, the Persian royal army was defeated by 11,000 Afghans at the Battle of Gulnabad. Victory went to the Afghans because of the tactical retreat by Amanullah's Gilzais and then the pursuing Persian cavalry was destroyed by fire of the *zamburaks*. The zamburaks fired balls weighing one to two pounds. As the zamburak volley dislocated Persian cavalry, the Afghan horsemen led a counter-attack, and victory was complete.[158] Seven years of Afghan domination of Persia resulted in the death of 1 million inhabitants of the country.[159] Afghan control over Persia was finally ended by Nadir Shah.

Nadir Shah was born on 6 August 1698 in north Khorasan. He belonged to the Qereqlu Afshar semi-nomadic Turkoman tribe.[160] At a young age, he led a band of robbers. The collapse of the Safavid monarchy enabled him to pillage the Persian frontier province of Khorasan. He seized the Kalat Fort by murdering the governor, his uncle. Then, he defeated the Afghans in Khorasan and captured Nishapur District. For defeating the Afghans, he became the national hero. And in 1727, he entered the service of Shah Tahmasp. On 26 August 1732, Shah Tahmasp was deposed by Nadir. The latter became the regent of the eight-month-old son of the Shah. When four years later the infant died, Nadir ascended the throne on 26 February 1736 as *Shahenshah*.[161]

Nadir gained Armenia and Georgia from the Ottomans and the provinces bordering the Caspian from the Russians. The Island of Bahrain was taken from the Arabs. Next, the predatory Bakhtiari tribe of the Shuster Hills was pacified and some were enrolled in his army. In 1737, Nadir with 80,000 men marched towards Kandahar. The Afghans at Kandahar posed a threat to Khorasan in particular and to Persia in general. Moreover, recovery of Kandahar was necessary in order to reclaim the full heritage of the Safavids. At that time, Kandahar was under the Afghan chief Hussein. On 30 March 1737, the Persian army invested Kandahar. The fort fell on 12 March 1738.[162]

Nadir then advanced towards Mughal-held Afghanistan and India for several reasons. First, the faction-ridden Mughal durbar, despite Nadir's repeated requests, failed to cooperate with the Persians against the rebellious Afghans in Kandahar. Actually, the faction-ridden Mughal durbar suffering from financial troubles and from Maratha threat in central India was in no position to launch a military expedition against the Afghans along the Indus. Second, the Mughal durbar refused to recognize Nadir as Shahenshah of Persia. The Mughals were not sure whether Nadir would last long in Persia's tortuous political scene. Third, the weak Mughal centre encouraged Nadir to invade India to plunder the country of its riches, a traditional motive of many Central Asian warlords including Amir Timur. Nadir commanded about 55,000 cavalry.[163] In June 1738, Nadir occupied Mughal Kabul.[164] At the Battle of Karnal (24 February 1739), the Mughals were defeated by the Persians. Rustam Ali, who composed his chronicle in 1741–42, noted: 'The Indian warriors ... fought with their cruel swords.... The Iranis ... firing their guns from a distance and from different quarters, made heaps of corpses of Indians'.[165] Another Mughal chronicler, named Muhammad Muhsin Sadiki, also noted the hailstorm of bullets unleashed by the Persians and the uselessness of the heavy Mughal cannons which cannot be used effectively in accordance with the changing tactical scenarios.[166] Superior Persian cavalry, long-range muskets, and zamburaks destroyed the indisciplined and ill-led Mughal force which depended on elephants and slow firing immobile large cannons. On 20 March 1739, Nadir entered Delhi.[167] After extracting a heavy indemnity in cash from the hapless Mughal emperor Muhammad Shah, Nadir annexed the Mughal provinces west of the Indus to his own empire. On 16 May 1739, Nadir left Delhi for Persia.[168] The regions west of the Indus were thus lost to Delhi government permanently. Not even the Raj would be able to conquer it permanently.

After Nadir's murder by his own soldiery in June 1747, one of his famous Afghan generals named Ahmad Shah Abdali (b. 1723–d. 1773; r. Afghanistan 1747–73) of the Durrani tribe established an independent realm centred around Afghanistan. Ahmad Shah is regarded by some scholars as the founder of the first 'national' Afghan monarchy. In 1747, near Kandahar, the Abdali tribes held a *jirga* and selected Ahmad Khan, then aged 24/25, as their ruler. A holy man (a Sufi master named Sabir Shah) declared him as *Dur-i-Durrani* (pearl of pearls).[169] Ahmad Khan, later known as Ahmad Shah Durrani/Abdali, was born in 1722/23 at Multan.[170] He was from the Saduzoi sub-tribe of the Abdalis.[171] In his sixteenth year, Ahmad Khan was appointed in Nadir's personal staff as a *yasawal* (orderly officer). Later, he rose to the rank of *bank-bashi* (treasury officer). As commander of the Afghan contingent, Ahmad accompanied Nadir in his Indian and Turkish campaigns.[172]

Ahmad Shah established a rudimentary civil and military administration which started to become dysfunctional the moment he closed his eyes. At the apex of the administration was the monarch. An important royal prerogative was the right to issue coinage; also, the *khutba* (religious sermon) was read in the name of the king. Moreover, the king was the commander-in-chief of the army. Theoretically, the monarch's power was unlimited, but in practice it was not. In fact, the king's authority was hemmed by the presence of powerful families and tribal plus clan leaders. Much depended on the charisma, personality, and military leadership of the monarch. Most of the officers of the polity, including those in the king's household, were hereditary in nature. The principal income of the state in peacetime was land revenue. Ahmad Shah, in order to placate the tribal sirdars, fixed the land revenue very lightly. None of his weak successors dared to increase the rate of land revenue. The king lacked the right to resume the grants issued by his predecessors. Only rarely after the civil wars, the victors resumed the land grants from the defeated party. In general, the administration was geared to mobilize manpower of western Afghanistan for manning the army and economic assets from the rich Indian provinces east of the Indus.[173]

The king was assisted in administration by the grand *vizir*/wazir. The grand wazir like the modern prime minister was in charge of supervising all the departments. This post was filled up either from Barakzai or Saduzoi clan. Below the grand wazir, came the *munshi bakshi* (chief secretary) who handled all the king's correspondence and the *hircarah bakshi* (head of intelligence department). All the mounted and foot messengers were under the latter officer. The other important officials were *nasakchi bakshi* (whose duty was to superintend all punishment) and *zabt bagi* (who was in charge of seizing property which had been ordered to be confiscated or sequestrated). The post of *mir akhur* (master of horses) was hereditary. The post of *ishikagzi bakshi* (royal doorkeeper, actually master of ceremonies) always went to the Poplazais. And the post of *arzbagi* was hereditary in the family of Akram Khan. The arzbagi was in charge of introducing the persons who came to the court in order to meet the monarch. The arzbagi had under him two officials: *jaurchi bakshi* and *chaus bakshi*. Other important officers of the royal households were *sunduktur bakshi* (keeper of the wardrobe or keeper of the jewels) and *hakim bakshi* (chief physician). The whole kingdom was divided into twenty-seven provinces excluding Baluchistan. Of the provinces, eighteen were governed by the *hakims*. These provinces were .Herat, Farah, Kandahar, Ghazni, Kabul, Bamiyan, Ghorband, Jalalabad, Lamghman, Peshawar, Dera Ismail Khan, Dera Ghazi Khan, Shikarpur,

Siwi Sind, Kashmir, Chach Hazara, Leia, and Multan. The hakims collected the revenue and commanded the militia in the provinces. The
revenue was not collected directly but through the tribal chieftains in
the provinces. The tribal chiefs in a province also controlled the police.
In each province, there was a sirdar, who was in charge of the regular
army. The sirdar reported to the hakim. However, when the hakim was
a Durrani chief then he also held simultaneously the post of sirdar in
that province. The administration of civil justice was conducted by the
qazi who also reported to the hakim. In the rest of the nine provinces,
instead of hakim, the provincial governor was known as sirdar who was
a Durrani chief. He generally ruled through a deputy, who collected the
revenue from the head of the tribes. In such provinces, the qazis were
appointed by the king.[174] Thus, we see that even at the height of power,
the Afghan monarchy was not an authoritarian institution but an arbitrary one. The Afghan royal administration was more dependent on
the hereditary principles and tribal sirdars rather than on impersonal
bureaucrats. The Afghan administration was more decentralized and
federal than that of the Mughals, Safavids, and the Ottomans.

Ahmad Shah built up a well-disciplined Afghan army. Besides
Afghans, Ahmad Shah also employed Qizilbash cavalry. These troopers
were Persians who had settled in western Afghanistan. He organized
his heavy cavalry in twenty-four corps and each of them numbered to
1,200 horsemen. In addition, Ahmad Shah also maintained *yatims*
(light cavalry) used for reconnaissance and harassing the enemy army.
Camels were used for transportation of military baggage and for the
zamburaks. Each zamburak was worked by two men and each such gun
was carried on the back of a camel.[175]

Ahmad Shah in his death bed warned his successor that they should
always remain defensive vis-à-vis Persia and Turkestan but should
launch periodic raids into India which was to function as a cash cow for
the cash-strapped Afghan monarchy. As regards Persia and Turkestan,
Ahmad Shah's aim was to defend Khorasan and Balkh. Ahmad Shah
noted that not only the Uzbeks were militarily powerful but they
also lacked economic assets which could be plundered after defeating them.[176] Ahmad Shah led several raids into India. In December
1747, he left Peshawar with 18,000 men. Besides the Afghans, the
frontier Pathans encouraged by the prospect of loot also joined Ahmad
Shah. With 30,000 Afghan cavalry, Ahmad Shah entered Lahore on

12 January 1748 and after staying there for a month moved towards Delhi. The Mughal wazir Qumaruddin came with an army of 60,000 to confront Abdali. On 11 March 1748, the Afghans and the Mughals met each other at Manupur, about 10 miles from Sirhind. The Mughals enjoyed artillery superiority over the Afghans.[177]

In the ensuing battle, Qumaruddin was killed but his son Mir Mannu, who took over command, forced the Afghans to retreat. The retreating Afghans were harried all the way back to the Indus by the Sikhs. Mir Mannu was appointed subadar of Punjab in April 1748. However, the Afghans still held Multan and the Raja of Jammu declared his independence from the Mughals and created an independent Dogra kingdom. Worse, Mir Mannu received no support from the Mughal wazir Safdar Jang (leader of the Irani/Persian mansabdars) who was trying to undermine the power of the Turani party, whose leader was Mir Mannu. Nevertheless, Mir Mannu ordered Adina Beg to curb the power of the Sikhs. And Kaura Mal (a feudatory of Mir Mannu) with a force of Sikhs and Turani mercenaries was ordered to eject the Afghans from Multan. In December 1748, Abdali left Peshawar again for India. Mir Mannu sent frantic appeals to Delhi for aid but Safdar Jang did not send him any aid. Mannu with his own force stopped the Afghans at Chenab, at a point 4 miles east of Wazirabad. Abdali realized that the coming summer would cause hardship for his soldiers in India in case he had to go for a long-drawn campaign. While with the main army Ahmad Shah faced Mir Mannu, the former sent a strong column under Jahan Khan to Lahore. Mannu's deputy at Lahore moved out from the city to confront Jahan Khan. This enabled Kapur Singh and the Sikhs under him to occupy Lahore temporarily. Jahan Khan was unsuccessful in Lahore and the Afghans wanted to return with whatever gain was possible. Since Mir Mannu had not received any help from Delhi, he decided to open negotiations. Abdali was given all the territory west of the Indus which was previously ceded to Nadir Shah. In addition, the revenue of the four districts of Punjab: Sialkot, Aurangabad, Gujarat, and Pasrur, which amounted to Rs 1,400,000, was also assigned to Abdali. Theoretically, Mir Mannu from a Mughal official became a feudatory of the Afghan ruler. Mir Mannu then returned to Lahore and engaged in the task of chastizing the Sikhs. When Mir Mannu failed to pay the revenue of the four districts of Punjab which had been ceded to the Afghans, Ahmad Shah launched his third invasion of India. In the

middle of November 1751, advance guard of the Afghan army under
Jahan Khan crossed the Indus and Ahmad Shah with the main body
followed behind. Mir Mannu paid Rs 900,000 to buy off the invaders.
The Afghans took the money but moved further into Punjab. No help
was forthcoming from the Delhi durbar.

Mir Mannu concentrated his force by calling Kaura Mal from
Multan and Adina Beg Khan from Jalandhar. Mir Mannu's army comprised 20,000 Sikhs. In December 1751, Mir Mannu crossed Ravi to
check the Afghans under Jahan Khan. Instead of joining Jahan Khan,
Abdali made a detour and closed in towards Lahore from the north-
east. Mannu returned to the city and entrenched himself outside the
city walls. This tactic proved to be a mistake as the Afghans controlled
the countryside from where they could draw provisions for their army.
In contrast, Mannu had to depend on the supplies stocked in the city
in peacetime. After six weeks, all the grain and fodder in his camp
was exhausted. Then, Mir Mannu called a council of war. Kaura Mal
counselled patience as it was already March and Abdali was bound to
go back to Afghanistan with the onset of the summer season in April.
But Adina Beg was for immediate action. Mir Mannu accepted Adina
Beg's advice. On 5 March 1752, Mannu attacked the Afghans. Kaura
Mal fell in the battlefield and Adina Beg with his contingent retreated.
Mir Mannu fought on as long as possible and then surrendered. The
Afghans extracted Rs 3,000,000 in cash from Mannu and by the terms of
the treaty which was ratified by the Mughal emperor on 13 April 1752,
Lahore and Multan were ceded to Ahmad Shah Abdali. Thus, Punjab
broke away from the declining Mughal system to the rising Abdali
empire. Before returning to Afghanistan, Ahmad Shah also conquered
Kashmir. Mir Mannu was appointed as governor of Punjab by Ahmad
Shah and ordered to check the rising power of the Sikhs. Mir Mannu
died in May 1754. At that time, the scenario in Punjab became chaotic.
Mir Mannu's widow, Mughlani Begum, controlled Lahore. Multan and
the four districts, Gujarat, Sialkot, Pasrur, and Aurangabad, continued
to pay the revenue to Abdali. But Jalandhar and Sirhind were under
Adina Beg.[178]

By this time, the Mughal empire had disintegrated into several semi-
independent *nawabi*s (like Awadh, Hyderabad, Bengal, and so on)
and the Marathas had emerged as the premier power in the subcontinent. The subadars had declared independence and styled themselves

as nawabs. They, however, accepted the de jure authority of the Mughal emperor in Delhi. In 1760, Ahmad Shah with 60,000 cavalry, 20,000 infantry, armed with jezails and 2,000 zamburaks and 200 pieces of heavy cannons, moved from Afghanistan with the objective of destroying the Maratha power in north India. The Rohillas (with 45,000 cavalry and infantry with 90 guns) and the Nawab of Awadh Shuja-ud-Daulah (with 30,000 infantry and cavalry and fifty artillery pieces) joined Ahmad Shah's side against the Marathas. On 12 January 1761, Ahmad Shah engaged the Marathas in a conventional set-piece battle known in history as the Third Battle of Panipat.[179]

The Jat ruler Raja Suraj Mal advised the Marathas to conduct guerrilla warfare against Ahmad Shah for several reasons. First, the 51,000-strong Maratha light cavalry force was suited for harassing attacks against the Afghans' LOC with Kabul. But against the heavy disciplined Afghan *sowar*s mounted on sturdy Turcoman horses, the Maratha ponies were useless in a battle. Again, Abdali was bound to go back in Afghanistan in summer. So, it was better for the Marathas to bide time by conducting attritional guerrilla warfare from their base at Jhansi. The Maratha sirdar Malhar Rao Holkar agreed with Suraj Mal's assessment of the scenario. However, the headstrong Maratha commander Sadashiv Rao Bhau and the Peshwa's son Viswas Rao did not pay any attention to Suraj Mal and decided to engage Abdali in a conventional battle. Bhau and Viswas Rao put their faith on the 9,000 soldiers, trained in the European method of warfare and equipped with handguns and field artillery, led by Ibrahim Khan in the Maratha force.[180] When the Maratha force encamped at Panipat in late 1760, Abdali used his superior cavalry to cut all communications between the Maratha camp and the surrounding regions. Soon, the Maratha soldiers and horses started suffering due to lack of provisions.[181] Abdali's generalship, infantry–cavalry cooperation, zamburaks, and superior logistics resulted in an Afghan victory over the Marathas at Third Panipat.

Ahmad Shah conquered Sind, Baluchistan, and Kashmir. The total population of his empire came to about 5 million and of them half were Pathans and the rest were a mixture of Hazaras, Qizilbash, and so on. When Ahmad Shah died in 1772/3, he was succeeded by his son Timur Shah (b. 1748–d. 1793; r. 1773–93).[182] Even the core of the empire was a motley collection of heterogeneous disparate groups, divided along ethnic, linguistic, religious, and racial lines. The principal five groups in Afghanistan were the Pathans, Tajiks, Uzbeks, Hazaras, and Aimaq (also known as Chahar Aimaq). The Pathans (Hanafi Sunni Muslims) dominated Afghanistan. The Pathans were divided into three major groups: Durranis (dominant in the north and west of Kandahar), Gilzais (dominant in Kabul and Zabul provinces), and the Indus frontier Pathans (which included Afridis, Waziris, Mohmands, Mashuds, Jaji, Mangal, Kakar, Orakzais, Shinwaris, and so on). Among the Durranis, the Barakzai clan of the Mohammadzai sub-tribe was most important politically.[183]

In order to reduce the power of the Pashtuns, Timur changed the capital from Kandahar to Kabul and made Peshawar, on the eastern, that is, Indian, side of the Khyber Pass, as his winter capital.[184] Under Timur's weak rule, the Durrani empire lost Sind, Balkh, and Afghan Turkestan. There were revolts in Kashmir and Turkestan. When he died after a reign of twenty years, he left behind twenty-three sons. Timur Shah belonged to the Saduzoi clan of the Durrani tribe. The next in importance were the Barakzai clan of the Durrani tribe. The Barakzai clan inhabited the region south of Kandahar and the banks of Helmand. Those who inhabited the fertile banks of Helmand practised agriculture but the rest of the tribe were shepherds. Under Timur Shah, the Barakzai clan numbered some 30,000 families. Haji Jamal Khan of the Barakzai clan was a noble of Ahmad Shah. When Haji died, he left behind four sons. Timur made the eldest one, named Rahimdad Khan, as leader of the Barakzai clan in place of Haji. However, due to pressure from the other tribal leaders, Timur was forced to remove Rahimdad, who was appointed as keeper of the government records. In place of Rahimdad, Powindah Khan, the second brother, was appointed.[185]

Powindah Khan, the leader of the Barakzais, served Timur Shah with efficiency. When Azad Khan, the governor of Kashmir, rebelled, Sirdar Madad Khan and Powindah Khan led an expedition and chastized the rebellious governor. A grateful Timur Shah appointed Powindah as leader of a section of Glizai tribe in addition to his other posts. When Prince Abbas, son of Timur Shah, rebelled, the rebellious prince was joined by Arsalan Khan Mohmand. Powindah Khan was ordered to crush the rebellion. At Lalpurah, the rebel force was destroyed and Timur Shah gave his loyal servant the title of Sarfaraz (Lofty) Khan. Meanwhile, the Uzbek tribes threatened north Afghanistan. Timur Shah lost his nerve and decided to leave Kabul for Herat. Powindah Khan dissuaded his master from taking such a cowardly step. Powindah with an army marched towards Balkh and patched up a fragile peace with the Uzbek chief and then returned to Kabul. For the time being, the Uzbek threat was contained.[186]

When Timur Shah died in 1793, his fourth son, named Zaman Shah (r. 1793–1800) by his first wife, ascended the throne with Powindah Khan's support. The Durranis actually wanted to place Prince Abbas on the throne. Zaman Shah rewarded Powindah by giving him command of a part of the Qizilbash force and an annual salary of Rs 80,000.[187] But Powindah Khan who hoped to become the wazir was sidelined and, in disappointment, he engaged in treason against his master. Powindah got in touch with Shah Shuja. Wufadar Khan, who wanted to become the wazir, instigated Zaman Shah to take drastic action against Powindah Khan. Powindah was caught and executed. The result was that the powerful Barakzai clan now became hostile to the royal Saduzois.[188] Powindah's son Fateh Khan, along with Zaman Shah's half brother Shah Muhammad, took refuge with the ruler of Bokhara, Shah Murad Beg.[189]

Though Zaman Shah ascended the throne at Kabul, his half brothers ruled various parts of Afghanistan in a semi-independent manner. The situation is somewhat similar to that of the Mughal empire after the death of Babur and rise of Humayun on the Mughal throne. Humayun (not to be confused with Babur's son and Mughal emperor Humayun) seized Kandahar; Abbas ruled Peshawar; Haji Firuz-ud-Din and Mahmud took Herat. Zaman Shah was able to defeat Humayun and occupy Kandahar. Abbas was forced to give up Peshawar and thrown in the prison.[190]

Long-distance trade between Central Asia and India during the eighteenth century was conducted through Afghanistan.[191] Grain trade in Afghanistan was in the hands of the Hindu Punjabi Khatris/Arora merchants. They gave loans at very high rates (50 per cent interest) to the Afghan rulers for launching military expeditions into India.[192] In order to solve the perennial economic problem of Afghanistan, Zaman Shah decided to invade Punjab. Moreover, the disgruntled princes of India encouraged Zaman Shah to invade the subcontinent and overthrow the British. Two of Tipu Sultan's (ruler of Mysore till 1799) agents named Mir Raza Ali and Mir Habibullah visited Kandahar in

May 1797 and encouraged Zaman Shah to invade India to overthrow the British and the Marathas. Tipu agreed to provide a contingent of 20,000 soldiers to cooperate with Zaman Shah and Rs 3 crore as expense for his Indian invasion. One Shaikh Rahim Ali, an intelligence agent for the British, reported that the rulers of Jammu, Kangra, Awadh, and Rohilkhand also encouraged Zaman Shah to attack India. In 1798, the Shah requested the nawab of Awadh's assistance for the impending military operations against the Sikhs and the Marathas. Zaman Shah's objective was to annex Punjab and to retain the Mughal Emperor Shah Alam II as a puppet ruler in charge of the region between the Jamuna River (including Delhi) and Chambal. In November 1798, the British EIC collected grains and troops at Allahabad to protect Awadh in case Zaman was able to break through the Sikh resistance in Punjab. Zaman Shah left Kabul in September 1798 and reached Peshawar. On 13 October, he left Peshawar after receiving tributes. The Indus was crossed at Attock. On 3 November, the Afghan army reached Rawalpindi and on 16 November, the Shah was at Rohtas.[193]

Due to lack of available cash, Zaman Shah was able to muster only 12,000 miserably equipped men. His corps of 500 zamburaks lacked *sarwans* (camel drivers). Zaman's attempt to crush the Sikh resistance by engaging them in a decisive set-piece battle failed due to Ranjit Singh's strategy. The latter encouraged the Sikh *misls* (Sikh territorial band organized around a particular leader or family) to conduct guerrilla attacks on the invading Afghan army. This time a conventional Afghan army was at the receiving end of guerrilla resistance by the Sikh light cavalry. Due to dispersed but intense Sikh resistance, Zaman Shah failed to raise adequate revenue to sustain his army. When Zaman Shah was engaged in Punjab against the Sikhs, the Barakzais instigated rebellions in Afghanistan. Hence, Zaman was forced to return to Afghanistan. Back in Afghanistan, Zaman was arrested and blinded, and Fateh Khan took over in Kabul.[194]

Shah Mahmud, Timur Shah's son by his second wife, was placed on the throne and he ruled from 1800 till 1803. In 1801, Shah Shuja, brother of Zaman Shah and in charge of Peshawar, assembled a military force and marched towards Kabul. Shah Shuja commanded 10,000 Afridis and Yusufzais. He was opposed by Shah Mahmud's 3,000-strong cavalry and infantry force. The battle was fought at Surkh-Rud, west of Jalalabad. Indiscipline resulted in Shah Shuja's defeat. The eagerness of

Shuja's troop to loot the royal treasure enabled Fateh Khan to launch a charge by the Barakzais which discomfited Shuja's force. Shah Shuja was defeated and took refuge first among the sirdars of Khyber and then among the Afridis.[195] In 1802, Shuja with 12,000 Afridis attacked Peshawar which was under Mahmud's control. The confrontation which occurred in midsummer ended with a mass slaughter of the Shuja's soldiers. Shuja escaped to Chora and then took refuge in Tirah. Shuja then went from Zhob to Quetta and took money from some caravan traders. Then, he again advanced to Kabul with his rag-tag force and found Mahmud besieged in Bala Hissar. Fateh Khan with his 10,000-strong army retreated from the vicinity of Kabul, leaving the city to Shuja.[196] In July 1803, Shah Shuja became the ruler. Shuja ruled from 1803 till 1809 when he was driven out by Shah Mahmud. In 1809, Shah Mahmud returned from Herat and got support from his powerful *wazir* Fateh Khan of the Barakzai tribe. Shah Mahmud defeated Shah Shuja at the Battle of Nimla fought between Kabul and Peshawar. Though Shah Mahmud became the ruler of Afghanistan, Shuja (whose mother was of Yusufzai tribe) retained support among the tribes which bordered between India and Afghanistan.[197] Shuja would later become a pawn in the British attempt of controlling Afghanistan. Shah Mahmud continued to rule till 1818.[198] In 1809, Mountstuart Elphinstone arrived in Peshawar. At that time, Ranjit Singh's Khalsa kingdom's frontier ran between Hasan Abdal and Rawalpindi on the Margalla Pass.[199]

* * *

The Mughals, Safavids, and the Uzbeks, despite being Muslim themselves, faced tough opposition from the Afghans. This is not to argue that Islam had played no role in Afghan insurgency. Rather, the point we are trying to make is that Islam in general and jihad in particular were not crucial components of Afghan opposition to external invaders in their homelands. From the medieval era, the control for Afghanistan represented a sort of Great Game for controlling the heart of Eurasia. The Mughals were more successful than the British in maintaining a permanent presence in Afghanistan. The two principal Mughal bases for controlling Afghanistan were Kabul and Kandahar. The distance between Kabul and Kandahar was about 325 miles.[200] The Mughals were never able to capture Herat and control western and north-west

Afghanistan. This region was alternately under the influence of the Persians and the Uzbeks of Central Asia. The next chapter will show that British control over Afghanistan was transitory. Moreover, the Mughals, unlike the British, used Afghanistan as a springboard for projecting power in Central Asia.

As this chapter has shown, road building, subsidies to the tribes, construction of military outposts, forts, establishments of thanas, and military recruitment are the characteristic features of Mughal COIN which evolved over two centuries. Despite the passage of time and changes in military hardware, certain Mughal COIN techniques remained operational even under the British Indian empire, the imperial successors of the Mughals. The Mughals realized that border management of the frontier tribes is inseparable from the related and greater Afghan 'problem'. The Mughal technique of subsidies to placate the Afghan tribes, as the next chapter shows, continued in the British period. When the subsidy amount was cut, rebellions broke out which in turn cost the imperial power much more. So, reduction of tribal subsidies proved to be a false economy. Moreover, both the imperial powers through limited military recruitment tried to co-opt the potentially rebellious manpower of Afghanistan. Nevertheless, during the nineteenth century, certain innovative COIN techniques also evolved.

NOTES

1. George MacMunn, *Afghanistan from Darius to Amanullah* (1929; reprint, Lahore: Sang-e-Meel Publications, 2002), 2–3.

2. Robert F. Baumann, *Russian-Soviet Unconventional Wars in the Caucasus, Central Asia, and Afghanistan,* Leavenworth Papers, 20 (Fort Leavenworth, Kansas: Combat Studies Institute Press, 1993): 134; Larry P. Goodson, *Afghanistan's Endless War: State Failure, Regional Politics and the Rise of the Taliban* (Seattle/London: University of Washington Press, 2001), 19–20; Thomas Barfield, *Afghanistan: A Cultural and Political History* (Princeton/Oxford: Princeton University Press, 2010), 44.

3. MacMunn, *Afghanistan,* 6.

4. Jos J.L. Gommans, *The Rise of the Indo-Afghan Empire, c. 1710–1780* (Leiden: E.J. Brill, 1995), 11.

5. MacMunn, *Afghanistan,* 13; Barfield, *Afghanistan,* 47.

6. Nirodbhusan Roy, *Niamatullah's History of the Afghans* (n.d.; reprint, Lahore: Sang-e-Meel Publishers, 2002), 17. Mohan Lal considered the theories

of Israelite or Armenian origin of the Afghans as spurious. Mohan Lal, *Life of the Amir Dost Mohammaed Khan of Kabul with His Political Proceedings towards the English, Russian, and Persian Governments including the Victory and Disasters of the British Army in Afghanistan*, 2 vols (1846; reprint, New Delhi: Asian Educational Services, 2004), vol. 1, pp. 1–7.

7. H.W. Bellew, 'A New Afghan Question', *Journal of the United Service Institution of India*, 47 (1881): 49–97.

8. Olaf Caroe, *The Pathans: 550 BC–AD 1957* (London: Macmillan, 1958), 10, 12–13, 15.

9. Barfield, *Afghanistan*, 24, 89.

10. Roy, *Niamatullah's History of the Afghans*, 8, 20–1.

11. Caroe, *The Pathans*, 9–10.

12. Barfield, *Afghanistan*, 40.

13. Major G.F. MacMunn, *The Armies of India* (1911; reprint, New Delhi: Heritage Publishers, 1991), 153–4.

14. Patrick Macrory, *Kabul Catastrophe: The Story of the Diasastrous Retreat from Kabul, 1842* (Oxford: Oxford University Press, 1986), 19.

15. Gommans, *The Rise of the Indo-Afghan Empire*, 16, 21.

16. Barfield, *Afghanistan*, 36.

17. Macrory, *Kabul Catastrophe*, 19.

18. *Babur-Nama (Memoirs of Babur)*, tr. from the Original Turki Text of Zahir ud din Muhammad Babur by A.S. Beveridge, 2 vols (n.d.; reprint, New Delhi: Saeed International, 1989), vol. 1, p. 1; Stanley Lane-Poole, *The Emperor Babur* (n.d.; reprint, New Delhi: Sunita Publications, 1988), 28.

19. *Babur-Nama*, vol. 1, pp. 105, 134.

20. Lane-Poole, *Babur*, 56–7.

21. Mansura Haidar, 'Military Organization under the Uzbeks', in Haidar, *Medieval Central Asia: Polity, Economy and Military Organization (Fourteenth to Sixteenth Centuries)* (New Delhi: Manohar, 2004), 304.

22. *Babur-Nama*, vol. 1, pp. 185, 196.

23. *Babur-Nama*, vol. 1, p. 232.

24. Roy, *Niamatullah's History of the Afghans*, xxxiv.

25. Stephen F. Dale, *The Garden of the Eight Paradises: Babur and the Culture of Empire in Central Asia, Afghanistan and India (1483–1530)* (Leiden: E.J. Brill, 2004), 187–8. Pashai, Paraji were dialects of Persian or other Iranian languages.

26. *Babur-Nama*, vol. 1, pp. 199, 217.

27. Dale, *The Garden of the Eight Paradises*, 187–8.

28. Barfield, *Afghanistan*, 49.

29. Lane-Poole, *Babur*, 98–9, 101.

30. Dale, *The Garden of the Eight Paradises*, 189.

31. Barfield, *Afghanistan*, 44.

32. Barfield, *Afghanistan*, 32, 36.

33. *Babur-Nama*, vol. 1, pp. 227, 253; Barfield, *Afghanistan*, 26.

34. Abul Fazl, *The Akbar Nama*, tr. from the Persian by H. Beveridge, 3 vols (1902–39; reprint, New Delhi: Saeed International, 1989), vol. 1, p. 238.

35. *Babur-Nama*, vol. 1, p. 383.

36. Jayashree Vivekanandan, *Interrogating International Relations: India's Strategic Practice and the Return of History* (London/New York/New Delhi: Routledge, 2011), 161; Fazl, *The Akbar Nama*, vol. 1, pp. 236–7.

37. *Babur-Nama*, vol. 1, pp. 327–8.

38. Dale, *The Garden of the Eight Paradises*, 188–9.

39. Lane-Poole, *Babur*, 137.

40 *Babur-Nama*, vol. 1, p. 202; Macrory, *Kabul Catastrophe*, 20; Gommans, *The Rise of the Indo-Afghan Empire*, 16–17.

41. *Babur-Nama*, vol. 1, p. 328.

42. *Babur-Nama*, vol. 2, p. 519.

43. Zain Khan, *Tabaqat-i-Baburi*, tr. S. Hasan Askari, Annotation, B.P. Ambastha (Delhi: Idarah-i-Adabiyat-i-Delli, 1982), 187; Henry Steinbach, *The Country of the Sikhs* (n.d.; reprint, New Delhi: KLM Book House, 1977), 6.

44. *Babur-Nama*, vol. 2, p. 452; Fazl, *The Akbar Nama*, vol. 1, p. 240.

45. Barfield, *Afghanistan*, 26.

46. *Babur-Nama*, vol. 2, p. 457; Roy, *Niamatullah's History of the Afghans*, liv.

47. Barfield, *Afghanistan*, 29.

48. William Maley, *The Afghanistan Wars* (2002; reprint, London: Palgrave Macmillan, 2009), 10.

49. Khan, *Tabaqat-i-Baburi*, 7, 21.

50. Roy, *Niamatullah's History of the Afghans*, 208.

51. Roy, *Niamatullah's History of the Afghans*: 12–13, 23, 32.

52. Khan, *Tabaqat-i-Baburi*, 25.

53. Roy, *Niamatullah's History of the Afghans*, xlii.

54. *The History of India as Told by its Own Historians: The Muslim Period, The Posthumous Papers of the Late H.M. Elliot, Ed. and Continued by John Dawson*, 8 vols (1876–77; reprint, Delhi: Low Price Publications, 2001), 5; *Tarikh-i-Salatin-i-Afghana* of Ahmad Yadgar, 25, 28.

55. Roy, *Niamatullah's History of the Afghans*, xxviii, xxx.

56. *Babur-Nama*, vol. 2, pp. 472–5.

57. Khan, *Tabaqat-i-Baburi*, 22.

58. *Babur-Nama*, 2: vol. 2, p. 480.

59. *The Jahangirnama: Memoirs of Jahangir, Emperor of India*, tr., ed., and annotated by Wheeler M. Thackston (New York: Oxford University Press in association with the Smithsonian Institution, Washington DC, 1999), 23.

60. *Babur-Nama*, vol. 2, pp. 480, 534.

61. Haidar, 'Military Organization under the Uzbeks', in Haidar, *Medieval Central Asia*, 304–5.

62. Haidar, 'The Administrative Structure under the Uzbeks', in Haidar, *Medieval Central Asia*, 122.

63. Fazl, *The Akbar Nama*, vol. 1, pp. 287, 307, 326–7, 346, 367.

64. *The Tezkereh Al Vakiyat or Private Memoirs of the Mughal Emperor Humayun, Written in Persian Language by Jouher*, tr. by Major Charles Stewart (London: Oriental Translation Fund, MDCCCXXXII), 20–38.

65. *Tezkereh Al Vakiyat*, 54, 68, 71, 73, 77.

66. *Tezkereh Al Vakiyat*, 78–9; Iqtidar Alam Khan, *The Political Biography of a Mughal Noble: Munim Khan-i-Khanan, 1497–1575* (New Delhi: Munshiram Manoharlal, 1991), 7.

67. Khan, *The Political Biography of a Mughal Noble*, 7–8, 11.

68. *Tezkereh Al Vakiyat*, 85.

69. Dale, *The Garden of the Eight Paradises*, 187–8.

70. Khan, *The Political Biography of a Mughal Noble*, 12.

71. *Tezkereh Al Vakiyat*, 87.

72. *The History of India as Told by its Own Historians*, 5: *Tazkirat-ul-Wakiat* of Jauhar, 147–9.

73. Goodson, *Afghanistan's Endless War*, 15.

74. Khan, *The Political Biography of a Mughal Noble*, 10.

75. *Tezkereh Al Vakiyat*, 108.

76. *The History of India as Told by its Own Historians*, 5: *Tarikh-i-Jahan Lodhi*, 108.

77. *Tezkereh Al Vakiyat*, 108–16.

78. Andre Wink, *Akbar* (Oxford: Oneworld, 2009), 24.

79. Fazl, *The Akbar Nama*, vol. 2, pp. 80–1.

80. Fazl, *The Akbar Nama*, vol. 1, p. 357; Lieutenant William Barr, *Journal of a March from Delhi to Peshawar and from Thence to Kabul with the Mission of Lieutenant-Colonel C.M. Wade, Including Travels in the Punjab, a Visit to the City of Lahore and a Narrative of Operations in the Khyber Pass Undertaken in 1839* (1844; reprint, New Delhi: Munshiram Manoharlal, 2003), 94.

81. M. Athar Ali, 'Jahangir and the Uzbeks', in M. Athar Ali, *Mughal India: Studies in Polity, Ideas, Society, and Culture* (New Delhi: Oxford University Press, 2006), 316.

82. *The History of India as Told by its Own Historians*, 6: Appendix, Note A, 457.

83. Sunita Zaidi, 'Akbar's Annexation of Sind—An Interpretation', in Irfan Habib (ed.), *Akbar and His India* (1997, reprint; New Delhi: Oxford University Press, 2002), 25, 27.

84. Fatima Zehra Bilgrami, 'The Mughal Annexation of Sind—A Diplomatic and Military History', in Habib (ed.), *Akbar and His India*, 33–6, 39–43.

85. Fazl, *The Akbar Nama*, vol. 2, pp. 39–41, 43, 45, 56, 59–60, 81–4, 289.

86. Wink, *Akbar*, 22.

87. Haidar, 'The Administrative Structure under the Uzbeks', in Haidar, *Medieval Central Asia*, 123.

88. Vincent A. Smith, *Akbar the Great Mogul: 1542–1605* (n.d.; reprint, New Delhi: S. Chand, 1962), 141–4.

89. M. Athar Ali, 'The Objectives behind the Mughal Expedition into Balkh and Badakshan, 1646–7', in Ali, *Mughal India*, 327–9.

90. *The History of India as Told by its Own Historians*, 6, *Akbar Nama* of Abul Fazl, 80–4.

91. *The History of India as Told by its Own Historians*, 6, *Zubdatut Tawarikh* of Shaikh Nurul Hak, 191–2.

92. Jadunath Sarkar, *A Short History of Aurangzeb* (1930; reprint, New Delhi: Orient Longman, 1979), 116.

93. Ali, 'Jahangir and the Uzbeks', in Ali, *Mughal India*, 317.

94. *Tezkereh Al Vakiat*, 53, 59.

95. *The History of India as Told by its Own Historians*, 6: *Wakat-i-Jahangiri*, 302.

96. MacMunn, *Afghanistan*, 17.

97. *The Empire of the Great Mogul, De Laet's Description of India and Fragment of Indian History*, tr. by J.S. Hoyland and Annotated by S.N. Banerjee (1928; reprint, New Delhi: Munshiram Manoharlal, 1974), iii.

98. *The Empire of the Great Mogul, De Laet's Description of India and Fragment of Indian History*, 55.

99. *The Empire of the Great Mogul, De Laet's Description of India and Fragment of Indian History*, 56–7, 70.

100. *The Jahangirnama*, 21.

101. *The Jahangirnama*, 58.

102. *The Jahangirnama*, 58.

103. Percy Sykes, *A History of Afghanistan*, 2 vols (1940; reprint, New Delhi: Munshiram Manoharlal, 2002), vol. 1, pp. 311–12.

104. *The Jahangirnama*, 58.

105. *The Jahangirnama*, 66.

106. *The Jahangirnama*, Prince Khusrau had rebelled against his father Jahangir.

107. *The Jahangirnama*, 59.

108. *The Jahangirnama*, 66, 89.

109. Sykes, *A History of Afghanistan*, vol. 1, pp. 312–13.

110. Sykes, *A History of Afghanistan*, vol. 1, p. 313.

111. *The Empire of the Great Mogul, De Laet's Description of India and Fragment of Indian History*, 56.

112. Sykes, *A History of Afghanistan*, vol. 1, p. 314.

113. Sykes, *A History of Afghanistan*, vol. 1, p. 314.

114. Sykes, *A History of Afghanistan*, vol. 1, p. 314.

115. Inayat Khan, *The Shah Jahan Nama*, An Abridged History of the Mughal Emperor Shah Jahan, compiled by his Royal Librarian, ed., and completed by W.E. Begley and Z.A. Desai (New Delhi: Oxford University Press, 1990), 323.

116. Khan, *The Shah Jahan Nama*, p. 323.

117. Khan, *The Shah Jahan Nama*, 323, 327–8; Sykes, *A History of Afghanistan*, vol. 1, pp. 314–15.

118. John F. Richards, *The Mughal Empire, The New Cambridge History of India*, I: 5 (1993; reprint, New Delhi: Foundation Books, 2002), 132.

119. Khan, *The Shah Jahan Nama*, 328–30.

120. Khan, *The Shah Jahan Nama*, 331.

121. Abul Fazl, *The Akbar Nama*, vol. 1, p. 250.

122. Khan, *The Shah Jahan Nama*, 332.

123. Sykes, *A History of Afghanistan*, vol. 1, p. 315.

124. Richards, *The Mughal Empire*, 132–3; Sykes, *A History of Afghanistan*, vol. 1, p. 315.

125. Wink, *Akbar*, 78; Sykes, *A History of Afghanistan*, vol. 1, p. 318.

126. Sykes, *A History of Afghanistan*, vol. 1, p. 315.

127. *The History of India as Told by its Own Historians*, vol. 7, *Shah Jahan Nama* of Inayat Khan, pp. 87–9.

128. *The History of India as Told by its Own Historians*, vol. 7, *Shah Jahan Nama* of Inayat Khan, pp. 89–90.

129. *The History of India as Told by its Own Historians*, vol. 7, *Shah Jahan Nama* of Inayat Khan, p. 90; Sykes, *A History of Afghanistan*, vol. 1, p. 316.

130. *The History of India as Told by its Own Historians*, vol. 7, *Shah Jahan Nama* of Inayat Khan, 90–4.

131. *The History of India as Told by its Own Historians*, vol. 7, *Shah Jahan Nama* of Inayat Khan, pp. 95–6.

132. *The History of India as Told by its Own Historians*, vol. 7, *Shah Jahan Nama* of Inayat Khan, pp. 99–101.

133. *The History of India as Told by its Own Historians*, vol. 7, *Shah Jahan Nama* of Inayat Khan, pp. 101–2.

134. Sykes, *A History of Afghanistan*, vol. 1, p. 318.

135. Wink, *Akbar*, 23–4.

136. *The History of India as Told by its Own Historians*, vol. 7, *Majalis-us-Salatin* of Muhammad Sharif Hanafi, 138.

137. *The History of India as Told by its Own Historians*, vol. 7, *Miral-i-Alam, Miral-i-Jahan Nama* of Bakhtawar Khan, 164.

138. Wink, *Akbar*, 57–9.

139. Stephen Tanner, *Afghanistan: A Military History from Alexander the Great to the Fall of the Taliban* (New York: Da Capo Press, 2002), 113.

140. Saqi Mustad Khan, *Maasir-i-Alamgiri*, tr. into English and annotated by Jadunath Sarkar (1947; reprint, Calcutta: The Asiatic Society, 1990), 37–8.

141. George MacMunn, *Vignettes from Indian War* (1901; reprint, New Delhi: Low Price Publications, 1993), 184.

142. Sarkar, *A Short History of Aurangzeb*, 116.

143. Khan, *Maasir-i-Alamgiri*, 40–1; *The Empire of the Great Mogul: De Laet's Description of India and Fragment of Indian History*, 5.

144. Khan, *Maasir-i-Alamgiri*, 41.

145. Ishwardas Nagar, *Futuhat-i Alamgiri*, tr. and ed. by Tasneem Ahmad (New Delhi: Idarah-i-Adabiyat-i-Delli, 1978), 103–5, 124.

146. Nagar, *Futuhat-i Alamgiri*, 105–6; Khan, *Maasir-i-Alamgiri*, 72.

147. Nagar, *Futuhat-i Alamgiri*, 106–8.

148. Nagar, *Futuhat-i Alamgiri*, 108–10; Khan, *Maasir-i-Alamgiri*, 81.

149. Nagar, *Futuhat-i Alamgiri*, 110.

150. Khan, *Maasir-i-Alamgiri*, 81.

151. Nagar, *Futuhat-i Alamgiri*, 111–12; Khan, *Maasir-i-Alamgiri*, 82–4.

152. Khan, *Maasir-i-Alamgiri*, 89–90.

153. Sarkar, *A Short History of Aurangzeb*, 115–16.

154. Nagar, *Futuhat-i Alamgiri*, 113–14.

155. Satish Chandra, *Parties and Politics at the Mughal Court: 1707–40* (1959; reprint, New Delhi: People's Publishing House, 1979).

156. M. Athar Ali, 'The Passing of the Empire: The Mughal Case', in Ali, *Mughal India*, 340.

157. Ganda Singh, *Ahmad Shah Durrani: Father of Modern Afghanistan* (Bombay: Asia Publishing House, 1959), 9.

158. Michael Axworthy, *The Sword of Persia: Nader Shah from Tribal Warrior to Conquering Tyrant* (London and New York: I.B. Tauris, 2006), 45–9.

159. William Irvine, *Later Mughals*, 2 vols (reprint, New Delhi: Taj Publication, 1989), vol. 2, p. 318.

160. Axworthy, *The Sword of Persia*, 17–18.

161. Irvine, *Later Mughals*, vol. 2, pp. 317–19.

162. Irvine, *Later Mughals*, vol. 2, p. 319.

163. *The History of India as Told by its Own Historians*, vol. 8, *Tarikh-i-Hindi* of Rustam Ali, 61.

164. Paddy Docherty, *The Khyber Pass: A History of Empire and Invasion* (London: Faber and Faber, 2007), 180.

165. *The History of India as Told by its Own Historians*, vol. 8, *Tarikh-i-Hindi* of Rustam Ali, 61–2.

166. *The History of India as Told by its Own Historians*, vol. 8, *Jauhar-i-Samsam* of Muhammad Muhsin Sadiki, 74.

167. M. Athar Ali, 'Recent Theories of Eighteenth Century India', in Ali, *Mughal India*, 350.

168. Axworthy, *The Sword of Persia*, 15.

169. Tanner, *Afghanistan*, 117–18; Shah Mahmoud Hanifi, 'Quandaries of the Afghan Nation', in Shahzad Bashir and Robert D. Crews (ed.), *Under the Drones: Modern Lives in the Afghanistan-Pakistan Borderlands* (Cambridge, Massachusetts/London: Harvard University Press, 2012), 88.

170. Singh, *Ahmad Shah Durrani*, 15.

171. Tanner, *Afghanistan*, 118.

172. Singh, *Ahmad Shah Durrani*, 18.

173. M. Elphinstone, *An Account of the Kingdom of Caubul, and its Dependencies, in Persia, Tartary, and India Comprising a View of the Afghan Nation and a History of the Dooraunee Monarchy*, 2 vols (London: Richard Bentley, 1842), vol. 2, pp. 243–7.

174. Elphinstone, *An Account of the Kingdom of Caubul*, vol. 2, pp. 251–7.

175. *The History of India as Told by its Own Historians*, vol. 8, *Nigar-i-Nama-i Hindi* by Sayid Ghulam Ali, 398–9.

176. Elphinstone, *An Account of the Kingdom of Caubul*, vol. 2, p. 247.

177. Singh, *Ahmad Shah Durrani*, 57, 59–60.

178. Khushwant Singh, *A History of the Sikhs*, vol. 1, *1469–1839* (1963; reprint, New Delhi: Oxford University Press, 1989), 131, 133–6, 137–41.

179. *The History of India as Told by its Own Historians*, vol. 8, *Tarikh-i-Manazilul Futuh* by Muhammad Jafar Shamlu, 148–9, 152–3.

180. *The History of India as Told by its Own Historians*, vol. 8, *Tarikh-i-Ibrahim Khan, Tamadus Saadat* of Mir Ghulam Ali, 274–5.

181. *The History of India as Told by its Own Historians*, vol. 8, *Tarikh-i-Ibrahim Khan*, 280.

182. Macrory, *Kabul Catastrophe*, 17–20; Tanner, *Afghanistan*, 122.

183. Goodson, *Afghanistan's Endless War*, 14.

184. Tanner, *Afghanistan*, 124.

185. Lal, *Dost Mohammad Khan*, vol. 1, pp. 10–12.

186. Lal, *Dost Mohammad Khan*, vol. 1, pp. 12–15.

187. Lal, *Dost Mohammad Khan*, vol. 1, pp. 15–16.

188. Macrory, *Kabul Catastrophe*, 21; James Atkinson, *Afghan Expedition: Notes and Sketches from the First British Afghan War of 1839–1840* (1842; reprint, London, The Long Riders' Guild Press, 2007), 7; Lal, *Dost Mohammad Khan*, vol. 1, pp. 16–18.

189. Atkinson, *Notes and Sketches from the First British Afghan War of 1839–1840*, 7.

190. Atkinson, *Notes and Sketches from the First British Afghan War of 1839–1840*, 6–7.

191. Gommans, *The Rise of the Indo-Afghan Empire*, 5.

192. Stephen Frederick Dale, 'Indo-Russian Trade in the Eighteenth Century', in Sugata Bose (ed.), *South Asia and World Capitalism* (New Delhi: Oxford University Press, 1990), 140–50.

193. Hari Ram Gupta, *History of the Sikhs*, vol. 4, *The Sikh Commonwealth or the Rise and Fall of Sikh Misls* (New Delhi: Mushiram Manoharlal, 1982), 486–7, 491, 493–5.

194. Macrory, *Kabul Catastrophe*, 23, 27.

195. Atkinson, *Notes and Sketches from the First British Afghan War of 1839–1840*, 8; Caroe, *The Afghans*, 272.

196. Caroe, *The Afghans*, 272–3.

197. Tanner, *Afghanistan*, 125.

198. Victoria Schofield, *Afghan Frontier: At the Crossroads of Conflict* (2003; reprint, London: I.B. Tauris, 2010), 33.

199. Caroe, *The Pathans*, 274.

200. MacMunn, *Afghanistan*, 115.

2

BRITISH INDIAN EMPIRE AND WARFARE IN AFGHANISTAN
1810–1947

THERE HAVE BEEN SEVERAL STUDIES of British involvement in Afghanistan[1] and some scholars have also analysed British policy towards the Indus tribes.[2] Most of them have analysed British policy towards the Indus tribes as the product of 'Forward' and 'Masterly Inactivity' policies. Christian Tripodi notes that there were four stages with regards to British North-West Frontier Policy. According to Tripodi, between 1843 and 1874, the Raj followed a Closed Border Policy (i.e., Masterly Inactivity). In mid 1870s, the Forward Policy took over. In 1901, Lord Curzon (governor general/viceroy of India) initiated modified Closed Border Policy. From 1922 till 1947, modified Forward Policy operated.[3] The reality was probably messy and could not be categorized so nicely. British India's policy towards its North-West Frontier is also evaluated by using John S. Galbraith's 'Turbulent Frontier' hypothesis. For Galbraith, the presence of unruly frontiers forced the imperial state like Britain to devolve much power in the hands of the local officials managing the borders. Long distance from the metropole and bad communications with the centres of imperial power allowed these men on the spots to expand the imperial domains by using the autonomy devolved on them. British India's policy was made mostly in India rather than in Britain. The introduction of telegraph and the opening of the Suez Canal failed to totally eliminate the autonomy in the realm of decision making enjoyed by the men on the spots. And even the governor generals had problems in controlling their aggressive subordinates deployed at the margins of the empire. The local officials took advantages of disorders beyond the borders to expand in pursuit of glory and material profit. And the home authorities, as Galbraith writes, at times grumbled, but accepted expansion of the imperial frontiers, if it came cheaply.[4]

What the above-mentioned scholars have missed is the interconnections between British policy towards Afghanistan and the British policy vis-à-vis the tribes along India's North-West Frontier. This chapter attempts to fill this historiographical gap. Further, while Tripodi focuses mostly on the role of the 'politicals' in the making of frontier policy, this chapter focuses on tactics, technology, and logistics of conventional and sub-conventional warfare conducted by the British and Indian troops in Afghanistan and the North-West Frontier. Rather than merely the border officials, British policy vis-à-vis Afghanistan was also partly shaped by the actions of Afghanistan's neighbours and internal conditions within the country. Hence, due attention is given to Russian and Persian manoeuvrings towards Afghanistan and fluctuating political conditions within the mountainous, economically underdeveloped country. Now, let us focus on the origin of 'Afghan problem' in British official mind.

PRELUDE TO INTERVENTION

The successful conclusion of the Third Anglo-Maratha War (1817–18) brought the whole of the subcontinent except Punjab under British control. As a paramount power, the British debated whether an independent Punjab should be retained as a strong buffer against the 'unruly' tribes who inhabited the region between the Indus and Afghanistan, or whether Punjab should be annexed to the British Indian empire and a secure frontier along the Indus established. After British victory in the Second Anglo-Sikh War (1848–9), British India's frontier reached the Indus and the British officials in India realized that they had to deal with the Afghan 'problem' in a much more systematic manner. By this time, as far as the Great Game for the control of Afghanistan was concerned, the Uzbek Khanate and Persia/Iran were down and out. The big players were Czarist Russia (which then was in the process of absorbing the Uzbek realm) and the British empire (which had succeeded the Mughals and was in the process of reducing the autonomy of Iran). By 1830, Czarist Russia had replaced France as the principal power threatening the Raj through Afghanistan. Throughout the nineteenth century, the British made an error in thinking that the Russians could move large number of troops through the deserts and mountains of Central Asia to Afghanistan to attack India.[5]

Unlike the indigenous powers, the British freed themselves from supply of war horses through Afghanistan by importing horses from Britain and Australia.[6] In March 1809, Mountstuart Elphinstone was sent to Shah Shuja's winter capital at Peshawar in order to seal off possible Russian and French influence in Afghanistan. At that time, Shah Shuja was engaged in reconquering the rebellious province of Kashmir.[7] The rebels defeated Shuja's two commanders Akram Khan and Madud Khan. Shah Shuja lost power due to the shifting Afghan politics and, in November 1815, finally took refuge in the British cantonment at Ludhiana.[8] As early as the 1820s, several Afghan *sirdars* realized that the British were a rising power in South Asia and attempted to deal with the *feranghis*. Dost Muhammad (b. 1791–d. 1863), the ruler of Ghazni, captured Kabul in 1826. In 1827, Dost Muhammad became the ruler of Afghanistan.[9] In 1829, Sultan Muhammad Khan of Peshawar wanted to negotiate with the British as an independent chief. When in 1834, Shah Shuja advanced on Kandahar, and the Khalsa kingdom increased pressure on the Indus frontier. Dost Muhammad appealed to Great Britain for aid in order to recover Peshawar. His nephew, son of Jabbar Khan, was sent to Ludhiana to establish diplomatic relationship with the EIC state.[10]

In 1834, Ranjit Singh was able to capture Peshawar from Afghanistan. The Sikhs remembered the atrocities committed by Abdali's troops in Punjab. Hence, Sikh rule in the Afghan city was indeed harsh. In the 1830s, one Colonel Leslie/Rattray was the Khalsa kingdom's governor of the Khyber Pass. He converted to Islam, and accepted the title of Fida Muhammad Khan. He established his headquarters at the Ali Masjid Fort and levied tolls on the caravans which moved through the Khyber Pass.[11] In 1837, the Khalsa kingdom's governor of Peshawar, General Paulo Avitabile (an Italian mercenary), set up open gallows in the city to deter the miscreants.[12] On the road between Rohtas to Peshawar (200 miles east of Kabul), Ranjit Singh built a mud fort at Khairabad. Its garrison was ordered to maintain control over the surrounding heights. Another mud fort for the same purpose was built at Nowshera/ Naushera. Overall, Ranjit Singh took care to make the road to Peshawar safe for travellers. Through fire and sword against the marauders and the villages around the city of Peshawar, which harboured them, the Khalsa kingdom was able to maintain a semblance of order along the highway.[13] In 1837, when Dost Muhammad Khan made an unsuccessful attempt to wrest Peshawar from the Sikhs, Alexander Burnes of Bombay Political Department was at Kabul on a commercial mission. Burnes was ordered by the governor general to establish British influence in Afghanistan. However, Burnes perceived that Russian and Persian influence were dominant in Kabul.[14]

FIRST ANGLO-AFGHAN WAR: 1839–42

Henry Durand came to India in May 1830, as lieutenant of the Corps of Engineers. In 1836, he was in charge of bridging the Indus near the fort of Bhakkar.[15] This was done in anticipation of a campaign in Afghanistan. In 1837, Lieutenant General Henry Fane, the commander-in-chief of India (5 September 1835–6 December 1839), warned against any military adventure in Afghanistan.[16] But he was overruled by his civilian superior, Governor General Lord Auckland. International events also went against Fane's view. In December 1837, a Russian envoy named Vitkevich arrived at Kabul.[17] Herat was under the Saduzoi chieftain Kamran Shah, who was Shah Shuja's nephew. The real power was in the hand of his wazir, Yar Muhammad Khan. In early 1837, Kamran Shah and Yar Muhammad were campaigning in Seistan in eastern Persia. Qajar Shah of Persia decided to besiege Herat. Muhammad Shah, ruler of Persia, not only claimed Herat but also Kandahar. The Board of Control of the EIC overreacted and urged the governor general of India to take strong action in order to safeguard the British Indian Empire. Overreaction on part of the metropolitan powers was a characteristic which will be evident both in late twentieth and early twenty-first centuries. On 17 September, Kamran and Yar Muhammad returned to Herat. On 23 November 1837, a large Persian army (10,000 infantry, 2,000 cavalry, and 30 guns) backed by

Russian advisers laid siege to Herat.[18] And this increased the anxiety of the British about probable Russian influence in Afghanistan, despite the fact that Herat is 2,000 miles from Calcutta. The Raj pressurized Ranjit Singh to cooperate in the British invasion of Afghanistan. Ranjit demanded some more territories west of the Indus in addition to Peshawar as the price for cooperation. This demand was refused by the Raj.[19] As a result, Khalsa co-operation with the EIC during the First Afghan War was half-hearted.

On 6 April 1838, the British envoy, John McNeill, arrived at Herat to initiate a ceasefire. On 4 June 1838, a squadron of five warships and two steamers with detachments from three regiments and a marine battalion set sail for the Island of Karrack (Kharg/Kharak), a few miles off the Persian coast. The Persian governor surrendered to the British force. On 9 September 1838, the Persian Shah raised the siege of Herat.[20]

Though the Persians had raised the siege of Herat due to the occupation of Kharak Island in the Persian Gulf by the troops of the Bombay army, the Raj under Governor General Auckland proceeded with the plan to install Shah Shuja at Kabul.[21] British India's highest authority and the London government in unison, and not merely the 'men on the spot', took the decisive decisions. Patrick Macrory asserts that instead of trying to install the discredited Shah Shuja, Auckland should have tried to strengthen Dost Muhammad's reign. Dost Muhammad was suspicious of Russian expansion in Central Asia and would have welcomed British aid in this respect. However, Dost was an avowed enemy of Ranjit Singh of Punjab since the latter had occupied Peshawar. Auckland could not support Dost due to the good relations which existed between the Khalsa kingdom and the Raj.[22]

Two regiments of regular infantry, two troops of horse artillery, and two regiments of irregular cavalry were raised under the command of the British officers for serving with Shah Shuja. Shah Shuja's contingent comprised Hindustani, Sikh, and Gurkha recruits, and some British officers seconded from the EIC's armies. This body was raised at Ludhiana and numbered to 5,600 men. In November 1838, Shuja left Ludhiana for Shikarpur. The army in India, assembled at Ferozepur, was ordered to join Shuja at Shikarpur. In 1839, British India mobilized about 39,000 soldiers against Amir Dost Muhammad.[23] In February 1839, the Bombay column was at Larkana, and the two brigades of the Bengal army under Major General Willoughby Cotton moved from Shikarpur towards Kandahar. The Bengal army's contingent comprised some 9,500 soldiers. The Bombay column numbered some 5,600 soldiers. On 4 March 1839, John Keane (commander-in-chief of the Bombay army) assumed command of both the columns. These two columns united at Quetta, in the province of Shaul, during the first week of April 1839.[24] The forces destined for the invasion of Afghanistan together was known as the Army of the Indus.

Dost Muhammad's kingdom yielded an annual revenue of about Rs 2,262,943 (226,294 sterling).[25] Theoretically, Dost Muhammad commanded 38,000 feudal cavalry (of them 8,000 were Durranis). Most of the regular units along with the tribal levies were put under the command of Dost's son, Akbar Khan.[26] Under his direct command, Dost Muhammad had 12,000 cavalry organized in two divisions. One division known as *Khud Aspah* comprised personnel who rode their own horses. The other division known as *Amlah Sarkari* comprised personnel who rode on the horses provided by the government. These two divisions were subdivided into parties comprising 200 horses. Several such parties were put under the charge of various sons of the Amir. For instance, Muhammad Akbar Khan was given command of 2,000 such cavalry, Muhammad Afzal Khan commanded 600 cavaliers, and Ghulam Haidar Khan commanded 1,000 cavaliers.[27]

The infantry of the Army of the Indus was equipped with Brown Bess musket. It was a muzzle loader (ML) effective to 150 yards and one could fire two rounds per minute. In contrast, the Afghan jezail was effective up to 800 yards when fired from a rest, and could kill a horse when fired from a distance of 600 yards.[28] Each jezail was about 7 feet long and a fork was used while firing.[29] The Afghans had an advantage over their British Indian opponents in hand-held firearms, which would vanish only during the late nineteenth century.

Shah Shuja's contingent moved from Ludhiana to Ferozepur.[30] The Army of the Indus entered Afghanistan through the Bolan Pass and a small British Indian and Khalsa force moved through the Khyber Pass under Claude Wade. Due to objections of Ranjit Singh, the principal invasion force moved into Afghanistan through Sind. From the very first, heat and lack of adequate supply of water troubled the British Indian military column.[31] George Lawrence (later lieutenant general), who was then a coronet in the 2nd Light Cavalry Regiment, describes the arduous journey in the following words:

> On the 23rd February we marched from Shikarpur for Dadur, distant 146 miles, crossing the desert which commences at a place called Rajghan. This sterile tract, extending for twenty-three miles, is pestilential during the extreme heats of summer, and becomes a swamp in the rainy season, in June or July…. We arrived at Dadur, the entrance of the Bolan Pass, on the 10th of March, and were delayed there some time owing to the desertion of many of our syces and dooly bearers.[32]

In March 1839, the British Indian detachment, which from Peshawar marched towards the Khyber Pass, numbered to about 3,950 soldiers (including the Sikh allies).[33] Lieutenant William Barr of the Bengal Artillery, who was with the column, writes about the 'notorious Khyberries':

> Their dress generally consisted of a long chupkun of a light brown colour, reaching to their knees, loose trousers, and grass sandals, or shoes with hobnails…. Their usual weapons are a long jezail, or rifle, with a wooden fork attached to its extremity, on which the piece is rested to secure a better aim; a sword; and a large knife stuck into the sash: some had a pistol in addition.[34]

The Afghans believed that the principal invasion force like that of the Mughals would invade Afghanistan from India through the Khyber Pass. On 17 May, Dost Muhammad's son Akbar Khan, with a large train of artillery, was at the vicinity of the Khyber Pass. On 5 July 1839, a COIN operation was undertaken by the British Indian force. Colonel Wade and Ferris with a detachment went to the region near the Kabul River, where Sadat Khan was inciting the population on the left bank of the Kabul River against the British. On 6 July, Lieutenant William Barr, with a howitzer of the Khalsa army, and Shah Zada Timur's bodyguard joined Wade and Ferris' force. Barr found out that from the shelter of the rocks, the Afghans fired their jezails, whose range outranged the matchlocks in the hands of Barr's contingent. Only a few rifles in the hands of the British soldiers were able to hit the boldest of those Afghans who refused the cover of the *sangars*. By 20 July 1839, Wade had at his disposal 10,000 men (including the 6,000-strong Khalsa contingent) for moving through the Khyber Pass. The British were anxious about the loyalty of the Khalsa contingent as most of its personnel were Muslims. Barr was also worried about the Afghan levies raised by the British. He feared that most of them had joined the British bandwagon for economic gain and would desert at the earliest opportunity. Further, many of them in secret espoused the cause of Dost Muhammad rather than the British stooge Shah Shuja.[35] Barr's anxiety would become a reality in one year.

The grain contractors at Ludhiana delivered some supplies at Bhawalpur.[36] For marching through Baluchistan, Lieutenant Mackeson constructed a military road through the Bhawalpur state.[37] In order to procure supply of grain and fodder, and to ensure safety of the LOCs stretching back to India, the British entered into political negotiations with the Baluchi chiefs. Conducting politics and diplomacy simultaneously, while waging military operations, was a characteristic of Small War. Mir Mehrab Khan of Kalat was acknowledged by the British as the ruler of his principality, and in return, he agreed to accept the authority of Shah Shuja. Further, Mehrab Khan was to keep the Bolan Pass open for the British and provide supply for the British Indian troops. Mohan Lal (Indian secretary of Alexander Burnes) recounts that though he paid Mehrab Khan Rs 2,000 in cash (his annual subsidy as determined by the British), Mehrab failed to provide forage and grain to the soldiers and the beasts of burden. The Baluchis and the neighbouring Kakar tribes intensified their predatory raids on the British *dak*s (posts), camels, and supply columns. Mehrab Khan was either unable, or unwilling to check his followers' plundering activities. Further, Mir Mehrab Khan's governor in Shal, instead of protecting the camels of the British Indian columns, stole them when they went for grazing, and these animals were then sold in Seistan rather than in Kalat to prevent any suspicion on part of the British authority.[38]

Soon, the British got wind of Mehrab Khan's disloyalty and decided to teach him a lesson. Captain Bean, the political agent, decided that force was needed to be used against Mehrab Khan. In response, on 31 October 1839, Thomas Wilshire was sent to Quetta with a detachment. Simultaneous conventional military operations against the hostile regular force and low-intensity policing operations against the recalcitrant tribal chiefs were a characteristic of Small War. On 12 November, Wilshire reached the Jiryani village, about 8 miles from Kalat. Wilshire then made his disposition to storm the town and the citadel. The storming party was led by Brigadier Bomgardt. Mehrab Khan died fighting heroically with his sword in hand.[39]

On 4 April 1839, the British Indian units reached Quetta. But no supplies were found there. The troops were put on half rations. On 7 April, the British Indian units left for Kuchlak.[40] The difficulties of marching through Baluchistan into south Afghanistan seemed to be increasing with time. George Lawrence jots in his autobiography: 'We marched on the 11th through the Pisheen Valley to the mouth of the Kojuk Pass, which we had to traverse before reaching Kandahar. This defile is, for four miles of the distance, so narrow, that even after all the efforts of our engineers, only a single camel could advance at a time.'[41]

As the British Indian force marched towards Kandahar, Sirdar Kohandil Khan with some 4,000 cavalry encamped at Dandi Gulai with the objective of checking the advance of the *kafir*s. However, the lesser chiefs of the Kandahar region were willing to treat with the British. On 20 April 1839, a messenger from a Kakar chief named Haji Khan came to Mohan Lal with a letter addressed to Alexander Burnes. Thanks to Mohan Lal's political management, Haji Khan deserted to the British. The coalition of the Barakzai chiefs in Kandahar started to fall apart. One Mulla Nasu advised that the best course for them was to retreat to Persia and seek the aid of the Persian monarch Muhammad Shah, or to get in touch with the shadowy Russian count, Simonich. Haji Khan's accommodation by the British encouraged certain other chiefs also to submit. For instance, Abdulmajid Khan, son of Shah Pasan Khan, the governor of Lash and Ghulam Akhund Zadah, a priest who previously preached hatred against the British, then submitted.[42]

On 25 April 1839, Shah Shuja with the British Envoy and Minister William H. Macnaghten (previously chief secretary to the Bengal government) reached Kandahar. Lord Keane, with the 7,500-strong detachment, followed the Shah the next day and encamped in the neighbourhood of the city.[43] George Lawrence, like most of the British officers, was dismayed after seeing Kandahar. Lawrence notes: 'The appearance of the town greatly disappointed me, as I expected to find the capital of western [actually South] Afghanistan a far larger and more imposing place, instead of being merely composed of mud houses, surrounded by a wall of sun-dried bricks.'[44] On 2 June, one of Shah Shuja's sons was appointed as the governor of Kandahar, and Major Leech was nominated as the political agent. That day proved to be an eventful one as Ranjit Singh breathed his last.[45]

Dost Muhammad's eldest son Afzal Khan with 5,000 cavalry conducted 'hit and run' attacks against the British columns.[46] During the Second Anglo-Afghan War, Afzal Khan's role would be replayed by Ayub Khan. On 27 June 1839, the British Indian units left Kandahar for their onward march to Kabul through Ghazni. Most of the heavy battering guns, along with a garrison, were left at Kandahar as the British military high command did not expect any opposition at Ghazni (230 miles distant from Kandahar). On 20 July, on John Keane's order, the Quarter-Master General Major Garden ordered George Lawrence with 30 troopers to make a reconnaissance of the fortress of Ghazni.[47] While coming back from the reconnaissance, George Lawrence's party fell with an Afghan trooper who told him:

> You are an army of tents and camels: our army is one of men and horses. What could induce you ... to squander crores of rupees in coming to a poor country like ours, without wood or water, and all in order to force upon us a kumbukht (unlucky person), as a king, who, the moment you turn your backs, will be upset by Dost Mahomed, our *own* king.[48]

George Lawrence provides a description of the city of Ghazni and its fortress in his memoirs:

> The city of Ghazni.... a poor place now, containing only about two thousand houses and a very scanty population. The fortress is situated on the western end of a range of hills, and is defended by a deep ditch. The citadel, an irregular square, is placed on a mound, with two ramps leading to it, the walls being loop-holed, and had it been defended, might have caused us much trouble to capture. The old town of Ghazni is three miles to the east, and contains the tomb of the famous Shah Mahmud [Mahmud of Ghazni].... The climate of Ghazni is said to be very fine, and the country abounds in fruits: grapes, melons, apples, plums.[49]

On the morning of 21 July, the British Indian army in five columns arrived before Ghazni at 7 a.m. The light companies dislodged the Afghans from some walled gardens. The heavy guns in the fortress opened up on the British Indian units. One of the heavy guns of the defenders was a 64-pounder and named *Zabur Zang*. The British soldiers called it 'Long Tom'. The British light guns bombarded the fortress for two hours but made no impression on the walls. In the night of

22 July the storming party under Colonel Dennie, supported by the main column under General Sale, moved near the main gate. Captain Peat of the Bombay Engineers, aided by lieutenants Macleod and Henry Durand of the Bengal Engineers, laid the powder bags at the gate. At 4 a.m. on 23rd morning, the gate was blown and the fortress was stormed.[50] On 23 July 1839, the British captured the Ghazni Fort. Of its garrison, 600 were killed and 1,600 became prisoners.[51] The storming of Ghazni cost the Army of the Indus 17 killed and 175 wounded.[52] In 1839, Henry Durand was in charge of blasting the gate of Ghazni Fort, which led to the capitulation of the fort's garrison. Durand was then appointed as engineer of the Shah's troops but he resigned his commission and returned to Punjab. Then, Durand was ordered by the chief engineer to utilize his cartographical skill in drawing maps with reports on the Afghan campaign.[53]

On 1 November 1838, Colonel A. Roberts (father of the future Field Marshal Frederick 'Bob' Roberts) of the Bengal army was appointed to the command of the 4th Brigade of the Army of the Indus (which comprised 1st European regiment and the 35th and 37th Indian infantry regiments). In a report submitted on 1844, he explained the reasons for the disaster in Afghanistan in the following words:

> I entreated that the number of Afghan levies may be limited until we had officers better qualified by a more perfect knowledge of their language, customs and feelings, to command them, and until from experience and observation to be well prepared to meet any emergency deep inside a hostile country. I was regarded as an alarmist, hence removed from the command of Shah's troops. Our Afghan troops became our bitter enemies and murdered the officers.[54]

A. Roberts also pointed out the logistical failure in his report. He penned: 'My plan to store grain for six months along with munitions and to strengthen the fortifications of Bala Hissar with more artillery was turned down.'[55]

Vincent Eyre was the commissary of ordnance to the Kabul Field Force in 1840.[56] The principal logistical vehicles for supplying the troops in Afghanistan, both in the Mughal and British eras, were mules, bullocks, elephants, and camels. For details regarding the carrying capacity, cost, and forage required by the beasts of burden, refer to Table 2.1. In 1869, the cost of a mule driver came to about Rs 7 per month. For three

Table 2.1 Carriage Animals of the Army in India for Operation in Afghanistan

Animal	Carrying Capacity (in maunds)	Food Required per Day	Marching Speed	Approximate Price of a Single Animal (in Rupees)	Remarks
Donkey	1.5		1.5 miles per hour	4	Price in 1839 in Bhawalpur
Bullock	2	2 seers of gram and 14 pounds of dry forage	1.5 miles per hour	70	Price in 1878
Mule	2.5	3 seers of gram daily	3 miles per hour	200	Cost in 1869
Pony	2.5		5 miles per hour		
Camel	5		2 miles per hour		
Elephant	12			580	Price in 1871

Source: From Brigadier General G. Bourchier, to the QMG, Army HQ, Simla, 22 June 1869, Records of Chief Commands, 1865–76, Notes and Minutes by Napier; From Lieutenant J. Cookesley, RE, Eurasian Battery of Artillery, to the Commissioner of Assam, Shillong, 4 June 1869, Enclosure B, Records of Chief Commands, Notes and Minutes by Napier, MSS.EUR.F.114, 5(2), IOR, BL; The Commander-in-Chief to the Viceroy, Letter to John Lawrence, 27 June 1865, John Lawrence Collection, MSS.EUR.F.90/59, IOR, BL, London; From secy. to govt. Punjab, MD, to Commissioner, Rawal Pindi, 13 September 1879, Copy of a Telegram dated 13 September 1879, from the secy. to the Punjab Govt., MD, to all the Commissioners in Punjab, Supply and Transport, December 1879, MD, NAI; James Atkinson, *Afghan Expedition: Notes and Sketches from the First British Afghan War of 1839–1840*: 44; Brigadier R.C. Butalia, *The Evolution of the Artillery in India: From the Battle of Plassey (1757) to the Revolt of 1857*: 231; T.A. Heathcote, *The Indian Army: The Garrison of British Imperial India, 1822–1922*: 63.

Note: As a point of comparison, infantry marched on an average at 3 miles per hour and cavalry's trot was 7 miles per hour.

mules, a grass cutter was appointed at the wage of Rs 9 per month.[57] The elephant could drag heavy siege guns. But the disadvantage with elephant was that it consumed more than either the bullock or the mule. Moreover, the elephants required lot of green forage and water, and these two commodities were not easily available in the dry terrain of Afghanistan. During 1581–2, the Mughal army which accompanied Akbar during the invasion of Afghanistan had 500 elephants.[58] Advance in technology has failed to overcome the geographical constraint of conducting military operations in Afghanistan. As Chapter 3 will show that the Soviet armour-heavy ground forces in the early 1980s, based on internal combustion engine, guzzled up a lot of fuel, which had to be imported from the Soviet Union through Salang Tunnel in the north of Afghanistan. And the airpower-heavy US–NATO–ISAF forces (whose COIN operations are the subject of Chapter 4) had to import a lot of aviation fuel in order to provide mobility and close air support (CAS) to the friendly ground forces.

However, camel was considered best for traversing the rocky and mountainous region of Afghanistan. Unlike elephants, camels thrive on dry scrubs and bushes available in Afghanistan. The British commanders considered camels as best equipped for the rocky terrain between Peshawar and Kohat.[59] A camel was able to drag a 18-pdr gun over the sandy terrain.[60] The British route of entry for moving into southern Afghanistan lay through Baluchistan. The mountain tract along the Bolan Pass, which runs north along the Suleiman Mountains and south towards the coast, was inhabited by the Baluch clans.[61] On 15 March 1839, the British Indian units entered the Bolan Pass.[62] James Atkinson (of the Bengal army), superintending surgeon of the Army of the Indus, describes the Bolan Pass in the following words:

> ... a rough and pebbly road, between sand hills, studded with flint and lime stones, small and large, the space in breadth between the hills varying from 300 or 400 yards to about 30. As the torrent runs deviously from one side of the gorge to the other, we had to cross it six or seven times. The bottom consisted of large round stones, which gave an uncertain footing for a horse, though the camels with their large spread of foot got through without much difficulty. The depth was not more, generally, than eighteen inches.[63]

For this terrain, camels were best suited. The Army of the Indus had 30,000 camels and 38,000 camp followers. The camels were drawn from north India, Punjab, Rajasthan (then Rajputana), Sind, and even included some brood camels from the Government Stud Establishment at Hissar. Of these 30,000 camels, 14,325 beasts carried 30 days' commissariat supplies, and the rest of the camels carried ordnance stores and baggage. However, the expedition ran into logistical troubles as soon as the British and Indian units entered Baluchistan. For instance, on 7 March 1839, the 2nd Brigade was halted at Shikarpur due to shortage of camels.[64]

The British officers travelled in style. A senior British officer had six servants, crockery, silver plate, wine chest, portable bathtub, and so on. In fact, for carrying the officers' baggage, some of the medical stores for the troops had to be left behind.[65] One brigadier required 60 camels to carry his personal kit. And the junior subalterns per regiment took upto 40 servants. The 16th Lancers took even their pack of foxhounds, and one British officer of this regiment had 40 servants.[66]

On 7 August 1839, the army in India reached Kabul and Shah Shuja was restored to the throne.[67] There was considerable opposition to Shah Shuja, which escalated into a full-blown insurgency by 1841.[68] M.E. Yapp in an article asserts that a series of uprisings erupted in eastern Afghanistan between 1839 and 1841. All these disturbances were local in nature. Clan rivalries and economic discontent were the principal factors behind these disturbances. Dost Muhammad used religious propaganda in order to utilize these uprisings against the British but without much success. There was no general conspiracy against British authority, nor was there the objective to promote the interests of Dost Muhammad. Further, there is no evidence that the Khalsa kingdom instigated these uprisings against the British. Actually, several parallel disturbances occurred. There was no sense of Afghan/Afghanistan among the different local rebel leaders. All the leaders relied on individual and tribal loyalties in mobilizing their retainers. However, the local rebels saw themselves as Muslims and justified their rebellion in terms of Islam. For instance, in March 1840, an uprising occurred in Bajaur. This uprising was directed against the chief, Mir Alam Khan, who was supported by the British officer Connolly. In January 1840, there was disturbances in Kunar (along the Kunar River and the chief town was Pashat, 50 miles north-east of Jalalabad) due to the attempt by the British and Shah Shuja to collect revenues. However, the rebels did not support Dost Muhammad. In the spring of 1840, disturbances broke out among the Gigiani tribe in Jalalabad area. These disturbances were suppressed only in August 1840.[69] As early as April 1840, the British garrison at Kahan, the principal town of the Marri tribe of Baluchistan, was attacked. By the end of September 1840, the British garrison commander, Captain Lewis Brown, retreated from Kahan and reached Pulaji on 3 October 1840. The series of local resistance not only weakened the British resources which were stretched thin but also delegitimized Shah Shuja's authority. In November 1840, Dost Muhammad surrendered to Macnaghten.[70] But this act did not stop the Afghan insurrection from getting stronger and wider. The Afghans were now reacting strongly against the presence of kafirs in their country. And Dost Muhammad's son Akbar Khan remained north of Hindu Kush and bided his time for maintaining a bid to the throne. In April 1841, Major General W.K. Elphinstone assumed command of the troops in Afghanistan.[71]

The Gilzai tribes who occupied a large portion of the region between Ghazni and Kandahar were not subdued. The Gilzai sirdars were further enraged due to reduction of the subsidies, a measure which was forced upon Macnaghten by Auckland.[72] Especially damaging was the cessation of the 3,000 sterling pound subsidy annually paid to the eastern Gilzais for keeping the Khyber Pass open. The immediate result was that they rebelled and severed British communication between Kabul and Peshawar. Further, they occupied the passes on the road to Jalalabad and conducted systematic pillage and plundering on the convoys moving between Kabul and Peshawar. Robert Sale's brigade, which was on the point of marching back to India, was ordered to bring the eastern Gilzais back into line. Monteith was ordered to move with the 35th Native (Indian) Infantry Regiment (NIR), a cavalry squadron, and some guns. Sale (nicknamed 'Fighting Bob') had fought in the First Anglo-Burma War (1823) and was the colonel commandant of the 13th Battalion. After the capture of Ghazni, he was promoted to the rank of major general. Sale followed with the 13th Light Infantry Battalion. Suppressing the eastern Gilzais proved to be a tough task. Sale himself was wounded. However, the Khurd–Kabul Pass was cleared and Sale halted at Gandamak.[73]

On 12 October 1841, the 13th Light Infantry and the 35th Native Infantry Regiment with two guns under Dawes moved forward. Sale's objective was to go through the Khurd–Kabul Pass and deploy the 35th NIR in an advanced position at Khurd–Kabul after which the

13th was to retire to Bhudkak. The Khurd–Kabul is a narrow defile enclosed by high and rugged rocks. The Afghans in this Pass did not exceed sixty men but they knew the terrain. Concealed behind the rocks, stones, and sangars, they especially targeted the British officers. Even Sale was wounded in the left leg. On 18 October 1841, a 400-strong *lashkar* launched a night attack on the Khurd–Kabul Pass.[74] In the west of Kandahar, Sirdar Aktar Khan collected about 7,000 cavalry and infantry, but was defeated at Girishk in July 1841 by a detachment of Shah Shuja's regular troops commanded by Captain Woodburn. Woodburn's detachment comprised one infantry regiment, two horse artillery guns, and two regiments of Afghan cavalry.[75]

By the end of October 1841, Macnaghten had received enough warnings about a possible uprising in Kabul. However, suffering from the 'victory disease', he refused to take such warnings seriously. On 1 November, the shopkeepers in Kabul bazaar put their shutters down and refused to sell any ware to the British troops.[76] Major General Sale's wife, Lady Florentina Sale, noted in her journal on 26 October 1841: 'The general impression is that the Envoy is trying to deceive himself into an assurance that the country is in a quiescent state.'[77] Mohan Lal had warned Burnes that Abdullah Khan was instigating the tribal chiefs who had assembled at Kabul to rebel against the British. Burnes influenced by Macnaghten refused to believe the warnings by the 'croakers'.[78] Actually, Macnaghten had been selected for this post partly for the fact that he was a 'moderate'. Moreover, Macnaghten had been appointed as governor of Bombay and he was eager to leave Kabul for his new posting. By late October 1841, both Macnaghten and Burnes agreed that Afghanistan was settling down under the British-supported ruler, Shah Shuja, and significant number of British troops could be withdrawn from this country.[79]

On 2 November 1841, a popular insurrection broke out in Kabul.[80] The insurgency which had hitherto been mostly rural then acquired an urban colour. The British and Indian troops were stationed in the indefensible cantonment which was constructed in 1840. It was situated in the low swampy ground about 2 miles from the citadel. The cantonment was defended only by a waist-high mud rampart and a narrow ditch. Further, the commissariat supplies were stored in a small fort without a proper wall. The cantonment without any natural and man-made protection did not offer much scope for defence to the

British and Indian troops against the attacks by the armed populace of Kabul. Worse, the Afghans easily captured the commisariat supply fort. The British Engineers urged that the troops must be stationed in the Bala Hissar citadel. However, Shah Shuja's harem was in the citadel. Ultimately, respect for the cultural sensibilities of their political client Shah Shuja overrode military requirements of the British Indian force. British response to the Kabul uprising between 2–25 November 1841 was fragmented due to inadequate coordination between Elphinstone, Macnaghten, and Brigadier John Shelton (second in command of the army in India's units in Kabul after the departure of Sale).[81] Lack of unified command of the COIN force had come to haunt the British in Kabul. Sale was ordered to bring up his brigade from the Khurd–Kabul Pass and Eldred Pottinger was asked to join the Kabul garrison with his detachment from Charikar, which was 60 miles north of Kabul. However, Sale had already moved towards Jalalabad in the opposite direction, and from Pottinger's detachment, only he along with one other person reached Kabul. To cap it all, Akbar Khan with a force moved out from Bamian for Kabul.[82]

The Afghan sirdars promised that they would allow the British and Indian garrison in Kabul to retreat safely to India. However, the British Indian column on its way out was attacked. The British Indian column that left Kabul on 6 January1842 comprised about 5,000 combatants and roughly 12,000 camp followers. On 13 January 1842, the last remnant of the retreating British Indian force was wiped out at Gandamak. Of the 16,500 British and Indians who left Kabul, about 100 men survived.[83] The single British survivor was Surgeon William Brydon, who rode alone to Jalalabad.[84]

Meanwhile, the Conservatives came to power in Britain and they appointed Lord Ellenborough as governor general in place of Auckland. When on 25 November, Auckland received letters from Mr Clerk and Captain Mackeson about the news of the disaster in Afghanistan, he wrote to Jasper Nicolls, the commander-in-chief of India (7 December 1839–7 August 1843), depreciating any plan of re-conquest of Afghanistan. Nicolls was also against the invasion of Afghanistan. However, Mr Robertson, the lieutenant governor of the North-West Provinces and Mr George Clerk, the agent on the North-West Frontier pushed forward some troops to Peshawar. On 16 November, Clerk wrote to Colonel Wild, commanding at Ferozepur and to Colonel Rich at Ludhiana, urging them to send the 30th, 53rd, 60th, and the 64th NIRs to Peshawar. In this regard, a case could be made of the frontier officials being partly responsible for displaying aggressive intentions in order to restore order along the 'turbulent frontier'. While Nicolls wanted to bring the troops east of the Indus, Clerk insisted on pushing new units west of the Indus deep into Afghanistan. Clerk wrote to General Boyd at Sirhind for the dispatch of another brigade. The Sikhs were asked to collect the boats around Sutlej for transportation of the EIC's reinforcements. And 5,000 Sikh troops under Kunwar Partab Singh were ordered to march from Chach Hazara. Mackeson also requested the Sikh authorities for sending 6,000 troops to Jalalabad but General Avitabile argued that he needed all the Sikh troops for the protection of the Khalsa kingdom. Auckland believed that instead of two brigades, one brigade would be able to maintain British presence in Afghanistan. Wild declined to push into Afghanistan without adequate number of guns. On 3 January, four guns were provided to him. The camel drivers started deserting and the Afridi *malik*s were yet to be bribed into submission by Mackeson. Further, the loyalty of the Sikhs towards the EIC was fragile. Moreover, the Sikhs tampered the loyalty of the sepoys and played on their fears. The 9th Foot was ordered to be ready, along with the 26th NIR. Some irregular cavalry, two 9-pounders and a howitzer were ordered to accompany these units. Later, the 10th Cavalry was ordered to join this brigade. On 4 January, a brigade comprising 3,000 combat troops crossed the Sutlej. General George Pollock commanding at Agra, who had entered the Indian army as a lieutenant of artillery in 1803, was appointed commander of this avenging force. Meanwhile, Wild at Peshawar faced a lot of difficulties. His four NIRs comprised large number of young soldiers, whom the Sikhs had discouraged to move into Afghanistan. Wild had only one troop of irregular horse and four indifferent artillery pieces. Ammunition was scarce and the carriage was beginning to fail. Further, Sale and Macgregor were requesting immediate advance of the brigade.[85]

The fortress at Ali Masjid lies 5 miles within the Khyber Pass and 25 miles from Peshawar. It consisted of two small forts connected by a small wall and built upon a rock. The whole structure was surrounded on the south and west by two hills. It is called the 'Key to Khyber'. This fort was held by Yusufzais and resisted the attack of the Afridis.

On 15 January, Colonel Moseley with the 53rd and 64th NIRs accompanied by Mackeson started at night and reached Ali Masjid next morning. However, instead of 350 bullocks, only 60 bullocks came with the rearguard. This meant that the two NIRs were without adequate provisions. On 19 January, the 30th and 60th NIRs with some Khalsa guns started their march towards Ali Masjid. Under jezail firing by the Afghans, one gun was abandoned and the NIRs retreated to Jamrud. Meanwhile, the troops at Ali Masjid were suffering from lack of provisions, water, bedding, and tents. On 24 January 1842, Ali Masjid was abandoned to the Afridis and Colonel Mosley retreated to Jamrud. On 31 March 1842, Pollock pitched the camp at Jamrud. Brigadier Wild was ordered to command the advance guard and M'Caskill the rearguard. The flanking columns were ordered to advance in detachments of two companies at an interval of 500 yards.[86]

After receiving reinforcements, Pollock with some 8,000 soldiers marched west from Jalalabad. At Tezeen Valley, Akbar Khan's force of 16,000 men was defeated. Akbar Khan escaped to Goriband Valley. On 15 September, Pollock reached Kabul and on 17 September, he was joined by Nott's detachment from Kandahar. On 9 and 10 October, the Army of Retribution burnt the bazaar of Kabul as a mark of revenge. It was in this bazaar that the headless and limbless body of Macnaghten had been suspended by the unruly Afghan mob. On 11 November 1842, the British Indian force started its withdrawal from Afghanistan. In the end, Akbar Khan seized the throne for his father and Dost returned from India to reclaim his hereditary possession.[87] The first British adventure in Afghanistan except for a temporary power projection proved to be futile in the long run.

Under the second reign of Amir Dost Muhammad, Afghanistan became a stable political entity. In the 1850s, Dost Muhammad attempted to establish control over the Tokhi and Hotak Gilzais and toyed with the idea of annexing Kandahar. Meanwhile, Kuhandil Khan of Kandahar with the aid of the Persian government was trying to increase his sway towards Herat. In March 1852, Kuhandil was in control of Lash Juwain, Farah, and Sabzawar. On 30 March 1855, Dost Muhammad's son Ghulam Haidar concluded a treaty of friendship with the British Chief Commissioner of Punjab John Lawrence, in Peshawar. This diplomatic development along with an emerging power vacuum in Kandahar aided Dost's move. The death of Kuhandil Khan in

August 1855 brought a power struggle between the Kandahari sirdars. Rahmdil Khan and the sons of Purdil Khan and Mihrdil Khan were pitted against Muhammad Sadiq Khan and his brothers. In September 1855, Dost Muhammad started his march against Kandahar. He arrived in the city on 14 November, took possession of the citadel, and announced that the local contestants were to receive compensations. In September 1856, Dost handed over the control of the city to his son Ghulam Haidar and returned to Kabul.[88]

Back at Kandahar, Ghulam Haidar faced problems in administering the city. Rahmdil Khan had demanded a jagir worth Rs 500,000, and ultimately, in 1857, his allowance was raised to Rs 80,000 annually. Meanwhile, Ghulam Haidar faced problems in providing provisions to the garrison. In May 1856, there was a shortage of wheat, barley, and hay. Most of the cavalry was malnourished. Ghulam Haidar imported substantial amount of grain from Ghazni in the north-east, and Sabzawar, 300 miles distant in the north-west. In January 1857, Rs 90,000 was fixed as allowance for the 2,000-strong garrison at Farah. The monthly pay of each sowar (horseman) and infantry was Rs 10 and Rs 5, respectively. However, payments for the troops remained irregular. And desperate troops plundered the countryside. In administering the province of Kandahar, Ghulam Haidar was assisted by his brother Sher Ali Khan, the governor of Ghazni, and nephew Jalal Din Khan, who was in charge of Zamindawar and Girishk.[89]

Meanwhile, Herat, which the Persians had laid siege in April 1856, surrendered to the invaders on 26 October of the same year. In August 1856, Governor General Lord Canning supplied Dost Muhammad Khan with 4,000 muskets, bayonets, and ammunition, as well as a subsidy of Rs 500,000. However, this does not mean that Afghanistan had become a 'rentier state'. On 26 January 1857, the chief commissioner of Punjab and the *amir* signed the Anglo-Afghan Treaty of Friendship, which stipulated that the Afghan government was to receive an immediate subsidy of Rs 100,000 per month and an additional 4,000 muskets. A group of British officials (Kandahar Mission of 1857–8) was to supervise the expenditure of the subsidy for modernization of the Afghan army. The treaty also provided for permanent exchange of non-European representatives (*wakils*: Asian diplomatic agents in the service of the British-Indian state) at Peshawar and Kabul. Initially, the subsidy was for the duration of the Anglo-Persian War, but it continued for 18 months after the Anglo-Persian Peace Treaty on 4 March 1857. Between August 1856 and October 1858, the British government paid Rs 2.6 million to Afghanistan and supplied the country with equipment and ammunition worth Rs 164,115.[90] One of the conditions behind this monetary grant was that Dost should use it for strengthening his army, which would enable him to stabilize his regime in Afghanistan. The amir was supposed to maintain 18,000 infantry, of which 13,000 were to be regulars organized in 13 regiments.[91] This subsidy discouraged Dost from following an aggressive policy when British India was engaged in suppressing Bengal army's Hindu and Muslim mutineers during 1857–8.

On 27 May 1863, Dost brought Herat (which was independent since 1818) under his control. For his achievements, Dost was known as the Great Amir (*amir-e-kabir*). When he died of asthma on 9 June 1863, at the age of 72, Dost ruled over a region which extended from the Oxus River in the north to the plains of Peshawar. After Dost's designated heirs—Sirdar Muhammad Akbar Khan and Sirdar Ghulam Haidar Khan—died one after another in 1847 and 1859, respectively, his third son, Sirdar Sher Ali Khan, was appointed as the heir apparent (*waliahd*).[92] Dost's government was decentralized in nature. The Pathan tribes considered themselves partners rather than subjects of the monarch. Dost mostly depended on his siblings for the administration of his realm. Except the governor of Jalalabad, named Shahmard Khan (d. 1878), all the provincial governors were sons of the amir. Most of the provincial governors behaved as 'little kings'. They maintained their own military contingents, and were independent in their methods of revenue collection and fixing the allowances of their subordinate sirdars and their own household retainers.[93] Despite the presence of a comparatively stable neutral Afghanistan, there was no peace in the 'badlands' of the Indus, where the British Indian government had to conduct Small War.

SMALL WAR ALONG THE INDUS FRONTIER: 1843–77

The region between British Punjab and eastern Afghanistan was a no man's land. This region, roughly along the banks of the Indus, was inhabited by Pathan tribes who pillaged and plundered western Punjab. When the British and Indian troops pursued them, they escaped into eastern Afghanistan through the porous border. At times, these tribes also received official and unofficial encouragement from the Afghan government and the Pathan tribes in Afghanistan to pillage and plunder British territory. As a result, the Government of India (GOI), till the end of the Raj in 1947, had to conduct frequent 'Butcher and Bolt' expeditions (also known as Small War) against these frontier tribes. The fluid nature of tribal dynamics shaped the tribes' behaviour towards the British Indian empire. Each clan had their own perspective which was distinctive, unwritten, and unpredictable, built on a series of precedents. Further, the perspective of the clans was also shaped by the ever-changing political context.[94]

In general, the Mughal chroniclers described all the tribes between the Indus and Herat as Afghans. But, in contrast, the British attempted to identify and categorize the important tribes along the Indus frontier. In general, Tripodi writes, the British regarded the Pathans as 'noble savages'.[95] The British officers concluded that the Pathan tribes were divided into many clans and each clan was further subdivided into several sub-clans. Each sub-clan was in turn divided into families. And all the Pathans spoke Pushtu/Pashto. The British officers concluded that many Pathans were Afghans and the rest were Rajputs who had converted to Islam. In British format, life in the rugged mountains, difficulties of livelihood, and the Islamic ethos, made the Pathans and the Afghans good soldiers. The British officers tried to map the territorial localities of the different frontier tribes. The Yusufzais (also mentioned in the Mughal chronicles) inhabited the Peshawar Valley, Buner, Swat, Malakand Hills located east of the Indus in the Hazara District (Black Mountain). The Afridis inhabited the Khyber Hills and the British belief was that they were converted Rajputs. The Orakzais inhabited the valley north of the Samana Range. The Khattaks inhabited the Khattak Hills. Since their territory lies within British India's border, they were more manageable. The Bangash were in Miranzai. And the Turis were in Kurram Valley. Most of the tribes were Sunnis but a few like the Turis, Bangash, Hazaras, and so on, were Shias.[96] The Waziris were divided into three groups—Ootamanzis, Ahmudzais, and Mashuds. The Ahmudzais took partly to agriculture. Some of them also engaged in salt trade and grazing.[97] The Ahmudzais passed the summer in the region round Wana and moved during the winter to the grazing land on the western border of the Bannu District. And the

Ootamanzis inhabited the Tochi Valley.[98] The northern Waziris had very few villages. They generally inhabited the banks of the rivers and made temporary habitations with loose stones. In the mountains, they made an encampment known as *kizdhee*. These encampments were constructed with woollen blankets supported by sticks with coarse matting at the sides. These blankets were impervious to rain and not easily inflammable. The cattle and sheep guarded by dogs were also kept within such tents.[99] Iron ore was available in the Waziri Hills. The principal site was Koh-i-Mahsood near Mulkin. The ore was dug out and then crushed. Every village had a smelting apparatus. Smelting furnace was constructed with a conical roof planted nearly vertically on the ground with long holes. Iron was extracted by smelting the ore with charcoal. This was used for making swords, daggers, and barrels of jezails. In the Mashud region, the artisans who manufactured weapons were located at Kanirgorum Town.[100] And Khanki Valley was identified as the region inhabited by the Orakzais.[101] The three main branches of the Mashuds were Alizai, Shaman Khel, and Bahlozai. Each was divided into numerous sections and sub-sections. They occupied the region around Razmak, Wana, and Jandol.[102]

Shah Mahmoud Hanafi, taking a postmodernist approach, asserts that present-day knowledge about the tribes in Afghanistan is actually a product of British colonialism, and all classifications and categorization of the tribes and sects are actually 'constructions'. The term 'Afghanistan' was absent in Ahmad Shah's lexicon and in his worldview. The term was mainly the product of British empire building in the periphery. The British colonial project started with Mountstuart Elphinstone (1779–1859) whose book *An Account of the Kingdom of Kabul* (1815) was the first step in the British-initiated 'Oriental' project. Henry George Raverty (1825–1906) was the colonial official who studied Pashto language in order to carry forward British Indian Empire's Afghanistan project.[103] What is important for our purpose is the classification and categorization of the different frontier tribes as believed by the Raj officials.

In 1844, mountain batteries were raised specifically for service along the North-West Frontier and beyond it if required. Each battery had four 12-pdr howitzers and four 3-pdr guns along with two farriers, 168 syces, and 168 mules. The howitzer had a curved trajectory; hence, it was useful for firing behind the enemy fortification like the sangar.[104]

The Quetta town in northern Baluchistan constituted the southernmost post of British India's 'scientific' frontier.[105] And the northern anchor of the British defensive line was Peshawar. Like the Mughals in late sixteenth century, in order to secure the southern end of the scientific frontier, the EIC annexed Sind in 1843. The Baluchis of Baluchistan were believed by the British officers to be a Muslim hill community of Arab descent. They had entered Baluchistan from the Persian Gulf.[106] Their favourite weapons were their 28-inch-long knives, and they engaged frequently in nocturnal raiding.[107] At that time, the Baluchi chiefs were ruling Sind and they had Afghan retainers. Against the EIC troops' artillery and muskets, the matchlocks and knives of the Afghan retainers proved inadequate.[108]

After the First Anglo-Sikh War, the Khalsa durbar was dominated by the British officials of the EIC. Henry Lawrence was selected by the Governor General Lord Hardinge as the political agent of Punjab. In 1847, Henry Lumsden raised the Corps of Guides from the younger sons and relations of the headmen of the villagers. The initial recruits were Yusufzais, Khattaks, and Muhammadzai tribes. Later, the Guides also recruited Afridis, Waziris, Hazaras, Kafirs, Sikhs, and Gurkhas. The Guides Corps included both cavalry and infantry. A *malik* (head of clan/*khail*) or a Sikh sirdar with his retainers constituted a *risala*. Herbert Edwardes pacified Bannu between 1847–8, by balancing the Sikh sirdars of the durbar and making political agreements with the Khans (Muslim tribal chiefs) of the frontier. In order to concili-ate the tribal sirdars, the British resorted to symbolic compromise. Herbert Edwardes dressed like the Pathans and talked their language. The submission of the influential chiefs was stage-managed for the maximum symbolic effect.[109] However, permanent submission of the tribes remained a chimera. For instance, in 1850, the Kabul Khel section of the Ootamanzi Waziris attacked the salt mines at Bahadur Khel.[110]

Meanwhile, the GOI kept the restored Dost in good humour. Afghanistan was given a gift of muskets and money. This kept Dost neutral, when the 'Devil's Wind' blew across north India in the summer of 1857.[111] In the summer of 1857, most of the Hindustani sowars and the sepoys of the Bengal army rebelled. Along the North-West Frontier, the rebellion of the Bengal army units stationed at Peshawar, Rawalpindi, Sialkot, and so on, put the British in a difficult situation.

In order to replace the manpower loss and also to augment their military strength in a time of crisis, the British recruited the Pathans in auxiliary as well as regular units.[112]

However, some Pathan sirdars tried to raise the religious war cry and attempted to raid the border of British India thinking that as the British were moving most of their military assets into Hindustan to confront the rebellious *Pandies*, the raiders would have easy pickings. The British detachment was attacked at Khyber Pass on 27 August 1857 by an insurgent force led by Shahzada Mahmud.[113] After the Bengal army's mutiny was crushed in 1859, the British transferred military units back to the Indus frontier. John Lawrence believed in following a closed border policy. He wanted a 'no intervention' policy towards Afghanistan and minimum interaction with the tribes on the west side of the Indus.[114] Nevertheless, sporadic attacks by the Pathan tribesmen continued. In retaliation, in 1860, Brigadier General Chamberlain led an expedition comprising 5,196 men against the Mashud Waziris. As punishment, livestock from their villages were seized.[115]

The Sittana colony inhabited by the Hindustani fanatics near the Hazara frontier proved to be a source of trouble for the GOI. The Sittana fanatics supported by the Hussunzai tribe threatened the territory of the British-protected chief of Umb. It was decided to deploy a combined force comprising infantry, artillery, and cavalry units of about 5,000 personnel to teach the fanatics and the wayward tribes a lesson. Brigadier General N. Chamberlain was appointed as the commander of the Yusufzai Field Force. Inadequate supply of boats required for crossing the Indus at Topi delayed the mobilization of the force. The Raj's troops entered hostile territory on 18 October 1863 and reached the Umbeyla Pass on 20 October. The political officers accompanying the troops, as per the requirement of Small War, entered into communications with the local tribes and informed them that British India had no intention to interfere with their internal conditions or to annex these regions. The sole purpose of the government was to move the troops through their territory in order to punish the Hindustani fanatics of Sittana. Despite the efforts of the 'politicals', the Bonair tribe inhabiting the region of Umbeyla Pass displayed hostile attitude. From 25 October, the tribesmen started collecting towards the Umbeyla Pass. In early November 1863, the troops were used for road making in order to improve the LOC. From mid November, tribesmen started receiving reinforcements from Bajaur. As in the case of advance through the Bolan Pass during the First Afghan War, while operating in the Umbeyla Pass also, British officers found out that camels were the best logistical vehicles in this zone of operation. Many hostile villages were destroyed. On 17 December 1863, the tribes tendered their submission to British authority. The Umbeyla Campaign officially came to an end on 23 December 1863.[116]

In John Lawrence's view, the Russian danger to India was merely a phantom menace.[117] However, the North-West Frontier tribes had to be managed. In the post-Mutiny period, the units designated for fighting along the North-West Frontier started recruiting the 'unruly' Indus tribes in greater numbers in a systematic manner. For instance, in 1862, the Corps of Guides had Qizilbash, Pathans (Yusufzais, Khattak, Mohmand, and Gilzai clans), Afridis (Zakka Khel, Basi Khel, Sepai, and Koki Khel), and Kafirs in its ranks.[118] In November 1862, Lieutenant Colonel H.W. Norman (military member of the Viceroy's Council) warned that the number of Muslims coming from tribes beyond the Indus frontier should never be allowed to exceed one-eighth of the regiment's strength.[119] Obviously, the British were anxious about the loyalty of the tribes beyond the Indus. The British were aware of the game of playing off the different 'races' against each other to prevent the emergence of any anti-British coalition among the 'native' soldiery. In 1860, Major General S. Cotton commanding the Peshawar Division spelled out the *divide et impera* policy in the following words: 'To produce and bring into operation that feeling of antagonism naturally existing between the castes or races of which the Indian army is composed, by the formation of corps of distinct races, so that one would become an effective check on the other.... Thus regiments of Malwa Sikhs, Manjha Sikhs, Dogras, Mazbis, Afridis, Punjabi Muslims, etc., should be established.'[120] The British also tried to recruit the Baluchis. But they disliked wearing uniform and cutting their hair short.[121] So, Baluchi recruitment was not a success. Thus, the mentality of the colonized and not always imperial policy shaped military recruitment. Overall, in 1876, the number of Muslims from the Indus region, both in the infantry and cavalry, amounted to 3,800 men of about 44,685 personnel in the Bengal army.[122] In 1879, the Punjab Frontier Force (PFF, previously known as the PIF) numbered to 14,000 men.[123] It comprised Sikhs, Punjabi Muslims, and Gurkhas. It was a regional army geared for 'Butcher and Bolt' expeditions across the North-West Frontier. In 1886, the PFF was transferred from the control of the Punjab government to the commander-in-chief of India.[124]

By 1868, the Indian soldiers were equipped with smooth bore Enfield rifles whose effective range was about 200 yards.[125] Towards the end of the nineteenth century, the GOI calculated the number of fighting males among the Waziris were about 40,275.[126] In February 1878, the GOI decided to follow the policy of disarming the Hazaras. Registration of arms in the Peshawar and Kohat districts was carried out and carrying of arms was prohibited. Village police was recruited from the frontier tribes who were tasked to carry out policing duties. They to an extent relieved the army from its task of policing the border. The village militia got two grooved Brunswick rifles and the border police and the border militia were equipped with short Enfield carbines and swords. The border police were men of the districts, uniformed and armed by the GOI, whereas the militia comprised men of trans-border tribes who possessed their own arms and had no uniform. Gradually, the militia men were absorbed into the border police.[127]

Besides the border police, the GOI also raised certain paramilitary formations for guarding the North-West Frontier. During November 1881, the Khaibar Rifles was set up. In January 1888, a company was raised from the Zakka Khels of Bazar Valley. The total strength of the Khaibar Rifles came to about 836 personnel of whom there were 14 Viceroy's Commissioned Officer, also known as 'Native' Officers or VCOs (including *subedars* and *jemadars*), and 64 Indian non-commissioned officers (NCOs) (*havildars* and *naiks*). Except 30 personnel who were mounted, the rest of the men functioned as infantry. Their uniform comprised khaki turban and khaki loose trousers, and the men were equipped with rifles.[128] These militias remained the GOI's first line of defence. If they failed, then the GOI sent the regular units. And the military establishment of British India took care to maintain qualitative advantage in weaponry vis-à-vis the frontier tribes. During the Jowaki Expedition in 1877–8, the regulars were equipped with breech loading (BL) Snider rifles capable of accurate firing to 1,000 yards.[129]

PRELUDE TO THE SECOND ANGLO-AFGHAN WAR

Britain's policy towards Afghanistan was shaped not only by what was happening in Afghanistan and its neighbouring regions, but also due to the changing power politics within Britain. The death of

Dost and ensuing civil war in Afghanistan, and the slow but steady Russian expansion in Central Asia also triggered British anxiety vis-à-vis Afghanistan. The rise of Disraeli's Conservatives in the 1870s led to a reappraisal of the Russian threat to Afghanistan. The London government not only encouraged a Forward Policy towards Afghanistan but also authorized intrusion of direct British administration in Baluchistan in 1877.[130]

By 1875, both the London government and the GOI concluded that due to continuous advance of Russia in Central Asia, Afghanistan (especially its foreign policy) needs to be brought under firm control. Amir Sher Ali, it was decided, must be coerced to enter into closer diplomatic relation with the GOI. The British·considered the March 1855 Treaty, which was signed between Amir Dost Muhammad Khan (father of Sher Ali) and the GOI, needed to be updated. This treaty, which stated in general terms that Afghanistan and British India should remain friends, was considered inadequate for ensuring the Raj's security in the context of continuous Russian expansion in Central Asia. In 1863, when Dost Muhammad Khan died, his son Sher Ali ascended the throne. Muhammad Afzal Khan, Dost's eldest son and governor of Afghanistan's northern Turkestan provinces commanded a force of 25,000 men and also eyed the throne. Afzal's army was reorganized with the aid of a British officer named William Campbell. Campbell was taken prisoner in 1834 when Dost Muhammad fought Shuja. Later, Campbell accepted Islam, took the name of Sher Muhammad, and joined Afzal's service. Afzal was ruling Turkestan since 1855. Afzal refused to pay revenue and read the *khutba* (Friday sermon) in Sher Ali's name. In June 1864, Sher Ali confronted Afzal Khan. Sher Ali and Afzal fought an inconclusive battle at Bajgah in June 1864. Afzals' son Abdur Rahman shot dead Sher Ali's son and heir apparent Muhammad Ali Khan.[131] Sher Ali was able to arrest his brother Afzal and keep him in Kabul. Afzal's son Sirdar Abd al-Rahman escaped to Bokhara.[132]

The three Muslim khanates of Khokand, Bokhara, and Khiva, with a population between 5–6 million (they were mostly in the oases along Amy Darya and Syr Darya), were located in a semi-desert region. These polities lacked internal cohesion. These khanates had no settled boundaries and went to war with each other for establishing political supremacy. The rulers in theory were absolute, but in reality exercised limited authority over their multi-ethnic populace. In 1853 and

1854, the Russians captured Ak-Mechet and Vernyi. Then, the Special Committee took the decision to link the Siberian Line with Syr Darya. Such a linkage, assumed the Russian policy makers, would create a contiguous defensive line south of the Kazakh Steppe. This decision was confirmed by Czar Nicholas. Due to the onset of the Crimean War and the serf emanicipation reforms of Czar Alexander II, only in 1864, the Russians started implementing their 1854 decision. Only 4,000 troops were deployed for this mission. Colonel Cherniaev captured Aulie-Ata and Colonel Verevkin marched from Ak-Mechet and joined force with Cherniaev. The latter then on his own responsibility captured the city of Chimkent, a move which was not included in the original plan. In November 1864, Russian Foreign Minister Prince Gorchakov and Minister of Defence D.A. Miliutin recommended that no further advance should be made. The Czar approved the recommendation.[133]

However, Cherniaev, in defiance of instruction from Moscow, captured Tashkent. With a populace of about 100,000, Tashkent was the richest town in Central Asia and a long-time trading partner of Russia. Till 1864, Russia's policy was to keep Tashkent under Russian influence but not annexation of the city. However, war between Khokand and Bokhara in 1864 provided an opportunity to Cherniaev. He argued that the city was threatened due to Khokand–Bokhara conflict. In late 1864, Cherniaev advanced towards the town but failed to take it. He moved again and despite orders to the contrary, assaulted the town and captured it against heavy odds after two days' fighting. When Cherniaev was ordered to vacate the town by General Kryzhanovsky, he refused saying that it would hamper Russia's prestige. The Czar supported Cherniaev's action. Cherniaev then sent a mission to Bokhara. The amir of Bokhara was ordered to accept the Syr Darya and Naryn rivers as the Russian frontier. The amir detained the delegation and then Cherniaev started hostilities against Bokhara. But St Petersburg stepped in and relieved Cherniaev of his command. General Romanovsky was placed in charge. Nevertheless, Romanovsky continued military operations against Bokhara and occupied the town of Khojand in the Ferghana Valley. He was then replaced. The Turkestan region, however, was formally incorporated within the Russian empire, and in 1867, a separate province under General K.P. Kaufman, a protégé of Miliutin, was created. In March 1868, Bokhara declared a jihad against Russia. Kaufman occupied Samarkhand and Bokhara's force was routed.

Bokhara Khanate was declared as a Russian dependency. The Russsians took control of Bokhara's commercial, political, and external affairs.[134]

Though mostly the 'men on the spots' were responsible for expanding the Russian frontier towards Pamirs and Hindu Kush, the British government in India and Britain concluded that expansion of Russia in Central Asia was the product of a master plan chalked out in Moscow. The Russian military officers were interested in expanding the frontier both due to material and non-material reasons. Expansion brought glory, honour, promotion, and loot for themselves, and the men under their commands. Further, expansion also enhanced Russia's prestige and furthered their self-proclaimed 'civilizing mission'.[135]

Some hard-liners within the Russian General Staff, of course, dreamt about the invasion of India. In 1854, General Chikhachev planned a force of 30,000 soldiers advancing from Astrabad and Turkestan with the cooperation or acquiescence of the Persians and the Afghans. In 1857, a Russian Mission under Colonel Ignatiev was sent to Khiva and Bokhara. The Khivans were disturbed by the appearance of Russian steamers at the mouth of Syr Darya. At Bokhara, a treaty was concluded with the amir. Ignatiev perceived the military weakness of these two khanates. Ignatiev argued a preemptive move by Russia to annex these two khanates before the British could absorb them. After a mission to China, Ignatiev returned to Moscow as head of the Asia Division in the Foreign Ministry. He and the other hawks in Moscow were further aggravated when Dost Muhammad with indirect British support extended his influence over Afghan Turkestan (the region between upper Amy Darya and Hindu Kush). In 1858, a Russian agent named Nikolai Khanikov reached Herat with the objective of proceeding to Kabul in order to establish diplomatic relationship with Dost Muhammad. However, the latter due to his commitment to the British refused to receive the Russian agent.[136]

In March 1865, the khanate of Bokhara, in order to defeat the Khokandis, made a defensive treaty with the Russians. As a result, Russian cantonments were established at Charjui on the Oxus.[137] Meanwhile, in 1865, Sher Ali marched towards Kandahar because his younger brother Muhammad Amin Khan, governor of that city, had rebelled. Amin also occupied Kalat-i-Gilzai. In June 1865, at Kabaj, Amin Khan and his son, Ali Khan, died. Overcome by grief, Sher Ali took refuge in the world of mysticism. Meanwhile, the rebels gathered around

Muhammad Azam Khan who was the governor of Zurmula (Zurmut) before being exiled to India in 1864. Azam Khan joined hands with Abd al-Rahman who had moved from Bokhara to India. Both these sirdars planned to occupy Kabul. In May 1866, they occupied Kabul and released Afzal Khan and made him the amir. Sher Ali then reentered the scene with his army. However, Sher Ali's force was defeated repeatedly at Saidebad (May 1866), Muqur (January 1867), and in Panjsher (September 1867). Saidebad was comparatively a big battle, as in this confrontation, the total casualties of both sides amounted to 8,000 soldiers. Sher Ali Khan retreated to Herat. Luckily, Muhammad Afzal Khan died in October 1867. The latter was succeeded by his full brother Muhammad Azam Khan.[138]

Sher Ali moved towards Kandahar, and then to Ghazni, where Muhammad Azam Khan was engaged in a battle. An uprising occurred in Kabul against Azam Khan and several sirdars occupied the capital for Sher Ali. Azam Khan and Abd al-Rahman left Afghanistan. Azam Khan died on his way to Teheran and Abd al-Rahman moved into Samarkhand where he lived as a Russian pensioner for the next 11 years. On 8 September 1868, Sher Ali entered Kabul and started his reign as amir for the second time. The civil war occurred among the sons and grandsons of Dost Muhammad Khan because the latter had divided the kingdom among his sons just as Babur and before him Timur had done it. So, each son and grandson regarded himself as autonomous ruler, subject only to their father. Each of them maintained their own force and collected taxes and, after defraying the expenses, sent the surplus to Kabul. Further, Dost's numerous sons were of different wives and this increased rivalry among the siblings.[139] Besides the defective political structure, Pathan culture also played an important role in destabilizing Afghanistan. Hassan Kakar writes:

> However, competitiveness and rivalry were not confined to the families of the governing sirdars; they were characteristics of the Pashtuns among whom it was said that in the tribe you may not be without cousins, among cousins not without brothers, and among brothers not without sons. All this is due to the custom of *tuburi* or rivalry among paternal cousins that exists among them with force even to the present day.[140]

During the civil war, many sirdars also joined the warring princes. This was possible because the sirdars, enjoying rent-free lands, commanded private contingents. Further, they received extra allowances for providing military service during emergencies. And many tribal leaders who were deprived of their privileges by the amir also joined in the fray.[141] So, instability was inbuilt within the Afghan political cultural system.

The conquest of Khiva by Russia, in 1873, left them facing Turcoman tribes who inhabited the region between Caspian Sea and Amu Darya. The Turcomans were semi-settled nomadic tribes. Some functioned as slave traders and freebooters. Until 1861, these tribes were under Persian control. But in 1861, they defeated the Shah's army. The most formidable of these tribes were the Tekke Turcomans who inhabited the Akhal Oasis near the Persian border. After Samarkhand had fallen to the Russians in 1868, the Shah expressed alarm and requested British intervention to secure an agreement with the Russians guaranteeing Persia's northern frontier. The British Minister Charles Alison was told not to induce the Shah to expect any British aid. After the fall of Khiva to the Russians, the Shah again made the request. Alison's successor at Teheran, Taylor Thompson, argued that Persia could be subsidized and used as a barrier against Russian expansion towards Afghanistan and British India. British India's viceroy, Lord Northbrook, claimed that Persia was so unreliable that British aid to that country to act as a barrier against Russia's expansionism would be totally futile. However, Lord Napier of Magdala, commander-in-chief of British India (9 April 1870–9 April 1876), argued that Persia should be supported. In London, the India Office was for action but the Foreign Office was dead against such a plan.[142]

In 1876, the Khokand Khanate was annexed as a province of Ferghana.[143] The British again overreacted in 1878 as in 1838. In 1877, Russia declared war against Ottoman Turkey. It seemed that Britain might join the war on the side of Turkey. About 5,000 troops of the British Indian army were sent from Bombay to Malta to aid the British army in the probable forthcoming operations. In response, Russia pressurized Britain by increasing its activities along Central Asia. In June 1878, Major Cavagnari (deputy commissioner of Peshawar) reported that a Russian envoy of the same rank as the governor general of Tashkent was about to visit Kabul. And General Kaufmann had written to the amir of Afghanistan that the envoy must be treated as an ambassador deputed by the Czar himself. The Russian troops also established cantonments on the ferries of Kilif and Kerki on the Oxus River. On 13 June 1878, when the Berlin Congress was meeting, General

Stolietoff's Mission reached Kabul. According to British reports, the Russian Mission met with an enthusiastic response from the Afghan government. Sher Ali, along with the other senior dignitaries of the state, received General Stolietoff at Bala Hissar.[144]

The British were following 'carrot and stick' policy in order to bring the amir under control. In 1868, a free grant of money and arms was made to Sher Ali by Lord Lawrence, the governor general of India, to prevent the Kabul durbar from slipping away completely from British influence. In March 1869, Sher Ali Khan visited India. At Ambala, he was given a grand civic reception. In the conference held at Ambala between the amir and Lord Mayo (Lawrence's successor), the latter assured the former that British India would aid him in case of trouble and no attempt will be made to intervene in the internal affairs of Afghanistan. On 12 July 1873, the Afghan envoy, who met the viceroy at Simla, asked for British guarantee against Russian encroachments in northern Afghanistan. However, the GOI was non-committal at this juncture. In 1874, the amir arrested his eldest son, Yakub Khan, the governor of Herat.[145] Later, Sher Ali refused permission to a British envoy who had gone on a mission to Kasghar. Sher Ali also did not use the money which the GOI had forwarded to him for his use. Sher Ali probably realized that utilization of British financial grant would encourage the GOI to intervene in Afghanistan. Further, if British envoys were allowed in Afghanistan, then he also could not refuse such requests from the Russians. Hence, Sher Ali refused to admit the reception of a British mission when insisted upon by Lord Lytton, the governor general of India. On 21 September 1878, the British mission for Afghanistan left Peshawar for Kabul. Amir Sher Ali (who died in February 1879) was informed that if by 20 November 1878, the British mission was not allowed entry through the Khyber Pass, Afghanistan's stance will be interpreted as hostile by the GOI. Lord Cranbrook (who had succeeded the Marquis of Salisbury as secretary of state for India) on 25 October 1878 insisted that the amir must apologize and accept a permanent British mission in Afghanistan; otherwise, the British Indian troops would cross the India–Afghanistan boundary. Meanwhile, the GOI started concentrating troops at Peshawar, Thul, and Quetta.[146] On 19 November 1878, the amir wrote the following letter to the governor general:

> I assure your Excellency that, on the contrary, the officials of this God granted Government, in repulsing the Mission, were not influenced by any hostile or inimical feelings towards the British Government, nor did they

intend that any insult or affront should be offered. But they were afraid that the independence of this Government might be affected by the arrival of the Mission, and that the friendship which has now existed between the two Governments for several years might be annihilated…and if, in accordance with the custom of allied States, the British Government should desire to send a purely friendly and temporary Mission to this country, with a small escort, not exceeding twenty or thirty men, similar to that which attended the Russian Mission, this servant of God will not oppose its progress.[147]

However, both the GOI and the British government were in no mood to contemplate peace except on their own terms. Cavagnari was ordered to encourage the Afridis in the Khyber region to rebel against the amir.[148] In this case, rather than the 'men on the spots', the top decision makers at metropole and Kolkata took the aggressive decisions.

SECOND ANGLO-AFGHAN WAR: 1878–APRIL 1881

British India mobilized three columns. Major General Donald Stewart commanded the Kandahar Field Force (265 British officers, 12,599 men and 78 guns). Its advanced portion was under Major General Biddulph. The Peshawar Valley Field Force included 325 British officers, 15,854 troops, and 48 guns. And finally, the Kurram Field Force under Fred Roberts had 116 British officers, 6,549 men, and 18 guns. In total, British India concentrated 706 British officers, 35,002 men, and 144 guns. As per the requirements of conducting Small War, a political officer also accompanied the military column. Colonel Garrow Waterfield, commissioner of Peshawar, was appointed as Roberts' political advisor. Waterfield had a large number of Indian gentlemen in his staff. The duty of the Indian gentlemen was to conduct political negotiations with the frontier tribes.[149] The Afghan regular army comprised 56,173 troops organized into 73 infantry regiments, 42 cavalry regiments, and 48 artillery batteries. Most of the officers and soldiers were drawn from the Gilzais and the Pashtuns of Wardak area. The regular army consumed between 25 per cent to 40 per cent of Afghanistan's revenue.[150] An Afghan detachment which numbered to 18,000 men with 11 guns left the Habib Kila Cantonment for Peiwar Kotal, in order to block any probable advance by the British Indian units. On 1 December 1878, Roberts overcame the Afghan defensive position at Spingawi

Kotal, defended by 400 men. The Afghan units retreated across Alikhel Road pursued by British cavalry. At Peiwar, the casualties of Roberts' force numbered to two British officers and eighteen men killed and three British officers and seventy-five men wounded. As usual, casualties remained quite low in such Small Wars. On 8 December, Roberts' force reached Shutargardan and Alikhel on 12 December. On 31 December 1878, Sher Ali fled to Turkestan and his son Yakub Khan was released from the jail and became the amir. He professed friendship with the British Indian government.[151]

The principal objective of the Treaty of Gandamak was to have a British representative at Amir Yakub Khan's (grandson of Dost Muhammad) durbar at Kabul. The British representative's job would be to prevent Afghan foreign policy from taking an anti-British colour, especially in collusion with the Russians. On 24 July 1879, Louis Cavagnari was received at Kabul as the British rresident. Cavagnari's last message to the governor general sent on 2 September concluded with the words 'All well'. Within the next twelve hours, the residency was attacked. Cavagnari's escort of seventy-five men was annihilated by the Afghan army. The execution of the British envoy after an uprising by the Afghan soldiery at Bala Hissar in Kabul and, then, hanging the dead body in the bazaar of the city was an action replay of a similar scene which was enacted almost forty years ago.[152]

The GOI reacted quickly. The operational plan was to launch three columns simultaneously. One was to move through the Khyber Pass, one through the Kurram Valley, and another through Pishin Valley. The first two columns constituted the northern division. They were to capture Dakka and the Peiwar Pass. And the third column, with rein-forcements from Multan, comprised the southern division and was ordered to capture Kandahar.[153]

On 5 September 1879, Brigadier General Dunham Massy, then commanding the Kurram Field Force at Peiwar Kotal, was ordered to move with 10 days' supplies and capture the Shutargardan Pass, before the regular Afghan troops or the tribesmen could fortify the pass and entrench themselves strongly to deny entry to the British and Indian troops. The 72nd Highlanders and the 5th Punjab Infantry was ordered to secure the road between Ali Khel and the Shutargardan Pass and the 7th Company of Bengal Sappers and Miners was ordered to improve the road beyond Shutargardan.[154]

The army of invasion comprised the Peshawar Valley Field Force under Lieutenant General Sam Browne, Kurram Valley Field Force under Major General F.S. Roberts, and the Kandahar Field Force under Lieutenant General D.M. Stewart. Sam Browne commanded about 10,000 men and 30 guns, and Roberts had with him some 5,500 men and 24 guns. Stewart commanded some 7,300 men. In addition, Major General M.A.S. Biddulph's 6,250 men and 18 guns at Quetta were also put under Stewart's command. Sam Browne started from Peshawar and Roberts from Kohat. Stewart started from Multan and then advanced to Quetta through Dera Bhukti and Bolan Pass. Major General F.F. Maude commanded 6,000 men as a reserve division to protect the rear of the Peshawar Valley Field Force. Major General J.M. Primrose commanded another reserve division of about 6,000 soldiers to protect the rear of the Kandahar Field Force. These two reserve divisions later engaged in extensive COIN duties while the three field forces fought the regular soldiers of the Afghan army. The lines of communication were protected by 5,000 Imperial Service Troops (mainly drawn from the Sikh feudatory states) under Colonel J. Watson. Thus, about 17,000 soldiers were engaged in COIN against the rebellious tribes and about 29,000 men were deployed for conventional warfare against the amir's army.[155]

On 23 September 1879, Roberts' force moved from Kurram.[156] The Kurram Valley is about 60 miles long and between 3–10 miles wide. It is surrounded on all sides by high mountains with vegetation on them. In the north-west is the spur which runs down from Sika Ram, the highest peak of the Safed Koh Range (more than 14,000 feet high). This spur is crossed by Peiwar Kotal. A river which varies from 100 to 500 yards in width flows through the valley and the road then becomes a track which runs along its rocky bed.[157] The landscape was described by one British cavalry officer in the following words:

Fifteen miles up the stony track brought us to our first camping ground, Habib Killa, the hills...lie north and south of the valley.... Next morning we marched to Zuburdust Killa, our road at first leading over rocky ground, and through the new dry beds of torrents, alternating with tracts of thorny scrub jungle, from the depth of which we were occasionally saluted by the cry of...patridge. After six miles of this we reached the foot of the ascent to the Peiwar Kotal, a very steep rocky narrow gorge, the sides...sparsely clad with bushes and stunted pines, and the path only just broad enough for a gun-carriage. On the right (north) of the path rises the snow clad peak of Sita Ram, towering to a height of sixteen thousand feet.[158]

On 27 September, the Kurram Force ascended the Shutargardan. The depth of the river was, however, only three feet. All the men were dressed in khaki and wore putties. The latter were bandages of woollen stuff rolled round the leg from the knee to the ankle. It was considered better than the long boots for dismounted work in the rocky terrain.[159]

Five days' provision for the men and the horses were carried in canvas bags. This measure was necessitated due to scarcity of supplies between the Kurram and Logar river valleys.[160] Despite logistical preparation made by the GOI in advance, the Kurram Valley Field Force suffered from inadequacies as regards supplies. When news of the massacre of the British envoy's party was received, there were only 1,500 mules, 500 camels, and 800 pack bullocks in the Kurram Valley. They were adequate just for furnishing supplies to the winter garrison in the Kurram Valley. All the available animals at Peshawar and other border towns were bought by the British military authorities and sent to the army's commissariat post at Ali Khel. On 14 October, at Kabul, the British Indian force possessed 1,973 mules, 675 camels, and 604 bullocks. In addition, 230 *yabu*s were purchased at Kabul.[161]

In September 1879, for the troops under Roberts advancing towards Kabul and for those in the Kurram Valley, the responsibility for carriage was made over to the transport department. And it became the responsibility of the transport department rather than the commissariat to feed the animals and pay the attendants dealing with the animals. The general transport officer became responsible to pay compensation for losses of hired cattle by death, theft, and so on. He also paid the *chaudhuri*s, who in turn were responsible for hiring the animals.[162] The general transport officer was given credit from the treasury at Peshawar and his expenditure was adjusted by the special audit office at Ambala.[163] The general transport officer set up a depot at Thul for collecting and treating the sick animals. For every 1,000 animals, one transport officer was appointed. All the transport officers reported to the general transport officer. Further, a transport officer was stationed at Kurram and another at Ali Khel in order to look after the supply of animals for the force invading Afghanistan.[164]

In fact, the Raj had made some preparations in advance for creating the logistical infrastructure of the force which finally moved into

Afghanistan. In 1878, the lieutenant governor of Punjab instructed the divisional commissioners in charge of the divisions to collect information about the number of camels, mules, bullocks, and donkeys available for purchase and for hire in their administrative divisions, respectively. Some commissariat and transport department officials were deputed to the district headquarters of Punjab, so that the former group of officials could aid the district officials of Punjab in acquiring different types of animals in healthy conditions in the required numbers. The British officers realized that the camels acquired from the plains of Punjab were unable to operate deep inside Afghanistan effectively. So, the Indian camels were used till Thul, Kurram, Landi Kotal, and Dakka. For operation beyond these points, Waziri, Powinda, and other hill camels were used. The hill camels belonging to the Waziris were favourites of the British officers. In addition, much attention was given for hiring the *sarwans* (camel drivers) and the mule drivers. As an incentive they were offered free rations and warm clothing in addition to their pay when the army crossed the border of British India into Afghanistan. Contractors were engaged who received a certain sum of money in return for acquiring a certain number of mules. Each mule was hired on the basis of its capability to carry 2.5 maunds at the rate of Rs 15 per month. The transport and supply department considered the asses as better than the pack bullocks for operation across the frontier as the former could stand cold and hardship better.[165] In December 1879, the commissary general ordered the purchase of 20,000 camels from the Peshawar and Kurram districts. In addition, orders were sent out to purchase and hire mules. If mules in adequate numbers were not available, then pack bullocks were hired.[166] For the transport of grain from the Bannu District to Thul, Afridi coolies were hired.[167] Each camp follower was allowed only 25 pounds of baggage.[168]

In addition to the reorganization and bureaucratization of the logistical infrastructure during the Second Afghan War, British logistics to a great extent depended on indigenous support. Several tribal sirdars aided the British logistical apparatus. The Gajis, Turis, and the Gilzais sent their animals and local drivers. Padshah Khan, a Gilzai sirdar, declared his support for the British and sent animals and drivers for the British Indian army.[169] Again, Sirdar Tara Singh contacted the commissioner of Rawalpindi and offered 200 mules at Rs 250 each, 200 ponies at Rs 150 each, and 1,000 donkeys at Rs 70 each. Not only

within fifteen days was he able to supply these animals to the government, but also accompanied the army invading Afghanistan in order
to look after the animals provided by him.[170] The tribesmen and their
sirdars were aware of the GOI's requirements for their animals. So, they
hiked the price and the authorities had to bow down. To an extent,
imperial expeditions regenerated the local economies of certain localities. This encouraged certain sirdars to collaborate with the British. At
Thul, the Waziri and Powinda camels were available for hire at the rate
of Rs 15 per month. However, for use in Kabul (due to dangers of wear
and tear, and also likely casualties related with warfare), the Waziris
doubled the price to Rs 30 per month. Observing this, the Jowaki and
Afridis also increased their rate to Rs 30 per camel per month. As a
point of comparison, a sepoy's pay varied between Rs 7 to Rs 9 per
month. Regardless of cost, these camels did good work with the Kurram
Valley Field Force.[171]

Meanwhile, the amir was on the horns of a dilemma. The sirdars had
thrown their lots with the rebellious Afghan army and were pressur-
izing him to raise the cry of a jihad. Simultaneously, news reached him
that Major General Frederick Roberts, with a force, had already crossed
Ali Khel.[172] Yakub Khan took the plunge, escaped from Kabul, and
on 27 September presented himself in the camp of Roberts.[173] Major
R.C.W. Mitford describes the amir in the following words:

> He is a man of about six or seven and thirty, with a light almond complex-
> ion and a very long hooked nose, the lower part of the face hidden by a
> black moustache and beard, the eyes having a dazed expression like a freshly
> caught owl. This is said to have been caused by the five years' confinement
> in a dark cell to which his father, Sher Ali subjected him for conspiring.[174]

Roberts planned to march to Kabul through Kushi and Logar
Valley.[175] On 28 September, Roberts' force marched through a fertile
valley near the banks of the Logar stream to Zurgun Shahr. The Logar
Valley was one of the chief granaries of north Afghanistan and was
thickly sprinkled with walled villages. On 29 September, the 5th Punjab
Infantry, which constituted the rear guard, was subjected to firing while
it was marching. It was decided to launch a small COIN campaign. In
the evening of 30 September, a cavalry regiment was sent to surround
the village just before dawn and to allow no one to leave the hamlet.
At 7 a.m. in the morning, an officer from the political department

(a department in British India for dealing with pacification of the frontier area) came and seized the maliks to ensure 'proper' behaviour from the villagers in the near future.[176] On 1 October, Roberts issued the following proclamation at Kushi: 'The future comfort and well being of the force depend largely on the friendliness of our relations with the districts from which our supplies must be drawn; prompt payment is enjoined for all articles purchased by departments and individuals, and all disputes must be at once referred to a political officer for decision.'[177] The British COIN technique of using 'minimum force' for winning the 'hearts and minds' was in vogue.

The army in India both during the First and Second Anglo-Afghan Wars had to conduct conventional operations against the regular Afghan soldiers and unconventional operations against the armed tribesmen simultaneously. This pattern was repeated during the Third Anglo-Afghan War also. Some instances of COIN operations are necessary. The region between Shagai and Kata Kushtia was infested with the Afridis who engaged in robberies and assassinations. During November and early December 1878, in this region, raids on the convoys, cutting of telegraph wires, and so on, became common both during day and night. On 27 November at 8 p.m., the British camp and the picquets were attacked. After an hour of severe fighting, the insurgents were repelled. Subsequently, a large lashkar advanced and closed the Khyber Pass for two days. Brigadier General Appleyard, with two infantry regiments and some artillery, was dispatched from Landi Khana to aid Brigadier General Browne, so that the latter's force could reopen communication with Jamrud.[178]

A section of the Afridi tribe (Zakka Khels) attacked the British camp at Ali Masjid and they also conducted numerous raids in the Khyber Pass. They inhabited the region south of the Khyber Pass (Bazar and Bara Valley) and their valley was separated from the pass by a mountain range. The seeming immunity of their habitation had encouraged their predatory habits. So, it was decided to send an expeditionary force under General Maude to surround their strongholds and capture their leading headmen. Mutually supporting columns were sent from Ali Masjid and Dakka. Dakka was a small village on the southern bank of the Kabul River situated on a level plain surrounded by rocky hills. The Ali Masjid Column consisted of three guns of RHA, 11th and 13th Bengal Lancers, 300 infantry of the 1st Battalion of 5th Foot Regiment,

200 of the 51st Foot, the 2nd Gurkhas, and the Mahairwarra Battalion under the command of Brigadier General Doran. Thus, we see that a COIN detachment was a combined arms force. Maude and Doran with their force started marching on 19 December. Through ill-defined mountainous tracks, they reached the Chura Village. At Chura, some headmen of Malikidin Khel section submitted to Maude. Next day, the column pushed along the bank of the Chura River. Though no hostile parties were met except some stray shots from the mountaintops, still to avoid ambushes both sides of the mountains were crowned with flanking parties, and reconnaissance parties were sent forward before the advance of the main body. The Walli Village in the Bazar Valley was reached but it was deserted. Here, the force camped for the night. At 9 in the morning of 21 December, it was decided that if the terms provided to the inhabitants by the Political Officer Captain Tucker was not accepted, then the villages will be destroyed.[179]

At that time, Brigadier General Tytler with the Dakka Column arrived. His column consisted of two RA guns, 300 men of the 1st Battalion 17th Foot, 263 men of the 7th NIR and 114 men of the 45th Sikhs. This column had started its march from Dakka on 19 December. They halted at the villages of Chunar and Sitsobi and some headmen who submitted to Tytler, agreed to act as guides. Maude ordered Tytler to move to Nekai Village and burn it, and then return to Dakka. Doran's Column was ordered to burn the villages of Chinar and Halwai. However, when the British Indian troops reached these villages, they found that all these villages were deserted and the tribesmen had vanished into the mountain fastness with their families and domestic animals.[180]

In 1880, the army in India comprised 220,000 British and Indian soldiers.[181] In total, during this war, the GOI mobilized 70,000 soldiers.[182] The news of the defeat of General Burrow's brigade at Maiwand and the withdrawal of the Kandahar Force within the walls of that city reached Kabul by telegraph on 28 July. Donald Stewart decided to send a force immediately to Kabul under Lieutenant General Frederick Roberts. The GOI ordered that the force should leave Kabul on 3 August and reach Kandahar latest by 2 September. Roberts' Kabul-Kandahar Force comprised 9,987 British and Indian combatants. The commander-in-chief of India advised Roberts that Ayub Khan had 36 guns including a battery of breech loaders. Hence, Roberts should march not only with mountain artillery but also with heavy field cannons. However, Roberts took a calculated risk stating that the difficult terrain of Afghanistan would prevent him from marching quickly to Kandahar. And, in Roberts' calculation, speed was everything. So, Roberts decided to plunge ahead only with light mountain guns. Even then the transport for this force included 1,589 yabus, 4,511 mules, 1,149 ponies, 912 donkeys, and six camels with hospital equipment. The hospital details comprised 2,192 bearers, 115 doolies, 286 ponies, 43 donkeys, and three bullocks.[183] The doolie bearers were supplied by the transport department.[184] Overall, by 7 August, Roberts' force was accompanied by 6,000 transport animals and 7,000 followers.[185]

On 1 September 1880, Ayub Khan took up a position at the outskirt of Kandahar. Ayub was able to concentrate 4,000 regular infantry, 800 regular cavalry, 3,000 irregular cavalry, and 5,000 tribesmen (of them, 1,500 had firearms). Ayub's defensive position rested round the villages of Gundigan, Gundi Mulla Sahibdad, and Baba Ali Kotal. Ayub's force comprised both the regular Afghan troops (Herat and Kabuli regiments) and tribesmen including a few *ghazis*. The ghazis were concentrated at Bab Ali Kotal and Ayub's cavalry held the lower hills and the slopes in front of it. From the two villages of Gundigan and Gundi Mulla Sahibdad, Afghan skirmishers started firing at the advancing British Indian force. At 9.30 a.m., British artillery opened up on the Afghans. Under shell fire of the batteries, the Afghan regular troops withdrew but the ghazis stayed behind to fight and die and were bayoneted when the British infantry charged them. Precise and concentrated artillery fire, and then, a timely infantry charge proved too much for Ayub's motley force. Ayub Khan escaped leaving behind his camp and 30 artillery pieces (six iron BLR 9-pdr guns, 16 bronze ML 6-pdr guns, two 12-pdr howitzers, two 4.5-inch mountain guns and four 3-pdr mountain guns). Brigadier General Charles Gough's cavalry pursued the retreating Afghans across the Arghandab Valley towards Khakrez and killed some 350 tribesmen who were with Ayub's force. The total casualties for Roberts' force due to the action on 1 September numbered to 35 killed and 213 wounded. The number of wounded in Ayub's force was not known but the British officers calculated that about 1,200 of his men had died.[186] Maiwand was avenged and the Afghan threat to the British garrison in Kandahar was over. Then, Roberts, the British 'hero' of the Second Anglo-Afghan War entered Kandahar in triumph.

After the Second Anglo-Afghan War, the military authorities in India and the British officers who participated in the campaign scrutinized their experience. Interestingly, they focused on how to defeat the Afghan regular army quickly but again skirted the issue of how to establish a friendly and stable regime in Kabul and pacify the Afghan countryside after victory over the Afghan regular force. Certain improvements in the equipment and changes in the organization of the army in India were initiated as a result of the Second Afghan War. In November 1878, during the attack on Peiwar Kotal, the RHA had four 9-pdr guns.[187] They were considered quite useful. Two Gatling guns were supplied to the British units in the Sherpur-Kabul region, but the guns proved unserviceable. In 1889, the army in India had 169 machine guns (Nordenfeldt, Gardner, and Gatling).[188] The British used 9-pdr field guns and mostly 7-pdr mountain guns during the Second Afghan War. Roberts emphasized the role of firepower while fighting west of the Indus. Further, he noted that for service beyond the North-West Frontier, mountain artillery was essential. And 25-pdr, or even 40-pdr, field guns drawn by bullocks or elephants were necessary for operation in Afghanistan.[189] In 1885, the commander-in-chief of India demanded 12-pdr BL guns for field artillery. From 1888 onwards, rearmament of horse and field artillery with this gun continued slowly due to inability of the British ordnance establishment to meet all the demands of the army in India quickly.[190] However, for reasons of mobility, mountain guns were the most important category of weapons for combat west of the Indus. In 1883, Roberts emphasized:

Mountain artillery is important for operations on and beyond the frontier of India. Royal Arsenal Woolwich was prepared to construct a jointed 9-pdr. MLR mountain gun weighing about 450 pounds, with a steel carriage in two parts, weighing 210 pounds and 215 pounds, respectively, and having a 'hydraulic buffer attached to it. These weights were not beyond the carrying power of the Indian mules.[191]

Roberts further pointed out that ML howitzers were less accurate than the BL howitzers.[192] In 1887, the question of re-tubing 9-inch Rifled Muzzle Loader (RML) guns was considered. This modification was geared to adapt them for high-angle fire in order to destroy the sangars. It was decided to send these guns to England for this purpose. However, till 1893, only three refurbished guns were sent from England to India.[193]

In the light of experience of military operations in Afghanistan and against the Boers, Roberts decided to raise the tactical effectiveness of the Indian army. In 1883, he noted:

> The Boers in South Africa taught us that straight shooting is of vital importance, and that it will, on occasions, compensate for inferiority in number, discipline, and even in courage. India possesses many advantages in the way of making our soldiers good marksmen. As a general rule, ranges are conveniently near the barracks and field firing can almost everywhere be carried on with safety.[194]

The imperial anxiety about the loyalty of the Muslim soldiers (especially those from beyond the border of British India) increased after the Second Anglo-Afghan War. On 8 October 1883, Roberts warned General Shadwell: '…a strong religious feeling existed amongst some of the Muslim sepoys in our Indian regiments, which made them very averse to fighting against the amir of Afghanistan.'[195] The Soviets almost a century later would face the same problem during their invasion of Afghanistan.

WATCH AND WARD ALONG THE INDUS FRONTIER: 1885–1913

After the Second Anglo-Afghan War, a son of Dost Muhammad, named Abdur Rahman, became the ruler of Afghanistan and he continued to rule till 1901.[196] In British imperial mind, the real anxiety was the slow and steady expansion of Russia in Central Asia. In 1846, some 2,000 miles separated Czarist Russia from British India. By 1885, this gap was less than 500 miles.[197] In 1880, General Skobelev with a powerful force marched towards Geok Tepe and besieged it. By end January 1881, the fortress, which was garrisoned by 10,000 troops and had 40,000 civilians, was stormed. At the cost of 268 men killed, Skobelev was able to capture the fortress. A railway line was built from Krasnovodsk to Qizil Arvat to Amu Darya in 1885. This railway line connected Samarkhand in 1888, Tashkent in 1899 with a feeder line to Kushk on Afghanistan's border. In 1885, when the British Frontier Commission visited Herat, they found it as a squalid, dilapidated city, and its inhabitants were impoverished. When the Commission explored the mountains in the north (Paropomisus Range), they found that the mountains in contrast to those which separate Afghanistan from Central Asia were easy to negotiate, and there were several passes which led to Herat from the north.[198]

According to Rob Johnson, Roberts as commander-in-chief of India (1885–93) followed the 'Forward Policy'. In Roberts' view, the Indus was an inadequate defensive barrier. Moreover, if the Afghans with Russian aid were allowed to reach the Indus, the Indian populace might regard them as liberators and stage uprising in the rear areas. Further, the Russians would be able to mobilize the 'fickle' Pathans under their fold. To prevent such a scenario from unfolding in case of a Russia-sponsored Afghan invasion, Roberts decided to fight deep inside Afghanistan in order to defend the scientific frontier. For Roberts, the scientific frontier extended from Hindu Kush in Kashmir in the north to Kandahar up to Baluchistan in the south. Roberts further believed that the Russians would encourage the Persians to occupy western Afghanistan and that region would be the springboard for invasion of India across eastern Afghanistan. In such a case, the army in India might have to operate in Central Asia with Afghan support from north Afghanistan. Further, to ward off the Persians, Herat must also be captured.[199] Roberts' plan was more ambitious than those of the Great Mughals who had a permanent base in Kabul but never dreamt of capturing Herat. On 13 June 1893, General George S. White, commander-in-chief of India (April 1893–March 1898), wrote to the Duke of Cambridge: 'Sir, we must maintain the Kabul, Kandahar, and Ghazni line against Russia. If Russia gets Chitral then she will be able to outflank right of the defensive line and then can enter India through Jowari Pass and the Swat Valley. However, Chitral is very infertile, hence expensive for operational campaigns.'[200] The Chitral River when it reaches the Afghan border is known as the Kunar River, which flows into the Kabul River near Jalalabad.[201]

In 1878, Aman-ul Mulk, the *Mehtar* of Chitral, being afraid of a probable invasion by the amir of Afghanistan, placed himself under the nominal suzerainty of the Maharaja of Kashmir. Since the Maharaja of Kashmir was a vassal of the GOI, indirectly Chitral came under the influence of GOI. In 1885, the GOI sent a mission under William Lockhart and in 1888, Colonel Durand, as a representative of GOI, visited Chitral. The GOI was interested in Chitral to prevent the intrusion of Afghans or Russian influence in the northern corner of British India's scientific border. In response to the two British missions, Aman-ul Mulk sent two of his sons to India in 1886 and 1888, respectively. In his reign, Aman-ul Mulk had acquired Yasin and Mastuj by conquest. On 30 August 1892, Aman-ul Mulk died. After Aman's death, one of his sons, Nizam-ul Mulk, who was the governor of Yasin, took refuge with the British agent in Gilgit. His brother Afzal-ul Mulk meanwhile seized the mehtership and in order to gain legitimacy in the eyes of the British, requested the stationing of a permanent British representative at Chitral. However, Afzal was killed by his uncle Sher Afzal. Then, Nizam hurried to Chitral and became the mehter and drove away Sher Afzal who escaped to Kabul. Now, Nizam requested the presence of a British mission in Chitral. Local politics and rivalry between Kabul and Chitral, as well as the latent Russian threat, brought the British into Chitral. In 1893, a British Mission visited Chitral. In 1895, the mehter was assassinated by his younger brother Amir-ul Mulk. George Robertson, the British agent in Gilgit, anticipated danger but held firm. During January 1895, some Indian soldiers sent as reinforcements, marched from Mastuj and joined Gordon in Chitral. In March 1895, the GOI decided that an expedition should be sent through Swat and Bajaur to relieve Chitral. The expedition was supposed to start on 1 April. The Yasin villagers were impressed to carry the baggage of the expedition. The guns were partly carried by the men and partly dragged on sledges. The sepoys suffered from snow blindness and frost bite. With their *pugris*, they tried to cover their heads and ears ineffectually. Without the *postheens*, they would have suffered much more severely. On 9 April 1895, at Chaklewat, about 500 Chitralis armed with Martinis and Sniders from the sangars tried to block the progress of the British Indian column. However, artillery fire enabled the British and Indian soldiers to overcome opposition.[202]

In 1896, the Intelligence Division of the War Office informed GOI that Russia would take about eight months for concentrating troops on the Afghan frontier in order to launch a full scale invasion of India across Afghanistan.[203] In 1897, the British constructed the road through Bolan Pass which cost Rs 22 lakh.[204]

By the late nineteenth century, the GOI relied on the tribal levies as the first line of defence to maintain peace along the Indus frontier. Major General E.F. Chapman, Quarter Master General in India, wrote on 12 September 1888: 'It is a matter to encourage these levies to fight for us, and to shed their blood in our behalf; but their position must even during prolonged hostilities be upon our lines of communication; they can only I think be allowed to feed our fighting line by passing as regular soldiers into the regiments of the Bengal Army.'[205] Chapman noted that the regular levy would afford a field of employment and distinction for the more highly trained and experienced officers of the Indian army and also enable the GOI to influence the tribal sirdars.[206]

In 1893, in an attempt to recruit larger number of Waziris and Gilzais, the regimental commandants were ordered to give direct commission to some influential Pathan sirdars, who could ensure that their retainers would serve in the rank.[207] It was a sort of political cooption of potentially hostile elements by the Raj. Besides political cooption, the GOI also tried to raise the firepower of the force at its disposal. In 1887, Indian mountain batteries had 2.5-inch guns and 7-pdr mountain guns. In 1892, each Indian mountain battery had four 2.5-inch screw guns of 200 pounds weight and two 7-pdr RML guns.[208] In 1893, the Derajat Battery and the Peshawar Mountain Battery were equipped with 2.5-inch RML guns and the Punjab Garrison Battery had 12-pdr RBL guns. The 2.5-inch guns were drawn by mules.[209] In 1892, Captain Aylmer argued about the superiority of mortars over guns for destroying the mud forts and the stockades. Mortars were lighter and had far sharper trajectories than howitzers. The army in India had brass mortars of 5.5-inch and 4.6-inch calibers which were able to shoot spherical shells weighing 16.5 pounds and 8 pounds, respectively. These shells were troublesome to pack and were very inaccurate. The ordnance authorities in England were engaged in constructing a jointed 12.5-pdr howitzer which would supplant the 7-pdr gun which weighed about 200 pounds.[210] In the 1890s, the Indian troops were equipped with Martini–Henry BL rifles and the British troops with .303 Lee–Metford rifles. The Martini–Henry's effective range was 1,200 yards and the .303 Lee–Metford rifle, which used smokeless ammunition, had a range of 2 miles.[211]

In 1896, the Durand Commission established the border known as the Durand Line between British India and Afghanistan. The result was the Pathan tribes were divided between British India and Afghanistan. The amir was neither consulted over this division by Britain nor accepted this division as final. As a result of the new line, British India had to police 26,000 square miles of mountainous terrain with a population of two and a half million. This region included Chitral, Bajaur, Swat, Buner, Dir, Khyber, Kurram, and Waziristan.[212]

During 1897–8, COIN operation against the frontier tribesmen escalated almost to the level of a conventional war like the Second Anglo-Afghan War. Both during the Second Anglo-Afghan War and during the 1897–8 Frontier Campaign, the GOI mobilized about 70,000 troops.[213] Table 2.2 shows the nature of wound sustained by the soldiers of the army in India in action against the frontier tribesmen during the Malakand expedition. The table also enables us to see the nature of weapons used by the Afghans to inflict casualties on the Malakand Field Force. It is evident that more casualties were due to use of jezails and other hand-held firearms rather than due to swords, knives, and stones. The Afghans, instead of close-quarter combat, engaged in long-distance firefight with the personnel of the army in India. Since the British were engaged in a COIN, the casualties were not very high unlike in the case of an inter-state war. The Malakand Field Force with a strength of about 1,760 combatants operated for seven weeks.[214] The breakdown of casualties of the Malakand Field Force for different periods follows. Between 26 July 1897 and 1 August 1897, the Malakand Field Force due to the fighting at Malakand, suffered 23 Killed in Action (KIA) and 150 Wounded in Action (WIA) from all causes. On 2 August 1897, the casualties of the army in India after the action at Chakdara numbered another 11 WIA and five KIA. On 17 August, after the fighting at Landaki, the Malakand Field Force counted eight WIA and four KIA.[215]

An attempt must be made to portray the face of Small War. Nocturnal actions were common. One British officer of the Malakand Field Force noted that on 13 August 1897, darkness was pierced by the continuous noise of firing.[216] Lieutenant H.B. Ford, acting Adjutant General (ADG) of the 31st Punjab Infantry, noted: 'The fighting was constant for a week and was of such a close nature as to demand incessant exertions from the officers. They had to exhibit courage and gallantry to keep the morale of the troops intact.'[217] Dispersed small-scale actions required a great degree of coherence among the small subunits of the army. And this in turn required the officers displaying personal heroics often at the cost of their lives in order to maintain combat morale. There were several cases when British officers risked their lives in order to carry wounded sepoys back to the lines. Such actions

Table 2.2 Casualties in Action at Malakand from 26 July 1897 till 1 August 1897

Nature of Weapons Used	Nature of Casualties	
	Sword/Knife/Spear/Stone	Bullet Wound/Gunshot
WIA	1 captain, 1 lieutenant, 1 subedar, 1 resaidar, and 1 jemadar	1 lieutenant-colonel, 1 major, 1 captain, 3 lieutenants, 1 second-lieutenant, 1 subedar, 1 jemadar
KIA	1 sergeant of the Madras Sappers and Miners, 20 sepoys of the 31st Punjab Infantry, 2 sepoys of the 24th Punjab Infantry, 3 sepoys of the 45th Sikhs, 11 sappers from the Queen's Own Sappers and Miners, 2 drivers and 2 gunners of Number 8 Bengal Mountain Battery, 4 sowars of the Queens Own Corps of Guides	2 sergeants of the Madras Sappers and Miners, 6 sepoys of the 31st Punjab Infantry, 29 sepoys of the 45th Sikhs, 3 sepoys of the Guides, 12 sepoys of the 24th Punjab Infantry, 22 sepoys of 31st Punjab Infantry, 1 sepoy of the 31st Dogras, 1 gunner of Number 8 Bengal Mountain Battery, 3 sowars of the 11th Bengal Lancers, 2 sappers of the Queen's Own Sappers and Miners, 23 sepoys of the Queen's Own Guides
Total Casualties	50	113

Source: Return of Casualties in Action at Malakand from 26 July to 1 August 1897, Progs. No. 671, Expeditions, Proceedings of the Government of India, Malakand, 1897–8, S.No. 13, MD, NAI.

created strong loyalty bonds between the sahibs and the sepoys, which in turn held the small subunits together in midst of the firefight.[218] The officers' reports made clear that the jemadars displayed conspicuous courage and coolness under fire. And this resulted in the combat effectiveness of the sections.[219] To a great extent, COIN remains a junior officers' and subaltern's game. It must be noted that the failure of the American field officers to show courage and risk death in the fighting zone resulted in a drop in the morale and combat effectiveness of the American army in Vietnam in the late 1960s and in the early 1970s.[220] During the Tirah Campaign (1897–8), the tribesmen had about 100 Lee–Metford rifles and several thousand round of ammunition. The tribesmen's tactics was to pick off every possible British officer. For this job, selected Mohmand marksmen equipped with Martini–Henry rifles went to work.[221] For instance, the 36th Sikh Regiment which participated in this campaign had all except one British officer becoming casualties.[222] The Pathans realized that the British officers constituted the backbone of the regiments' fighting strength. In 1897, the British regiments for the first time used Lee–Metford and smokeless powder in the frontier fighting. This surprised the Bunerwals at the Tanga Pass.[223] During the 1898 expedition against the Afghans and the Mohmands, DumDum ammunition was used.[224]

In November 1901, Lord Curzon, the governor general of India, established the North-West Frontier Province (NWFP). It included five districts, each administered by a deputy commissioner. Previously, these districts were under Punjab government. The five districts were Hazara, Peshawar, Kohat, Bannu, and Dera Ismail Khan and the seven political agencies included Dir, Swat, Chitral, Khyber, Kurram, Tochi, and Wana. The NWFP had its own civil police (for dealing with day-to-day ordinary crime) and frontier constabulary (armed police).[225] The NWFP's tribal territories comprised 18,000 square miles and extended from the Himalayan foothills to the Gomal River, separating South Waziristan from Baluchistan.[226] The seven political agencies which bordered on the Durand Line were tribal territory (at present Pakistan's FATA). Here, the GOI did not levy any taxes nor did the Indian Penal Code operate. The seven political agents kept in touch with the tribes through the jirgas. If the tribesmen engaged in unlawful activities and the jirgas could not control them, then the political agents used the scouts (Tochi Scouts, Kurram Militia, and so on).

BRITISH INDIAN EMPIRE AND WARFARE IN AFGHANISTAN   119

These paramilitary forces could operate up to the Durand Line. The Scouts were organized in platoons and commanded by the VCOs. One British officer was put in charge of 200 Scouts. Compared to the regular troops, the Scouts were lightly armed and their effectiveness rested on their mobility. They were as good as the tribesmen in taking cover and marksmanship.[227]

In 1904, several Afridis visited Kabul and received monetary gifts from the amir. With this money, the Afridis bought arms and ammunition and returned to their villages. Throughout 1904, the Afridis, especially the Zakka Khels (who inhabited Tirah's border with Afghanistan), conducted raids into British Punjab. The Kuki Khel Afridis fortified their villages. Moreover, each village displayed an old muzzle-loading cannon. However, the supply of cannon balls was limited to 13–14 balls per gun. The Shinwari mullahs too encouraged the tribes to rebel against British authority. The Mohmands were also disaffected with the British due to construction of rail lines through their territory. In 1907, one Sufi Sahib and Abdul Karim preached jihad in Tirah. And one Lala Pir, an agent in the pay of Kabul government, stirred up troubles in Waziristan. Lala Pir was in communication with Mulla Powindah and Hamzullah Mulla and tried to incite the Waziris and the Mashuds into rebellion. A Gilzai lashkar was raised from the Ghazni District with the objective of attacking the Kurram Valley. On 28 January 1908, the Zakka Khels raided the Hindu quarter of the Peshawar city and looted the *banias*. Since the Afridi maliks proved incapable of controlling the Zakka Khels and despite deployment of police, tribal raids occurred, the GOI decided to launch a military expedition. Major General James Wilcocks was put in charge of the expedition and his political officer was lieutenant colonel Roos-Keppel. It was planned to send two brigades into Bazar Valley and hold one brigade in reserve at Naushera. While the first brigade occupied Chura, the second brigade entered the Bazar Valley by the Chura Pass through Malikdin Khel region and advanced to Walai.[228]

Arnold Keppel describes the features of Small War conducted by the Afridis against the British Indian troops:

> Mountain warfare, as carried on the north-west frontier, does not lend itself to impassioned descriptions of bloody fields of battle, of cavalry charges and heroic actions done in the limelight before the astounded gaze of two armies. The Afridi does not rush down into the open to certain death,

but retires gracefully before a stronger force sent against him, skulking along the sky-line, and ready to take advantage of the smallest mistake on the part of the opponents, or to cut off any straggler. He has been described as the finest natural skirmisher in the world. It is when the retirement of the British troops begins that he is at his best.[229]

An attritional guerrilla war in the mountains was tiring for the troops and they suffered from combat fatigue. After arduous hill climbing in daylight, the tired soldiers cooked and ate their food in the dark, as no lights were allowed to prevent the enemy snipers from shooting at the bivouacs. Then, the soldiers had to dig narrow trenches in the stony soil to take shelter in daylight when the tribesmen shot from the mountain tops. Even while taking rest in the night, the soldiers were apprehensive that the tribesmen might launch a night attack across the perimeter. For most of the soldiers, the blood curdling howling and shouting of the tribesmen during nocturnal attacks were indeed nerve-racking.[230]

In 1912, there was an uprising in Khost, and Amir Habibullah suppressed it with 4,000 regulars and 18,000 tribesmen.[231] By the beginning of the second decade of the twentieth century, the GOI assessed that the principal threat to British India would come from Afghanistan. They believed that besides an invasion by the Afghan regular force (supported by Russia), a combination of Afghan intrigues, moral and material support for a jihad would also simultaneously result in large-scale uprising of the frontier tribes. In 1912, British India's military authorities calculated that the fighting strength of the North-West Frontier tribes was about 334,000 men. Worse, between 1909 and 1912, the GOI assumed that the tribesmen had acquired 90,000 modern rifles. William Nicholson noted that as regards skirmishing, taking cover, climbing over the rocks, marksmanship, the Afridis were better than the Boers. Moreover, the Afridis in the regiments of the Indian army had acquired Western military training and they could desert during an uprising. In George Roos-Keppel's view, the Swatis, Afridis, and the Waziris were not only hostile to the British but they were fanatical and mullah-ridden. And pan-Islamic movements were bound to affect adversely the loyalty of the army in India's Muslim soldiers.[232] The GOI tried to keep a tab on the Pathan soldiers recruited from beyond the border of British India through the political agents.[233] The GOI concluded that the amir of Afghanistan occupied a venerable position in the Muslim world (somewhat like a mini caliph). In their anxiety, British India's top brass concluded that the amir was crafty and treacherous, and if he gave a call for jihad, then not only the frontier tribes but also the Muslims within India (and even the Muslims serving in the British-officered Indian army) would rebel against British authority.[234] It is to be noted that the core of the army in India comprised the British Indian army besides the British regiments stationed in the subcontinent. And, as Table 2.3 shows, the Muslims constituted a considerable chunk of the British-officered Indian army. Between 1885 and 1912, the number of Pathans (both in absolute and in percentage terms) in the Indian army increased. In fact, during the 1907–8 frontier expedition, many Pathan reservists, pensioners, and soldiers of the Indian army on *furlough* fought with the rebellious tribesmen against the British Indian force. However, the British had one card up their sleeve. Those pensioners and reservists who were suspected of fighting with the lashkars against the army of India had their pension and reservists' pay stopped.[235]

In 1912, there were about 34,000 frontier militia and levies but not much faith was put on them.[236] The British played the divide and rule policy as regards organizing the frontier militias. The Kurram Militia was composed of Shias, and General William Birdwood assumed that they would remain loyal to the British and fight the Sunni tribesmen. The Khyber Rifles was geared to guard the Khyber Pass, and in 1908, they successfully fought the Zakka Khels. Birdwood was confident that even if the Afridis rebelled, the Khyber Rifles would fight with the British. The Northern Waziristan Militia comprised only one-fourth Waziris drawn from the districts under British control. The rest of the militia comprised Afridis and Khattaks. The Southern Waziristan Militia was Waziris in name only, as most of the personnel were Yusufzais, Bangash, and Afridis from outside Waziristan. So, the British were confident that these two militias could be used successfully against the Waziris and the Mashuds.[237] In 1913, British India's military authorities concluded that in case of a future war with Afghanistan or with the frontier tribes, gross wastage for the infantry, cavalry, and the artillery would be 65 per cent, 50 per cent, and 40 per cent, respectively. Gross wastage included casualties (killed and wounded) but some of it were recoverable in the long run. The net wastage for the three above-mentioned branches were calculated at 52 per cent, 40 per cent, and 32 per cent, respectively.

Table 2.3 Social Composition of the Indian Army between 1885 and 1912

Communities Recruited from Different Regions	Date			
	1885		1912	
	Number	Percentage	Number	Percentage
Pathans from the Indus region	5,765	4.5	12,201	8
Muslims from west Punjab (Salt Range)	8,799	7	25,299	16
Muslims from north India	21,196	16.5	9,054	6
Muslims from other parts of India (i.e., especially Deccan)	9,529	7.5	8,717	5.5
Gurkhas from central Nepal	6,684	5	18,100	12
Dogras and Garhwalis from eastern Punjab foothills (now Himachal Pradesh)	3,964	3	10,421	8
Rajputs from Rajasthan and north India	8,291	6	12,051	8
Jats from east Punjab and North-West Province and Marathas from Maharashtra	9,246	7	5,685	3
Other Hindus (Middle Castes)	24,898	15	10,252	7
Indian Christians/Eurasians	3,304	2	1,491	1
Jews, Assamese from Assam, Chins from Chin Hills, and Karens from west Burma	5,202	4	306	.24
Sikhs from central Punjab	17,774	13.5	32,702	21
Total	131,019		158,603	

Source: Proceedings of the Army in India Committee, 1912, vol. 1-A, *Minority Report*. Simla: Government Central Branch Press, 1913, p. 156.

Note: Slight discrepancies in the total percentage and absolute numbers are present in the original document.

Net wastage meant permanent loss of combatants to the army. Absence of a large reserve was accepted as a shortcoming of the British Indian military establishment in case of an attritional war.[238]

In March 1914, the GOI estimated the net annual military expenditure to be about Rs 30.75 lakh. Of this amount, 130,300 sterling pounds was set aside for rearmament of the field artillery with Quick Firing (QF) guns and howitzers for the mountain artillery.[239] The Anglo-Russian Treaty of 1907 stipulated that Afghanistan lay outside the Russian sphere of influence. Russia agreed to confer all the matters relating to Afghan–Russian relation with Britain. And Britain agreed not to occupy or annex any part of Afghanistan or interfere in the internal affairs of Afghanistan. The amir of Afghanistan refused to recognize this treaty but Russia and Britain honoured the terms of this treaty till 1919.[240]

FIRST WORLD WAR AND THE THIRD ANGLO-AFGHAN WAR: 1914–19

Relation between British India and Afghanistan remained tense during the First World War due to mistrust on both sides. Further, German meddling in Afghanistan did not help matters. General E.G. Barrow, Military Secretary at the India Office London, noted in June 1914:

> There is undoubtedly unrest on the frontier, more particularly on the Waziri and the Mohmandi borders. There are mutterings of 'jihad' all along the Afghan marches, and though the Amir is believed to be loyal to us, that safeguard depends on his life. At any moment he may be assassinated or die a natural death, in which case we may expect an upheaval in Afghanistan. If this occurs the whole frontier may be in a blaze, so that the imperative necessity for a watchful policy and preparation for instant action is obvious.[241]

In 1915, the GOI deployed 22 infantry battalions, 21 cavalry squadrons, eight batteries of 48 guns, and two sapper companies (equivalent to two divisions) in order to deter the North-West Frontier tribes and Afghanistan. Out of these units, mobile columns were established at Tank, Miranshah, Kohat-Kurram line, Adozai, Shabkadr, Abazai, Rustam, Chakdara, and Oghi, for possible operations.[242]

In 1916, a German Mission came to Kabul. Its leader was Wilhelm von Hentig. Later, this person would head the oriental section of the

Nazi Foreign Office. The objective of this mission was to encourage the Muslim Afghans to join a jihad against the Allies in order to create a diversion at Britain's backyard, that is, NWFP. However, the advance of the German troops to the Don River and Crimea in 1917 opened up more ambitious opportunities in front of the Second Reich.[243] In January 1917, the British government believed that Ottoman and German agents were present in Afghanistan. The London government concluded that their activities inside Afghanistan would be successful if the Ottoman–German forces got military victories in Mesopotamia (Iraq), Syria, and in the Caucasus.[244] In the first month of 1917, British intelligence gathered information about the reorganization of the Afghan army. The *kandak* organization was introduced in the army. One kandak was equivalent to one-third of a brigade. One kandak comprised 600 infantry, 200 cavalry, 200 gunners, six machine-guns, and six mountain guns. Meanwhile, the GOI strengthened its defensive infrastructure in Baluchistan. Attention was given to complete the Nushki-Dalbandan railway.[245] However, the good news for the Raj was that the pro-German party in Afghanistan under Nasrullah was sidelined by the amir. In 1915–16, it was estimated that some 27 lakh Kabuli rupees were spent in anti-British propaganda.[246] Mir Habibullah Khan, the amir of Afghanistan from 1901 to 1919 was able to maintain good relations with British India till the end of the First World War. However, his successor Amanullah (r. 1919–28) failed to maintain peace with GOI especially after the end of the First World War.[247] Habibullah was pro-British and was murdered on 20 February 1919. Amanullah owed his position to the anti-British lobby of the Afghan army.[248]

The amir's troops comprised regulars and irregulars. The irregulars came with their own rifles, ammunition, knives, and a supply of flour in bags made of undressed sheep skin leather. The problem with the irregulars (followers of the tribal chiefs) was that they could not fight for a long time away from their villages due to supply problems. The Afghan army comprised 78 infantry battalions, 21 cavalry regiments, 280 BL guns, and about an equal number of MLs. The latter were mainly deployed along the Persian and Russian border. In total, there were 38,000 infantry, 8,000 cavalry, and 4,000 artillery men. The Kabul Arsenal had a store of 15,000 small bore rifles and 400,000 Martinis. Afghanistan was divided into ten military districts. In eastern Afghanistan, the districts which bordered on India were Jalalabad, Khost, Ghazni, Mukur, and Kandahar. In these five districts, some 35 infantry battalions, 4.5 cavalry regiments, and 107 BL guns were deployed. In the Kabul Military District, the garrison comprised 17 infantry battalions, 3 pioneer battalions, 7.5 cavalry regiments, and 108 BL guns. However, in terms of staff organization, the Afghan army remained weak. In Kabul Military District, there were four mixed brigades and each brigade comprised one cavalry regiment, one field battery, one pack artillery battery, three infantry battalions, and three machine guns.[249] It seems that the kandak organization was rejected in favour of the traditional brigade organization.

The Afghan soldiers displayed lot of courage and a high level of endurance. However, they were not trained well. Weapon training, tactical exercise, and capability to manoeuvre in the battlefield were almost absent among the regulars. No bayonet instruction was given to them. About half of the infantry battalions in eastern Afghanistan were equipped with .303 rifles. And the rest had Martinis and Sniders. And none of the battalions had more than 75 per cent of their authorized strength. During the war, armed tribesmen were used to fill up the ranks.[250] But they lacked training and regimental traditions. These two factors resulted in incoherence among the Afghan regular battalions during firefight.

The British Indian Field Army for service in the North-West Frontier composed of 1st, 2nd, 16th, and 4th divisions with 1st, 4th, and 10th cavalry brigades and the 12th Mounted Brigade. A division of the Field Army consisted of three infantry brigades (each of one British and three Indian battalions), one squadron of Indian cavalry, one field artillery brigade (two 18-pdr batteries and one 4.5-inch howitzer battery), one mountain (pack) artillery brigade (two batteries of 2.75-inch guns), two companies of machine guns (16 guns each), two companies of sappers and miners, one pioneer battalion, one divisional signal company, and a divisional ammunition column. The 12th Mounted Brigade comprised newly raised Indian units mounted on undersized country-bred horses. In addition to the Field Army units, certain other formations were also available for internal defence and rear area security. They were the Kohat, Bannu, and the Derajat independent brigades, the garrisons at Malakand and Chitral, Peshawar and Quetta, and units in the Zhob Valley. These units were used for internal security. Each of the three independent brigades comprised one regiment of Indian cavalry, one battery of mountain artillery, one armoured car battery of three cars (two in Bannu Independent Brigade), and four battalions of Indian infantry (three in the Derajat Independent Brigade).[251] On 1 February 1919, about 76,908 British soldiers were stationed in India, and of them, 15,186 were non-effective due to sickness.[252]

In 1919, the GOI was faced with both conventional and unconventional war, simultaneously. On 27 April 1919, the amir's agents at Peshawar were ordered not to issue any passports for Kabul to any British subjects. The postmaster of the Afghan Post Office at Peshawar was one of the principal agents deputed to raise rebellion among the Indus tribes. A copy of the amir's *firman* inciting all the border tribes to rise against the British was intercepted and then sent to the Secretary of State for India on 4 May 1919. To an extent, the amir was forced to give the call for jihad in order to avert an internal rebellion against him. Several Indus tribes like the Mohmands also pledged their support to the amir's cause. A party of Afghan soldiers occupied Bagh and Kafirkot which were well within the boundary of the British Indian empire. The Afghan plan of action was a three-pronged attack on Dakka, Khost, and Onetta by ghazis and regular troops.[253] While the Afghan army crossed British India's border, an uprising also occurred in Waziristan. Conflagration flared up along the whole border from Chitral in the north to Baluchistan in the south.[254] On 6 May, the Afghan forces moved within 5 miles of Landi Kotal. At that time, the numerically superior Afghan forces could have launched a successful attack on the small British Indian forces at Dakka. However, the indecisive Afghan military leadership let that opportunity slip.[255]

On 6 May 1919, the army headquarter of India ordered general mobilization. The forces for defending North-West Frontier comprised the North-West Frontier Force, Baluchistan Force, and the Central Reserve. The North-West Frontier Force under General A.A. Barratt comprised the 1st and 10th cavalry brigades, 1st and 2nd divisions, Peshawar Area Troops, Malakand and Chitral garrisons, Northern LoC Troops, Kohat Force (Kohat Independent Brigade), and Waziristan Force (Bannu and Derajat independent brigades). Lieutenant General R. Wapshire commanded the Baluchistan Force which comprised the 12th Mounted Brigade, 4th Division, Zhob and Quetta Area Troops, Meshed Force, and East Persian LoC Troops. The Central Reserve under General Headquarter India was composed of the 4th Cavalry Brigade,

16th Division, 46th and 47th mobile brigades, and 1st Special Brigade.[256] On 8 May 1919, the Afghan troops moved from Kabul towards Jalalabad, Khost, and Kandahar. And the region between Jalalabad and Dakka was full of ghazi tribesmen. On 9 May, the British Indian troops attacked Bagh.[257]

Combat in Afghanistan and in the North-West Frontier required high level of training, especially among the platoon and company commanders. But most of the veterans had been sent overseas due to the demands of the First World War. About 182 Indian infantry battalions and 131 Indian cavalry squadrons were sent overseas. They left behind depots to train the recruits in order to meet the wastage and also to manage the administrative affairs of the units. Some of the units were in the process of disbandment after the end of the First World War in October 1918. Most of the personnel who fought in the Third Afghan War came from these not-so-well-trained recruits in the depots. And the units which were in the process of disbandment were hastily brought to strength and thrown into the fray. However, the British Indian military establishment was lucky in one respect. Several British officers, who were en route from Mesopotamia to Britain for demobilization, were detrained in India due to shortage of shipping. These officers were utilized to meet the Afghan crisis in 1919.[258]

At the early stage of the war, telegraph and telephone lines were sabotaged. On 26 July, heavy rain storm and sabotage by the tribesmen damaged the railway track and the culverts on the narrow gauge railway line from Khanai. The line north-east of the Murgha Mehtarzai Pass became unfit for traffic.[259] In the Third Anglo-Afghan War, besides armoured cars, aircraft were used for the first time against the Afghans. The Royal Air Force (RAF) had arrived in the North-West Frontier during the 1916 Mohmand Campaign. In 1919, the 31st Squadron was stationed at Risalpur, east of Peshawar, and the 114th Squadron was at Quetta. Both these squadrons were equipped with BE2C aircraft. It was a two seater used both for reconnaissance as well as a light bomber, and had a maximum speed of 72 miles per hour and the ceiling was 10,000 feet. It was armed with one to four Lewis Guns and carried upto 230 pounds of bomb.[260] On 28 July, a tribal lashkar numbering 4,000 men laid siege to Fort Sandeman. Frictions among the sirdars prevented a coordinated attack by the different contingents within the lashkar. On 3 August, an aircraft from Quetta bombed the lashkar. Due to lack of adequate food supply, in the next few days, the lashkar dispersed. The total casualties suffered by the army in India from all causes due to the war in 1919 numbered to 1,751, including 182 British officers and men.[261] The Third Afghan War came to an end on 8 August 1919 with the signing of the Peace Treaty at Rawalpindi between the representatives of the amir of Afghanistan and the GOI.[262] However, troubles continued in Waziristan.

The terrain of Waziristan is characterized by the rugged Suleiman Range which comprises brownish mountains with deep twisting valleys. The district is about 120 miles long and some 60 miles wide at one point, shaped roughly like a quadrilateral of some 4,500 square miles. The Waziristan district stretches from Kurram Valley in the north up to the Gomal River in the south. Actually, Waziristan is between Kurram and Baluchistan. On the west of Waziristan lies the Durand Line. The Bannu basin and the Indus lie in the east.[263] The Tochi and Gomal rivers flow through Waziristan. Tochi in the north has two tributaries named Kazha and Margha.[264] The Gomal separates Waziristan from Baluchistan and points the way towards the Gomal Pass.[265] In the 1930s, the population of Waziristan numbered to some 200,000 semi-nomadic Wazirs.[266] The South Waziristan Militia rebelled and captured Wana. Pursued by a small force under Major Russell, the mutineers crossed the Gomal River and escaped towards Fort Sandeman.[267] COIN operations in Waziristan continued till 1920.

COIN IN THE NORTH-WEST FRONTIER REGION: 1920–47

In 1920, the General Staff in India noted:

> North-West Frontier as being the greatest and most immediate anxiety.... The defection of the frontier militia has thrown an increased burden on the regular army. The tribesmen of the future will be better armed, will have an abundance of ammunition and will evince greater tactical skill and knowledge.... The organization and equipment of the Afghan regular army will tend to approximate more and more to European model.[268]

The General Staff continued:

> The policy of holding the frontier outposts with tribal militia had failed.... The regular forces located on the frontier should be strong enough to hold their own, and to take such offensive action in their own areas as will

prevent tribal unrest and aggression from spreading unduly or interfering with the concentration of the field army. Their role is in fact, that of 'covering troops' and their presence on the frontier should afford the field force greater liberty of action.[269]

The General Staff proposed that the army in India should be divided into three categories. Firstly, the covering troops will replace the three frontier brigades. Secondly, there will be a field force, and thirdly, there will be a garrison for checking internal unrest. The covering troops will comprise 12 infantry brigades. The field force will be highly mobile and should comprise five cavalry brigades and four divisions. This force during a war with Afghanistan will be geared to occupy Jalalabad and Kandahar.[270] In 1920, the RAF in India comprised two scout squadrons, two bomber squadrons, and four reconnaissance squadrons.[271]

In 1920, the USSR sponsored the Congress of Peoples of the East in Baku. The Congress called for a holy war against British imperialism. In 1921, the Soviets signed the Afghan-Soviet Treaty in accordance with which the USSR agreed to provide economic and military aid to Afghanistan.[272] As a reaction to the Third Afghan War and simultaneous tribal uprising in Waziristan, British India from 1922 onwards deployed elements of the army in India in South Waziristan.[273]

In 1930–1, the GOI decided to initiate some measures in order to strengthen the defensive capabilities of the region around Peshawar. One brigade was to advance from the Bara River (which was a source of drinking water) into the Khajuri Plain, while the sappers constructed a pipe line. Detailed deployments of the pickets, sentries, and patrols were carried out in order to avoid any surprise by the hostile tribesmen. During November 1931, the Number 2 Field Company of Sappers stationed at Peshawar was used for building a blockhouse at one of the peaks overlooking the Khyber Pass. For carrying out construction works, the sappers were put in the Ali Masjid Fort.[274] Building of blockhouses along the ever-turbulent North-West Frontier by the British was a continuation of the Mughal policy. Lieutenant Colonel M.C.A. Henniker, who was a subaltern in the Number 2 Field Company in Peshawar in late 1931, provides an interesting piece of information about the Pathans' sense of chivalry while conducting Small Wars in his memoirs:

A curious thing was the water supply for the blockhouses. This came by pipe-line laid over the hills from the pumping station below. The pipe could easily have been cut by the Afridis, but this was never done. They considered rules as necessary in warfare as we did. Cutting the water-pipes of the Raj would be as immoral as the use by us of poison gas.[275]

Despite all the romanticization of the Pathans, they were danger-ous enemies. Their innate 'martial' culture and modernization of their weaponry caused anxiety to the British military officers stationed along the North-West Frontier. One British officer noted in his autobiogra-phy: 'Pathans must live by sword in a way undreamed of in England. Rifles are treasured possessions, and they have recourse to all kinds of devices to get them.'[276] On the road between Kohat and Peshawar, there was a factory which manufactured rifles for the Pathans. Such rifles were known as Pass-made Rifles. However, due to the softness of the metal used, these rifles became inaccurate after repeated firings. For this reason, while a Pass-made Rifle cost Rs 80 (six pounds) in 1931, stolen British rifles were sold at Rs 800 at the Thieves Bazaar in Peshawar.[277] Henniker describes the mode of construction of the Pass-made Rifles in the following words:

> Perhaps the manufacture of the barrel is the most cunning. A long square piece of metal is first cut to the right length. It is then mounted in a lathe and rotated by a small boy spinning a bicycle wheel from which a belt runs to the 'chuck' which grips the barrel. At one end (the muzzle end) a knitting needle with a piece of a file soldered to it is pulled against the appropriate spot by a weight on a string. As the boy revolves the steel barrel the knitting needle with the file on it gradually eats into the end. And then…(by God's grace) it emerges some weeks later, having penetrated the whole length of the bore. The outside is then turned concentrically with the bore and the rifling is done by another ingenious maneuver.[278]

COIN duty did not involve continuous low-key fighting. During the intermittent period of peace, the British officers relaxed by engaging in duck and snipe shooting. For the ordinary soldiers posted in the North-West Frontier, when there was no fighting, summers were gener-ally hot, dusty, and dull.[279]

Like the Mughals, the GOI maintained control over the tribes by providing them subsidies. The Tori Khel demanded an increase in the tribal allowance. The Tori Khel was the principal sub-tribe of the Ootamanzai Wazirs. They inhabited the region from Spinwam on the Kaitu River across the Tochi and Khaisora Valleys to the Shaktu River.

In March 1935, the GOI agreed to increase the tribal allowance in return for access in the Lower Khaisora Valley. However, several sections of the tribe refused to accept the GOI's conditions. In 1936–7, large-scale disturbances again broke out along the North-West Frontier. The immediate cause for trouble was the Islam Bibi case, which brought the *faqir* of Ipi (the precursor of Mullah Omar) into prominence. His original name was Mirza Ali Khan. He was of the Bangal Khel clan of the Tori Khel Waziris and was born in 1897 in a village near Khajuri Post at the western end of the Shinki Defile. In 1922, Mirza Ali and his brother purchased some land in the Sham Plain area and built a house and a mosque. At that time, Mirza Ali Khan frequently visited the village named Ipi in order to get training under the mullah of that place. In 1926, Mirza Ali Khan settled at Ipi. In 1928, he performed the Haj and on his return lived a religious life visiting shrines and religious leaders. Thus, he acquired a reputation for saintliness and influence among the Daurs and Tori Khel Waziris.[280]

A minor Hindu girl eloped with a Muslim student. She converted to Islam and took the title of Islam Bibi. The girl's relative brought a charge of abduction against the student and the girl was recovered. As a result, communal tension was heightened at Bannu. On 7 April 1936, the date fixed for the trial of the student, over 2,000 Muslims assembled in the court. In the meantime, the Duars who lived in the Tochi Valley, west of Bannu, were stirred by the mullahs. The Duars threatened to march to Bannu and the faqir of Ipi provided them leadership. The Duar ringleaders were arrested but the faqir moved into Sham in the Shaktu area.[281]

On 11 May 1936, at the invitation of the Zarina Tori Khel, the faqir moved into Biche Kashkai on the lower Khaisora River, where he built a mosque and preached hatred against the British. He persuaded his brother Shah Zaman to give up government service and join him. Shah Zaman agreed and then became the right-hand man of the faqir. In his subversive activities, the faqir received strong support from the Tori Khels. He was able to manage an alliance between the feuding Tori Khels, Bhittanis (they inhabited the region between Bannu and Dera Ismail Khan) and the Mashuds by raising the cry of 'Islam in danger'. The GOI pressurized the Tori Khels either to surrender the faqir to the British authorities or to force him to leave their territory. The maliks of Tori Khel replied that they lacked the authority to forcibly remove the faqir. Worse, if any British and Indian troops entered their territory, then they could not guarantee the soldiers' safety. Amalgamation of local grievance with pan-Islamic cry, prospect for loot and plunder, as well as the idea that the Raj was weakening due to progressive devolution of power to the Indian politicians encouraged the Waziris to fight the government. In November 1936, the British resident in Waziristan recommended military operation. As part of the minimum force requirement, the troops were to carry out a 'peaceful demonstration' and were to take no offensive action unless they were attacked.[282]

The army in India's military operation could be divided into two parts. The first part involved pacification of the Tori Khel area, occupation of the Sham Plain, and construction of roads in this region. This region lies between Bannu, Spinwan, Mir Ali, Datta Khel, and the Shaktu River up to the Jani Khel Post. The terrain was crisscrossed with numerous watercourses which were thickly strewn with rocks and boulders. In the dry weather, the watercourses were small streams but after rain, they became dangerous torrents. And the second part involved operations west of the Razmak-Jandola Road. West of the Razmak-Jandola Road, the two main rivers are the Tank Zam flowing beside the Central Waziristan Road and the Gomal River, which flows south-east of Wana. In this region, there are many hills cut by valleys of varying size. The hills are high and covered with trees and thick scrub.[283]

The Razmak Column (named Razcol) was ordered to start from Damdil and the Bannu Column (named Tocol) from Mir Ali, and they were to meet at Biche Kashkai. Razcol was to move through the Khaisora River and Tocol through Husain Khel, the Katira River to Jaler Algad. The resident (as per the requirement that a civil/political official should accompany the force engaged in COIN) and the assistant political agent of Waziristan accompanied the Razcol and Tocol, respectively. The route for the Razcol was especially rough and they had to march through the boulder-strewn river bed and the stream had to be crossed several times. At several places, the river bed was only 50 yards wide and the exits were dominated by commanding features, from the top of which the tribesmen could fire at will. One section of armoured cars (Light Tank Company) was detailed to protect the advancing troops till Asad Khel. About eight platoons of Tochi Scouts were ordered to provide protection to both the flanks of the columns. Another six platoons of Tochi Scouts were to move to Biche Kashkai before the column's arrival. At Zerpezai, a *khasadar* informed the Tochi Scouts that the ridges were held by hostile tribesmen. The platoons were immediately fired upon. The khasadar's information saved the platoons from an ambush. With the help of artillery, the Scouts cleared the ridges. In the night, through lamps, whistle, and verbal sound, communication among the dispersed piquets was maintained. When the British officers became casualties, the VCOs took command of the companies. On the morning of 27 November, a 400-strong lashkar opposed the Tochi Scouts. Due to casualties and shortages of ammunition, both the columns decided to return to Mir Ali. Total casualties numbered to 115, at the cost of 41 hostile tribesmen killed and 32 wounded.[284] In order to pacify Waziristan, the GOI constructed 115 miles of road in the disaffected areas and each section of the tribe was fined a number of rifles and a sum of money.[285]

In February 1939, Major D.B. Mackenzie of the 5th Battalion of the 13th Frontier Force Rifles, while writing the Preface to the fourth edition of General Andrew Skeen's *Passing It On* noted that the 1937 operations in Waziristan was fought by the troops trained in accordance with the 1925 *Manual of Operations*. The materials in the 1925 manual was amplified and presented in an interesting manner by Skeen in his monograph titled *Passing It On*. In fact, Skeen, while writing the Preface to the first edition of his book in July 1932, noted that he has written this book because the manuals were 'indigestible' to the young soldiers. The book proved to be enormously popular. In October of the same year, the second edition was printed. The third edition came out in September 1934. Mackenzie noted that despite the fact that Skeen's account is based on the 1919–20 operations, it still retains validity. In fact, 'minor tactics' on the North-West Frontier had remained more or less the same.[286]

Skeen emphasized that frontier fighting mainly centred around the infantry and it was mostly junior officers' game. And the fate of the campaigns depended on the 'on spot' decisions taken by the junior officers.[287] Skeen warned in his book that the Mashuds were adept in using the terrain of the frontier to their great advantage. Their mobility on the cliffs and steep slopes was remarkable. With great patience and due to innate knowledge of the terrain, they were able to hide their movement and melt away in the natural landscape with agility. In contrast, the superiority of the British and Indian troops was in the sphere of discipline and firepower. Even if the imperial troops combined fire and movement, in terms of forward and backward mobility, they were never able to catch up with the nimble Pathans. The imperial soldiers were handicapped by army boots and heavy equipments. Worse, the initiative as regards timing and place of attack remained with the tribesmen.[288] In a somewhat pessimistic tone, Skeen notes: 'Their power of moving concealed is astounding, not only in moving from cover to cover, but in slipping from light to shadow, and background to background. It has to be seen to be believed. And their stillness in cover is equally striking. You can never train your men to the same pitch.'[289] Partly, the problem could be solved, argued Skeen, if the British officers took care to observe the natural game and the folds in the terrain with the vegetation cover, when they went for hunting in Kashmir, and in the Kulu and Chamba (now in Himachal Pradesh). It seems that just before the Second World War, the frontier Pathans acquired a sort of 'hill supermen' status among the British officers just as the Japanese soldiers acquired the status of 'jungle supermen' among the British officers between 1942 and 1944. The favourite tactic of the tribesmen was ambushing the British and Indian troops. From their childhood, when they grazed their livestock, they knew the terrain. Further, it was claimed that they had very good eye sight. In Skeen's paradigm, the Pathans were culturally conditioned for conducting guerrilla warfare in this terrain. Skeen claimed that being born and brought up in the land of constant inter-tribal war and blood feuds, the tribesmen, in general, had a well-honed instinct for danger without which they could not survive in the 'badlands' of the frontier. One is reminded of the Western ethnocentric view just before Pearl Harbour that the Japanese in general have very bad eye sight, and hence, they cannot be good pilots. A product of the 'keen' eye sight of the Pathans and their familiarity with the terrain enabled them, argued Skeen, to take potshots on particular British officers. The Pathans' marksmanship is highlighted by Skeen. Keeping in mind the First World War, Skeen writes that while in a conventional warfare, massed firing was impersonal, in frontier campaigns, the Pathans fired aiming at particular targets.[290]

In 1936, the Secretary of State for Foreign Affairs in Britain expounded British policy towards Afghanistan and British India's North-West Frontier in the following words:

> The policy of the Government of India in regard to their tribal territory is to preserve the peace of the border, foster good relations with the tribes, and gradually to introduce standards of civilization and order into the

tribal area, together with the improvement of their economic conditions. Moreover, it is their policy to pursue these ends by peaceful means and by agreement with the tribes and not to resort to military action, except when it is necessary to do so in order to preserve the peace and to repel attacks on British and protected areas...or on friendly tribes.[291]

Meanwhile, the Third Reich was becoming interested in Afghanistan, probably to strike at the 'soft' underbelly of the British empire: India. The Afghan delegation to the 1936 Berlin Olympic Games was impressed by German power which the Afghan delegates compared with Britain's 'flabby pacifism'. By 1938, Germany had placed Organization Todt (OT) in Afghanistan with the objective of construction of roads and bridges. Lufthansa established a direct air link between Kabul and Berlin. The German firms Siemens and Telefunken provided telecommunications equipment to Afghanistan. The British Minister at Kabul, Kerr Fraser-Tytler concluded that the Afghan army was equipped with German military equipments.[292] Moreover, the other Axis partner, Italy, also showed interest in developing the Afghan Air Force. Raids by the Afghan Air Force into India, with encouragement from hostile Great Powers (either Third Reich or Soviet Russia), warned the Expert Committee for the Defence of India under the chairmanship of Lord Chatfield in January 1939, will cause more psychological than material damage to the prospect of British rule in South Asia. Further, such an act will also embolden the frontier tribes. However, the Expert Committee concluded that the principal problem remained the tribal irregulars rather than the Afghan army.[293]

In September 1939, the GOI was anxious that Germany might use Persia as a base for stirring up trouble in India. The Nazi–Soviet Pact revived the late nineteenth-century British fear of a Russian-sponsored Afghan invasion of India. Since Russia's western border was made secure by arrangement with Adolf Hitler's Germany, Moscow, assumed the London government, might turn attention in the southern direction to get a warm water port in the Indian Ocean. The same logic would excite the state department officials at the height of Cold War in the 1970s and 1980s. In order to keep Afghanistan in good humour, the secretary of state for India on 12 September 1939 elaborated on the details of British policy:

In recent years we have been helping the Afghan Government with sales of rifles and of aircraft, by training their Air Force personnel in India, and with a commercial credit of 500,000 sterling pounds. A political credit of 250,000 sterling pounds is under consideration.... There is, however, a potential danger to our interests in the country and on the frontier in the relatively large number of Germans (96 excluding wives and families) employed in Afghanistan. The Afghan Prime Minister who has always been nervous of Russian interference, recently sounded us to an assurance or mutual pact against aggression. The Afghan desire for this will have been increased by the Russo-German Pact. A proposal is being submitted to offer the Afghan Government an agreement for mutual consultation and assistance. Some of the advantages of this from our point of view would be to strengthen the position of the Afghan Government and to make sure of their cooperation... in rendering the German Colony harmless.[294]

In a memorandum dated 21 September 1939, Lord Zetland, the secretary of state for India, noted that if Russia creates a diversion through Afghanistan, then the army in India would be unable to hold India. The strength of the army in India was adequate to stop the Afghan army and the North-West Frontier tribes. But against a first-class military power, argued the secretary of state for India, the army in India would wither away. However, the GOI have very little solid information about Russian plans and activities vis-à-vis India's North-West Frontier. The secretary of state for India assumed that instead of a full-scale invasion, Russia might start an air raid against India through Afghanistan. India's anti-aircraft defence, he noted, was almost non-existent. India had only eight 3-inch guns. Worse, the political and psychological effect of such raids on the subject populace would have been disastrous. In case of such a scenario, warned the secretary of state for India, British prestige would sink not only in India but also in the Middle East and it would have a negative effect on London's conduct of global war.[295]

In response to the GOI's anxiety about the probable Russian threat to India's North-West Frontier through Afghanistan, the Chief of Staff Committee (hereafter COSC) issued a memorandum which somewhat underplayed the probable Russian threat. C.L.N. Newall, Dudley Pound, and Edmund Ironside, the members of the COSC, rightly emphasized that rather than Afghanistan, eastern Europe and Manchuria were more important to the Soviets. Further, the Soviets lacked both the doctrine and the tools for conducting a strategic bomber offensive against India. The COSC's memorandum noted:

...what little evidence we have indicates that Afghan fears may not be totally unjustified. On the other hand it is doubtful whether the Soviet, in view of her preoccupation in Europe and the Far East, is prepared at this stage to embark on operations which would bring her into open conflict with the British Empire. Present information indicates that the Russian air garrison of the Central Asian Military District is still at its peace strength of 58 aircraft. This force includes only 18 bombers of the obsolete type which are incapable of attacking objectives in India.... Modern Soviet bombers have a radius of action to enable them to attack Kabul, and the North-West Frontier Province and to penetrate further into India. Owing however, to the standard of efficiency of the Russian Air Force and to their policy of not employing their air force against distant objectives unconnected with land operations, it is very doubtful if in fact the Soviets would attack objectives beyond the North-West Frontier.[296]

Meanwhile, the Afghan government decided to drag its foot over the issue of British influence in Afghanistan. In early 1940, the GOI was still anxious that after the costly failure in Finland, the Red Army might try to win an easy victory over Afghanistan. The Kabul government informed GOI that the scheme proposed by the British military officer G.N. Molesworth, for training the Afghan army cannot be implemented immediately. The Afghans, the GOI was told, needed more time to get accustomed to the idea of being trained by the foreigners. The Afghan government was rightly afraid of excessive British influence in their country. Nevertheless, the prime minister of Afghanistan requested financial subsidy and supply of arms. And he told the GOI that such measures will prepare the way for a British Military Mission in Afghanistan in the near future.[297]

Low level of troubles continued along the North-West Frontier. In February 1940, in the Bannu District along the Bannu-Tochi Road, a military convoy was ambushed by a lashkar which resulted in the death of a British officer and a sergeant, three being wounded and three lorries were burnt. In addition, there were three cases of kidnapping. The GOI thought of sending troops into the Ahmudzai Salient. A brigade for reconnaissance was sent towards the hills in north-west of Bannu. On 12 February, a lashkar comprising 200 tribesmen encountered it. The losses of the brigade amounted to one British officer and one VCO killed and five sepoys wounded.[298] The tribesmen were itching for a fight. When news filtered among the tribesmen that troops will show the flag at Ahmudzai Salient, the former started collecting there. On 21 February 1940, a British Indian column started moving towards the Ahmudzai Salient against tribal opposition. In the first two days,

19 men of the lashkar were killed and 25 wounded. On the night of 24–25 February, two platoons of Frontier Constabulary on patrol duty were ambushed by a lashkar comprising 500 men. Only 28 Scouts were able to escape the ambush.[299] In March 1940, five new Afridi platoons were inducted in order to strengthen the Frontier Constabulary.[300] In an attempt to buy the passive loyalty of the Kabul government, during April 1940, the GOI decided to offer Afghanistan a credit of Rs 10 lakh a year for two years for improving the roads. On 6 April, in North Waziristan, the Scouts assisted by aircraft dispersed a lashkar. In South Waziristan, in the Kotkai area, the troops confronted the hostile tribesmen who took position within the caves.[301]

As the global military situation deteriorated for the Allies, the GOI stepped up its appeasement policy towards Afghanistan. The GOI became nervous because of one Mashud leader Musa Khan, who offered to raise a force of 20,000 Mashuds in support of Moscow in case the Godless Soviets decided to march into India through Afghanistan. The ruling elites of British India anticipated the emergence of an unholy alliance between the 'God fearing mullahs' and the 'Godless Bolsheviks' indirectly supported by the Nazis. The secretary of state for India believed that the Afghan Foreign Minister was pro-Allied but the ruler was pro-Axis. In May 1940, the GOI offered a free gift of 5,000 rifles and .25 million rounds of small arms ammunition to the Kabul government for equipping the Afghan Northern Army. In case of a Russian invasion, this force was to bear the brunt of attack. The pill was sweetened by an offer of 2.5 million sterling pounds as credit which will be spread over five years for industrial development in Afghanistan and purchase of armaments by the Kabul government. Of the financial subsidy, 50 per cent was earmarked for making roads. And 25 per cent of the grant was reserved for agricultural development including construction of canals and bridges. For industrial development of Afghanistan, especially for buying textile production machinery, iron and steel, and so on, the rest 25 per cent of the grant was kept aside.[302] Such sporadic attempt at funding the Afghan state does not mean that it had become a rentier state. Next month, in June 1940, information reached the GOI that the Russians in Kabul were receiving German and Italian backing. And due to Axis pressure, the Afghan government was afraid of accepting GOI's 'gift' of rifles and small arms ammunition.[303] The GOI persisted in its effort to woo the 'not so interested' Afghan government. In July

1940, the London government decided to buy 8,000 tons of Afghan wool and the GOI another 10,000 tons of Afghan wool in order to aid the Kabul government to tide over financial difficulties. Due to fear of Russia, Kabul was unwilling to enter into military conversation with the GOI. To avoid provoking the Soviet 'Bear', Kabul did not allow the Indian and British contractors to start the road development project.[304] The London-GOI's 'sterling diplomacy' failed, argued the British officials due to fear generated by the Soviets in Afghan mind. One could speculate that the Kabul government was using the Soviet menace as a ploy to prevent any British intrusion into Afghanistan. It was a prelude of the game played by the 'neutral' countries to play off the USSR and the USA against each other for their own benefits during the heydays of the Cold War.

In January 1943, the GOI considered it dangerous to teach the local *mistries* of the ordnance establishment, located in Peshawar, the skill of making automatic handguns. The British authorities feared that they may go back to the tribal areas and start manufacturing such guns for the tribesmen.[305] Tommy Guns and Sten Guns, which were ideal for close-quarter assault between 50–100 yards, would have increased the lethality of the Indus tribesmen vis-à-vis the units of the army in India stationed in that region.[306] In fact, many Punjabi mistries, who had learnt their skill at Rawalpindi Arsenal, manufactured arms illegally at the Kohat Pass.[307] In mid-May 1944, the followers of faqir of Ipi were dispersed in central Waziristan. However, on 16 May, the road running north from Razmak was attacked by the tribesmen.[308] During December 1944, rocket firing aircraft of the RAF was used against the Mashuds and the Waziris.[309] Heavy snowfall in the middle of January 1945 and bitter cold restricted all military activities along the North-West Frontier during the first month of 1945.[310]

* * *

For both the Mughal and British Indian empires, the principal threat in Afghanistan remained the probable conventional threat posed by rival great power(s). From nineteenth century onwards, extra Asian powers (like Britain) also participated in the Great Game. Britain like the Mughals maintained a permanent power base (i.e., formal empire) in southern Asia for conducting warfare in Afghanistan. The British

and the Mughals were dependent on South Asian military manpower
for projecting power in Afghanistan. The British relied on Indians and
the Indus tribes for manning the Indian army, which was the principal
instrument for projecting power in Afghanistan. The Mughals and the
British realized that management of the frontier tribes was inseparable
from the related and greater Afghan 'problem'. The British officers of
the late nineteenth and early twentieth centuries as well as civilian
intellectuals unlike the Mughals believed that jihad and mullahs were
crucial components of Afghan culture. Despite the passage of time
and changes in military hardware, certain COIN techniques remained
operational during the last five centuries. Both the Mughals and the
British used subsidies to placate the Afghan tribes. When the subsidy
amount was cut, rebellions broke out which in turn cost the imperial
power much more. So, reduction of tribal subsidies proved to be a false
economy. Moreover, both the imperial powers through limited military
recruitment tried to co-opt the potentially rebellious manpower of
Afghanistan. Nevertheless, with time, certain innovative COIN techniques also evolved. For instance, the Mughals, unlike the British, did
not possess 'politicals', frontier police, and paramilitary units geared
especially for specialized COIN duties.

The British experience during the three Afghan Wars was that it was
easier to defeat the Afghan regular army in conventional battles and
sieges, but almost impossible to permanently subjugate the militias
and the armed tribesmen who conducted hit-and-run attacks. In other
words, it was easier to win the conventional campaigns in Afghanistan,
but extremely difficult to maintain a lasting peace. Both the British and
the Mughals found out that it was logistically difficult and financially
expensive to maintain a large force in Afghanistan for a long period.
But fighting the dispersed groupings of armed Pathans to secure
peace required the maintenance of a large force for a long period. The
Americans and the Soviets would have certainly agreed with such views.

NOTES

1. T.A. Heathcote, *The Afghan Wars: 1839–1919* (1980; reprint, Gloucestershire: Spellmount, 2007); Brian Robson, *Crisis on the Frontier: The Third
Afghan War and the Campaign in Waziristan, 1919–20* (Staplehurst: Spellmount,
2004).

2. T.R. Moreman, *The Army in India and the Development of Frontier Warfare: 1849–1947* (Houndmills, Basingstoke: Macmillan, 1998); Charles Allen, *Soldier Sahibs: The Men Who Made the North-West Frontier* (London: John Murray, 2000); Alan Warren, *Waziristan: The Faqir of Ipi and the Indian Army, The North-West Frontier Revolt of 1936–7* (Karachi: Oxford University Press, 2000); Andrew M. Roe, *Waging War in Waziristan: The British Struggle in the Land of Bin Laden, 1849–1947* (Lawrence, Kansas: University Press of Kansas, 2010). The most recent monograph by Christian Tripodi titled *Edge of Empire: The British Political Officer and Tribal Administration on the North-West Frontier, 1877–1947* (Surrey: Ashgate, 2011) emphasizes on the political aspect of border management.

3. Tripodi, *Edge of Empire*, 15–17.

4. John S. Galbraith, 'The "Turbulent Frontier" as a Factor in British Expansion', *Comparative Studies in Society and History*, 2, 2 (1960): 150–68.

5. Pierce G. Fredericks, *The Sepoy and the Cossack* (London: W.H. Allen, 1972), 28.

6. Breeding of Horses, Remount Horses, Minutes by Napier, Notes and Minutes by Lord Napier of Magdala, Commander-in-Chief of Bombay, 1866–9, MSS.EUR.F114, 1C, IOR, BL, London.

7. Victoria Schofield, *Afghan Frontier: At the Crossroads of Conflict* (2003; reprint, London: I.B. Tauris, 2010), 63.

8. James Atkinson, *Afghan Expedition: Notes and Sketches from the First British Afghan War of 1839–1840* (1842; reprint, Long Riders' Guild Press, 2007), 10, 19.

9. George MacMunn, *Afghanistan from Darius to Amanullah* (1929; reprint, Lahore: Sang-e-Meel Publications, 2002), 87; Jules Stewart, *Crimson Snow: Britain's First Disaster in Afghanistan* (2008; reprint, Stroud, Gloucestershire: History Press, 2010), 11. Dost Muhammad assumed the title of *Amir* in 1834. M. Hassan Kakar, *A Political and Diplomatic History of Afghanistan: 1863–1901* (Leiden: Brill, 2006), 9.

10. MacMunn, *Afghanistan*, 102.

11. Paddy Docherty, *The Khyber Pass: A History of Empire and Invasion* (2007; reprint, London: Faber and Faber, 2008), 199.

12. MacMunn, *Afghanistan*, 109.

13. Lieutenant William Barr, *Journal of a March from Delhi to Peshawar and from Thence to Kabul with the Mission of Lieutenant-Colonel C.M. Wade, including Travels in the Punjab, a Visit to the City of Lahore and a Narrative of Operations in the Khyber Pass Undertaken in 1839* (1844; reprint, New Delhi: Munshiram Manoharlal, 2003), 97–8, 114, 120–1.

14. Atkinson, *Notes and Sketches from the First British Afghan War of 1839–1840*, 2.

15. From Major Henry Durand to the President of the Board of Control, 15 Feb. 1834, para 1&7, Memorandum of Services of Henry Durand, Major,

Engineer, Bengal Army, Letters from Miscellaneous Correspondence, Charles Wood Collection, MSS.EUR.F.78/1b-2, IOR, BL, London.

16. Brigadier Humphry Bullock, *History of the Army Service Corps, Vol. 1, 1760–1857* (1952; reprint, New Delhi: Sterling, 1976), 106.

17. Docherty, *The Khyber Pass*, 200.

18. Stewart, *Crimson Snow*, 13, 19–21; Percy Sykes, *A History of Afghanistan*, 2 vols (1940; reprint, New Delhi: Munshiram Manoharlal, 2002), vol. 1, p. 2.

19. Atkinson, *Notes and Sketches from the First British Afghan War of 1839–1840*, 3.

20. Stewart, *Crimson Snow*, 22, 24–5.

21. Atkinson, *Notes and Sketches from the First British Afghan War of 1839–1840*, 3.

22. Lady Florentina Sale, *A Journal of the First Afghan War*, ed. by Patrick Macrory (1969; reprint, Oxford: Oxford University Press, 2002), Introduction by Macrory, xiv–xv.

23. Heathcote, *The Afghan Wars: 1839–1919*, 25.

24. Atkinson, *Notes and Sketches from the First British Afghan War of 1839–1840*, 5; Bullock, *History of the Army Service Corps*, vol. 1, pp. 107–8.

25. Mohan Lal, *Life of the Amir Dost Mohammad Khan of Kabul with His Political Proceedings towards the English, Russian, and Persian Governments including the Victory and Disasters of the British Army in Afghanistan*, 2 vols (1846; reprint, New Delhi: Asian Educational Services, 2004), vol. 1, p. 236.

26. Rob Johnson, *The Afghan Way of War: Culture and Pragmatism, A Critical History* (London: Hurst & Co., 2011), 51.

27. Lal, *Life of the Amir Dost Mohammad Khan*, vol. 1, p. 240.

28. Fredericks, *The Sepoy and the Cossack*, 65–6.

29. Barr, *Journal of a March from Delhi to Peshawar and from Thence to Kabul*, 144.

30. Bullock, *History of the Army Service Corps*, vol. 112, p. 1.

31. Lal, *Life of the Amir Dost Mohammad Khan*, vol. 2, p. 185.

32. Lieutenant-General George Lawrence, *Reminiscences of Forty-Three Years in India* (1874; reprint, Lahore: Sang-e-Meel Publications, 1999), 6.

33. Barr, *Journal of a March from Delhi to Peshawar and from Thence to Kabul*, 127–8.

34. Barr, *Journal of a March from Delhi to Peshawar and from Thence to Kabul*, 139.

35. Barr, *Journal of a March from Delhi to Peshawar and from Thence to Kabul*, 139, 177–9, 183–84.

36. Bullock, *History of the Army Service Corps*, vol. 1, p. 110.

37. Atkinson, *Notes and Sketches from the First British Afghan War of 1839–1840*, 40.

38. Lal, *Life of the Amir Dost Mohammad Khan*, vol. 2, pp. 193, 197, 199–200.

39. Lal, *Life of the Amir Dost Mohammad Khan*, vol. 2, pp. 200–1.

40. Lawrence, *Reminiscences of Forty-Three Years in India*, 8.

41. Lawrence, *Reminiscences of Forty-Three Years in India*, 9.

42. Lal, *Life of the Amir Dost Mohammad Khan*, vol. 2, pp. 205–8.

43. Lal, *Life of the Amir Dost Mohammad Khan*, vol. 2, p. 210.

44. Lawrence, *Reminiscences of Forty-Three Years in India*, 11.

45. Lal, *Life of the Amir Dost Mohammad Khan*, vol. 2, p. 215.

46. Heathcote, *The Afghan Wars*, 33.

47. Lawrence, *Reminiscences of Forty-Three Years in India*, 12.

48. Lawrence, *Reminiscences of Forty-Three Years in India*, 12–3. Italics in original. *Kambakht* means useless person.

49. Lawrence, *Reminiscences of Forty-Three Years in India*, 17.

50. Lawrence, *Reminiscences of Forty-Three Years in India*, 14, 16.

51. Heathcote, *The Afghan Wars*, 34.

52. Sale, *A Journal of the First Afghan War*, Introduction, xv.

53. From Major Henry Durand to the President of the Board of Control, 15 Feb. 1834, para 8&10, Charles Wood Collection.

54. Statement of the Services of Colonel Roberts, Bengal Army, 27 July 1853, Charles Wood Collection.

55. Statement of the Services of Colonel Roberts, Bengal Army, 27 July 1853, Charles Wood Collection.

56. Lieutenant Vincent Eyre, *The Military Operations at Kabul: The Retreat and Destruction of the British Army, 1832* (1843; reprint, Stroud, Gloucestershire: Nonsuch, 2005), 8.

57. From Brigadier-General G. Bourchier, to the QMG, Army HQ, Simla, 22 June 1869, Records of Chief Commands, 1865–76, Notes and Minutes by Napier, MSS.EUR.F.114, 5(2).

58. Vincent Smith, *Akbar: The Great Moghul, 1542–1605* (n.d.; reprint, Delhi: S. Chand, 1962), 142.

59. John Lawrence to Blane, Miscellaneous Letters to Colonel L.S. Blane, Military Secy., 1865–6, John Lawrence Collection, MSS.EUR.F.90/60, IOR, BL.

60. Brigadier R.C. Butalia, *The Evolution of the Artillery in India: From the Battle of Plassey (1757) to the Revolt of 1857* (New Delhi: Allied Publishers, 1998), 225.

61. MacMunn, *Afghanistan*, 122.

62. Lawrence, *Reminiscences of Forty-Three Years in India*, 6.

63. Atkinson, *Notes and Sketches from the First British Afghan War of 1839–1840*, 56.

64. Atkinson, *Notes and Sketches from the First British Afghan War of 1839–1840*, 52–3; Bullock, *History of the Army Service Corps*, vol. 1, p. 113.

65. Fredericks, *The Sepoy and the Cossack*, 68.

66. Sale, *A Journal of the First Afghan War*, Introduction, xv; Lawrence, *Reminiscences of Forty-Three Years in India*, 7.

67. Sale, *A Journal of the First Afghan War*, Introduction, xv.

68. Eyre, *The Military Operations at Kabul*, 7.

69. M.E. Yapp, 'Disturbances in Eastern Afghanistan, 1839–42', *Bulletin of the School of Oriental and African Studies*, 25, 1/3 (1962): 499–523.

70. Heathcote, *The Afghan Wars*, 41, 43.

71. Eyre, *The Military Operations at Kabul*, 21; Sale, *A Journal of the First Afghan War*, Introduction, xv.

72. Eyre, *The Military Operations at Kabul*, 21, 29.

73. Mowbray Morris, *The First Afghan War* (London: Sampson Low, 1878), 74–5; Sale, *A Journal of the First Afghan War*, Introduction, xviii–xix.

74. Sale, *A Journal of the First Afghan War*, 6–7.

75. Eyre, *The Military Operations at Kabul*, 21.

76. Morris, *The First Afghan War*, 75–6.

77. Sale, *A Journal of the First Afghan War*, 9.

78. Morris, *The First Afghan War*, 76.

79. Sale, *A Journal of the First Afghan War*, 9.

80. Eyre, *The Military Operations at Kabul*, 11.

81. Morris, *The First Afghan War*, 72–3, 79; Sale, *A Journal of the First Afghan War*, 11.

82. Morris, *The First Afghan War*, 80–1.

83. Eyre, *The Military Operations at Kabul*, pp. 7, 11.

84. Sale, *A Journal of the First Afghan War*, Introduction, xiii.

85. *Frontier and Overseas Expeditions from India*, vol. 3, *Baluchistan and the First Afghan War* (1910; reprint, Quetta: Nisa Traders, 1979), pp. 385–7.

86. *Frontier and Overseas Expeditions from India*, vol. 3, pp. 388–9, 397–8.

87. Morris, *The First Afghan War*, 99–101, 104–5.

88. Christine Noelle, *State and Tribe in Nineteenth Century Afghanistan: The Reign of Amir Dost Muhammad Khan (1826–1863)* (1997; reprint, Oxon/New York: Routledge, 2008), 241–3.

89. Noelle, *The Reign of Amir Dost Muhammad Khan (1826–1863)*, 244–7.

90. Noelle, *The Reign of Amir Dost Muhammad Khan (1826–1863)*, 248–50.

91. Lieutenant-Colonel B.N. Majumdar, *History of the Army Service Corps, Vol. 2, 1858–1913* (New Delhi: Sterling, 1976), 108.

92. Kakar, *A Political and Diplomatic History of Afghanistan: 1863–1901*, 9–10.

93. Noelle, *The Reign of Amir Dost Muhammad Khan (1826–1863)*, 251, 254–5.

94. Tripodi, *Edge of Empire*, 12.

95. Tripodi, *Edge of Empire*, 3.

96. G.F. MacMunn, *The Armies of India* (1911; reprint, New Delhi: Heritage Publishers, 1991), 146–8, 150–3.

97. Waziris, Description of the Various Sections of the Three Great Divisions of Waziris, 4: 1–3, MSS.EUR.F.163/3, IOR, BL.

98. *Official History of Operations on the N.W. Frontier of India 1936–7* (n.d.; reprint, Uckfield, East Sussex: Naval and Military Press, n.d.), 2.

99. Waziris, 4: 13.

100. Waziris, 4, Report by Lieutenant-Colonel C.W. Macgregor.

101. George MacMunn, *Vignettes from Indian War* (1901; reprint, New Delhi: Low Price Publications, 1993), 187.

102. *Official History of Operations on the N.W. Frontier of India 1936–7*, 2.

103. Shah Mahmoud Hanifi, 'Quandaries of the Afghan Nation', in Shahzad Bashir and Robert D. Crews (ed.), *Under the Drones: Modern Lives in the Afghanistan-Pakistan Borderlands* (Cambridge Massachusetts/London: Harvard University Press, 2012), 89–91.

104. Butalia, *The Evolution of the Artillery in India*, 222, 225–6.

105. Schofield, *Afghan Frontier*, 53.

106. MacMunn, *The Armies of India*, 155.

107. Fredericks, *The Sepoy and the Cossack*, 69.

108. MacMunn, *Vignettes from Indian War*, 103–11.

109. Allen, *Soldier Sahibs*, 69–70, 94–6, 98, 103, 126–7, 139, 149.

110. Waziris, 4: 2.

111. Johnson, *The Afghan Way of War*, 87.

112. From offg. secy. to chief commander, Disturbances among the Native Troops in Punjab, 2, 3 October 1857, List of Letters addressed to govt. subsequent to 29 June 1857, FSP, NAI, New Delhi.

113. List of Letters, 45, 28 August 1857, FSP.

114. Charles Chenevix Trench, *The Frontier Scouts* (London: Jonathan Cape, 1985), Foreword by Philip Mason, xii.

115. Waziris, 4: 7–8.

116. Majumdar, *History of the Army Service Corps*, vol. 2, pp. 22–8.

117. K.M.L. Saxena, *The Military System of India: 1850–1900* (New Delhi: Sterling, 1974), 127–8.

118. Memo of the Composition of the Corps of Guides, Lieutenant-Colonel H.B. Lumsden, 17 Jan. 1862, Records of Chief Commands, Notes and Minutes by Napier, MSS.EUR.F.114, 5(2).

119. From Lieutenant-Colonel H.W. Norman, Secy. to the GOI, MD, to the offg. ADG of the Army, Fort William, 25 Nov. 1862, Records of Chief Commands, Notes and Minutes by Napier of Magdala.

120. From Major-General S. Cotton, Commanding Peshawar Division, to the ADG of the Army, Calcutta, 26 July 1860, 723, Records of Chief Commands, Notes and Minutes by Napier.

121. Memorandum by Major R.E. Boyle Commanding 11th Bengal Lancers, Ethnic Elements of the Indian Army, Records of Chief Commands, 1865–76, Notes and Minutes by Napier, MSS.EUR.F.114, 5(4).

122. Annual Army Caste Return of the Indian Troops of Bengal Presidency, 1 Jan. 1876, Records of Chief Commands, 1865–76, Notes and Minutes by Napier.

123. Peter Lumsden, 15 Nov. 1879, Records of Chief Commands, 1865–76, Notes and Minutes by Napier, MSS.EUR.F.114, 5(3).

124. Saxena, *The Military System of India: 1850–1900*, 88, 130.

125. Confidential, Major-General Chalmers Reid to the ADG of the Army, Calcutta, 7 Feb. 1868, Records of Chief Commands, Notes and Minutes by Napier.

126. Waziris, 4: 12.

127. *Memorandum on the Different Systems Adopted on the North-Western Frontier for the Employment of Local Levies* (Simla: Government Central Branch Press, 1888), 4–6, MSS.EUR.F.163/7, IOR, BL.

128. *Memorandum on the Different Systems Adopted on the North-Western Frontier for the Employment of Local Levies*, 9–10.

129. T.R. Moreman, 'The Arms Trade and the North-West Frontier Pathan Tribes, 1890–1914', *Journal of Imperial and Commonwealth History*, 22, 2 (1994): 190.

130. Tripodi, *Edge of Empire*, 16.

131. Johnson, *The Afghan Way of War*, 91; Kakar, *A Political and Diplomatic History of Afghanistan: 1863–1901*, 10–11.

132. Kakar, *A Political and Diplomatic History of Afghanistan: 1863–1901*, 11.

133. Martin Ewans, *Securing the Indian Frontier in Central Asia: Confrontation and Negotiation, 1865–95* (London/New York: Routledge, 2010), 13.

134. Ewans, *Securing the Indian Frontier in Central Asia*, 17, 19–20.

135. Ewans, *Securing the Indian Frontier in Central Asia*, 18.

136. Ewans, *Securing the Indian Frontier in Central Asia*, 18–19.

137. Johnson, *The Afghan Way of War*, 93.

138. Kakar, *A Political and Diplomatic History of Afghanistan: 1863–1901*, 11–2.

139. Kakar, *A Political and Diplomatic History of Afghanistan: 1863–1901*, 12–3.

140. Kakar, *A Political and Diplomatic History of Afghanistan: 1863–1901*, 13.

141. Kakar, *A Political and Diplomatic History of Afghanistan: 1863–1901*, 14.

142. Ewans, *Securing the Indian Frontier in Central Asia*, 77–8.

143. Ewans, *Securing the Indian Frontier in Central Asia*, 78.

144. Field-Marshal Roberts, *Forty-One Years in India: From Subaltern to Commander-in-Chief* (1897; reprint, New Delhi: Asian Educational Services, 2005), 341.

145. Majumdar, *History of the Army Service Corps*, vol. 2, pp. 111–12.

146. Sydney H. Shadbolt, *The Afghan Campaigns of 1878–1880 Compiled from Official and Private Sources* (London: Sampson Low, Marston, 1882), 1–4; Roberts, *Forty-One Years in India*, 347.

147. Roberts, *Forty-One Years in India*, 351–3.

148. Roberts, *Forty-One Years in India*, 345.

149. Roberts, *Forty-One Years in India*, 346, 350.

150. Johnson, *The Afghan Way of War*, 98–9.

151. Roberts, *Forty-One Years in India*, 353–4, 357–9, 363–5, 368–9.

152. Howard Hensman, *The Afghan War of 1879–80* (1881; reprint, Lahore: Sang-e-Meel Publications, 1999), 1, 3–4.

153. Shadbolt, *The Afghan Campaigns of 1878–1880 Compiled from Official and Private Sources*, 4.

154. Hensman, *The Afghan War of 1879–80*, 4–5.

155. Shadbolt, *The Afghan Campaigns of 1878–1880 Compiled from Official and Private Sources*, 4–6.

156. Major R.C.W. Mitford, *To Cabul with the Cavalry Brigade: A Narrative of Personal Experiences with the Force under Lieutenant-General F.S. Roberts with Maps and Illustrations from Sketches by the Author* (n.d.; reprint, New Delhi: Bhavna Books and Prints, 2000), 3–4.

157. Roberts, *Forty-One Years in India*, 352–3.

158. Mitford, *To Cabul with the Cavalry Brigade*, 5.

159. Mitford, *To Cabul with the Cavalry Brigade*, 4, 12.

160. Mitford, *To Cabul with the Cavalry Brigade*, 3.

161. Hensman, *The Afghan War of 1879–80*, 5.

162. From Lieutenant-Colonel J.I. Willes, Commissary General, Bengal, to Lieutenant-General M. Kennedy, Controller General of Supply and Transport, MD, Simla, Progs., 34, 29 September 1879, Military Proceedings, Supply and Transport, December 1879, MD, NAI.

163. From Colonel T.B. Harrison, Controller of Military Accounts, Bengal, to Lieutenant-General M. Kennedy, Controller General of Supply and Transport, MD, Calcutta, Progs., 37, 8 October 1879, From Lieutenant-General M. Kennedy, Controller General of Supply and Transport, MD, to the Commissary General, Bengal, Progs., 42, 21 October 1879, Military Proceedings, Supply and Transport.

164. Scheme and Rules for the Transport Service in the Kurram Valley, Progs., 44, Supply and Transport, MD, December 1879.

165. Progs., 49, 13 September 1879, Supply and Transport, MD.

166. From Colonel S. Black, Secy. to Punjab Govt., MD, to the Controller General, MD, Simla, 13 September 1879, Progs., 49, Supply and Transport, MD.

167. Progs., 49, Supply and Transport, MD.

168. Mitford, *To Cabul with the Cavalry Brigade*, 2.

169. Hensman, *The Afghan War of 1879–80*, 6.

170. Progs., 49, Supply and Transport, MD.

171. Telegram from Deputy Commissioner Bannu, to secy. to the Punjab Govt., MD, 10 September 1879, Copy of a Telegram from secy. to Punjab Govt., MD, to Deputy Commissioner, Bannu, 13 September 1879, Supply and Transport, MD.

172. Hensman, *The Afghan War of 1879–80*, 7.

173. Hensman, *The Afghan War of 1879–80*, 8. Major R.C.W. Mitford writes that Amir Yaqub Khan with some 20–5 Afghan horsemen surrendered to Roberts' force on 28 September. Mitford, *To Cabul with the Cavalry Brigade*, 15.

174. Mitford, *To Cabul with the Cavalry Brigade*, 16.

175. Hensman, *The Afghan War of 1879–80*, 11.

176. Mitford, *To Cabul with the Cavalry Brigade*, 16–7.

177. Hensman, *The Afghan War of 1879–80*, 18.

178. Shadbolt, *The Afghan Campaigns of 1878–1880 Compiled from Official and Private Sources*, 10.

179. Shadbolt, *The Afghan Campaigns of 1878–1880 Compiled from Official and Private Sources*, 10–12.

180. Shadbolt, *The Afghan Campaigns of 1878–1880 Compiled from Official and Private Sources*, 12.

181. General Lord Roberts, *Short Report on Important Questions Dealt with during the Tenure of Commander of the Army in India* (Simla: Government Central Printing Office, 1893), 3, L/MIL/17/5/1613, IOR, BL.

182. Note by the commander-in-chief on the financial member's proposal for reduction in the Native Army, para 9, 1Q/21, 4 Aug. 1894, George White Collection, MSS.EUR.F.108/24, IOR, BL.

183. *The Second Afghan War: 1878–80*, Compiled by Major-General Charles MacGregor, and revised by F.G. Cardew (reprint, Rawalpindi: Army Education Directorate, 1975), pp. 548, 553–7.

184. From Willes, to Kennedy, Progs. No. 34, 29 Sept. 1879, Military Proceedings, Supply and Transport, December 1879.

185. *The Second Afghan War: 1878–80*, 557.

186. *The Second Afghan War: 1878–80*, 574–80.

187. General Frederick Roberts, *Correspondence with England while Commander-in-Chief in Madras: 1881–5* (Simla: Government Central Printing Office, 1890), 116, L/MIL/17/5/1615, PT 2, IOR, BL.

188. Roberts, *Short Report on Important Questions Dealt with during the Tenure of Commander of the Army in India*, 7.

189. Roberts, *Correspondence with England while Commander-in-Chief in Madras: 1881–5*, 46–7, 115.

190. Roberts, *Short Report on Important Questions Dealt with during the Tenure of Commander of the Army in India*, 8.

191. General Frederick Roberts, *Correspondence with India while Commander-in-Chief in Madras: 1881–85* (Simla: Government Central Printing Office, 1890), 90, L/MIL/17/5/1615, Part 3, IOR, BL.

192. Roberts, *Correspondence with India while Commander-in-Chief in Madras: 1881–85*, 91.

193. Roberts, *Short Report on Important Questions Dealt with during the Tenure of Commander of the Army in India*, 7.

194. Roberts, *Correspondence with England while Commander-in-Chief in Madras: 1881–5*, To Field-Marshal, the Duke of Cambridge, 24 April 1883.

195. Roberts, *Correspondence with England while Commander-in-Chief in Madras: 1881–5*, 115.

196. Schofield, *Afghan Frontier*, 33.

197. Roe, *Waging War in Waziristan*, 1.

198. Ewans, *Securing the Indian Frontier in Central Asia*, 77–9.

199. R.A. Johnson, '"Russians at the Gates of India"? Planning the Defence of India, 1885–1903', *Journal of Military History*, 67, 3 (2003): 711–13.

200. Geo S. White to the Duke of Cambridge, Simla, 13 June 1893, George White Collection.

201. Robson, *Crisis on the Frontier*, 40.

202. H.C. Thompson, *The Chitral Campaign: A Narrative of Events in Chitral, Swat, and Bajaur* (London: William Heinemann, 1895), 1–3, 3–5, 7, 10, 114, 125–8, 131–2, 136.

203. Note by E.H.E. Collen, 7 July 1896, 1Q/26, George White Collection.

204. Appendix IV, 6 Feb. 1905, George White Collection, MSS.EUR.F.108/87&88.

205. *Memorandum on the Different Systems Adopted on the North-Western Frontier for the Employment of Local Levies*, 3.

206. *Memorandum on the Different Systems Adopted on the North-Western Frontier for the Employment of Local Levies*, 3.

207. From Lieutenant-Colonel W.G.H. Macbay, Commanding 26th Baluchistan Regiment, Bombay Infantry, to the Asst. ADG, 18 April 1893, Military Collection, Confidential Reports of the Regiments, L/MIL/7/17008, IOR, BL.

208. Roberts, *Short Report on Important Questions Dealt with during the Tenure of Commander of the Army in India*, 8–12.

209. From ADG in India, to secy. GOI, MD, Simla, Enclosure No. 1, 9 June 1893, Annual Confidential Inspection Reports on the Regiments and Battalions of the Bengal Army, 1892–3, L/MIL/7/17008, IOR, BL.

210. General Frederick Roberts, *Correspondence with the Viceroy of India (The Marquess of Lansdowne): 26 November 1888–2 April 1893* (Calcutta: Superintendent

of Government Printing, 1893), L/MIL/17/5/1615, IOR, BL; Butalia, *The Evolution of the Artillery in India*, 222.

211. Moreman, 'The Arms Trade and the North-West Frontier Pathan Tribes, 1890–1914', 190–1.

212. Roe, *Waging War in Waziristan*, 3.

213. *Proceedings of the Army in India Committee, 1912*, 1-A, *Minority Report* (Simla: Government Central Branch Press, 1913), 30.

214. From Major-General Bindon Blood to the ADG in India, 27 October 1897, Appendix A, Malakand Field Force, 16 September 1897, Proceedings of the GOI, Malakand, 1897–8, S.No. 13, MD, NAI.

215. Despatches from Brigaider General Meiklejohn and Major-General Blood, on the Operations of the Malakand Brigade and the Malakand Field Force up to 26 August 1897, Progs. No. 671, From Bindon Blood, Commanding Malakand Field Force to the ADG in India, 20 Aug. 1897, Progs. 673, Return of Casualties in Action at Landaki, 17 August 1897, Proceedings of the GOI, Malakand.

216. From Brigadier-General W.H. Meiklejohn Commanding Malakand Field Brigade to the ADG in India through the officer commanding Malakand Field Force, 13 August 1897, Proceedings of the GOI, Malakand.

217. General Order No. 1089, 13 August 1897, Proceedings of the GOI, Malakand.

218. Field Operations Malakand, No. 1089, 13 August 1897, General Order, Proceedings of the Government of India, Malakand, 1897–8.

219. From Major-General B. Blood Commanding Malakand Field Force to the ADG in India, 20 August 1897, General Order, Proceedings of the GOI, Malakand.

220. Richard A. Gabriel and Paul L. Savage, *Crisis in Command: Mismanagement in the Army* (1981; reprint, New Delhi: Himalayan Books, 1986).

221. From Major-General B. Blood, to the ADG in India, 27 October 1897, Proceedings of the GOI, Malakand.

222. *Proceedings of the Army in India Committee, 1912*, 1-A, *Minority Report*, 109.

223. General Andrew Skeen, *Passing It On: Short Talks on Tribal Fighting on the North-West Frontier of India* (1932; reprint, New Delhi: English Book Store, 1965), 15.

224. *Papers regarding British Relations with the Neighbouring Tribes on the North-West Frontier of India and Punjab Frontier Administration* (London: HMSO, 1901), 52, MSS.EUR.F.163/15©, IOR, BL.

225. Roe, *Waging War in Waziristan*, 3; Trench, *Frontier Scouts*, Foreword, xiii.

226. Tripodi, *Edge of Empire*, 9.

227. Trench, *Frontier Scouts*, Foreword, xiii–xiv.

228. Arnold Keppel, *Gun-Running and the Indian North-West Frontier* (1911; reprint, Lahore: Sang-e-Meel, 2004), 7, 12, 20–2, 25–8.

229. Keppel, *Gun-Running and the Indian North-West Frontier*, 28.

230. Keppel, *Gun-Running and the Indian North-West Frontier*, 28–9.

231. *The Third Afghan War 1919 Official Account Compiled in the General Staff Branch, Army Headquarters India* (Calcutta: Government of India, 1926), 22.

232. *Proceedings of the Army in India Committee, 1912*, 1-A, *Minority Report*, 29, 32–3, 61, 71.

233. *Proceedings of the Army in India Committee 1912*, vol. 3, *Minutes of Evidence* (Simla: Government Central Branch Press, 1913), 641.

234. *Proceedings of the Army in India Committee, 1912*, 1-A, *Minority Report*, 32.

235. *Proceedings of the Army in India Committee 1912*, vol. 3, *Minutes of Evidence*, 537, 679.

236. *Proceedings of the Army in India Committee, 1912*, 1-A, *Minority Report*, 37.

237. *Proceedings of the Army in India Committee 1912*, vol. 3, *Minutes of Evidence*, 536–7.

238. *Proceedings of the Army in India Committee, 1912*, 1-A, *Minority Report*, 120–2.

239. To the Marquess of Crewe, Secy. of State for India, 26 March 1941, no. 41, Army Despatches to the Court, 1914, NAI.

240. Lester W. Grau, *The Bear Went over the Mountain: Soviet Combat Tactics in Afghanistan* (1996; reprint, London: Frank Cass, 1998), xxvi.

241. The Military Situation in India and the Middle East, Memorandum by General E.G. Barrow, Military Secretary, India Office, Committee of Imperial Defence, 3, 24 November 1915, CAB/24/1, PRO, Kew, Surrey, London.

242. The Military Situation in India and the Middle East, Memorandum by Barrow, 3, 24 November 1915.

243. Robert Strausz-Hupe, 'The Anglo-Afghan War of 1919', *Military Affairs*, 7, 2 (1943), 89.

244. Secret, Appreciation of the attached Eastern Report 1, 11 January 1917, 2, CAB/24/143, PRO.

245. Secret Eastern Report, 1, 10 January 1917, 11–12, CAB/24/143.

246. Secret Eastern Report, 1, 31 January 1917, 5, CAB/24/143.

247. Schofield, *Afghan Frontier*, 33.

248. Strausz-Hupe, 'The Anglo-Afghan War of 1919', 92.

249. *The Third Afghan War 1919 Official Account Compiled in the General Staff Branch*, 22–3.

250. *The Third Afghan War 1919 Official Account Compiled in the General Staff Branch*, 23.

251. *The Third Afghan War 1919 Official Account Compiled in the General Staff Branch*, 16–17.

252. Brian Robson, *Crisis on the Frontier: The Third Afghan War and the Campaign in Waziristan, 1919–20* (Staplehurst: Spellmount, 2004), 20.

253. Lieutenant Colonel B.N. Majumdar, *History of the Army Service Corps, Vol. 3, 1914–39* (New Delhi: Sterling, 1976), 138–40.

254. Robson, *Crisis on the Frontier*, xiii.

255. Majumdar, *History of the Army Service Corps*, vol. 3, 142.

256. *The Third Afghan War 1919 Official Account Compiled in the General Staff Branch*, 21–2.

257. Majumdar, *History of the Army Service Corps*, vol. 3, 140–2.

258. *The Third Afghan War 1919 Official Account Compiled in the General Staff Branch*, 18.

259. Lieutenant-General G.N. Molesworth, *Afghanistan 1919: An Account of Operations in the Third Afghan War* (Bombay: Asia Publishing House, 1962), 170–2.

260. Robson, *Crisis on the Frontier*, 27, 29.

261. Molesworth, *Afghanistan 1919*, vii, 170.

262. Majumdar, *History of the Army Service Corps*, vol. 3, 152.

263. Roe, *Waging War in Waziristan*, 15; MacMunn, *Armies of India*, 152.

264. Roe, *Waging War in Waziristan*, 16.

265. Schofield, *Afghan Frontier*, 52.

266. Alan Warren, 'Bullocks treading down Wasps'? The British Indian Army in Waziristan in the 1930s', *South Asia*, 19, 2 (1996): 38.

267. Molesworth, *Afghanistan 1919*, 156.

268. Memorandum on the Size, Composition and Organization of the Military Forces in India, General Staff April 1920, 1, Enclosure to Despatch 2, 24 June 1920, Army Department Miscellaneous, 141, NAI.

269. Memorandum on the Size, Composition and Organization of the Military Forces in India, p. 2.

270. Memorandum on the Size, Composition and Organization of the Military Forces in India, 2–3.

271. Memorandum on the Size, Composition and Organization of the Military Forces in India, Appendix D.

272. Grau, *The Bear Went over the Mountain*, xxvi.

273. Tripodi, *Edge of Empire*, 17.

274. Lieutenant-Colonel M.C.A. Henniker, *Memoirs of a Junior Officer* (Edinburgh/London: William Blackwood & Sons, 1951), 144–5, 155.

275. Henniker, *Memoirs of a Junior Officer*, 156.

276. Henniker, *Memoirs of a Junior Officer*, 175.

277. Henniker, *Memoirs of a Junior Officer*, 175–6.

278. Henniker, *Memoirs of a Junior Officer*, 176.

279. Henniker, *Memoirs of a Junior Officer*, 170, 179.

280. *Official History of Operations on the N.W. Frontier of India 1936–7*, 2–4.

281. *Official History of Operations on the N.W. Frontier of India 1936–7*, 3–4.

282. *Official History of Operations on the N.W. Frontier of India 1936–7*, 4–7.

283. *Official History of Operations on the N.W. Frontier of India 1936–7*, 1.

284. *Official History of Operations on the N.W. Frontier of India 1936–7*, 8–15.

285. Warren, 'Bullocks treading down Wasps'? The British Indian Army in Waziristan in the 1930s', 52.

286. Skeen, *Passing It On*, Preface.

287. Skeen, *Passing It On*, Preface.

288. Skeen, *Passing It On*, 2–3.

289. Skeen, *Passing It On*, 3.

290. Skeen, *Passing It On*, 3–4, 7, 14.

291. Report of the Expert Committee on the Defence of India 1938–39, 10, CAB/24/287, PRO, Kew, Surrey, UK.

292. Milan L. Hauner, 'Afghanistan between the Great Powers, 1938–45', *International Journal of Middle East Studies*, 14, 4 (1982): 482–83.

293. Report of the Expert Committee on the Defence of India 1938–39, 9.

294. India at the Outbreak of War, First Fortnightly Report submitted by the secy. of state for India covering the period upto 11 September, 12 September 1939, WP(39)5, CP, NMML, New Delhi.

295. Question of Russian Threat to India, Memorandum by the Secretary of State for India, 21 September 1939, WP(39)55, CP, NMML.

296. Russian Threat to India, Report by the Chiefs of Staff Committee, 29 September 1939, War Cabinet Papers, WP(39)55, CP.

297. Eleventh Fortnightly Report submitted by the Secy. of State for India covering the period 1–15 February 1940, Foreign and Frontier Relations, Afghanistan, 17 February 1940, WP(40)62, CP.

298. Eleventh Fortnightly Report submitted by the Secy. of State for India covering the period 1–15 February 1940, North-West Frontier.

299. Twelfth Fortnightly Report submitted by the Secy. of State for India covering the period 16–29 February 1940, North-West Frontier, 4 March 1940, WP(40)80, CP.

300. Reports for the Month of March 1940 for the Dominions, India, Burma and the Colonies, Protectorates and Mandated Territories, Report by the Secy. of State for India, para 31, 2 April 1940, WP(40)107, CP, NMML.

301. Reports for the Month of April 1940 for the Dominions, India, Burma and the Colonies, Protectorates and Mandated Territories, Report by the Secy. of State for India, para 27, 3 May 1940, WP(40)137, CP, NMML.

302. Reports for the Month of May 1940 for the Dominions, India, Burma and the Colonies, Protectorates and Mandated Territories, Report by the Secy. of State for India, para 27, 6 June 1940, WP(40)164, CP, NMML.

303. Reports for the Month of June 1940 for the Dominions, India, Burma and the Colonies, Protectorates and Mandated Territories, Report by the Secy. of State for India, para 24, 19 July 1940, WP(40)181, CP.

304. Reports for the Month of July 1940 for the Dominions, India, Burma and the Colonies, Protectorates and Mandated Territories, Report by the Secy. of State for India, para 19, 17 Aug. 1940, WP(40)186, CP.

305. Question of the manufacture of Tommy Guns and Sten Guns in Peshawar Factory, 21 January 1943, GOI, Police Branch, HD, NAI.

306. General Staff Branch Report by DCGS, 20 July 1943, GOI, Police Branch, HD, NAI.

307. From Lieutenant-Colonel G.L. Mallam, Chief Secy. to Govt. NWFP, to Addl. Secy. to the GOI, HD, 1 July 1943, GOI, Police Branch, HD, NAI.

308. Reports for the Month of May 1944 for the Dominions, India, Burma and the Colonies and Mandated Territories, Report by the Secy. of State for India, para 72, 29 June 1944, WP(44)352, CP.

309. Reports for the Month of December 1944 for the Dominions, India, Burma and the Colonies and Mandated Territories, Report by the Secy. of State for India, 31 January 1945, WP(45)74, CP.

310. Reports for the Month of January 1945 for the Dominions, India, Burma and the Colonies and Mandated Territories, Report by the Secy. of State for India, para 89, 22 February 1945, WP(45)108, CP.

3

THE SOVIET INVASION OF AFGHANISTAN
1979–88

THE PERIOD BETWEEN THE END of World War II and the beginning of the decade of the 1970s represented one of the greatest periods of stability in Afghanistan. However, by the late 1970s, the state in Afghanistan disintegrated both due to local faction politics and great power rivalry which occurred in the background of the Cold War. The USSR, which had invested much political and economic capital from the 1920s till the 1970s, was drawn into Afghanistan by the vortex of fractious Afghan power politics. The USSR also viewed the regional problem in Afghanistan through the lens of the Cold War which operated at the systemic level. This in turn heightened the paranoia of the stagnant superpower, resulting finally in the invasion. This chapter analyses the nature of unconventional warfare between the *mujahideen* and the Soviets, against the tortuous political background and state disintegration in Afghanistan.

Barnett R. Rubin's concept of 'rentier state' could be applied in case of Afghanistan during the second half of the twentieth century. Rubin writes that the state of Afghanistan developed as a buffer state between competing empires (Russian and British) and then between competing alliance systems (Soviet and American). Its rulers sought to mobilize resources from both the peoples of Afghanistan and international sources (both polities and markets). These rulers created new elites through a foreign-funded educational system in the hope that these new elites could control and transform indigenous society. The limitations of such a state became clear when regional instability and escalating tensions between the two Cold War giants resulted in the tearing apart of Afghanistan. State building with external resources occurred before domestic capitalist development. Such rentier states depended on foreign aids rather than on goods and services produced by their citizens. A rentier state like Afghanistan lacked sophisticated, differentiated apparatus capable of penetrating civil society, and a non-capitalist, non-monetized society posed hardy obstacles to state monitoring and information-gathering attempts.[1] Let us have a flashback to pre-1970 Afghanistan.

DISINTEGRATION OF THE AFGHAN STATE

The period between the end of World War II and the decade which ended in the 1960s was one of relative calm in Afghanistan. King Zahir Shah was crowned in 1933 at the tender age of 19, after the assassination of his father, Nadir Shah. Under King Zahir Shah, Afghanistan was ruled mostly by members of the royal family, especially by his cousin (later the king's brother-in-law) Prince Muhammad Daud Khan.[2] Two of Zahir Shah's paternal uncles, Muhammad Hashim Khan and Shah Muhammad Khan, served as prime ministers from 1933 to 1946 and from 1946 to 1953, respectively.[3]

In 1953, Lieutenant General Muhammad Daud Khan assumed the office of prime minister and undertook the task to modernize Afghanistan. He remained in office till 1963. Daud also developed ties with the USSR. In 1956, an accord was signed by which the Soviets undertook to equip and train the Afghan army. In 1961, Afghanistan was sending large numbers of cadets and officers to the USSR. And by 1963, many Soviet officers functioned as military instructors in Afghanistan.[4]

Rubin writes that during the half century before the end of the Cold War, decolonization increased the bargaining leverage of Afghanistan's rulers. Due to competition between two blocs, they had access to resources from foreign backers. Rubin notes: 'Such locational rents largely financed the expansion of the state apparatus in Afghanistan after 1955.[5] External resources strengthened the state's capacity to exercise despotic power (arbitrary coercion). But the state lacked infrastructural power. The latter meant the capacity of the state to penetrate civil society and to implement logistically political decisions throughout the realm. Infrastructural power required institutions for monitoring and surveillance more than coercion. Such capacities emerged out of state–society struggle over extraction and compliance in which organized groups in the civil society allowed the state access to resources, including information, in return for citizenship rights and social services. These sorts of bargains legitimized the state. Such developments did not occur in Afghanistan, but due to foreign funding, the state's rulers acquired technical capabilities in certain areas. Money, weapons, and military training from foreign backers allowed the Afghan state to become overdeveloped and autonomous with respect to society. So, arms were acquired without industrialization, revenue without capital accumulation and without any bargaining between the rulers and the ruled. This development to an extent also occurred in Pakistan which had access to US military aid as a 'frontline' state during and after the Cold War. The Musahiban rulers (Nadir Shah, Zahir Shah, and Daud Khan) of Afghanistan tried to create an export economy based on fruits and karakul lambskins. But the resource generated from such items was insignificant for the state-building enterprise to succeed. However, aid from the foreign states during the Cold War enabled the Afghan rulers to build an army, schools, roads, and so on, without confronting directly the power holders.[6] In 1961, the first girls' school was opened in Mazar-i-Sharif. It was known as Rabiah-I Balkhi Lycee. Actually, King Amanullah had opened a school for females at Kabul in the 1920s which, to an extent, contributed to his downfall.[7] The conservatives in the countryside under the leadership of the *mullahs* were alienated and rebelled against the modernizing government.

By 1953, in Afghanistan, taxes on land and livestock represented only 14 per cent of the government's domestic revenue and 39 per cent came from taxes on foreign trade. Overall, in that year, only seven per cent of the state's expenditure was funded by foreign aid, with 93 per cent funded from the domestic revenue. But by 1963, foreign aid funded 49 per cent of the state expenditure and domestic revenue covered 38 per cent of it only. The balance came from domestic borrowing.[8] The Soviets were interested in the natural gas from the Shibargham field in province of Jowzjan and constructed a 60-mile pipeline to the USSR's border in 1967.[9] Between 1955 and 1978, the USSR provided Afghanistan with $1.27 billion in economic aid and about $1.25 billion in military aid, while the USA during the same period offered $533 million in economic aid.[10] Before 1978, about 80 per cent of the Afghans lived in the villages. Agriculture remained the primary economic activity followed by animal husbandry.[11] In the 1970s, life expectancy was less than 40 years. Only half of the children survived beyond their fifth birthday.[12] The state elite became Westernized and established a patrimonial patronage network which radiated from Kabul. The elites' ties to the society were based on the largess (acquired from foreign donors) distributed by them.[13]

The Communist party in Afghanistan (People's Democratic Party of Afghanistan, i.e., PDPA) comprised two factions—Khalq and Parcham. The Parcham (Banner Wing), which was the moderate faction, had the support of the urban intellectuals, Tajiks, and the Uzbeks, and was led by Babrak Karmal (1929–96). Karmal was a Pashtun and son of an army general. He studied law at Kabul University and became a lawyer. He was a founder member of the PDPA, which came into existence on 1 January 1965. Later, he became a member of the parliament. The Parchams were gradualists. In 1978, only 11.7 per cent of the Afghan masses lived in the urban areas. The Khalq (masses), the more radical faction, drew support from the countryside and the Pashtun tribes. Its leaders were Nur Muhammad Taraki (1917–79) and Hafizullah Amin (1929–79). Amin studied at Kabul University and later at Columbia University in the USA. Taraki learnt English while working as a clerk in Bombay/Mumbai; later, he studied political economy at Kabul University and then became a journalist, and finally, a politician.[14] The PDPA received funding from the KGB (Committee for State Security) and maintained close ties with the Kremlin.[15]

In 1972, Afghanistan was struck by a famine and the state's response was inadequate. In July 1973, Zahir Shah's monarchy was overthrown by a palace coup initiated by the former prime minister, Muhammad Daud.[16] Feuds within the ruling elite and Daud's overweening ambition were the important factors behind the coup. Daud was aided by a group of rebellious Soviet-trained military officers with ties to the GRU (Main Intelligence Directorate, i.e., the Soviet Military Intelligence Agency). Daud viewed them as disposable allies to be discarded when convenient. Daud was a militant nationalist who believed that the king had betrayed Afghan interests by agreeing to a treaty giving Iran extensive access to the waters of the Helmand River, especially during a period of draught in Afghanistan. Further, the Pashtuns of Afghanistan were also angry over the king's failure to retaliate against Islamabad for its repression of the Pashtun and the Baluchi ethnic minorities in Pakistan.[17] Since the Afghan state was not dependent for resources on domestic production organized by the property-owning classes under its rule, the state officials sought autonomy in their own interests. This autonomy became partly predatory. The officials organized collectively with the aid of military officers and captured power to initiate a revolution from above. The objective of such revolution was to restructure society in order to usher in modernity. Such revolutionaries attempted to legitimize their action by emphasizing the ideology of progress.[18] In Rubin's words, 'Unlike the revolutionaries of France, Russia, or China, however, their structure of opportunities—like that of the rulers—permitted them to seek support from sources in the international system, not only from the discontented in their own society. A rentier state produced rentier revolutionaries.'[19]

On the surface, everything appeared normal after this bloodless coup. In the words of one Afghan civilian (later turned *jihadi*): 'This was still a time of law and order when you could travel freely around the country. Murder was unheard of.'[20] However, this coup was the first step in the breakdown of the state in Afghanistan. Till that date, the Afghan monarchy represented the focus of legitimate loyalties over and above clan and tribal loyalties. Now, as the symbol of that loyalty vanished, divided loyalties engulfed the state's civilian and military bureaucrats. Initially, Daud included some members from the Parcham faction of the PDPA in his cabinet. However, with time, Daud tried to distance himself from the Parcham faction, and purged several Parcham ministers in 1976.[21] In the 1970s, the Iranian monarch Reza Shah's son wanted to link the Iranian and Pakistani rail systems. It was planned that the three Persian cities—Herat, Kandahar, and Kabul—were to be interconnected to this new Trans-Persian Railway. For this purpose, the Shah offered President Daud a $2 billion credit. If completed, the Shah's new railway system would have redirected the flow of Afghanistan's trade away from the Soviet border towards the Middle East. It might have resulted in the rise of Tehran–Kabul–Istanbul alliance. This new lateral axis would soon have connected to China which was then completing the 1,200-km-long Karakoram Highway across the Himalayas from Kasghar to Islamabad. Milan Hauner speculates that Moscow took a dim view of such developments.[22] Daud's attempt to establish good relationship with the Western countries resulted in Leonid Brezhnev turning against him.[23] On 12 April 1977, during a state visit to the USSR, Brezhnev demanded the removal of experts of the NATO countries from north Afghanistan. Daud, a nationalist, retorted that he will never tolerate Soviet interference in the internal affairs of Afghanistan.[24]

The Communists also infiltrated the Afghan army. In 1974, one Colonel Abdul Kadir, who had played a significant role in replacing the king in 1973 and a supporter of the Khalq, set up a secret United Front of Afghan Communists within the army. So, some elements of the army were loyal to the Khalq faction. Due to constant Soviet pressure, the two factions of the PDPA agreed to unite. In July 1977, the two factions met at Jalalabad. They elected a new Central Committee and a Politburo. Taraki was appointed as general secretary and Karmal as his deputy. However, Amin's candidacy was contested. Amin's opponents claimed that he was a CIA stooge. Amin argued that when he was studying in the USA, he was short of money and he merely played the CIA along.[25]

On 27 April 1978, a small leftist group of Soviet-trained Afghan officers seized control of the government and founded the Democratic Republic of Afghanistan (DRA), which became a client state of the USSR.[26] The rebel Afghan officers belonged to the PDPA and they called the military coup as the Saur/Sawr (April) Revolution.[27] The role of the USSR in instigating this coup remains ambiguous. At that time in Afghanistan, 85 per cent of the populace was peasants or nomads, and agriculture accounted for 60 per cent of production. Most of the agricultural land was divided into small holdings. The peasants paid no taxes and the state paid its soldiers and bureaucrats with revenue generated from foreign aid, sales of natural gas, and taxes on some export commodities.[28]

According to one version, the planning for coup started as early as 1975. At that time, the Parcham faction had considerable influence over the republican government. Amin's task was to recruit the army and air force officers who would mobilize units to seize the centres of communications in order to paralyse the Daud government. Then, its leaders would be removed by a surgical strike before the loyal elements of the regime could rally and attempt a strike back. The immediate factor behind the Khalq-Parcham coup was Abdul Qadir Nuristani's (Daud's Minister of the Interior) crackdown on the left-wing radicals which led to the assassination of Mir Akbar Khyber, an important leader of the Parcham faction on 17 April. Khyber's death started a chain reaction, which the Daud government was unable to contain. The two Marxist factions jointly mounted demonstrations in the streets, mourning Khyber, and defying the government. At times, the number of demonstrators exceeded 10,000 people. The government responded by arresting more Marxist leaders. Taraki was arrested in the night of 25–26 April. On 26 April, Amin was arrested.[29]

On the morning of 27 April 1978, the rebel 4th Armoured Division started to move towards Kabul from its Puli Charki base located south of the city. It was led by Colonel Muhammad Aslam Watanjar. Once the armoured division had moved inside Kabul, it aided the Air Force Colonel Abdul Kadir to seize the airport. Kadir then flew a helicopter to Begram, 40 miles north of Kabul, to take over the air headquarters there. Once in command, Kadir ordered air strikes on the president's palace. Meanwhile, Watanjar's force, joined by rebel infantry units, strengthened rebel control over Kabul. Throughout the day, scattered actions occurred between the loyal and rebel forces, as the rebels took over the communications, foreign affairs, and the interior ministries. General Ghulam Haidar Rasuli, the army chief of staff, attempted to rally the loyal units from the palace. He found out that most of the units and their commanders were sitting on the fence to find out who would win in the end. Detachments from the loyal Rishkhor division moved into Kabul from the south and engaged the rebels. In the early afternoon, the MIGs from Begram Air Base made their rounds at the palace. The presidential guards, who were fighting courageously against the rebels, found that bombs and rocket strikes were too much for them. Earlier in the day, Daud had ordered the loyal air units at Shindand Air Base (500 miles west of Kabul) to aid him. They arrived early in the afternoon. When they came they had only ten minutes of flying time before they had to return to Shindand. They could not establish radio command with Daud's government, and hence, could not identify the rebel units. Thus, they had to return without dropping a single bomb. In late afternoon, the tanks broke into the president's palace and the presidential guards fled. It is not clear whether Daud died in a gun battle or committed suicide.[30]

The Khalq regime lasted from 27 April 1978 to 27 December 1979. The USSR favoured the Parcham faction over the Khalq. The expulsion of Karmal and other Parcham leaders from the cabinet and their banishment abroad enabled Taraki and Amin to consolidate their hold over power by late 1978. From that point of time, the Khalq initiated several reform programmes, which increased popular opposition. When popular resistance against the Khalq increased, the USSR felt the future of Marxism in Afghanistan and its own influence were gravely threatened. This was the principal factor behind the Soviet invasion on 27 December 1979 and the subsequent execution of Hafizullah Amin, the principal leader of the Khalq by Soviet Special Forces.[31]

Besides the objective of putting a puppet government in Kabul, the Soviet invasion of Afghanistan probably was also driven by the desire to get closer to a warm water port and within a striking distance of the Persian Gulf. The Soviets expanded and fortified the airbase at Shindand in south-west Afghanistan which put the Soviet bombers within close range of the Persian Gulf. Further, the aim was to encircle China and to prevent a hostile Afghanistan from allying itself with China and the USA in order to encircle the USSR completely.[32]

Diego Cordovez and Selig S. Harrison claim that Soviet objectives in Afghanistan were 'limited' from the start. Moscow did not have any master plan to dominate the Middle East or the Persian Gulf. Rather, the Soviets invaded Afghanistan in order to prevent the emergence in their eyes of an American-supported 'Afghan Tito' on their southern flank.[33] Selig S. Harrison continues that the timing of the 1978 Revolution was decided not by Moscow but by the local Communist leaders. The Afghan Communists who emerged in control of the new regime were not the trusted Afghan protégés of the KGB. And Leonid Brezhnev viewed Amin as a potential Tito who was plotting with the USA, Pakistan, and China to establish an anti-Soviet regime.[34] In fact, the Afghan Communist leader Babrak Karmal fed Soviet fear of American links of his rival Hafizullah Amin.[35] Further, the Soviet leaders were worried about the possible spread of Islamist influence from Afghanistan into their Muslim republics in Central Asia and Caucasus.[36] The rising number of Muslim population made the Soviet ruling elite nervous. The Soviet census of 1979 counted 43.7 million

Muslims, which amounted to 16.7 per cent of the total population. Of the Muslims, the various groups were Uzbeks (12.5 million), Kazakhs (6.5 million), Tatars (6.3 million), Tajiks (3 million), and Kirghiz and Turkmen (about 2 million each), and so on. It was estimated that by 2000, the Muslims in the USSR would have numbered between 65 and 80 million. In contrast, the slower growth rate of the Slavic population meant that by 2000, they would have numbered between 190 to 195 million. So, between 1979 and 2000, the Slavic share of the total Soviet population would have declined from 72 per cent to 65 per cent and that of the Russians from 52.4 per cent to 46.7 per cent. According to one calculation, if the Soviet Union survived in the twenty-first century, then by 2050, the Muslims would have achieved demographic parity with the Russians.[37]

Initially, the Soviets were anxious that invasion of Afghanistan would stand in the way of East–West détente. However, opposition to SALT II agreements in the US Senate hardened Soviet stance towards Afghanistan. The NATO's announcement that strategic arms deployed in West Europe would be further increased was the last straw. The growing rapprochement between Washington and Beijing made Kremlin more uncomfortable.[38]

The decision to move into Afghanistan was taken in a secret meeting convened by General Secretary Leonid Brezhnev (who had come to power in 1964) on 12 December 1979. The meeting was attended by Chief Party ideologue Mikhail Suslov, KGB Chairman Yuri Andropov, Foreign Minister Andrei Gromyko, and Defence Minister Ustinov. Most of the decisions in the USSR at that time were taken by a triumvirate comprising Andropov, Gromyko, and Ustinov. In the above-mentioned meeting, Andropov criticized Amin's mass repression and feared that Amin was moving closer to the 'West'.[39]

Some 85,000 Soviet troops participated in the invasion.[40] About 75 per cent of the Soviet armed forces' personnel were conscripts who served between two to three years. Annually, some 37.7 per cent of the Soviet military manpower had to be replenished by new 18-year-old conscripts. The Soviet officer corps was dominated by the Russians who constituted 80 per cent of the officers.[41] According to Edgar O'Ballance, just before the invasion, the Soviet army, in the units destined to move into Afghanistan, replaced most of the Muslim soldiers with Slavic conscripts in order to prevent any empathy between the Muslim

Soviet soldiers and their religious compatriots in Afghanistan.[42] A new battalion of paratroops and Spetsnaz troops from the Central Asian republics was formed in May 1979. It was based in Uzbekistan and was initially designed to guard the Afghan President Taraki but never used for this purpose. This battalion, named as Muslim Battalion, comprised Tajiks, Uzbeks, Turkmen, and so on, and would be used later in order to soften the impact of Soviet presence in Afghanistan.[43] On 27 December 1979, the Soviet forces started moving into Afghanistan. The invasion had begun. The initial aim of the Soviets was to replace Amin with Karmal, and to secure the major cities like Kabul, Herat, Kandahar, and Jalalabad, as well as the LOCs with the USSR (especially the Salang Tunnel).[44] Gradually, the Soviets were drawn into military operations against the Afghan rebels.

Meanwhile, the new government installed by the Soviets after the execution of Amin failed to stand on its own legs. Karmal under Soviet pressure was forced to accept several leaders of the Khalq faction as his colleagues in the new government. Asadullah Sarwari, who had served as Taraki's Secret Police Chief, was installed as deputy prime minister. Muhammad Ismail Danish, the minister of mines, had served in Amin's final cabinet. Khalqi Sayyid Muhammad Gulbazoi, was installed as minister of interior. Major General Abdul Kadir became a member of the Revolutionary Council's Presidium. And Colonel Muhammad Aslam Watanjar served in the Revolutionary Council Presidium's Committee, and was the minister of communications as well. Another member of Karmal's Cabinet, Colonel Sherjan Mazduryar, the minister of transport, fell out with Amin in September 1979.[45]

SOVIET COIN IN AFGHANISTAN

The Soviets faced opposition from the dispersed groups of mujahideen, who conducted a classic guerrilla war tinged with Islamic flavour. In 1979, the population of Afghanistan was about 13.05 million, including about 800,000 nomads.[46] In the 1980s, one scholar noted that there were fifty-five ethnic groups in Afghanistan. Pushtuns/Pasthuns (Pathans) comprised the largest single ethnic group followed by the Tajiks, Uzbeks, and the Hazaras. The Pasthuns numbered to about 6 million and inhabited mostly south-eastern and south-central Afghanistan.

The Tajiks numbered to about $3^{1/2}$ million.[47] Overall, there are hundreds of tribes belonging to more than a dozen ethnic groups in Afghanistan and in the neighbouring areas of Iran and Pakistan. Most of these tribes are loosely organized. In some cases, the power of the tribal chiefs is more or less dominant. While some of the tribes have a few thousand members, others might have several hundred thousand members. Some of the tribes are nomadic and some are settled.[48]

According to a CIA document dated 23 September 1980:

> Those who cling most closely to the traditional tribal ways are the least likely to be influenced by Communism. To the extent that the tribesmen have an ideology it is a belief that a combination of Islam and even older tribal traditions is the proper guide for action. Among most tribes, the traditional views include such things as the obligation to seek revenge, masculine superiority, an emphasis on personal bravery and honour and suspicion of outsiders. Tradition also tends to sanctify everything from rules governing property ownership to ways of treating illness. Any change in the traditional way of life is considered wrong, and modern ideas—whether Communist or Western—are seen as a threat.[49]

A secret CIA report dated 23 September 1980 noted that the insurgency was strongest in the most traditionally minded Pashtuns of province of Paktia and in Nuristan, and also among the Tajiks further north. They resisted the Afghan Marxists and the Soviets in order to preserve their old ways rather than fight Communism. Some of the reforms which had incensed the tribes are education of women, and so on. Such reforms were opposed to the worldview of the Afghans. Many tribes assisted the insurgents because gun smuggling boosted their income.[50]

In recent times, many modern scholars have argued that the so-called *Pashtunwali/Pushtunwali* code is merely a construction of the Orientalist scholars. One scholar named Thomas Ruttig writes:

> Although Pashtunwali is often described in its ideal form and as static, it actually evolves and differs in time and space.... With its core principles of 'honor' and 'courage' (*nang* and *tora*), 'hospitality' (*melmastia*), 'seeking shelter by submission' and revenge (*nenawata* and *badal*), 'a moratorium on a conflict and the deposit to guarantee it' (*tiga* and *baramta*), its tribal institutions like 'the tribal leader and the village elder' (*khan* and the *malek*), the tribal assembly and its reinforcement institution (*jirga* and the *arbakai*), as well as the Pashtuns' notorious fragmentation, embodied in the principle

taburwali (the enmity between 'cousins'), Pashtunwali is a complicated—and unwritten—system.[51]

Ruttig goes on to write that there is actually nothing unique about the Pashtuns. What has been written about the Pashtuns applies to the Somalis as well. Ruttig continues that the place of a tribe and a sub-tribe always fluctuate in the so-called Pashtun genealogical tree. Sometimes, a whole tribe disappears. There are no eternal unchanging tribal institutions. Versions of Pashtunwali differ by locale. What has been written about the Pashtuns' Pashtunwali is mostly hoax, myths about an idealized golden past frozen in time.[52]

Pashtunwali/Pushtunwali is not totally a construction. Masood Farivar, a mujahideen who was born in 1969 at Sheberghan in north Afghanistan,[53] writes in his autobiography: 'People lived their lives according to the guiding principles of Pashtunwali—the way of the Pashtun. Its main tenets required showing hospitality to all, providing shelter for those in need, and retaliating against those who have wronged you. Pashtunwali made no distinction between rich and poor, landlord and peasant.'[54] Learned scholars trained in the Western academician might consider the Pashtuns' concept of Pashtunwali and jihad as hoary myths. But for the jihadis themselves, the concept of jihad, interrelated with the Pashtunwali, was not a false consciousness or purely instrumental. As a young Afghan, who turned into a jihadi, writes in his autobiography:

> Jihad was being waged first and foremost in defence of our *namoos*—our women, our honour. Namoos is what defines every male Afghan. The worst insult he can suffer is *beenamoos*—a man whose womenfolk have been violated. Back in Sheberghan, shortly after the Soviet invasion, I'd overheard my father recite to a relative the famous Afghan motto about the three most important things to every Afghan man's honour: women, land, and gold (in Farsi, they all start with the letter z—*zan, zameen,* and *zar*). The easiest way to provoke an Afghan is to violate one of the z's, he said, and the Russians had violated all three.[55]

The Islamic doctrines of jihad and *shahadah* motivated the insurgents. In Neamatollah Nojumi's view, jihad gave the mujahideen a moral duty to defend their home and family against the Godless Soviets. And shahadah encouraged one to sacrifice his life for establishing safety and peace of the *qaum* (Islamic community). The concept of *ghazi/gazi* gave the commanders of the resistance group high moral superiority to exercise political and military leadership. If the ghazi died, his death glorified his victory. Frequently, the locals cheered the mujahideen as *ghazian*.[56]

After the 27 April 1978 coup which brought the Communists to power in Afghanistan, Afghan resistance groups started sprouting up along the Afghanistan–Pakistan border. And the Jimmy Carter administration made Pakistan partially a US base of operation for supporting the Islamic guerrillas who were fighting the Soviets.[57] In June 1981, the resistance groups united to form the Islamic Unity of Afghan Mujahideen (IUAM). In August 1981, the latter group split into the Group of Seven (IUAM-7) and the Group of Three (IUAM-3). While IUAM-7 was a union of fundamentalist organizations, IUAM-3 was a union of traditionalist organizations. In May 1985, both the IUAM-7 and IUAM-3 joined as the Peshawar Seven. It comprised *Hizb-i-Islami* Gulbuddin (HIH/Islamic Party), *Jamat-i-Islami* (JIA/also known as Islamic Society), *Harakat-i-Inqilabi-i-Islami* (Islamic Revolutionary Movement, IRMA), *Ettihad-i-Islami* (Islamic Union for the Liberation of Afghanistan, IUA), *Hizb-i-Islami Khalis* (Islamic Party, HIK), *Mahaz-i-Milli Islami* (National Islamic Front of Afghanistan, NIFA), and *Jeb-i-Nejat-i-Melli* Afghanistan (Afghanistan National Liberation Front, ANLF).[58]

The HIH wanted to establish an Islamic state in Afghanistan and spread the message of Islam throughout the world. Most of its personnel were Tajiks and Pashtuns of north-east, east, central, and south-west Afghanistan. The central committee was headed by Gulbuddin Hekmatyar, a Pashtun from the Kharoti tribe. He was born in the Imam Shabi region, in the province of Kunduz in 1944, and graduated from the engineering faculty of Kabul Polytechnic Institute. The JIA comprised Tajiks, Pashtuns, Turks, and Uzbeks. This organization was powerful in Herat, and led by the Professor of Theology Burhanuddin Rabbani. He was a Tajik born in 1941, and graduated from the Kabul Theological Lycee, and then from the Theological Faculty of Kabul University. The HIK split off from the HIH in 1975. The leadership of this party comprised old mullahs and *ulemas*, who fanatically wanted to go back to the preaching and practices of medieval Islam. This party mainly comprised Pashtuns engaged in barbarous sabotages, terrorism, and so on. Its leader was Mawlawi Mohammed Yunis Khalis, a Pushtun from the Khugiani tribe. He was born in 1920 in the Wazir Kuchiyani in the province of Nangrahar. He was known among the Pashtun tribes as a poet and a religious authority. From 1963 to 1973, he led a group of mullahs called the Taliban who conducted propaganda in the mosques of Kabul.[59] This name would come back to haunt the world after 20 years.

The IUA came into existence in March 1982. It was headed by Abd Al-Rab Abdul-Rasul Sayaf, a professor of theology. He was born in 1945 in the Paghman region of Kabul province. He hailed from a poor peasant family. After graduating from the Theological Faculty of Kabul University, he attended Al-Akhzar Muslim University in Egypt in 1970. He then taught for some time at the Theological Faculty of Kabul University. He was a supporter of Gulbuddin Hekmatyar.[60]

The ANLF was founded in Pakistan in 1979. Its objective was to establish an Islamic society and observance of the principles of *Sharia* laws. The ANLF was powerful in the provinces of Kabul, Logar, Kunar, Nangrahar, Paktia, and in the eastern border areas of Afghanistan among the Pushtun pockets. Some detachments of the ANLF also fought in the provinces of Faryab, Takhar, and Kunduz. The ANLF leader was Sebghatullah Mojaddidi who was born in Kabul in 1925 in a hereditary spiritual Sunni family called the *Hazarats*. He graduated from Al-Azhar University in Cairo. The NIFA was founded in 1978 in Pakistan by *Pir* Sayid Ahmad Gailani. He was born in 1931 in a hereditary family of Hazarat of Arabian descent. His family belonged to the Qadria Sufi branch.[61]

The IRMA came into existence in 1973 in the province of Baluchistan in Pakistan. The founder was Muhammad Nabi Mohammadi born in 1920 in the province of Logar. The second-tier leadership comprised ulemas and mullahs who whipped up support in the rural regions. The IRMA had 10,000 members and about 25,000 followers. It was mostly a Pashtun organization. It was active in the provinces of Kabul, Logar, Ghazni, Paktia, and Zabol. The warriors of the IRMA's armed detachments were fanatical and comprised mostly peasants of southern Afghanistan. The total strength of all these organizations fluctuated between 40,000 to 60,000 men.[62]

Two important mujahideen leaders were Gulbuddin Hekmatyar and Ahmad Shah Masud/Massoud. While Hekmatyar was a Pashtun, Masud was a Tajik from the Panjshir Valley in the north-east of Kabul. The Soviets launched several attacks to capture Panjshir but ultimately failed. The Panjshir Valley with high ridges, narrow canyons, and winding cliffs bordering on the Hindu Kush is certainly not an ideal terrain for the Soviet conventional ground force.[63]

To a great extent, the Soviets did not win the war in Afghanistan because they fought the mujahideen with conventional doctrine and tactics suited for conducting a conventional war in central Europe against the NATO forces. In 1980, a Vietnamese delegation came to Afghanistan and advised the Soviets to use small sub-units of Special Forces supported and supplied by helicopters for conducting the war against the mujahideen. However, Marshal Sokolov rejected this recommendation.[64] Very often, Soviet COIN operations took the shape of small and medium-grade conventional operations.

The first major Soviet military operation against the mujahideen occurred in March 1980 when the guerrilla forces in the Kunar Valley were on the verge of capturing Asadabad, the capital of the province of Nangrahar, which was then under the control of the Afghan army. The Soviet 40th Army launched its attack with indiscriminate shelling of the valley which warned the guerrillas of the coming offensive. Armoured regiments moving across the valley's main roads were able to supply the Afghan army detachments. However, no attempt was made to block the withdrawal of the guerrillas and to destroy them. So, when the Soviet detachments went back, the guerrillas again resumed their operations.[65]

Major A.P. Pivovarenko describes a Soviet action in May 1980 in Bamian city and the surrounding countryside:

> ...one of our battalions was structured as a raiding detachment. The battalion was reinforced with a tank company, a self-propelled artillery battery from division artillery, the regiment's reconnaissance company, a platoon of ZSU-23-4s and a squad of sappers. The reconnaissance company carried out its first raid in the area of Ghorband during the pre dawn hours of 20–21 May and arrived at the village at daybreak.... On the following day, the entire raiding detachment finally began to move onto the city of Bamian. The detachment moved by road and fell into a mujahideen ambush, losing one BMP and one ZSU-23-4.... The detachment conducted further raids which combed outlying villages and canyons. But, again the mujahideen had successfully withdrawn and the battalion swept empty blocks and areas.[66]

The Soviet motorized columns were easily disabled in the long narrow winding roads by the Afghan insurgents who pushed boulders from mountain tops. This was a tactic which the Pathans had followed against the British and the Mughals also. Then, the blocked Soviet motorized columns were destroyed by Molotov cocktails and machine-gun fire.[67]

In Soviet doctrine, combat helicopters were regarded as ground attack systems and operated in direct support of the ground forces. The combat helicopter shared this role with SU-25 Frogfoot fixed-wing aircraft. In Soviet doctrine, the concept of vertical envelopment was considered essential for striking the enemy throughout his depth. In accordance with this concept, for specific missions, troops (known as *desanti*) were inserted far behind the enemy lines (i.e., about 50 miles behind the enemy frontline) with the help of troop carrying helicopters which in turn were protected by combat helicopters, and at times, by the fixed-wing aircraft. The desanti cooperated with forward detachments which comprised a combined arms group that included tanks, motorized rifle units, and artillery.[68]

The mujahideen closed the road from Gardez to Khost in 1981. This was the main LoC to Khost. The threat to Gardez-Khost Road was also posed by the mujahideen supply and armament complex at the caves of Zhawar. In September 1985, the DRA forces tried to seize Zhawar but failed. During February 1986, the DRA and the Soviet 40th Army launched a campaign which lasted for 57 days and resulted in the capture of Zhawar. The DRA and the Soviet forces held it for five hours, destroyed whatever they could, and then withdrew.[69] In April 1986, during the Second Battle for Zhawar, the Soviet aircraft used smart munitions against the caves. The Pakistani instructors unsuccessfully tried to bring down the Soviet aircraft with Blowpipe missiles.[70]

During the Battle of Khost fought in December 1987, 10,000 Soviet and Afghan troops, supported by bomber aircraft, helicopter-borne Spetsnaz units, and artillery, moved out from Gardez towards Khost on 27 December. Part of the Gardez-Khost Road lay through the Kanay Valley, where the twisting ravines were ideal for ambush. The heights on both sides of the road were picketed by the loyal Afghan troops (a tactic which would have won the approval of the officers of British Indian army) and helicopters flew overhead. The Afghan commandos were also deployed ahead of the column to trap any mujahideens if possible.[71]

The air base at Begram, north of Kabul, was best equipped for the operation of Soviet aircraft like MIG-23 Flogger, SU-25 Frogfoot, and MIG-29 Fulcrum.[72] Paucity of maps and reliable intelligence data resulted in only 25 per cent of the ordnance being delivered on the targets. The MIG-21 was the principal bomb hauler of the Soviet Air Force. These Mach 2 high-altitude interceptors were forced to fly low and slow to fire rockets and drop bombs on the mujahideen. Needless to say, MIG-21 was not suited for such ground attack missions. The TU-16 medium and SU-24 light bombers were used to carpet-bomb suspected guerrilla zones.[73] Such aerial tactic alienated the neutral Afghans from the Soviets. According to one author, the mujahideen's acquisition of Stinger missiles in 1986 put the Soviet Air Force in Afghanistan on a defensive posture and, to an extent, hastened Soviet withdrawal from Afghanistan in 1989.[74] Even before the advent of the Stingers, due to provision of surface to air missiles by the US to the insurgents, the Soviet Air Force from late 1982 resorted to bombing raids from higher altitudes and used heat flares as counter-measures to mislead the heat-seeking missiles fired by the insurgents.[75] In total, the USSR lost over 2,000 aircraft in Afghanistan by 1989. As a point of comparison, during the Vietnam War, the USA lost over 7,000 fixed-wing and rotary aircrafts (including fighter and attack aircrafts) from all causes over the 10-year-period. Around 50 per cent of the above-mentioned figure was combat-related losses.[76]

Neamatollah Nojumi tells us that the bulk of the mujahideen's economic resources (financial and food supply) came from the local communities, especially the rural areas.[77] From 1980 to 1985, the Soviets attempted to eliminate the mujahideen support in the countryside. The rural population provided food and shelter to the mujahideen, and the Soviets bombed the rural villages and destroyed the granaries, irrigation systems, and crops. Further, the Soviet sweeps in the countryside resulted in conscription of the young males and destruction of their herds. The result was 7 million Afghan refugees who fled to Pakistan and Iran.[78] According to another estimate, 5.5 million Afghans (one-third of Afghanistan's pre-war population) became refugees, 2 million Afghans were forced to migrate from one part of the country to another, and 1.3 million died.[79] Ivan Arreguin-Toft notes: '...the main causes of Afghanistan's high noncombatant casualty and refugee rates were due to the systematic and deliberate targeting of noncombatants and their food, water, and shelter. These attacks were intended to weaken the mujahideen by disrupting their logistical and intelligence base among the broader civilian population.'[80]

The US military aid to the mujahideen increased steadily. In 1980, it amounted to only $30 million, and in 1981, it became $50 million.[81] The rugged terrain and limited manpower of the Soviets prevented them from sealing off the routes from Pakistan through which the mujahideen got supplies of weapons. In November 1982, the US intelligence estimated that even with a surge of 50,000 troops and subsequent concentration of such numbers in a particular zone, the Soviets might only be able to temporarily pacify a particular region, but not the whole country. The US decided to provide the insurgents with more anti-tank mines, man pack mortars, radios, heavy machine guns, surface-to-air missiles, and anti-aircraft guns.[82] The Reagan administration from 1983 onwards started supporting the mujahideen seriously and systematically. Reagan's CIA Director William Casey was rabidly anti-Communist and an expert in covert warfare (he had served in the Office of Strategic Services, which was CIA's predecessor during World War II). Casey actively supported the policy of arming the mujahideen.[83]

Meanwhile, the Soviets were also growing tired of the unending Afghan War. Mikhail Gorbachev critiqued Soviet involvement in Afghanistan as a 'bleeding wound'.[84] Despite being a festering wound, the Soviet intervention in Afghanistan continued due to lack of decisive political will in Moscow. General Secretary Brezhnev became incapacitated in 1980 but did not die until 11 November 1982. He was succeeded by the ailing Yuri Andropov. He lasted for less than two years (November 1982–February 1984), and was in turn, succeeded by the sick Konstantin Chernenko in February 1984. He died in March 1985.[85] However, Andropov was ready to withdraw from Afghanistan, provided Pakistan accepted the legitimacy of the regime in Kabul. Andropov was eager to co-operate with the UN and was ready to replace Karmal with another person, and to include the non-Communists in the Kabul government. But hard-liners in both the USA and Pakistan shot down this proposal.[86] While in office, Andropov's search for a diplomatic initiative occurred simultaneously with a policy of resisting military escalation. His aim was to minimize casualties and to scale down operations while looking for a negotiated settlement. For instance, while in 1982, two major division-level offensives occurred at Panjsher Valley and in Herat; Soviet offensives in 1983 were confined to battalion and regimental-level attacks supplemented by aerial bombings of the resistance strongholds. Under Chernenko (February 1984–March 1985), Soviet military operations escalated. Six military offensives (each involved between 5,000 to 10,000 soldiers) were conducted.[87] With the accession of Gorbachev in March 1985, the political leadership got a grip on the situation. He ordered the military to get victory in Afghanistan within a year and, failing that, he would find a way out of the impasse by withdrawing from the 'hell on earth'.[88]

Between April 1985 and April 1986, there was a huge surge in the Soviet 40th Army in Afghanistan like the last flicker of a dying flame. The Soviets had some 6,000 tanks, Armoured Personnel Carrier (BTRs) and Self-Propelled Air Defence Weapon System (BMPs). The number of personnel rose from 81,000 to 108,000. Of the 108,000 soldiers, there were some 73,000 combatants. The cutting edge of the 40th Army was provided by the airborne, air assault, Spetsnaz soldiers and two motorized rifle brigades. The other motorized forces were used in security missions like guarding the lines of communication, airfields, and major cities. Overall, some 85 per cent of the Soviet soldiers were tied up in such security missions.[89] Two important communication links for the Soviets were across the Hindu Kush. The Salang Road, made possible by the Soviet construction of the Salang Tunnel in the late 1960s, ran north from Kabul to Termez in the Soviet frontier. Another route was the Shibar Road west of Kabul and was functioning from the 1930s.[90] Large numbers of Soviet soldiers were tied up in guarding the communication routes.

The Soviet failure was also due to inadequate troop density. In Vietnam, at the point of maximum surge, the USA had 500,000 troops. And in Afghanistan, which is five times the size of Vietnam, the maximum strength of Soviet troops never exceeded 104,000 soldiers.[91] The four motorized rifle divisions comprised mostly third echelon Central Asian reservists. This represented Soviet underestimation of the mujahideen combat capacity.[92] More to the point is Lester W. Grau's assertion: 'The Soviet Army was trained for large-scale, rapid tempo operations. They were not trained for the platoon leaders' war of finding and closing with small, indigenous forces which would only stand and fight when the terrain and circumstances were to their advantage.'[93] Similarly, the

American military officer turned analyst Matt M. Matthews concurs: 'One of the primary reasons the other motorized rifle forces were not used more aggressively was because of their inability to adapt to the challenges of counterinsurgency warfare.'[94] Geography also came to the aid of the mujahideen. Afghanistan is a dry and rugged land, dominated by the Hindu Kush Mountains in the east and centre, and by the plateaus and deserts of the west and south. In the mountainous country, the modern mechanized Soviet army was constrained to move along a few vulnerable winding passes, and its combat effectiveness was limited by the dust and sand of the desert.[95]

After the withdrawal, the Soviets assessed mujahideen's combat performance. The Soviets concluded that the mujahideen were influenced by the Basmachi movement. The Basmachi were resistance fighters in Central Asia who resisted the imposition of Bolshevik regime between 1918 and 1933. The Basmachis conducted hit-and-run raids and ambushes against the Red Army. The mujahideen always used surprise, knew the terrain well, and were natural scouts. The tactical strong points of the guerrillas comprised conducting night actions, ability to move rapidly and secretly through the mountains. Further, the *mujahid*s were supported by large number of agents who provided reconnaissance for them.[96] The point to be noted is that the nineteenth-century British officers also emphasized night actions and ability of the light-footed Pathan insurgents to move quickly and secretly across the mountainous terrain.

To sum up, the Soviet army, writes Pavel Baev, failed in Afghanistan because the officers thought about total victory in the physical sense and failed to grasp the political and propagandistic steps.[97] Not all was negative with the Soviets. The Communist regime's reforms aided the landless labourers who got land, and the women acquired education and better health care. But the Soviets did not use propaganda properly to win over a big chunk of the tribesmen. Further, the Soviets never played the Pasthunistan card which, in turn, would have turned the Pasthuns in Pakistan against the Punjabi governing elite of that country.[98]

At a broader level, the Soviet strategy in Afghanistan was faulty. The Soviets and their client, the PDPA government, attempted to hold the cities and destroy the mujahideen's economic resources. Not only such a strategy alienated the rural people, but also made the PDPA regime hollow. In such circumstances, the PDPA could only survive by depending on flow of aid from the USSR.[99] Ivan Arreguin-Toft asserts:

> Barbarism should have been an ideal COIN strategy because the Soviets were not vulnerable to domestic or interstate political costs associated with its prosecution. Moreover, it should have devastated the intelligence and logistical capacity of the mujahideen and to a large extent it did.... Barbarism didn't work in Afghanistan because the mujahideen were able to rely on foreign intelligence and logistical support and operated from sanctuaries in Pakistan and Iran.[100]

In a way, the mujahideen functioned as partly 'rentier guerrillas'. The insurgency flourished because the USSR failed to destroy these rentier guerrillas' main base: Pakistan.

On 5 July 1977, General Zia-ul-Haq (Chief of Army Staff Pakistan), arrested Prime Minister Z.A. Bhutto and later executed him. Zia Islamized the Pakistan army. The army officers were encouraged to join communal prayers with their troops. And the promotion boards were ordered to review the moral and religious behaviour of the officers besides assessment of their military professionalism.[101] Pakistan's dictator General Zia-ul-Haq's policy of supporting the Afghan mujahideen was designed to meet several aspects. Firstly, this move would raise Zia's legitimacy among the fundamentalist elements within Pakistan and also among the fundamentalist Muslim countries like Saudi Arabia. Secondly, fighting the Soviets would enable Zia to curry favour with the USA due to the ongoing Cold War. Thirdly, Zia was troubled with the threat posed by the USSR along Pakistan's north-western border and India (Soviet ally) along Pakistan's eastern border. By installing a friendly regime in Afghanistan, Pakistan aimed to gain strategic depth. The Zia government was afraid that a hostile Afghanistan would encourage secessionist movement among the Pathan inhabitants of Pakistan's north-west region. The Afghanistan–Pakistan border problem could be traced back to the creation of Durand Line in 1893. Pakistan accepted it but Afghanistan never accepted this line as the ultimate frontier. Afghanistan actually voted against Pakistan's admission into the United Nations in 1947.[102] In 1955, a *loya jirga* held in Kabul rejected the inclusion of Pashtun areas as part of Pakistan. Afghanistan also claimed the province of Baluchistan in Pakistan. Kabul's claim to Baluchistan was based on Ahmad Shah Durrani's control over the Khanate of Kalat.

Further, Kabul was aware that control over Baluchistan would provide the country with access to the sea. Soviet support for Pashtunization policy of Kabul before the 1970s also threatened Pakistan's security elite. As early as 1960, First Secretary of the Soviet Communist Party Nikita S. Khrushchev asserted that historically Pashtunistan had always been a part of Afghanistan.[103] In fact, Zia sold the idea to the Reagan administration that the USSR intended to grab a warm water port in the Indian Ocean by overrunning both Afghanistan and Pakistan. Further, both the Zia government and the USA were unnerved by the Shia Revolution in Iran in 1978. While the pro-US regime of the Iranian Shah disintegrated, Zia was disturbed by the unrest among the Shia minority within Pakistan. The Shia dissidents in Pakistan also received support from Tehran. Just as the USSR overreacted about the developments in Afghanistan after 1978, the USA overreacted and assumed Moscow's 'sinister' hand behind the collapse of the Reza Shah regime.[104]

In 1979, Zia selected a Pashtun named Lieutenant General Akhtar Abdur Rahman Khan as head of the ISI. The ISI's Director General Akhtar Abdul Rahman had direct access to Zia. Akhtar maintained strong ties with the CIA and the Saudis. Under Akhtar, the staff of the ISI rose from 2,000 in 1978 to 40,000 in 1988. As early as 1978, when the Marxist officers of the Afghan army overthrew the Daud government, the Afghan countryside exploded. The rural Pashtuns of Afghanistan had contact with Pakistan's religious party named Jaamat-i-Islam. Zia ordered Akhtar to arm the Pashtun guerrillas. Zia also sent Akhtar to Riyadh (capital of Saudi Arabia) to request assistance for arming and financing the mujahideen. Prince Turki bin Faisal, Intelligence Chief of Saudi Arabia, ordered General Intelligence Directorate (GID) to get in touch with the ISI. Thus, the ISI-GID alliance came into existence, which later would become a CIA-ISI-GID tripartite alliance.[105]

Muhammad Yousaf, a brigadier in the infantry branch of the Pakistan army, was ordered in 1983 to take over the Afghan Bureau of ISI. From October 1983 till August 1987, Yousaf's job was not only to train and equip the mujahideen, but also plan operations inside Afghanistan. Yousaf had a staff of 60 officers and 300 senior NCOs in order to carry out his job. Yousaf's headquarter was located on the northern outskirts of Rawalpindi about 12 km from Islamabad. While the main headquarters and the warehouses were located in Rawalpindi, there were two forward detachments at Peshawar and

Quetta, respectively. Supplies which arrived at Karachi in ships were moved at the warehouses in Quetta, and then, to the warehouses at Rawalpindi.[106] Yousaf writes in his memoirs: 'To the Mujahideen I could issue no orders.... I had to achieve operational results by cajoling and convincing, not commanding.'[107] Yousaf claimed that in the four years of his tenure, his organization had trained more than 80,000 mujahideens. The ISI drew the mujahideen recruits from the 2 million Afghan refugees who were spread in the borderland stretching from Chitral in the north to Quetta in the south. They lived in squalid mud huts or in tents.[108] In the ISI training camps along the Durand Line, the mujahid guerrillas were trained for 10 days and the better students among them were selected for three-month training course. Pakistan army's elite Special Services Group (SSG), in which Pervez Musharraf (later general-turned-dictator) had served earlier, also participated in training the Afghan guerrillas.[109] Besides the USA and Pakistan, the mujahideens were also aided by China and Iran. China especially equipped the Tajik insurgents, while Iran trained the Shia militants.[110]

In February 1982, Agha Shahi, the foreign minister of Pakistan, resigned and was succeeded by the hard-liner Sahibzada Yaqub Khan. General Yaqub Khan, after a distinguished military career, functioned as an ambassador in Washington, Paris, and Moscow (where he was stationed during the invasion). On 21 March, Yaqub was sworn in as the minister.[111] While negotiating with the UN, Yaqub's demand was that Karmal should vanish from the scene, and that would allow the Soviets to withdraw from Afghanistan with minimal bloodshed.[112] While Pakistan showed extraordinary interests in Afghanistan in order to gain strategic depth vis-à-vis India, in New Delhi's perspective, Kabul was marginal.

After 1947, Jawaharlal Nehru, independent India's first prime minister, followed a 'myopic' foreign policy. In his framework of grand strategy, there was no place for Afghanistan and Central Asia. And it proved to be a cardinal error.[113] Afghanistan would come back to haunt India with Zia's forward policy in Afghanistan during the 1980s and the rise of the Taliban in the 1990s. From the 1970s, India was acquiring 90 per cent of the weapon systems from the USSR. The USSR provided India with easy interest rate for repayment of the arms supplied and also greater time period for repayment. Further, repayment was allowed to be made in local currency or goods. On the other hand, the Western companies demanded hard currency on the basis of 'cash and carry' principle. As a tactical ploy, the Indian bureaucrats with military experts toured the Western countries for buying arms. In 1982, despite India's refusal to give basing rights to the Soviets in Vishakhapatnam Port, Moscow gave massive amount of weapons to Delhi. India had some 85 million Muslims. So, it could not afford to support the USSR totally on the issue of Afghan invasion. However, India could neither afford to alienate the USSR in order to get military aid in the near future. So, Delhi's condemnation of the Soviet invasion was muted. The Soviet invasion of Afghanistan raised Pakistan's value in USA's eyes. Pakistan received a number of F-16s and other military goods. The F-16s were capable of delivering nuclear weapons. While the US planners wanted Pakistan to deploy these weapons along the Afghanistan border against a possible Soviet threat, Islamabad deployed them along the India–Pakistan border.[114]

Gorbachev wanted a new leadership in Kabul, and in May 1986, Karmal was replaced by Dr. Najibullah, who was head of the KHAD (Afghan Government's Security Agency). Najibullah, previously a boxer, was known by the nickname of 'the Bull'.[115] On 13 November 1986, Gorbachev and the Politburo decided to withdraw from Afghanistan.[116] The UN in 1988 aided Soviet withdrawal. By February 1989, the Soviet retreat from Afghanistan was completed.[117]

SOVIET DEFEAT IN AFGHANISTAN: ASSESSMENT AND CONSEQUENCES

Did Afghanistan prove to be the Soviet Union's Vietnam? Abdulkader H. Sinno seems to imply yes. The Soviet dead and missing in Afghanistan numbered to 15,000 soldiers (13,833 killed) out of the 642,000 men, who served during the 10-year period. Of these troops, 525,000 were in the Soviet armed forces, another 90,000 were in the KGB, and 5,000 were in the Soviet Ministry of Internal Affairs (MVD). However, 415,932 soldiers were victim to disease (115,308 suffered from hepatitis and 31,080 from typhoid). Dysentery was another killer. The total number of sick and wounded numbered to 469,685 and of them 10,751 became invalids.[118] Like the American soldiers in Vietnam, the Soviet troops, by 1985, were suffering from drug and alcohol abuse.[119] One author argues that many Muslim reservists, used in non-combat roles during the invasion, fraternized with the fellow Muslims in Afghanistan.[120]

The morale of the Soviet soldiers was also shaky by 1985. At the training centres, the Soviet conscripts were told that they were going to fight the Chinese and American mercenaries. When they reached Afghanistan, they found out that they were unwelcome occupiers in a hostile land.[121] In terms of military hardware, besides the aircraft and helicopters, the Soviets lost 147 tanks, 1,314 armoured personnel carriers, 433 artillery pieces and mortars, 1,138 radio sets and command and communications vehicles, 510 engineering vehicles, and 11,369 trucks.[122] The Afghan misadventure cost the Soviets 8 billion roubles annually, which was about 10 per cent of the 1989 Soviet defence budget. And the Soviet defence budget consumed between 15 per cent to 25 per cent of the Soviet GNP. So, the Afghan policy cost the USSR somewhat between 1.5 to 2.6 per cent of its GNP.[123]

In contrast, Mark Galeotti asserts that the Afghan misadventure did not destroy the USSR. The war was a minor, ill-conceived, and uncomfortable military adventure, which resulted in a negligible drain on Soviet economy. The Afghan War was not a critical factor in the transformation of the Soviet system.[124] In fact, compared to the Afghanistan invasion in 1979, Moscow used three times the number of troops for invading Czechoslovakia in 1968. In the much easier terrain, with better road and rail networks, the USSR deployed 250,000 Soviet army personnel in Czechoslovakia.[125] Some 65,000 died annually on Soviet roads. The 60 billion roubles which the Afghan War cost in total up to 1988 (official figure) was equivalent to the amount spent in one year for subsidizing basic foodstuffs. The USSR spent 1 per cent to 2 per cent of its budget on the Afghan War. As a point of comparison, the USA spent 23 per cent (in 1969) of its defence budget for the war in South-East Asia. In 1969, the USA had 500,000 men in Vietnam, and the force–space ratio was more than 7 troops per square mile. And during the time of maximum troop concentration, the Soviets in Afghanistan had less than 150,000 soldiers and the ratio was .7 troops per square mile. The USA lost 40,000 men in Vietnam and the USSR lost only 15,000. The true cost of the war, concludes Galeotti, for the USSR was psychological and political.[126] So, as regards adverse material effects of the Afghan misadventure on the USSR, the jury is still out but nevertheless the whole 'incident' was a psychological blow for the Soviets.

Yousaf claims that after the Soviet withdrawal, the mujahideen could have achieved outright victory. But this was not so because US interest was against such a victory. In fact, it suited the interests of both the superpowers to have a chaotic stalemate in Afghanistan. Further, the accidental death of Zia also removed one of the strongest and consistent supporters of the mujahideen from the equation. On 17 August 1988, the Pakistan Air Force's Lockheed C-130 transport aircraft crashed after taking off a few miles north of Bhawalpur. Besides Zia, General Akhtar Abdul Rahman Khan, then chairman of the joint chiefs of staff committee and head of ISI until 1987, also died. Zia was on the hit list of KHAD, which was trained by the KGB. Even for the US government also, after the withdrawal of the USSR from Afghanistan, Zia was becoming a liability. After the Soviet withdrawal, the USA did not want Communist rule in Afghanistan to be replaced with an Islamic fundamentalist regime. In the US government's eyes, Zia's aim was exactly that and he attempted to create an Islamic Block stretching all the way from Middle East to Central Asia.[127] Zia reportedly told Selig S. Harrison:

> We have earned the right to have a friendly regime there.... We took risks as a frontline state, and we won't permit it to be like it was before, with Indian and Soviet influence there and claims on our territory. It will be a real Islamic state, part of a pan-Islamic revival that will one day win over the Muslims in the Soviet Union, you will see.[128]

Yousaf speculates that either the KGB or KHAD or RAW (Research and Analysis Wing, i.e., Counter-Intelligence Agency of India) through its Soviet contacts or the CIA or a small caucus within the Pakistan army with links to the CIA might have supplied the ultra sophisticated poison gas which killed the pilots of the C-130, resulting in its crash.[129] After Zia's death, a general election was held and Benazir Bhutto (daughter of prime minister Zulfiqar Ali Bhutto who was executed by Zia) became the prime minister, and the new head of ISI was Hamid Gul. They continued to support the fundamentalist mujahideen against the Soviet-backed regime in Kabul.[130] However, it could be argued that their support was not that intense as it was under Zia's regime.

After withdrawing from Afghanistan, the annual Soviet aid to its client regime, according to one estimate, was US$ 1.5 billion.[131] Iavn Arreguin-Toft writes that the mujahideen were so dependent on external aid that when the tap was turned off in 1989, they failed to defeat the Najibullah regime.[132] The American 'tap' was probably not turned off completely. According to one author, in 1991, the US aid to the mujahideen amounted to $500 million annually.[133]

The mujahideen confronted the Najibullah government's forces. The Battle of Jalalabad fought in April 1989 was a landmark event in the mujahideen's road to victory against the Soviet client government. The wounded mujahideen soldiers were taken by trucks across the Pakistan frontier for medical treatment. The logistics and liaison officers among the mujahideen were responsible for arranging several hundred Arab volunteers to fight in Afghanistan.[134] Masood Farivar, a young Afghan refugee who joined the resistance, writes in his memoirs: 'Since joining the resistance in 1987, and later working as a combat reporter, I'd meet dozens of Arab volunteers: young, naïve, and fanatically religious men drawn to the battlefields of Afghanistan by the promise of eternal life.'[135] Farivar writes:

> Young and overzealous, these Arabs were war tourists who had bought their way into our country—and most Afghans resented their presence. While we called our struggle a jihad, a holy war, we were fighting first and foremost to liberate our country. The Arabs, who saw us as lesser Muslims, were seeking heavenly rewards. The more politically minded of these fighters declared, with a fierce conviction I could never understand, that 'jihad will go on until the green flag of Islam flutters over Moscow and Washington'.... In a sense, these men symbolized what the war had morphed into by 1989. This was no longer a jihad, a war of liberation against the godless Soviets; it had degenerated into a conflict manipulated by outsiders; each with very different ambitions.[136]

In fact, the Arabs came to Afghanistan in larger numbers after the Soviet withdrawal. For them, victory in Afghanistan was the first step in a global jihad.[137]

The Soviet-backed government led by President Najibullah collapsed in 1992. The UN's plan to form a post-Najib provisional government failed. Benon V. Sevan, the UN Secretary General's personal representative in Afghanistan and Pakistan, selected Phillip Corwin to tackle the Afghan problem. Previous to his assignment in Afghanistan, Corwin was a member of the UN Secretary-General Boutros Boutros-Ghali's speech-writing unit. Corwin's duty was to assist in organizing a loya jirga which will be held outside Afghanistan, especially at Vienna. This is because better security could be provided at Vienna than in Kabul.

The Secretary General's idea was that the loya jirga should have 150 representatives acceptable to all the parties from all segments of Afghan society. The representatives should be from political parties, opposition groups, should be religious and tribal leaders, militia commanders, prominent personalities, émigrés, and so on. On 18 March 1992, Najib publicly declared that he will resign as soon as a government could be designated to replace him. The UN was negotiating with various opposition groups to nominate 15–20 names that would take over as provisional authority, once Najib resigns. The majuhideen groups' financial backer was Saudi Arabia and military backer was the USA. The USA, Saudi Arabia, and Pakistan did not want any Communist participation in the post-Najib provisional government. In order to secure Najib's resignation, the UN Secretary General had to guarantee Najib's safety.[138] Phillip Corwin writes:

> By securing Najib's resignation and then being unable to get him out of the country, the UN had contributed to, even augmented, the creation of a power vacuum in Afghanistan. Like the negotiator who tries to broker the release of hostages and then becomes a hostage himself, the UN was sucked into a power vacuum it had helped to create.[139]

About the reasons behind UN's failure in Afghanistan, Corwin writes:

> Of course, diplomacy must be backed by credible military force, and the international community did not have any military force to support its diplomatic efforts in Afghanistan during the period covered in this book.... Quite simply, the UN does not have the military capacity to intervene in major conflicts, and never will have, because the big powers will never give it that authority, which might conceivably undermine their own sovereignty.[140]

At that time, the Tajik forces were under Burhanuddin Rabbani and his military commander Ahmed Shah Masud. They were aided by the Uzbek Commander in north Afghanistan, named General Abdul Rashid Dostum.[141] Dostum was a *jang salar* (warlord). To most of the Afghans, he was known as the *Pasha* (commander). Dostum's power base was the Uzbek community who comprised 10 per cent of Afghanistan's population. The Uzbeks are the Turco-Mongols who have descended from the Golden Hordes Mongols.[142] However, in January 1992, Dostum turned against the Afghan government which previously had supplied him with arms.[143]

In the collapse of the regime of President Najibullah in April 1992, a group of Afghan army generals and militia commanders under the leadership of General Rashid Dostum played an important role. They formed a faction known as *Junbesh-i-Milli Islami* (National Islamic Movement). The units of the Afghan regular army constituted the largest chunk of the Junbesh's army of the north. In mid-1992, the regular units were the best equipped among the different armies operating in Afghanistan. Dostum inherited five divisions, several independent brigades, police, and armed units belonging to the WAD (Ministry of State Security), and a number of militias. Theoretically, Dostum had some 120,000 men under arms, and in reality, the troops numbered to 60,000 men. The regular units had a large number of armour and artillery, and a small air force spread over the seven provinces of Afghanistan.[144]

The first president of post-Najibullah Afghanistan was Sebghatullah Mojaddidi. He was the elderly leader of Jabh-i-Nejat-i-Milli. He served for two months and was succeeded by Professor Rabbani, the leader of Jamiat. He was supposed to serve for four months before handing over the post to a designated successor. However, Rabbani refused to hand over the post and the civil war in Afghanistan continued. Each of the factions had their particular views about the criteria to be used for determining the weight of various groups within the new government. Neither the factions could agree among themselves nor was there any international backer (after the failure of UN's mission) forcefully encouraging them to agree.[145]

As the international community's attention waned on Afghanistan (especially that of the USA after the retreat of the USSR from that country), the mujahideens continued their 'armed *buzkashi*'. When Hizb-i-Islami declared in 1991 its opposition to the US First Gulf War, the organization lost the financial support of most of its patrons in the Arab Gulf states. After 1992, the Hizb-i-Islami was not well funded, though it had stockpiled a lot of weaponry for probable military operations. After the capture of Shindand airport, Hizb-i-Islami proclaimed the formation of its air arm. Hekmatyar failed to pay the salaries of Shindand airport's air force officers. Hizb-i-Islami's militia officers introduced road taxation to sustain themselves. Hekmatyar soon lost the air assets to Ismail Khan, the autonomous ruler of Herat. Dostum and Masud also had considerable air assets. The Afghan government's air force officers and specialists offered their services to the highest bidders after the collapse of Najib government. In May 1992, Hizb-i-Islami launched a rocket attack on Kabul which resulted in the death of 50 people. By early June, fighting occurred between the Khomeinist Hizb-i-Wahdat front and the Sunni radicals of Ittehad in Kabul. In January 1994, the tripartite alliance of Hizb-i-Islami, Wahdat, and Junbesh was announced, and Junbesh launched an attack towards Kabul. The offensive did not result in significant success as Dostum's partners failed to support the offensive adequately and Masud had been warned beforehand. In order to avert financial difficulties, the Kabul government (or whatever was left of it) went on a printing spree. And, inflation skyrocketed. While in 1992, 1,000 Afghanis were equivalent to 1US$; in 1996, 17,800 Afghanis were equivalent to 1US$.[146]

US policy/grand strategy towards Afghanistan in particular and South Asia in general, at that time, was faulty on two aspects. First, after arming and financing the mujahideen groups, Washington DC forgot all about them when the Soviet 'Bear' retreated north of Hindu Kush. This was because the policy makers in the USA looked at the Afghan conflict through the lens of a bipolar conflict between the two Cold War warriors. Firstly, the US policy makers failed to take into account the collateral repercussions of their policy of supporting the mujahideen through Pakistan. Afghanistan's civil war became in the US eyes a sort of 'forgotten war'. Secondly, there were long-term implications of leaving the battle hardened orthodox ideologically motivated bearded mullahs with training in covert warfare and high-technology weapons. Robert Gates (CIA's Deputy Director for Intelligence under William Casey, Director of CIA in the Reagan Administration) notes:

> Years later, these fundamentalist fighters trained by the mujahideen in Afghanistan would begin to show up around the world, from the Middle East to New York City, still fighting their Holy War—only now including the United States among their enemies. Our mission was to push the Soviets out of Afghanistan. We expected post-Soviet Afghanistan to be ugly, but never considered that it would become a haven for terrorists operating worldwide.[147]

Gates wrote these words in 1996, just five years before 9/11.[148]

* * *

To sum up, Soviet intervention in Afghanistan was the product of an amalgamation of global superpower rivalry in the Cold War era with fractious regional faction politics in Afghanistan. The Soviet defeat was not inevitable. In fact, there was no outright defeat of the Soviet armed forces like the French army in Vietnam. The mujahideen won like all the successful guerrillas by holding out and not getting defeated. The clan structure of the Afghans, terrain, and lifeline from Pakistan prevented the Soviet COIN from becoming successful. Given adequate political will and military assets, the armed forces of the USSR would have been able to contain but not destroy the mujahideens. However, by the mid-1980s, the Soviet leadership found the game not worth the gamble. Hence, the Soviet withdrawal occurred under Gorbachev's leadership. But the ball for withdrawal had been set rolling albeit at a slow speed under Gorbachev's predecessor Andropov. The heavily armed mujahideen, mostly the creation of Zia and the CIA, prevented the rise of a stable Afghanistan in the post-Soviet withdrawal era. And this in turn gave rise to the Taliban and resulted in subsequent US–NATO intervention, the subject of the next chapter.

NOTES

1. Barnett R. Rubin, *The Fragmentation of Afghanistan: State Formation and Collapse in the International System* (1995; reprint, New Haven/London: Yale University Press, 2002), x, 13.

2. Gregory Feifer, *The Great Gamble: The Soviet War in Afghanistan* (2009; reprint, New York: Harper Perennial, 2010), 21.

3. William Maley, *The Afghanistan Wars* (2002; reprint, Houndmills, Basingstoke: Palgrave Macmillan, 2009), 13.

4. Robert F. Baumann, *Russian-Soviet Unconventional Wars in the Caucasus, Central Asia, and Afghanistan*, Leavenworth Papers, No. 20 (Combat Studies Institute, Fort Leavenworth, Kansas: US Army Centre of Military History, Washington D.C., 1993), 131.

5. Rubin, *The Fragmentation of Afghanistan*, 9.

6. Rubin, *The Fragmentation of Afghanistan*, 12–13, 20.

7. Masood Farivar, *Confessions of a Mullah Warrior* (London: Atlantic Books, 2009), 18.

8. Maley, *The Afghanistan Wars*, 13.

9. Edgar O'Ballance, *Afghan Wars: Battles in a Hostile Land 1839 to the Present* (2002; reprint, Oxford: Oxford University Press, 2003), 78.

10. Rubin, *The Fragmentation of Afghanistan*, 20.

11. Neamatollah Nojumi, *The Rise of the Taliban in Afghanistan: Mass Mobilization, Civil War, and the Future of the Region* (New York: Palgrave, 2002), 18.

12. Mark Galeotti, *Afghanistan: The Soviet Union's Last War* (1995; reprint, London: Frank Cass, 2001), 4.

13. Rubin, *The Fragmentation of Afghanistan*, 21.

14. Rodric Braithwaite, *Afghantsy: The Russians in Afghanistan, 1979–89* (2011; reprint, London: Profile Books, 2012), 38; Feifer, *The Great Gamble*, 21–2; O'Ballance, *Afghan Wars*, 87.

15. Feifer, *The Great Gamble*, 22.

16. Maley, *The Afghanistan Wars*, 15.

17. Selig S. Harrison, 'How the Soviet Union Stumbled into Afghanistan', in Diego Cordovez and Harrison, *Out of Afghanistan: The Inside Story of the Soviet Withdrawal* (New York/Oxford: Oxford University Press, 1995), 14.

18. Rubin, *The Fragmentation of Afghanistan*, 14.

19. Rubin, *The Fragmentation of Afghanistan*, 81.

20. Farivar, *Confessions of a Mullah Warrior*, 44.

21. Baumann, *Russian-Soviet Unconventional Wars in the Caucasus, Central Asia, and Afghanistan*, 131–2.

22. Milan Hauner, *The Soviet War in Afghanistan: Patterns of Russian Imperialism* (Lanham, Maryland: University Press of America in association with Foreign Policy Research Institute, 1991), 77.

23. David Loyn, *In Afghanistan: Two Hundred Years of British, Russian and American Occupation* (New York: Palgrave Macmillan, 2009), 138.

24. Maley, *The Afghanistan Wars*, 20.

25. Braithwaite, *Afghantsy*, 39–40.

26. Lester W. Grau (ed.), *The Bear Went over the Mountain: Soviet Combat Tactics in Afghanistan* (London: Frank Cass, 1998), xxvii.

27. Braithwaite, *Afghantsy*, 37.

28. Rubin, *The Fragmentation of Afghanistan*, 19.

29. Braithwaite, *Afghantsy*, 40.

30. Nancy Peabody Newell and Richard S. Newell, *The Struggle for Afghanistan* (Ithaca/London: Cornell University Press, 1981), 67–71.

31. Newell and Newell, *The Struggle for Afghanistan*, 66–7.

32. Abdulkader H. Sinno, *Organizations at War in Afghanistan and Beyond* (Ithaca/London: Cornell University Press, 2008), 108.

33. Diego Cordovez and Selig S. Harrison, 'Overview: Afghanistan and the End of the Cold War', in Cordovez and Harrison, *Out of Afghanistan*, 4.

34. Harrison, 'How the Soviet Union Stumbled into Afghanistan', in Cordovez and Harrison, *Out of Afghanistan*, 13.

35. Cordovez and Harrison, 'Overview: Afghanistan and the End of the Cold War', in Cordovez and Harrison, *Out of Afghanistan*, 5.

36. Sinno, *Organizations at War*, 110–11.

37. Hauner, *The Soviet War in Afghanistan*, 42, 48.

38. Newell and Newell, *Struggle for Afghanistan*, 116.

39. Feifer, *The Great Gamble*, 9–12.

40. Bruce Riedel, *Deadly Embrace: Pakistan, America, and the Future of the Global Jihad* (New Delhi: HarperCollins, 2011), 23.

41. Hauner, *The Soviet War in Afghanistan*, 43, 46.

42. O'Ballance, *Afghan Wars*, 97.

43. Feifer, *The Great Gamble*, 16–17.

44. Ivan Arreguin-Toft, *How the Weak Win Wars: A Theory of Asymmetric Conflict* (Cambridge: Cambridge University Press, 2005), 173.

45. Newell and Newell, *Struggle for Afghanistan*, 120, 122–3.

46. Maley, *The Afghanistan Wars*, 8. According to another calculation, Afghanistan's population was 15 million. Baumann, *Russian-Soviet Unconventional Wars in the Caucasus, Central Asia, and Afghanistan*, 134.

47. Maley, *The Afghanistan Wars*, 9; Baumann, *Russian-Soviet Unconventional Wars in the Caucasus, Central Asia, and Afghanistan*, 134.

48. Memorandum, The Soviets and the Tribes of South-West Asia, 23 September 1980, Georgetown University online documents. http://www.gwu.edu/~nsarchiv/NSAEBB/NSAEBB57/us1.pdf; accessed on 20 August 2011.

49. Memorandum, The Soviets and the Tribes of South-West Asia, 23 September 1980.

50. Memorandum, The Soviets and the Tribes of South-West Asia, 23 September 1980.

51. Thomas Ruttig, 'How Tribal Are the Taliban?', in Shahzad Bashir and Robert D. Crews (eds), *Under the Drones: Modern Lives in the Afghanistan-Pakistan Borderlands* (Cambridge Massachusetts/London: Harvard University Press, 2012), 104.

52. Ruttig, 'How Tribal Are the Taliban?', in Bashir and Crews (eds), *Under the Drones*, 105–7.

53. Farivar, *Confessions of a Mullah Warrior*, 7–9.

54. Farivar, *Confessions of a Mullah Warrior*, 13.

55. Farivar, *Confessions of a Mullah Warrior*, 83.

56. Nojumi, *The Rise of the Taliban in Afghanistan*, 22.

57. Strobe Talbot, *Engaging India: Diplomacy, Democracy and the Bomb* (New Delhi: Viking, 2004), 18.

58. *The Soviet-Afghan War: How a Superpower Fought and Lost*, The Russian General Staff, tr. and ed. by Lester W. Grau and Michael A. Gress (Lawrence, Kansas: University Press of Kansas, 2002), 53.

59. *The Soviet-Afghan War: How a Superpower Fought and Lost*, 53–4.

60. *The Soviet-Afghan War: How a Superpower Fought and Lost*, 54.

61. *The Soviet-Afghan War: How a Superpower Fought and Lost*, 54–5.

62. *The Soviet-Afghan War: How a Superpower Fought and Lost*, 55, 57.

63. Loyn, *In Afghanistan*, 137.

64. O'Ballance, *Afghan Wars*, 101.

65. Selig S. Harrison, 'Soviet Occupation, Afghan Resistance, and the American Response', in Cordovez and Harrison, *Out of Afghanistan*, 59.

66. Grau (ed.), *The Bear Went over the Mountain*, 11–2.

67. Arreguin-Toft, *How the Weak Win Wars*, pp. 193–4.

68. Major James F. Holcomb, 'Developments in Soviet Helicopter Tactics', in Air Commodore E.S. Williams (ed.), *Soviet Air Power: Prospects for the Future* (London: Tri-Service Press, 1990), 165, 167–71.

69. Lester W. Grau, 'The Battle for Hill 3234: Last Ditch Defence in the Mountains of Afghanistan', *Journal of Slavic Military Studies*, 24, 2 (2011): 218–19.

70. Lester W. Grau and Ali Ahmad Jalali, 'The Campaign for the Caves: The Battles for Zhawar in the Soviet-Afghan War', *Journal of Slavic Military Studies*, 14, 3 (2001): 81–3.

71. O'Ballance, *Afghan Wars*, 175.

72. Philip Towle, 'Air Power in Afghanistan', in Williams (ed.), *Soviet Air Power*, 187.

73. Mark A. O'Neill, 'Air Combat of the Periphery: The Soviet Air Force in Action during the Cold War, 1945–89', in Robin Higham, John T. Greenwood, and Von Hardesty (eds), *Russian Aviation and Air Power in the Twentieth Century* (London: Frank Cass, 1998), 230.

74. Towle, 'Air Power in Afghanistan', in Williams (ed.), *Soviet Air Power*, 184.

75. Afghan Resistance, by Gordon Negus, 5 November 1982, Directorate for Research, S-26553/DB-2C, George Washington University, online archives, accessed 20 August 2011. http://www.gwu.edu/~nsarchiv/NSAEBB/NSAEBB57/us1.pdf; accessed on 20 August 2011.

76. Richard A. Pawloski, 'Lanes, Trains and Technology', in Williams (ed.), *Soviet Air Power*, 129–30.

77. Nojumi, *The Rise of the Taliban in Afghanistan*, 18.

78. Grau and Jalali, 'The Campaign for the Caves: The Battles for Zhawar in the Soviet-Afghan War', 69–70.

79. Grau (ed.), *The Bear Went over the Mountain*, xviii.

80. Arreguin-Toft, *How the Weak Win Wars*, 183.

81. Harrison, 'Soviet Occupation, Afghan Resistance, and the American Response', in Cordovez and Harrison, *Out of Afghanistan*, 53.

82. Afghan Resistance, by Gordon Negus, 5 November 1982, Directorate for Research, S-26553/DB-2C, George Washington University, online archives, accessed on 20 August 2011.

83. Riedel, *Deadly Embrace*, 17.

84. O'Ballance, *Afghan Wars*, 177.

85. Grau (ed.), *The Bear Went over the Mountain*, xxviii.

86. Selig S. Harrison, 'Making the Russians Bleed', in Cordovez and Harrison, *Out of Afghanistan*, 91.

87. Selig S. Harrison, 'The War Escalates', in Cordovez and Harrison, *Out of Afghanistan*, 147.

88. Matt M. Matthews, 'We Have Not Learned How to Wage War There': *The Soviet Approach in Afghanistan, 1979–89*, Occasional Paper, No. 36 (Fort Leavenworth, Kansas: Combat Studies Institute Press, 2011), 45.

89. Matthews, 'We Have Not Learned How to Wage War There': *The Soviet Approach in Afghanistan, 1979–89*, 45–6.

90. Baumann, *Russian-Soviet Unconventional Wars in the Caucasus, Central Asia, and Afghanistan*, 131, 134.

91. Grau (ed.), *The Bear Went over the Mountain*, xii.

92. Arreguin-Toft, *How the Weak Win Wars*, 172.

93. Quoted from Grau (ed.), *The Bear Went over the Mountain*, xxviii.

94. Matthews, 'We Have Not Learned How to Wage War There': *The Soviet Approach in Afghanistan, 1979–89*, 46.

95. Galeotti, *Afghanistan: The Soviet Union's Last War*, 3–4.

96. Grau (ed.), *The Bear Went over the Mountain*, 197.

97. Pavel K. Baev, *The Russian Army in a Time of Troubles* (London: SAGE Publications, 1996), 22.

98. Memorandum, The Soviets and the Tribes of South-West Asia, 23 September 1980.

99. Nojumi, *The Rise of the Taliban in Afghanistan*, 19.

100. Arreguin-Toft, *How the Weak Win Wars*, 215.

101. Riedel, *Deadly Embrace*, 19–21.

102. Diego Cordovez, 'From Breakthrough to Breakdown', in Cordovez and Harrison, *Out of Afghanistan*, 124–5.

103. Amin Tarzi, 'Political Struggles over the Afghanistan-Pakistan Borderlands', in Bashir and Crews (ed.), *Under the Drones*, 22–3.

104. Riedel, *Deadly Embrace*, 17, 22.

105. Riedel, *Deadly Embrace*, 21, 23.

106. Mohammed Yousaf and Mark Adkin, *The Battle for Afghanistan: The Soviets versus the Mujahideen during the 1980s* (1992; reprint, Barnsley: Pen & Sword, 2001), 1–3, 26–8.

107. Yousaf and Adkin, *The Battle for Afghanistan*, 2–3.

108. Yousaf and Adkin, *The Battle for Afghanistan*, 4, 25.

109. Riedel, *Deadly Embrace*, 24.

110. Sinno, *Organizations at War*, 106.

111. Diego Cordovez, 'My Mission Begins', in Cordovez and Harrison, *Out of Afghanistan*, 80–1.

112. Cordovez, 'From Breakthrough to Breakdown', in Cordovez and Harrison, *Out of Afghanistan*, 132.

113. Jaswant Singh, *Defending India* (Chennai: Macmillan, 1999), 111.

114. Chris Smith, *India's Ad Hoc Arsenal: Direction or Drift in Defence Policy?* (New York: Oxford University Press in association with SIPRI, 1994), 22, 96, 107–8, 111–12.

115. Loyn, *In Afghanistan*, 155.

116. Sinno, *Organizations at War*, 109.

117. Grau (ed.), *The Bear Went over the Mountain*, xxix.

118. Grau (ed.), *The Bear Went over the Mountain*, xiv, xix.

119. Matthews, 'We Have Not Learned How to Wage War There': The Soviet Approach in Afghanistan, 1979–89, 46.

120. Hauner, *The Soviet War in Afghanistan*, 45–6.

121. Matthews, 'We Have Not Learned How to Wage War There': The Soviet Approach in Afghanistan, 1979–89, 47.

122. Grau (ed.), *The Bear Went over the Mountain*, xix.

123. Sinno, *Organizations at War*, 106.

124. Galeotti, *Afghanistan: The Soviet Union's Last War*, 2.

125. Riedel, *Deadly Embrace*, 23.

126. Galeotti, *Afghanistan: The Soviet Union's Last War*, 224–5.

127. Yousaf and Adkin, *The Battle for Afghanistan*, 6, 8, 12.

128. Quoted from Harrison, 'Making the Russians Bleed', in Cordovez and Harrison, *Out of Afghanistan*, 92.

129. Yousaf and Adkin, *The Battle for Afghanistan*, 15.

130. Loyn, *In Afghanistan*, 160.

131. Loyn, *In Afghanistan*, 164.

132. Arreguin-Toft, *How the Weak Win Wars*, 198.

133. O'Ballance, *Afghan Wars*, 225.

134. Farivar, *Confessions of a Mullah Warrior*, 1–3.

135. Farivar, *Confessions of a Mullah Warrior*, 4.

136. Farivar, *Confessions of a Mullah Warrior*, 5.

137. Farivar, *Confessions of a Mullah Warrior*, 5.

138. Phillip Corwin, *Doomed in Afghanistan: A UN Officer's Memoir of the Fall of Kabul and Najibullah's Failed Escape, 1992* (New Brunswick, New Jersey: Rutgers University Press, 2003), xv, 1–4, 8, 12.

139. Corwin, *Doomed in Afghanistan*, 13.

140. Corwin, *Doomed in Afghanistan*, 17–18.

141. Daniel Marston, 'Lessons in 21st Century Counterinsurgency: Afghanistan 2001–7', in Daniel Marston and Carter Malkasian (eds), *Counterinsurgency in Modern Warfare* (Oxford: Osprey, 2008), 221.

142. Brian Glyn Williams, 'Report from the Field: General Dostum and the Mazar-i-Sharif Campaign: New Light on the Role of Northern Alliance Warlords in Operation Enduring Freedom', *Small Wars & Insurgencies*, 21, 4 (2010): 611–12.

143. Seth G. Jones, *In the Graveyard of Empires: America's War in Afghanistan* (New York/London: Norton, 2010), 43.

144. Antonio Giustozzi, 'The Demodernization of an Army: Northern Afghanistan, 1992–2001', *Small Wars & Insurgencies*, 15, 1 (2004): 1–2.

145. Antonio Giustozzi, *Empires of Mud: Wars and Warlords in Afghanistan* (London: C. Hurst & Co., 2009), 69.

146. Giustozzi, *Empires of Mud*, 70–75.

147. As quoted from Riedel, *Deadly Embrace*, 18.

148. Riedel, *Deadly Embrace*, 18.

4

US AND NATO INTERVENTION
IN AFGHANISTAN

THE WITHDRAWAL OF THE SOVIETS resulted in bickering among the various *mujahideen* factions. Ultimately, after a lengthy and chaotic civil war, the Taliban emerged supreme. The rise of the Taliban to a great extent was the 'blow back' effect of US policy towards the mujahideen during the 1980s. The Taliban's symbiotic relationship with Al-Qaeda resulted in 9/11, which brought the world's sole superpower, the USA, into Afghanistan. History repeated itself. The USA, like the USSR and the British empire, won the conventional war but failed in the uncon-ventional war. Meanwhile, the Taliban has resurrected itself like a Phoenix rising from the ashes. And this has repercussions along the Af–Pak border. Let us have a look at the origins of the Taliban.

THE RISE OF THE TALIBAN ·

Talib is an Arabic word, and its literal meaning is 'one who is seeking something for himself.' This word is derived from the word *talab* meaning 'desire'. In Urdu, Taliban is the plural of talib. In Pushto, the word Taliban denotes the students studying in *deeni madaris* (religious institutions). The talibs go to different *alim*s (religious scholars) in order to gain religious knowledge. A talib after completing several years of studies in a deeni madari is given the title of a *mullah*. A mullah is qualified to become an *imam, qazi*, and a *mufti*.[1]

When the Soviet troops moved into Afghanistan, the military dictator of Pakistan General Zia-ul-Haq (president and dictator of Pakistan from 1977 to August 1988) established a chain of deeni madaris along the Afghanistan–Pakistan border. The objective was to create a body of religious-oriented students who would fight the Soviet troops in Afghanistan. Soon, the deeni madaris spread across Pakistan's NWFP, Baluchistan, Punjab, and Sind.[2] The establishment of these religious schools was in line with Zia's policy of Islamizing Pakistan's identity on Sunni lines, which led to the introduction of the Sunni–Hanafi–Deobandi system of jurisprudence as evident from the promulgation of Hudood Ordinances in February 1979. It was followed by the *Zakat* Ordinance in 1980. By 1984, some 9.4 per cent of the Zakat fund was used to support 2,273 *madrasas* which catered to some 111,050 students. They, along with the semi-educated unemployed youth, became the foot soldiers of the extremist sectarian outfits.[3] According to one calculation, in May 1997, in the Rawalpindi Division of Pakistan's Punjab (west Punjab of British India), there were 169 deeni madaris with 17,533 talibs registered with them. Most of these schools were used as hideouts for the Afghan terrorists/insurgents who were fighting the Soviets.[4] Most of the Taliban ulema were educated in the ex-NWFP (now Khyber Pakhtunkhwa/KP) and Baluchistan during the war with the Soviets.[5] The rank and file of the Taliban was drawn from the Afghan refugee camps in Pakistan.[6]

Though Zia to a great extent was responsible for Islamization of Pakistan's side of the Durand Line, the roots of radical Islam in this region could be traced back to the colonial era. The Dar ul Ulm Deoband madrasa was established in 1867 at Deoband in United Provinces (now Uttar Pradesh in north India) in the late nineteenth century. The founders of the Deoband were concerned with how the study of the *hadith* and the Quran should be used for reforming the Muslim faith. The roots of the Deobandi ideology can be traced back to the writings and teachings of Shaikh Ahmad Sirhindi, a Sufi of the seventeenth century. He urged reform of the Sufi practices. Sirhindi's ideas formed the basis of Mujaddidiyya *shaakh* (branch) of the Naqshbandiyya Sufi philosophy, which was developed by Shah Wali Ullah of the eighteenth century. He argued for the reintroduction of the Quran and hadith into Sufi *tariqa*. Shah Wali Ullah's teaching was taken to the Pashtun regions in the NWFP and Afghanistan in the 1820s by his grandson Shah Ismail and Sayyid Ahmed of Rai Bareilly district of Uttar Pradesh. The Deobandi curriculum abandoned the Sufi premise for the prescriptions of Sirhindi and Shah Wali Ullah, and focused entirely on imparting knowledge in relation to the hadith, Quran, and interpretative method. But the use of *bait* (pledge/oath) between *murshids* (teachers) and their students was a Sufi practice, and this tradition survived in the Deobandi institution.[7] Gradually, the Deobandis and other ulemas were drawn into religious anti-colonial/anti-imperialist politics. Early twentieth-century India was a period characterized by intense nationalist writings as well as pan-Islamic activities. The ulemas trained in Deoband School conceived a plan to liberate India from the British by mobilizing the North-West Frontier Pathan tribes. The movement was called *Jamaat-e-Mujahideen*. Some of the notable leaders were Fazl Ilahi, Fazl Rabbi, Saif Al Rahman (b. 1859–d. 1949), all of whom had studied at Dar ul Ulm Deoband. The plan was discovered in 1916 and several conspirators from the Indian side of the frontier moved into Afghanistan.[8] Maulana Abdur Rahim Poplazai, a Pakhtun from Peshawar, who had descended from a line of Sufi *pirs*, attended the meetings of the ulema in his father's mosque Qasim Ali Khan. In 1929, along with other Khilafatists, Poplazai participated in the deputation of Peshawar ulema and mullahs of the tribal areas to Afghanistan in order to try and rally support for the deposed Amir Amanullah Khan, who was a patron of the Deobandis in Afghanistan.[9] After decolonization and partition of the subcontinent in 1947, several Deobandi ulemas who were located on the Pakistani side of the border attempted to create madrasas which would provide Hanafi curriculum taught at Deoband. They called themselves and their students as Deobandis. They were the most organized ulemas in Pakistan and occupied the central position in religious politics. In 1951, Pakistan's ulemas signed a 22-point declaration, which stated that law and the constitution of the country must not contradict Islamic principles. This was ratified in the 1973 Constitution.[10]

The capture of Afghanistan by Taliban was something short of a miracle. Initially, the Taliban, led by their teachers, organized themselves as madrasa or mosque-centred networks (fronts) linked to *Harakat-i-Inqilabi-i-Islami* and *Hizb-e Islami* (*Khales*). They were known as Taliban fronts. When the Taliban found that the mujahideens violated their own religious principles by not unifying to build an Islamic state after the collapse of Najibullah regime in February 1992 but fragmented (*shirk*, referring to a deviation in Islam) and competed for power, they established their own ultra-orthodox movement. Many mujahideen commanders had stopped fighting after the collapse of Najibullah regime and went back to their madrasas for study. With the establishment of the Taliban, these ex-mujahideen commanders became principal Taliban leaders.[11]

In 1994, Rabbani and Masud encouraged the rise of the Taliban as a potential ally in the Pashtun belt against the *Hezb-i-Islami*. But when Mullah Omar refused to ally with Rabbani–Masud, the latter party declared war on the Taliban. At that time, there were three autonomous polities (Antonio Giustozzi terms them as 'emirates') rather than a single state in Afghanistan. Ismail Khan's domain centred around Herat and Dostum's *Junbesh* controlled north Afghanistan. Rabbani and Defence Minister Masud controlled Kabul and Laghman, and Logar (eastern part of the country). There was no coordination among these three polities. These three polities had their separate financial bases and military contingents.[12] During October 1994, the Taliban took Spin Buldak. In November 1994, the Taliban emerged in Kandahar. Lashkargarh was occupied in January 1995. In September 1995, the Taliban captured Herat and Ismail Khan fled to Iran.[13] In early 1996, Gulbuddin Hekmatyar, Mojaddidi, Dostum, and Karim Khalili (the leader of *Hezb-i-Wahdat*) pressurized Burhuddin Rabbani to step down. The four leaders of the anti-Rabbani group constituted the Supreme Coordination Council. Moreover, Pakistan started supporting the Taliban instead of Hekmatyar (Hezb-i-Islami/Party of Islam). From 1994 onwards till that date, Hekmatyar's main backer was Pakistan. In June 1996, Hekmatyar joined the government as the prime minister.[14] In 1996, the Taliban captured Kabul. In May 1997, Dostum's subordinate, Abdul Malik revolted and occupied Mazar-i-Sharif with the aid of the Taliban troops. During the summer of 1998, the Taliban from Herat started spreading its tentacles in the provinces of Faryab and Jowzjan. They used funds provided by Osama bin Laden to buy off the local commanders. Some 8,000 Taliban troops, supported by tanks and armoured personnel carrier (APCs), captured Dostum's headquarter, at Shiberghan in early August. Bamiyan fell in September 1998. Kunduz and Taloqan were also captured in the same year.[15] During the Taliban's July 1999 offensive, between 5,000 to 8,000 Pakistani volunteers joined the fray. Some claim that even Pakistani regular troops, dressed as volunteers, fought for the Taliban. In addition, an Arab brigade (under Osama bin Laden) also fought with the Taliban.[16]

The Taliban aimed to impose a radical Sunni Islamic Caliphate in Afghanistan. Girls were not permitted to attend schools and women were prohibited from working. Women were forced to wear *burqa*. The Taliban also enforced Islamic dress for the men. The men were forced to grow beard and avoid Western haircut. The Taliban closed the cinemas and banned music. In the shops, hotels, and vehicles, music cassettes were prohibited. In case of deviation, the shopkeeper or the vehicle driver was imprisoned. On 28 September 1996, Radio Kabul announced that thieves will have their hands and feet amputated, adulterers will be stoned to death, and those taking liquor will be lashed.[17] The Taliban's philosophy was derived from the Deobandi school of thought.[18] The Taliban's attraction towards a rigid interpretation of radical philosophy was because both the leadership and the rank and file were brutalized and psychologically scarred. The Taliban's one-eyed leader, Mullah Omar, is not merely a mujahideen commander but also a religious teacher. Being a religious teacher gives him extra advantage in negotiating with the local and tribal communities.[19] Mullah Omar is from Tarin Kot in the province of Oruzgan. Probably, he was born in the village of Nauda in 1959. He belongs to the Gilzai Pashtun Hotak group and this community was overrepresented in the Taliban government. He had four wives (Osama had three) and four children (two sons and two daughters). One daughter was killed in August 1999 in a bomb blast.[20] There is an apocryphal story that one day in the late 1989, after a clash with the Soviet forces, when Mullah Omar lost his eyes due to explosion of a rocket, at a party of poetry and singing on the same night, he himself sang *ghazals*.[21] There are conflicting accounts about Mullah Omar losing his eye in battle. According to one account, he himself removed the badly injured eye with a knife (without anesthesia) and sewed it up. Another account states that he was taken to a hospital in Peshawar, where his injured eye was surgically removed. Till 1994, Mullah Omar was an imam of a mosque in a small village in Maiwand District, west of Kandahar. In October 1994, Mullah Omar was appointed *amir* (leader) of the Taliban. In 1996, in a grand *shura* (assembly), where 1,500 religious scholars came, Mullah Omar was appointed *Amir-ul-Momin* (commander of the faithful).[22] It seems that the Taliban had several one-eyed leaders. Nuruddin Turabi, who became the justice minister, and Muhammad Ghaus, who became the foreign minister, also had lost eyes in battle. In fact, several of the Taliban leaders were battle scarred. Abdul Majid, who later became the Mayor of Kabul, lost a leg and two fingers. And Mullah Dadullah Lang, a Taliban commander (who was killed by the US forces in May 2007) lost a leg while fighting the Soviets in the 1980s.[23] Most of the Taliban's foot soldiers were orphans from the refugee camps who had never known any kind of normal life.[24]

However, the Taliban failed to control whole Afghanistan. A group of Tajik, Uzbek, and Hazara warlords known as *Shura-i-Nazar* (the West called them Northern Alliance), differed with Taliban's orthodox radical Islamic policies and controlled parts of northern Afghanistan, especially the Panjshir Valley, north of Kabul. The Northern Alliance received support from Iran, France, and Russia.[25] The Northern Alliance was mainly the product of Dostum, Ahmad Shah Masud/Massoud (the Lion of Panjshir) and the Hazaras. In 1998, Dostum fled to Turkey.[26] In 1998, Masud led the Tajiks of Shura-i-Nazar. They had about 15,000 fighters in Badakshan and the strategically vital Panjshir Valley, the gateway to Salang Tunnel. In early 1998, the Uzbek militia of *Jumbesh-i-Milli* (led by Dostum and then Malik) numbered to 65,000 personnel. In 2000, the Shia forces (Hazara Shia *Hezb-i-Wahdat*) in Balkh and Samanghan provinces numbered to only 5,000 personnel. In early 2001, the Taliban controlled 29 of the 31 provinces of Afghanistan and had about 45,000 fighters at its disposal.[27] By this time, the Taliban drew recruits from the Deobandi madrasas located between Ghazni and Kandahar. These madrasas were highly politicized and militarized.[28]

Initially, the US remained indifferent to the Taliban because Pakistan advised Washington that the Taliban would be able to establish peace and stability within Afghanistan and, in addition, would allow the American companies (especially UNICOL) to exploit the energy resources in Central Asia. However, things changed with the arrival of Osama bin Laden.[29] In 1996, the Taliban provided sanctuary to Osama Bin Laden when the latter escaped from Sudan. When Osama was held responsible for the August 1998 US Embassy bombings in Africa (Tanzania and Kenya), the Taliban refused to extradite him.

Osama was also responsible for an attack against the US Navy destroyer USS Cole in Yemen during 2000.[30] Even after 9/11, the Taliban did not hand over Osama to the USA because the Al-Qaeda financed Taliban regime, and also due to the Afghan cultural tradition of *melmastia*.[31] Tim Bird and Alex Marshall write that it was not a realistic option for Mullah Omar to hand over Osama bin Laden to the Americans because Osama commanded a core of battle-hardened warriors. Moreover, after 9/11, Osama's popularity soared and many *jihadis* volunteered to join his rank. In fact, one captured Taliban soldier later joked that it was not possible for Mullah Omar to hand over Osama but it was possible for Osama to hand over Mullah Omar to the Americans.[32]

US INTERVENTION AND THE FALL OF THE TALIBAN

'I want bin Laden's head shipped back in a box filled with dry ice. I want to be able to show bin Laden's head to the President. I promised him I would do that.... Have I made myself clear?' (Cofer Black's [Director of the CIA's Counterterrorism Center] order to the first CIA team which entered Afghanistan after 9/11.)[33]

In response to 9/11, the USA launched OEF on 7 October 2001 to crush the Al-Qaeda network in Afghanistan and also to remove the Taliban regime which was playing host to the former organization's leader Osama bin Laden.[34] Even before 2001, the CIA maintained linkages with the Northern Alliance.[35] In fact, the Clinton administration (1993–2001), took the decision to bomb Al-Qaeda training camps with long-distance weapons. On 20 August 1998, US submarines and surface ships from the Arabian Sea launched several Tomahawk cruise missiles at Al-Qaeda training camps located outside Khost. The Pakistan government was not informed earlier about the American strikes in order to prevent the information leaking out to the Taliban and Al-Qaeda through Pakistan's ISI, which had ties with the terrorist organizations.[36] Strobe Talbott, who was deputy secretary in the state department in Clinton administration, notes in his memoirs:

> Joe Ralston had the awkward assignment of making sure that he was with General Karamat (General Jahangir Karamat, Chief of Army Staff, Pakistan) during the launch of the Tomahawks. That way, if the low-flying missiles showed up on Pakistani radar screens, Joe would be able to assure Karamat

that they were not the first wave of an Indian sneak attack. Toward the end of a dinner at the VIP lounge at Islamabad airport, Ralston checked his watch and told Karamat that about 60 Tomahawks had just passed through Pakistani airspace en route to their targets in Afghanistan. Shortly after, he thanked his host for dinner, shook hands, and departed.[37]

Initially, OEF was called Operation Infinite Justice. Since, Muslims believe that only God can compel infinite justice, the name was changed to OEF. Afghanistan as the area of operation came under US CENTCOM. Afghanistan being a landlocked country, the USA had to gain over flight rights as well as control over the air bases in the neighbouring countries in order to station its troops and aircraft. And this involved lot of diplomatic activities on part of the Americans. Shia Iran, though an opponent of Hanafi Sunni Taliban-controlled Afghanistan, opposed joining a US-led coalition claiming that the war was a pretext for helping Israel and extending American military power. In late September 2001, Iran's supreme leader, Ayatollah Ali Khomeni, claimed that the USA has tampered with Iran's interest and Iran would not go along with the arrogant Americans. At the south of Afghanistan lies Pakistan, and the Afghan–Pak border is some 2,430 km long. Most of Pakistan's population in September 2001 was sympathetic to the Taliban. According to one estimate, in 1999–2000, only 22 per cent Pakistanis have a favourable image of the USA, and in 2002, this per-centage dropped to only 10 per cent. Worse, Pakistan and India have serious disagreement over the issue of Kashmir. And the high tension between Pakistan and India, seemed at that time, could boil over into a conventional conflict which might escalate into a nuclear conflagra-tion.[38] At that time, only Pakistan was maintaining diplomatic relations with the Taliban.[39] US diplomacy towards Pakistan at that moment was not subtle. President Pervez Musharraf, the general-turned-dictator, who took power by replacing Prime Minister Nawaz Sharif, notes about Colin Powell's phone call to him on 12 September 2001:

> I was chairing an important meeting at the Governor's House when my military secretary told me that the US Secretary of State, General Colin Powell, was on the phone.... Powell was quite candid: 'You are either with us or against us.' I took this as a blatant ultimatum.... I told him that we were with the United States against terrorism, having suffered from it for years, and would fight along with his country against it. We did not negoti-ate anything.[40]

Not only Colin Powell but other top decision makers of the USA also threatened the Pakistani military establishment. Musharraf was in Islamabad on 13 September. He writes:

> ...our director-general of Inter-Services Intelligence, who happened to be in Washington, told me on the phone about his meeting with the US deputy secretary of state Richard Armitage.... Armitage...told the director-general not only that we had to decide whether we were with America or with the terrorists, but that if we chose the terrorists, then we should be prepared to be bombed back to the Stone Age.[41]

According to Musharraf, he along with his generals played a war game and concluded that in case of a conflict, the Pakistani military would be completely annihilated. On 13 September, US Ambassador to Pakistan, Wendy Chamberlain, demanded several concessions on part of Pakistan. These concessions included interdiction of all logistical supplies to Al-Qaeda and Taliban, allowing US blanket over flight and landing rights in order to conduct military and intelligence activities, public condemnation of 9/11, sharing of all intelligence activities with the USA, and cooperating with the USA in order to destroy the Taliban and Al-Qaeda. It must be noted that the relationship between Taliban and their handlers in ISI was never smooth. Mullah Omar was invited several times in Pakistan but he never came. Nor Mullah Omar allowed extensive contact between his field commanders and the ISI.[42]

Due to American pressure, on 13 September 2001, Musharraf announced that Pakistan would cooperate completely with the USA. America acquired the rights to use the bases near the Pakistani cities of Pasni, Dalbandin, and Jacobabad. These Pakistani bases became forward operating bases of the Americans. However, the Shahbaz Air Base in Jacobabad is too far away for the aircraft from European airfields. Hence, the USA and the Coalition required airfields in Central Asia.[43]

The states on the north of Afghanistan are Turkmenistan, Uzbekistan, Tajikistan, and Kyrgyzstan. They are actually ex-Soviet republics in which Russian influence is declining slowly but steadily. The Russian President Vladimir Putin asked these Central Asian polities to cooperate with the USA in its war against terror. This is probably because Russia is also feeling the pinch of pan-Islamic terrorism in Chechnya. Uzbekistan's border with Afghanistan is 137 km long but is very close to Mazar-i-Sharif and other Northern Alliance strongholds.

The airfields in Uzbekistan are necessary for providing logistical support to the Northern Alliance troops. The US Secretary of Defence Donald Rumsfield met with President Islam Karimov and secured the use of Uzbekistan's ex-Soviet air base Karshi-Khanabad (i.e., K2). The USA pledged military and financial support in return for basing rights. From $24.8 million in 2001, the general aid to Uzbekistan rose to $3 billion in 2002. Another reason for Uzbekistan cooperating with the USA is the fact that the former is also facing threat from the Islamic Movement of Uzbekistan, an insurgency supported by the Taliban and the Al-Qaeda. Tajikistan offered the use of three air bases and in December 2001, Kyrgyzstan offered the use of Manas Airport which became the principal logistical hub of the Coalition force.[44]

On 26 September 2001, a helicopter from Dushanbe in Tajikistan deposited the first seven-man CIA team into the Panjshir Valley in north-east Afghanistan. This team, codenamed JAWBREAKER, was led by the 59-year-old CIA veteran Gary Schroen. The team brought with it communication equipments and cash worth $3 million. In the next 40 days, Schroen spent $5 million in buying the local warlords in order to establish an anti-Taliban alliance. Schroen met Arif Sarwari, the head of Intelligence Operation of the dead Northern Alliance leader, Ahmad Shah Masud. Schroen also met General Muhammad Fahim, the Tajik leader who had succeeded Masud and Dr Abdullah Abdullah, foreign minister of the Northern Alliance. Fahim was paid $1 million.[45] Meanwhile, the Northern Alliance was rejuvenated with the return of Dostum from Turkey in April 2001. His enclave was the Dar-Y-Suf (River of Caves) Valley in the Hindu Kush Mountains. There Dostum rallied 2,000 Uzbek *cheriks* (horse-mounted guerrillas) and started a hit-and-run expedition against the Taliban.[46] The second JAWBREAKER Team known as Team Alpha was inserted on 16 October in order to establish contact with Dostum. This team found that near Mazar-i-Sharif, three Northern Alliance commanders were conducting operation. One was General Muhammad Atta (a Tajik), another was General Mohaqqeq (a Hazara), and of course, Dostum.[47]

One of the characteristics of this campaign was that a few Special Operation Force (SOF) personnel worked with the anti-Taliban Afghan forces to topple the Taliban government. In Lieutenant Colonel Craig D. Wills' view, the Afghan model of warfare comprises a combination of SOFs, Afghan auxiliary forces, and airpower. This combination was initially designed to prepare the battlefield for decisive operation by the conventional ground force. However, allied Afghan auxiliary force (15,000 Afghan Northern Alliance troops) supported by US airpower was able to lay siege to Kabul within five weeks after the start of the campaign and before the induction of a significant number of US ground troops. In fact, the US-led Coalition installed a friendly regime at Kabul within two months after the beginning of the conflict. On 19 October 2001, Rumsfield announced that US troops would provide direct assistance to the Northern Alliance. On 21 October, the SOF teams called in their first air strikes in support of the Northern Alliance towards Mazar-i-Sharif. Portable laser designators enabled SOF teams to direct the laser-guided weapons dropped from aircraft overhead. And the GPS-enhanced overland navigation allowed the SOF teams to pass precise targeting data to the orbiting aircraft.[48] In late November 2001, the 10th Mountain Division headquarters were deployed in Begram to take charge of all the military operations in Afghanistan. The 10th Mountain reported to the theatre land component headquarter, stationed in Uzbekistan, and the latter reported to General Franks in Tampa, Florida.[49]

When OEF unfolded, the Taliban disposed of somewhere between 40,000 to 60,000 personnel. And, of them, between 20 per cent to 25 per cent were foreigners (Al-Qaeda personnel and recently arrived volunteer jihadis). The Northern Alliance disposed of some 20,000 troops led by different commanders. The troops were tied to their commanders by personal and kinship bonds rather than any overarching ideology. A series of battles occurred at Mazar-i-Sharif and the principal confrontation occurred on 5 November 2001. The Taliban personnel dug into fortified defensive positions and waited the attack of Dostum's troops. The US Special Forces Team with the Northern Alliance identified the Taliban's positions and called for air support. The MC 130 aircraft dropped two BLU 82 bombs. These 15,000-pound daisy cutter bombs obliterated the Taliban's positions. Dostum then led a cavalry charge against the disoriented Taliban troops. Mazar-i-Sharif fell on 10 November. Bamiyan fell to Northern Alliance on 11 November.[50] On 13 November 2001, the Taliban lost Kabul.[51] General Fahim immediately occupied the city, and on the same day, Ismail Khan's troops occupied Herat. Dostum, Daud, and Baryalai Khan laid siege to Kunduz. Several Pakistani officers and ISI personnel were also trapped along with the Taliban and Al-Qaeda troops in this city. An agreement between the Pakistani and US governments allowed Pakistan to evacuate its personnel in two aircrafts on 23 November. It is probable that some senior Taliban and Al-Qaeda leaders also escaped in these planes.[52] On 26 November, about 5,000 Taliban and Al-Qaeda personnel surrendered at Kunduz. On 9/10 December 2001, the Taliban withdrew from Kandahar. This marked the end of the Taliban regime in Afghanistan.[53] Mullah Omar was last seen as escaping in a Honda motorcycle during the first week of December 2001.[54]

One of the principal objectives of the USA in this war was to capture and eliminate the top leadership of Al-Qaeda and the Taliban. Early in the war, a Ranger team was parachuted into Mullah Omar's compound in Kandahar. And units of Delta Force were positioned in Pakistan to prevent 6-feet-5-inch-tall Osama bin Laden from escaping through southern Afghanistan into Pathan dominated north-west Pakistan.[55]

Some hard ground fighting occurred especially at the Tora Bora cave complex. The Tora Bora borders on Pakistan's Federally Administered Tribal Areas in Pakistan (FATA). Pakistan government's reach is at best limited in this region. The inhabitants are mostly Pathans, like the inhabitants of southern and eastern Afghanistan, while the governing elite of Pakistan mainly comprised Punjabi Muslims. The Tora Bora is a combination of man-made and natural cave-and-tunnel complex near the Pakistani border, south-east of Kabul. This complex was constructed during the Cold War era by the USA. The complex was heated and ventilated by electrical generators and was designed to withstand overpressure from explosions. The Tora Bora cave complex occupies an area of about 5 miles from south to north and 7 miles from east to west. Entry into the caves is difficult due to terrain and hostile ground fire. Each cave is about 25–50 feet high and the entrances are at various altitudes and at an inclination of 45–60 degrees, making attacks by troops and artillery difficult. It takes about 17 hours to trek from the road to the caves. The mountains are sheer and the passes are covered by dense forest. Some of the cave openings could only be reached by climbing or by helicopters. From 30 November, US aircraft started hitting the Tora Bora with daisy cutter anti-personnel bombs, massive bunker buster bombs, and JDAMs which were guided by Global Positioning System (GPS) satellites. However, no US troops were involved in the ground assault and the Afghan auxiliary troops were not willing to launch a

frontal assault against the defensive complex at Tora Bora for fear of
heavy casualties among the attackers. The result was the Saudi 'villain'
who escaped into north-west Pakistan.[56]

Lakhdar Brahimi, the Special Representative of the UN Secretary
General, convened a meeting in Bonn which lasted from 27 November
to 5 December 2001 with the objective of starting the process for
establishing a non-Taliban government in Afghanistan. The Bonn
Conference agreed that an interim government will be established
upon the official transfer of power on 22 December 2001. And a Special
Independent Commission will convene an emergency *loya jirga*, a typical Pashtun institution. Hamid Karzai was selected as chairman of the
interim administration. Karzai came from a Pashtun family. His father,
being a moderate, was assassinated by the Taliban at Quetta in July
1999. Karzai served as Mohadiddi's spokesman at Peshawar and briefly
as a deputy foreign minister after the fall of Najibullah regime. The
emergency loya jirga met from 11–19 June 2002. Dr Zalmay Khalilzad,
the Afghan-born US ambassador to Afghanistan (2003–5) sabotaged
the attempt by a section of the delegates to promote the 87-year-old
ex-King Zahir Shah. Zahir Shah was too old to provide dynamic leadership. Due to Khalilzad's forceful backing, Karzai emerged as the leader.
A loya jirga was held between 14 December 2003 and 4 January 2004,
and it adopted a new constitution (*Qanun-e-Asai-i Afghanistan*).[57]
Karzai became the president of the interim government in June 2002
and became president formally in October 2004 after being elected in
a nationwide election.[58]

US–NATO COIN IN AFGHANISTAN

> You cannot stop us. We've been using these tactics for hundreds of years
> and they have always worked. After an attack fighters can easily stash their
> weapons among villagers sympathetic to their cause. They can melt in
> with the local population and move on to another village, where there are
> more caches of weapons available to them for mounting another attack....
> The foreigners have the watches, but we have the time.
>
> —Taliban leader Ashoor[59]

History seems to be repeating itself. Once the Taliban's conventional
forces were destroyed, insurgency like a hydra-headed monster reappeared to haunt the US-led Coalition. After the collapse of Taliban,

the USA had to conduct COIN operations for establishing security and peace in the country as part of the state-building policy with a friendly government installed in Kabul.

After the fall of the Taliban regime at the end of 2001, NATO agreed to take command of an internal stabilization force in 2003. Known as International Security Assistance Force in Afghanistan (ISAF), this force was located in Kabul, and comprised a British infantry battalion. The ISAF was originally an outcome of the decision taken by the UN's Security Council on 20 December 2001. The first commander of the ISAF was Lieutenant General John McColl of UK.[60] Initially, NATO's mission was confined to Kabul and kept separate from the US COIN operations in the south and east of Afghanistan.[61] In the beginning, the Coalition troop suffered from lack of unity of command. While the OEF is an American-led military-oriented force as part of the Global War on Terror (GWOT), the ISAF started as a UN-mandated European organization that evolved into a NATO-led mission mainly for Afghanistan.[62]

During February 2002, the US had the 10th Mountain and the 1st Airborne divisions for mopping up operations.[63] In mid-2003, the Coalition had over 12,000 troops representing 19 nations. It was led by the Combined Joint Task Force (CJTF) 180, formed in June 2002 and based at Begram (twenty minutes flight time from Kabul).[64] In 2004, there were only 25,000 Coalition troops in Afghanistan. By 2005, the USA had 19,000 soldiers in this country. In comparison, in the same year, the USA had 140,000 troops in Iraq as part of Operation Iraqi Freedom.[65] As the USA got engaged more and more in Iraq, NATO agreed to expand its operation in the north, west, and finally, south of Afghanistan. In August 2006, NATO troops assumed responsibility from the Americans in an area known as Regional Command South. This included the provinces of Oruzgan, Zabol, Kandahar, and Helmand.[66] Afghanistan is about 50 per cent larger than Iraq and has 4 million more people. The population of Afghanistan in 2003 was about 31 million.[67] According to one estimate, the population of Afghanistan in 2006 comprised 32 million.[68] Between 2005 and 2008, the USA increased its troops' share in Afghanistan but it never matched the troop level of Iraq. In 2008, the USA had 31,000 soldiers in Afghanistan.[69] In 2009, the Obama administration ordered the deployment of 21,000 additional US troops.[70] By late 2011, the US had fewer than 100,000 troops in Afghanistan. However, Washington decided to withdraw the 33,000 'surge troops' by September 2012.[71]

The Taliban after OEF was down but not out. It started reviving along the Af–Pak border and is known as the neo-Taliban. Its Pakistan branch is known as Tehrek-i-Taliban. Probably in early 2002, the moderate section within the Taliban was waiting for some offer of power sharing from Kabul; but no such offer came and they decided to reactivate the insurgency. The hardcore section decided to conduct insurgency due to ideological reasons. In late 2002, in a meeting which was chaired by Mullah Dadullah, the latter announced the continuation of the insurgency and delegated duties to the top 10 commanders. The neo-Taliban has some similarities as well as dissimilarities with the Taliban. Antonio Giustozzi asserts that the neo-Taliban is much more integrated with the international jihadist movement. The neo-Taliban uses rhetoric like 'Global Christian War against Islam' and stressed solidarity with other internationalist jihadist movements. Besides the internationalization of the neo-Taliban's ideology, the latter also makes more use of audio-visual media. The neo-Taliban utilizes propaganda VCDs and DVDs. The insurgents carry video cameras with them in the battlefield in order to film the fighting and use the footage for propaganda purpose. By 2005, the Taliban commanders from the ranks of district commander upwards are equipped with laptops.[72] Further, the neo-Taliban is also displaying realistic attitude by downplaying its earlier rigid ideological fervor. In 2010 and 2011, the neo-Taliban asserted that it would respect the Islamic rights of the people including the women. Further, they claimed that they want to provide equal opportunities to all the ethnic groups and would like to establish normal relations with the other countries of the world.[73] Whether it is a long-term strategic transformation or a tactical ploy in order to gain short-term mileage, only the future will tell. Like the old Taliban, the neo-Taliban also depends on the village mullahs who are opposed to the tribal leaders, to spread their ideological message and for recruitment of the rank and file.[74]

The insurgency is intense in the Konar and Nuristan provinces. According to the US military analysts, there are three types of insurgents: local fighters, dedicated core fighters of the Afghan fundamentalist groups and criminal cartels, and finally transnational foreign fighters. The local fighters are recruits from the localities. They are selected from the madrasas and the Afghan refugee population in Pakistan. They are young, unemployed, and poorly educated, and are mostly used as labourers and given rudimentary weapons training. Economic and material concerns motivate them. These young fighters are rewarded with cash and clothing. They also partly join for the excitement and to gain a reputation among their peers and communities. They are not ideologically motivated and can be gleaned away from insurgency through provision of regular employment and financial opportunities. If the fundamentalist organizations lose the support of these local youths, then the formers' logistical infrastructures will be seriously dislocated, especially in the sphere of transportation and heavy labour.[75]

The members of Gulbuddin Hekmatyar's Hezb-i-Islami, now known as *Hezb-i-Islami Gulbuddin* (HIG), are core fighters. This fundamentalist organization was originally founded to fight the Soviets and received much support from Pakistan's ISI. Several fundamentalist groups in Afghanistan are linked with the *Lashkar-i-Toiba*, a Pakistan-based militant organization which is fighting Indian security forces in Kashmir. Moreover, the timber, gem mining, and drug cartels also possess dedicated fighters. These cartels resist establishment of government control, especially the trade restrictions, regulations, and taxation by the central government.[76] Many drug lords are also local tribal leaders and have extensive international connections.[77] In 2001, the GNP of the Afghan economy was $5 billion, and most of it was raised through smuggling and drug trade.[78] The core insurgents are skilled, well trained, and equipped with state-of-the-art military equipments which are often captured from the coalition forces. They are strongly motivated by religious ideology. Like the local fighters, they have also grown up within the regional communities and speak the local dialects. They especially operate within their immediate home community, district, or at best, the province.[79]

The dedicated group of foreign insurgents comprises members of the Al-Qaeda. They operate across the international borders and are fighting for establishing a global Islamic Caliphate. These foreign fighters, who are mostly Arabs and Central Asians, hail from Saudi Arabia, Yemen, Chechnya, and western China. Most of them are based in Pakistan. They have considerable financial resources which they use to influence the local and dedicated Afghan insurgents. The foreign insurgents are dedicated to their cause and are unwilling to compromise.

According to one US military estimate, the foreign fighters who fought in Nuristan from 2002 to 2008 numbered to 200 men.[80]

There is no unified leadership among the insurgents. The Hezb-i-Islami is based in Nurestan, Konar, Laghman, and Nangarhar. The Lashkar-i-Toiba is also active in this region. The Central Asian and Arab insurgents are active along the Afghan–Pak border in Bajaur in FATA in Pakistan, to Khost and Paktia in Afghanistan. The resurrected Taliban (i.e., neo-Taliban) is active in Baluchistan and in the Afghan provinces of Helmand, Kandahar, Zabol, and Paktika. Between 2004 and 2006, there were about 5,000–10,000 Taliban fighters active in Afghanistan.[81] The hard-core militants spend two to three months in Afghanistan and then pass the remaining months of the year resting in Pakistan.[82]

According to the RAND Corporation analyst Seth G. Jones, the neo-Taliban comprises two tiers. The top tier includes the principal political leadership structure and the guerrilla commanders. They are motivated by a radical version of Islam and view the struggle as a fight between Islam and Western infidels, and their puppet governments. The Taliban leadership comprises Mullah Omar and his key leaders are based in Quetta. A second group of leaders is based in Pakistan's FATA and one of the principal leaders was Sirajuddin Haqqani. In 2006, he commanded several hundred fighters and was semi-autonomous of the Taliban leadership in Afghanistan. Haqqani's support is powerful in Khost, Logar, Paktia, and Paktika provinces of Afghanistan, as well as in Waziristan. Haqqani enjoys close cooperation with the Pakistan army and especially the ISI. Haqqani also runs the madrasas around Miranshah and Mir Ali. The bottom tier of Taliban guerrillas comprises thousands of local Afghan fighters. They are men from the villages who are paid to set up roadside bombs, launch rocket and mortar attacks. At best, they function as part-time soldiers. They are not ideologically committed to jihad. They are motivated by unemployment and anger over the killing and wounding of their friends and relatives by the Afghan government, US or NATO forces.[83] Antonio Giustozzi claims that by 2006, about 20 per cent of the neo-Taliban's combat warriors were volunteers from Pakistan.[84]

The British returned to Afghanistan after almost a century, not as a principal player, but as a subsidiary to its dominant partner, the USA. From 2004, the Coalition force used Provincial Reconstruction Teams (PRTs) to improve the living standards of the Afghans.[85] Kersti Larsdotter makes a comparative analysis of the German PRT in Kunduz in north-east Afghanistan with British PRT in Mazar-i-Sharif (in Balkh), in north-west Afghanistan between 1 March 2004 till 28 February 2006. While the British approach was emphasizing 'hearts and minds' and 'minimum force' approach, the German PRT emphasized 'show of force'. While the British conducted patrols with six to seven men, the Germans conducted patrols with 20–30 soldiers. And the German soldiers wore more heavy armour and carried more weapons compared to the British personnel while moving about in the villages. In addition, the German Quick Reaction Force was bigger than the British one. In contrast to Kunduz, at Mazar-i-Sharif, the intensity of insurgent-related attacks increased during the above-mentioned time period. Larsdotter concludes that this study should at least question the basic supremacy of British minimum-force approach for all the regions in all the times.[86]

Rod Thornton asserts that the British army uses minimum force in COIN operations. And this characteristic could be traced back to British involvement in the colonies during the late nineteenth century and early twentieth century. Protestant ethics and Victorian values shaped the mentality of the imperial gentlemen officers. At the heart of the Victorian values lies Christian sentiment. The moral principles of the evangelical Protestant movement that developed during the later seventeenth and eighteenth centuries constituted the basis of British liberalism. Among the American force, Calvinism (which is also derived from Protestantism) discourages the use of minimum-force philosophy. However, Calvinism is unpopular in Britain. The concept of chivalry was inculcated among the British officers through the public school system, juvenile literature, and films. The public school system emphasized Christian morality among the Christian gentlemen reared in the duty of chivalry. The ruling class was encouraged to bring the coloured heathens under the orbit of Christian civilization without undue cruelty and excess. In addition, the fictions, poetry, theatres, and paintings spread the public school values of manliness, patriotism, chivalry, comradeship, and courage. Rather than unnecessary torture and cruelty, true courage, portrayed in the fictions, included magnanimity and gentleness. The message spread by British cinema was that the British soldiers act with fairness and compassion. All these traits were derived from Protestant ethics, and refracted and reinterpreted through

Victorian sensibilities. The net result was focus on fairness, chivalry, and restraint. Thornton continues that the pragmatic demands of maintaining a large disparate empire with limited number of British soldiers also encouraged the use of minimum force in order to prevent alienation of the majority of the subjects.[87]

The decision to send 3rd PARA to Afghanistan formed part of Britain's agreement to take over responsibility of the province of Helmand and send a United Kingdom Task Force (UKTF) of 3,700 troops. The troops were drawn from the 16th Air Assault Brigade with the 3rd PARA forming the infantry element of the force. Besides its normal complements of three rifle companies and specialist platoons of heavy machine guns, anti-tank missiles, mortars, reconnaissance patrols, and snipers, the battalion expanded to become an all-arms unit of 1,200 men. The artillery was made up of a battery of six 105-mm light howitzers. The Scimitar reconnaissance vehicles and Spartan personnel carriers provided light armoured capability. The CH-47 Chinook troop carrying helicopters provided the battalion group with air mobility. CAS was provided by A-10 tank buster aircraft and AC-130 Hercules Spectre gunships from the US Air Force. The Apache helicopter gunships and Harrier jets of the RAF provided additional firepower.[88]

The mission of the 3rd PARA was to use force as the last resort. And hunting down Taliban was not the objective. Rather, 3rd PARA's role was to provide security to protect the development and reconstruction efforts of the PRTs that would deploy with the task force. This was made up of both military elements and development specialists from the Department for International Development (DFID) and the Foreign and Commonwealth Office (FCO). It was assumed that their efforts would win over the loyalty of the majority population of the Pashtuns and allow the Kabul government to extend its authority in this province.[89]

When the NATO decided to expand the ISAF to southern Afghanistan, Britain agreed to take responsibility for the province of Helmand. Helmand is sandwiched between the provinces of Kandahar in the east and Nimruz in the west along the Iranian border. Helmand is a flat featureless desert that extends southwards to the border near Pakistan. In the north, the rugged mountains of Hindu Kush rise sharply from the desert landscape. The Helmand River has water throughout the year and is fed by snow from the mountains. Wells and ditches suck water from the Helmand and are used to make the land fertile for a few hundred metres on either side of the river banks.[90] This province is highly underdeveloped and narco-economy is dominant; local support for the Taliban remains high.[91] Afghanistan's economy depends on poppy growing, with the country producing 90 per cent of the world's opium.[92] The opium trade made up 30 per cent to 50 per cent of Afghanistan's GDP. At its height, Colombia's cocaine trade comprised 5 per cent of its GDP. In the beginning of the new millennium, the Afghan opium trade was worth $4 billion annually.[93] According to another estimate, 93 per cent of the world's opium comes from Afghanistan and half of the crop is grown in Helmand. Most of it is converted into heroin and it supplies 95 per cent of Britain's addict. The local farmers, trapped in a cycle of poverty and intimidation by the feudal drug barons, have no other alternative except to grow poppies. The opium trade sustains Taliban insurgency by providing money for purchase of arms and munitions.[94] In 1997, 96 per cent of the Afghan poppy came from the area under the Taliban's control. Abdul Rashid, head of Taliban's Counter-Narcotics Force, asserted that poppy cultivation was permissible because opium was consumed by the *kafirs* (infidels).[95] According to one estimate, the Taliban and the Al-Qaeda derived revenue varying from $70 million to $400 million annually from the poppy cultivation and trade.[96] In July 2000, the Taliban banned the cultivation of opium poppy, though not trafficking, from existing stocks. The ban caused a temporary shortage in 2001 and rise in the prices in the global market.[97] After the fall of Taliban, poppy cultivation again spread in Afghanistan. When Colonel Stuart Tootal, commanding 3rd PARA in 2006 at the province of Helmand, asked the officials how they would be able to gain the consent of the people if they ban opium cultivation which constitutes the livelihood of the poor farmers, he did not get any clear answer.

Tootal describes the operation of the 3rd PARA Battalion in the following words:

> It was clear that the struggle that we were about to become engaged in would be psychological as well as physical; it would be a battle for the hearts and minds of the people. I doubted whether eradication would help achieve this. We would be operating in a guerrilla landscape, where our protagonist lived and operated among the civilian population. He would be indistinct from

them until he decided to attack us. He would do so at a moment of his own choosing, before melting back into the obscurity of the community from whence he had come. While we would be constrained by the norms and conventions of war, such as Geneva Convention, the insurgents would not.[98]

In April 2006, 1,200 soldiers of the 3rd PARA Battle Group started its journey to southern Afghanistan. They were the first British unit to be sent to Helmand. During its six-month tour of duty, the 3rd PARA fired over 479,000 rounds of ammunition. The action took place along the desert plains and the foothills of Hindu Kush. During the Afghan summer, the battle group attempted to protect the scattered district centres against the Taliban.[99]

Between 2006 and 2009, in the province of Helmand of southern Afghanistan, six British Task Forces were deployed, each one based around a brigade (with some supplementary units), which served a six months' tour. Between May 2006 and September 2007, three successive British brigades engaged in major combat operations against the Taliban. But in September 2007, the fourth British Task Force came up with a population-centric approach. The objective was securing and developing the key areas of Helmand.[100]

One British officer named Leo Docherty, who participated in the first phase of this campaign, is caustic about its effectiveness. Docherty was born in Scotland, attended the Royal Military Academy Sandhurst, and was commissioned into the Scots Guard in 2001. He fought in Iraq in 2004. He trained as a paratrooper and passed a language course in Pusthu. He was deployed as aide-de-camp to the commander of the British force deployed in Helmand in April 2006. However, he left the army in December 2006.[101]

The British Task Force in which Docherty served mainly comprised the 16th Air Assault Brigade.[102] Docherty writes:

At the tactical level—for the troops on the ground—the plan to use something called 'the Mosaic'. It demands that all British units be aware of all facets of Afghan society—the tribes, the economy and local politics—while working within it.... Strategically, the plan for province of Helmand as a whole is based on 'the Comprehensive Approach'.[103]

The objective is to improve the security in Lashkar Gah, the provincial capital, so that the Department for International Development (DFID) could start practical developmental projects and the Foreign and Commonwealth Office could focus on counter-narcotics and improvement in governance. An 'inkspot', a security haven, will be established, in which life can return to normal.[104] One DFID official informed Docherty that improving the livelihood of the Afghans is their objective. Polio increased in southern Afghanistan after 2001.[105] In Afghanistan, 20 per cent of the children die before the age of five and about 70 per cent to 75 per cent of the populace are illiterate. The objective is to provide electricity and drinking water. Through microfinance lending and quick impact projects, the DFID is trying to achieve its objectives.[106] Child mortality has declined a bit. From about 165 deaths for every 1,000 individuals aged five or less, during the last decade of the last century, the rate was now 130 per 1,000 in 2008.[107] It is to be noted that Afghanistan is the second poorest state in planet earth.[108]

Overall, the situation in Docherty's view was indeed grim. Docherty writes that the Afghan police with whom the British were supposed to be working were hand in gloves with the personnel associated with the opium industry.[109] Even the ANA was wobbling. In March 2002, the Bush administration submitted to the Congress a $50 million proposal to train and equip 18,000 Afghan soldiers in 18 months.[110] Recruitment in the ANA started in May 2002. Battalions were given a basic course of 10 weeks and the creation of fully disciplined units was expected to take about six months.[111] Muhammad Fahim Khan, the Defence Minister of Interim Afghan government led by Hamid Karzai, named 100 generals for the ANA. Out of them, 90 were Tajiks from the Panjshir Valley. Such an overrepresentation of the Tajiks alienated the Pashtuns.[112] About the ANA, Docherty notes: 'They wear soiled green camouflage fatigues donated by the US and plastic sandals or inferior black leather boots.'[113] The ANA actually was not well motivated and suffered from large desertions. Firstly, this was because many soldiers were not eager to serve far away from their homes. Secondly, low wages and the personnel's unwillingness to accept military regulations were other factors. Some elements of the ANA were actually involved in the narcotics trade.[114] The Governor of Helmand, Engineer Daoud, who was appointed by the Hamid Karzai government, was guarded by a private military company.[115] Docherty notes in his memoirs: 'In a country where family, kin, and tribe are of paramount importance in political affairs, it's suddenly very clear that he's relying on us to support his position.'[116] In fact, after Karzai survived an assassination attempt in Kandahar on 5 September 2002, for some years, he was guarded by bodyguards from the US DynCorp firm. And this elicited strong criticism from the Afghans.[117]

The weak administration of the Karzai government to a great extent was responsible for the spread of insurgency. Of the first group of 32 provincial governors appointed in 2002, 20 were militia commanders, warlords/strongmen. Most of the district governors were smaller militia leaders. A political system geared towards the accommodation of warlords, who had their private armed contingents and autonomous resource base, prevented the functioning of officials loyal to the central government and establishment of an impersonal bureaucratic machinery.[118] Such actions delegitimized the Kabul government in the eyes of the common Afghans.

The neo-Taliban is taking heavy losses but is still not cracking. In 2006, according to one estimate, about 3,000 insurgents were killed. The NATO estimated that in the same year, they had killed 2,500 insurgents. The reconciliation offers by the Karzai government fail to induce large-scale desertions from the neo-Taliban.[119] The insurgent-related attacks are increasing with time. According to one author, insurgent-inspired incidents rose by 50 per cent from 12.4 attacks per day in 2007 to 18.4 per day in 2008. At the beginning of 2008, indigenous security forces in Afghanistan numbered to only 130,000 men. In comparison, the Iraqi army had 130,000 personnel and the Iraqi police had 190,000 men. A decision had been taken in 2008 to raise the size of the ANA and ANP from 57,000 and 75,000 to 70,000 and 82,000 men, respectively.[120] As a point of comparison, the Soviets in Afghanistan maintained about 500,000 soldiers and uniformed militias but still they failed.[121] In 2008, fatalities among the Afghan National Security Forces (ANSF) exceeded 1,000 annually.[122] By October 2011, the ANA numbered to 171,600 personnel and the ANP had 134,000 men. Thus, the total number of personnel in the ANSF numbered to 305,600 men. In 2011, the attrition rate was above 2.7 per cent. Further, the ANSF has very few Pashtuns from south Afghanistan.[123]

Besides the NATO, the US military is also continuing its COIN operations. The US COIN is characterized by massive use of firepower, mostly delivered from air, lack of attention for developing local knowledge and familiarity, and a failure to maintain whatever knowledge gained due to successive rotation of the personnel. Lack of respect for local customs, arbitrary arrests, and killings are factors which resulted in deterioration of relations with the Afghans. Unauthorized home searches are the principal source of discontent. So, now the US depends on Afghan militias and security forces in order to conduct home searches. House searches and arrests without prior communication to the local leaders and government officials (who felt discredited and humiliated) not only weaken the base of the government but also ensure a steady flow of recruits to the ranks of the neo-Taliban.[124]

Some examples of US-led Small War could be narrated. In April 2006, Combined Joint Task Force 76 (CJTF-76), under the 10th Mountain Division, started Operation MOUNTAIN LION in eastern Afghanistan. The objective was to defeat insurgent operations and to establish Coalition control in this region through 'clear-hold-build-engage' approach. The first 'clear' step involved use of lethal military force to clear the targeted areas of any enemy presence/control. The next 'hold' step involved creation of lasting security by establishing Coalition presence in the area cleared. The next two phases of 'build' and 'engage' involved improving infrastructures and facilities for the local communities and establishment of a working relationship with the people by communicating with them and gaining their trust. In the early evening hours of 21 June 2006, 16 US soldiers from the 3rd Squadron of 71st Cavalry of the 10th Mountain Division were engaged in a firefight on a mountain ridge overlooking the Gremen Valley near the Gowardesh Village in the north-east part of Afghanistan as part of the 'clear' phase. After thirty minutes of combat, two US soldiers died and one was mortally wounded. The insurgents withdrew after suffering large number of casualties.[125]

In June 2009, General Stanley McChrystal took command of the ISAF from General David D. McKiernan. McChrystal worked closely with the new CENTCOM commander, General David Petraeus.[126] Petraeus is widely regarded as the 'father' of US COIN strategy and responsible for saving the situation in post-Saddam Iraq. In 2007, Petraeus was responsible for creation of a new COIN field manual for the US military. Petraeus emphasized on protecting the civilians over killing the enemy (influence of British General Rupert Smith whose views are discussed in the next chapter), assumption of greater risk, and use of minimum and not maximum force (influence of British COIN).

For the US military geared for decisive campaigns fought with high-technology weapons resulting in a quick victory, Petraeus' recommendations are indeed radical. Petraeus' COIN strategy seems to be redirecting the US military towards nation-building tasks.[127] The principles of the US new COIN strategy follow:

> The US military, designed to inflict overwhelming and disproportionate losses on the enemy, tends to equate victory with very few body bags. So does the American public. The new counterinsurgency doctrine upends this perceived immunity from casualties by demanding that manpower replace firepower. Soldiers in Afghanistan must get out among the people, building and staffing joint security stations with Afghan security forces. That is the only way to disconnect the enemy from the civilians. Persistent presence—living among the population in small groups, staying in villages overnight for months at a time—is dangerous, and it will mean more casualties, but it's the only way to protect the population effectively. And it will make US troops more secure in the long run. This imperative to get out among the people extends to US civilians as well. US Embassy staff are almost completely forbidden from moving around Kabul on their own. Diplomacy is, of course, about relationships, and rules that discourage relationships fundamentally limit the ability of American diplomats to do their jobs. The mission in Afghanistan is to stabilize the country, not to secure the embassy.[128]

McChrystal's strategy comprised four components—winning the hearts and minds of the Afghan people, training the ANSF, building governance capacity and accountability in Afghanistan, and making the US army a learning adaptable organization. McChrystal emphasized the people are the prize and focused on language training for his soldiers. In order to set an example, McChrystal did not wear battle dress uniform when he visited the Afghan communities.[129]

The Afghan conflict spilled over neighbouring Pakistan, especially in the provinces of NWFP (now known as Khyber Pakhtunkhwa/ KP) and FATA, and to an extent, also in Baluchistan. The NWFP is situated between the Indus River and FATA and comprises 24 districts. These districts are settled and governed by the rules and regulations of the Constitution of Pakistan like the latter's three other provinces: Punjab, Sind, and Baluchistan. The most important district of KP is Peshawar (also the provincial capital). The other important districts are Dera Ghazi Khan, Bannu, Kohat (which has border with FATA),

Mardan, Manshera, and Abbottabad. The FATA comprises seven tribal agencies: Bajaur, Mohmand, Khyber, Khurram, Orakzai, North and South Waziristan. Except Orakzai Agency, the other six agencies have border with Afghanistan.[130]

In FATA, armed conflict started in South Waziristan in 2002–3 and spread in North Waziristan in 2003–4. The Waziris and the Mashuds, the two main tribes in North and South Waziristan are deeply involved in armed conflicts. The Taliban attacked and killed the pro-Pakistan government secular tribal elders in these regions. Their relatives were kidnapped and the secular jirgas were attacked by Taliban suicide bombers. By 2005, the Taliban was in complete control of these two regions. In 2006, the Taliban spread its influence in the Bajaur Agency and then in the Mohmand Agency.[131] Religious militancy is also spreading in the core region of Pakistan. Farzana Shaikh is sckeptical of the assumption of several Western scholars and policy makers that Sufism represents the moderate face of Islam and might save Pakistan. In 2003, RAND Corporation reported that Sufis might be partners of the USA in building modern democratic Islam. In 2007, RAND repeated that Sufis are natural allies of the USA. The West's strategy is to use the Sufis against the radical orthodox Sunni Islam represented by the Deobandis and Ahl-e-Hadith traditions. In contrast to 'imported' Wahabi and Arabian Islam, Sufism was portrayed even by President Pervez Musharraf as 'indigenous' and the key signifier of Pakistan. In fact, before Musharraf, Pakistan's President Ayub Khan (military general cum dictator from 1958–69) tried to bring the Sufi shrines under state bureaucratic management. President Zia-ul-Haq (general-turned-dictator, 1977–88), himself strongly influenced by Deobandi traditions with the aid of the Sunnis, turned against the Sufis. Pakistani Sufi scholar Tahir ul Qadri (b. 1951) of Punjab is a strong defender of Sufi saints. He condemned the violent rhetoric of the Taliban and Al-Qaeda. He reaches out to the West through Minhaj ul Quran International which has offices in London, New York, and Toronto. Qadri blames Wahabi and Salafi Islam in Pakistan and elsewhere. In October 2001, Qadri denounced 9/11. However, in 2002, the Sufi leader of JUP and head of Ahl-e-Sunnat, Shaikh Ahmed Noorani (d. 2003), urged his supporters to take up arms on the side of Taliban to fight the Western forces in Afghanistan.[132]

A clear-cut division of Islam into moderate Sufis/Shias versus radical Sunnis is simplistic as the case of Noorani mentioned above and the

Red Mosque incident show. On 10 July 2007, the Pakistan army troops stormed the Red Mosque complex in Islamabad which resulted in the death of 200 people. This operation was named as Operation SILENCE. Faisal Devji says that the presence of armed veiled women at the Red Mosque represented revolutionary Shites trends rather than masculine Sunni militancy of the Taliban and Al-Qaeda. Moreover, unlike the Tehrek-i-Taliban, the leaders at the Red Mosque never made any anti-Shia statements. Further, the mosque's seminary was characterized by its co-educational character, as males and females stayed in close proximity.[133]

On 12 December 2007, in North Waziristan, some 40 tribal leaders with their militias coalesced to form the Tehrek-i-Taliban (Pakistani Taliban). Baitullah Mehsud was selected as the leader. The objectives were to fight the infidels in Afghanistan and to launch a jihad against the Pakistan state. The organization claimed that it had 40,000 militants under its command. This organization also drew recruits from Punjab and Sind. In 2008, 3,000 members of the Tehrek-i-Taliban drove away 12,000 Pakistani troops from Swat, blew up a girls' school and other public buildings, and caused exodus of one-third of Swat's 2 million people. The Swat Valley in the east opens to Indian Kashmir and in the west to Afghanistan. Dominance of Swat provided the Tehrek-i-Taliban and Al-Qaeda control over north Pakistan and the roads that run to the major cities including Islamabad, besides new routes to wage jihad in Kashmir and Afghanistan.[134] The year 2008 witnessed Pakistani military operations in Bajaur, Mohmand, and Waziristan. This region witnessed drone attacks by US Forces and suicide bombings by the neo-Taliban, as well as attacks on the NATO supply convoys in the Khyber Agency.[135] In 2008, Maulana Fazlullah was in control of Swat. It is reported that Fazlullah invited Osama bin Laden to come and live in Swat under his protection. The Pakistan government succumbed to his threats and passed the *Nizam-e-Adl* regulations in early 2009, which resulted in the imposition of the *Sharia* in the Malakand region.[136] On 7 May 2009, after evacuating most of the population, the Pakistan army launched a major air-ground offensive in Swat. About 4,000 militants prepared a fortified position around Mingora. While the aircraft dropped bombs, the artillery also rained down shells. Some 30,000 troops moved into Swat. The operation was reminiscent of Soviet COIN operations in Afghanistan during the 1980s. By June, the militants were pushed out of Swat. About 300 soldiers and 2,000 militants were killed during the operation. However, the leaders of Tehrek-i-Taliban escaped into FATA and Afghanistan. Some 1.5 million refugees from Swat, who had left the region earlier, started moving into the valley once again. In 2009, Pakistani civilian deaths at the hands of the insurgents numbered to 3,021, and the equivalent figure for Afghanistan is 2,412. Further, another 7,300 Pakistanis were wounded.[137]

In 2009, General Kayani agreed to rotate all the Pakistan army units through a six-week course on COIN. About 200 US and British officers trained the Pakistani trainers of the Frontier Corps (Pakistani paramilitary formation). The US Special Forces created a 700-man-strong Frontier Corps commando unit. As part of the US military aid, the 60,000 strong Frontier Corps received equipment for conducting COIN and the personnel's battlefield medical care was improved. To prevent the re-entry of the militants back into Swat Valley, the Pakistan army maintained 25,000 troops even during the summer of 2011. The noted journalist Ahmed Rashid opines that by 2009, the Pakistan army's COIN doctrine was shaped by General Petraeus's COIN doctrine, which emphasizes the principles of clear, hold, build, and transfer. While in Swat Valley, the Pakistan army targeted the Tehrek-i-Taliban; in FATA, the Haqqani network and local militia commander, Hafiz Gul Bahadur, were considered friendly to the Pakistani military establishment. On 7 August 2009, a US drone killed Baitullah Mehsud, the leader of Tehrek-i-Taliban, in North Waziristan. On 22 August 2009, a 40-member shura chose Hakimullah Mehsud, then aged 26 and a ruthless militant commander, as the leader of Pakistani Taliban.[138]

The status of the Islamic clergy, particularly the mullahs, rose both in Pakistan and in Afghanistan, due to their role during the anti-Soviet resistance. The Taliban regime made the mullahs their 'eyes and ears' in the villages and emphasized the collection of religious taxes (*ushr* and *Zakat*), which were traditional sources of income for the latter. This measure further strengthened the traditional power of the village mullahs: they are often the only literate persons in the villages and have the power of sermon. After the fall of the Taliban, some ulema, especially those at the top of the mujahideen *tanzims*, gained sacrosanct status as jihadi leaders. Under the Hamid Karzai government, they serve as an unofficial Supreme Advisory Council, which was gathered by the president occasionally to obtain their support and blessings for key government decisions. Without an official sanction, the Supreme Advisory Council appears similar to Iran's Council of Guardians.[139] Meanwhile, Karzai, who was re-elected president in 2009, was facing charges of corruption and under the present rules, could not stand for the election due in 2014.[140] Worse, it is reported that the American troops will be leaving Afghanistan in 2014. The last US troops left Afghanistan on 26 October 2014.

On 1 May 2011, Osama bin Laden was killed by the US Special Forces (Navy Seals) at Abbotabad in north-west Pakistan.[141] But the insurgency along the Af–Pak border is still continuing. US is using armed UAVs (Predator and Reaper drones armed with AGM-14 Hellfire missiles). The UAVs use precision weapons to kill suspected terrorists. According to one estimate, between 2007 and March 2011, 33 Al-Qaeda and Taliban leaders and between 1,100 and 1,800 insurgents were killed by the drones.[142] Compared to 135 drone attacks in 2010, in 2011, there were 79 drone attacks in FATA (mostly in North and South Waziristan).[143]

In 2011, one American academician and another Canadian military officer, in an article jointly written, asserted that throughout Afghanistan's history, Islam in general and the the mullahs in particular have played crucial roles. The objective of the mullahs is to establish a Deobandi Islamic Emirate in Afghanistan. And the mullahs have led opposition against foreign invaders in history. At times, the mullahs have also replaced the village elders and have taken control in various localities.[144] The British civilian official named Roos-Keppel, an important voice in the GOI before the beginning of the First World War, would have agreed with such an analysis.

Daniel Marston rightly says that the Afghan insurgency is not primarily religious. Rather the feelings among the Pashtuns (who had been traditionally dominant in Afghanistan) that they have been marginalized by the Uzbek and Tajik-led Northern Alliance supported by the Coalition and the presence of the foreign troops are giving strength to the insurgency.[145] Before 1979, the Pushtu-speaking Pathans, who mainly live in the south and east of Afghanistan, made up 42 per cent of the population. The Turkic and the Iranian minorities, including Tajiks, Uzbeks, and the Turcomans, are in the north of the country.[146] It should be noted that the resurgence of insurgency in Iraq after the collapse of Saddam regime is also partly for the fact that the Sunnis, who had been dominant till Saddam's time, now feel sidelined by the US-backed Shia regime. Secondly, the Sunnis also hate the presence of Western troops in their country.[147] Hence, power politics and ethnic rivalries, to a great extent, are shaping the insurgencies in both Afghanistan and Iraq.

* * *

The principal threats remain the neo-Taliban and the multilayered loose agglomeration of insurgent organizations along the Af–Pak border. What is dangerous is that the neo-Taliban is showing flexibility both in the spheres of doctrine and organizational framework. There seems to be no easy way of stabilizing Afghanistan. The threat posed by radical Islam is motivating the Western countries to pour manpower and resources into a country ravaged by three decades of civil war and foreign occupation. How long this massive infusion of foreign assets will continue is also questionable. It seems that there is no clear-cut formula for conducting a successful COIN in Afghanistan in particular, and in the troubled spots of the world in general. The effectiveness of much vaunted British minimum force approach is also partly challenged in Afghanistan. Despite this fact, there has been a shift in US COIN doctrine. Use of minimum force and security for the Afghan civilians are the dominant principles shaping the US COIN policy at present. In the time of writing this chapter, combat between US–NATO security forces and the insurgents are continuing in Afghanistan. According to a US combat personnel, they are conducting a 'Vietnam style war at high altitude' in Afghanistan. Whether the conflict represented a sort of New War or not is discussed in the next chapter.

NOTES

1. Kamal Matinuddin, *The Taliban Phenomenon: Afghanistan 1994–1997, With an Afterword Covering the Major Events since 1997* (1999; reprint, Karachi: Oxford University Press, 2001), 12–13, 15–16.

2. Matinuddin, *The Taliban Phenomenon*, 14; George Friedman, *America's Secret War inside the Hidden Worldwide Struggle between the United States and its Enemies* (London: Abacus, 2004), 200. For an alternate view, see Tahir Andrabi, Jishnu Das, and Asim Ijaz Khwaja, 'Madrasa Satistics Don't Support the Myth',

in Shahzad Bashir and Robert D. Crews (eds), *Under the Drones: Modern Lives in the Afghanistan–Pakistan Borderlands* (Cambridge, Massachusetts/London: Harvard University Press, 2012), 162–73. The three authors argue that though the rise of madrasas are more in Khyber Pakhtunkhwa compared to other regions of Pakistan, still the increase in the number of madrasas is less than public schools. Hence, rise of radical Islam along the Af–Pak border is not the direct result of increase in the number of madrasas and lack of alternate avenues of education.

3. Raghav Sharma, 'Sectarian Violence in Pakistan', in D. Suba Chandran and P.R. Chari (eds), *Armed Conflicts in South Asia 2009: Continuing Violence, Failing Peace Processes* (New Delhi/Oxon: Routledge, 2010), 42–3.

4. Matinuddin, *The Taliban Phenomenon*, 14.

5. Gilles Dorronsoro, 'The Transformation of the Afghanistan-Pakistan Border', in Bashir and Crews (eds.), *Under the Drones*, 39.

6. Seth G. Jones, *In the Graveyard of Empires: America's War in Afghanistan* (New York/London: W.W. Norton & Co., 2010), 57.

7. Sana Haroon, 'The Rise of Deobandi Islam in the North-West Frontier Province and its Implications in Colonial India and Pakistan 1914–1996', *Journal of the Royal Asiatic Society*, Series 3, 18, 1 (2008): 48; Jones, *In the Graveyard of Empires*, 54.

8. Sana Haroon, 'Religious Revivalism across the Durand Line', in Bashir and Crews (eds), *Under the Drones*, 46.

9. Haroon, 'The Rise of Deobandi Islam in the North-West Frontier Province and its Implications in Colonial India and Pakistan 1914–1996', 50.

10. Haroon, 'Religious Revivalism across the Durand Line', in Bashir and Crews (eds), *Under the Drones*, 53.

11. Thomas Ruttig, 'How Tribal Are the Taliban?', in Bashir and Crews (eds), *Under the Drones*, 114.

12. Antonio Giustozzi, *Empires of Mud: Wars and Warlords in Afghanistan* (London: C. Hurst & Co., 2009), 74, 78–9.

13. Larry P. Goodson, *Afghanistan's Endless War: State Failure, Regional Politics, and the Rise of the Taliban* (Seattle/London: University of Washington Press, 2001), 77.

14. Goodson, *Afghanistan's Endless War*, 77–8; William Maley, *Rescuing Afghanistan* (London: Hurst & Co., 2006), 8.

15. Goodson, *Afghanistan's Endless War*, 78–9; Jones, *In the Graveyard of Empires*, 58–9.

16. Goodson, *Afghanistan's Endless War*, 82–3.

17. Jones, *In the Graveyard of Empires*, 60–2.

18. Seth G. Jones, *Counterinsurgency in Afghanistan* (Santa Monica, CA: RAND Corporation, 2008), 38.

19. Neamatollah Nojumi, *The Rise of the Taliban in Afghanistan: Mass Mobilization, Civil War, and the Future of the Region* (New York/Houndmills, Basingstoke: Palgrave, 2002), 23.

20. Dorronsoro, 'The Transformation of the Afghanistan-Pakistan Border', in Bashir and Crews (eds), *Under the Drones*, 41; Pervez Musharraf, *In the Line of Fire: A Memoir* (New York: Free Press, 2006), 209.

21. James Caron, 'Taliban, Real and Imagined', in Bashir and Crews (eds), *Under the Drones*, 73.

22. Musharraf, *In the Line of Fire*, 210.

23. Jones, *In the Graveyard of Empires*, 58.

24. Maley, *Rescuing Afghanistan*, 21.

25. Sean M. Maloney, 'Conceptualizing the War in Afghanistan: Perceptions from the Front, 2001–2006', *Small Wars & Insurgencies*, 18, 1 (2007): 29.

26. Brian Glyn Williams, 'General Dostum and the Mazar-i-Sharif Campaign: New Light on the Role of Northern Alliance Warlords in Operation Enduring Freedom', *Small Wars & Insurgencies*, 21, 4 (2010): 614.

27. Goodson, *Afghanistan's Endless War*, 85–6.

28. Jones, *In the Graveyard of Empires*, 58.

29. Shanthie Mariet D'Souza, 'Afghanistan: Tipping Point', in Chandran and Chari (eds), *Armed Conflicts in South Asia 2009*, 20.

30. Shanthie Mariet D'Souza, 'Afghanistan: Turning the Tide', in D. Suba Chandran and P.R. Chari (eds), *Armed Conflicts in South Asia 2010: Growing Left-Wing Extremism and Religious Violence* (New Delh/Oxoni: Routledge, 2011), 19; Adrian R. Lewis, *The American Culture of War: The History of the US Military Force from World War II to Operation Enduring Freedom* (2007; reprint, Oxon/New York: Routledge, 2012), 391.

31. D'Souza, 'Afghanistan: Tipping Point', in Chandran and Chari (eds), *Armed Conflicts in South Asia 2009*, 20.

32. Tim Bird and Alex Marshall, *Afghanistan: How the West Lost its Way* (2011; reprint, New Delhi: Orient Blackswan, 2012), 77–8.

33. Quoted from Bird and Marshall, *Afghanistan*, 73.

34. Lieutenant-Colonel Craig D. Wills, *Airpower, Afghanistan, and the Future of Warfare: An Alternative View*, Cadre Paper No. 25 (Alabama: Air University Press, 2006), 35–6.

35. HY S. Rothstein, *Afghanistan and the Troubled Future of Unconventional Warfare* (Annapolis, Maryland: Naval Institute Press, 2006), 7.

36. Strobe Talbot, *Engaging India: Diplomacy, Democracy and the Bomb* (New Delhi: Viking, 2004), 115–16.

37. Talbot, *Engaging India*, 116. Brackets used are mine.

38. *The United States Army in OPERATION ENDURING FREEDOM, A Different Kind of War: October 2001-September 2005*, Donald P. Wright with the

Contemporary Operations Study Team (Fort Leavenworth, Kansas: Combat Studies Institute Press, 2010), 27, 35–6, 39.

39. Musharraf, *In the Line of Fire*, 200.

40. Musharraf, *In the Line of Fire*, 201.

41. Musharraf, *In the Line of Fire*, 201.

42. Musharraf, *In the Line of Fire*, 201–2, 204–5, 211.

43. *The United States Army in OPERATION ENDURING FREEDOM*, 39–40, 58.

44. *The United States Army in OPERATION ENDURING FREEDOM*, 37–9.

45. Bird and Marshall, *Afghanistan*, 74.

46. Williams, 'General Dostum and the Mazar-i-Sharif Campaign: New Light on the Role of the Northern Alliance Warlords in Operation Enduring Freedom', 614.

47. Bird and Marshall, *Afghanistan*, 75.

48. Wills, *Airpower, Afghanistan, and the Future of Warfare*, 35–9.

49. Rothstein, *Afghanistan and the Troubled Future of Unconventional Warfare*, 13.

50. Bird and Marshall, *Afghanistan*, 79–81.

51. Maley, *Rescuing Afghanistan*, 30.

52. Bird and Marshall, *Afghanistan*, 81–2.

53. D'Souza, 'Afghanistan: Turning the Tide', in Chandran and Chari (eds), *Armed Conflicts in South Asia 2010*, 19; Lewis, *The American Culture of War*, 408.

54. Musharraf, *In the Line of Fire*, 217.

55. Friedman, *America's Secret War*, 192.

56. Friedman, *America's Secret War*, 194–5, 200.

57. Maley, *Rescuing Afghanistan*, 30–1, 33–5, 43.

58. Lewis, *The American Culture of War*, 409.

59. Quoted from Emily Spencer and Bernd Horn, 'Introduction', in Spencer (ed.), *The Difficult War: Perspectives on Insurgency and Special Operations Forces* (Toronto: Dundurn, 2009), 16.

60. Lewis, *The American Culture of War*, 409.

61. Colonel Stuart Tootal, *Danger Close: Commanding 3rd PARA in Afghanistan* (London: John Murray, 2009), 22.

62. Maloney, 'Conceptualizing the War in Afghanistan', 27–8.

63. Lewis, *The American Culture of War*, 409.

64. Lieutenant-General David W. Barno, 'Fighting "the Other War": Counterinsurgency Strategy in Afghanistan, 2003–5', *Military Review*, 87, 5 (2007): 33.

65. *Wanat: Combat Action in Afghanistan, 2008, The Staff of the US Army Combat Studies Institute* (Fort Leavenworth, Kansas: Combat Studies Institute Press, 2010), 10, 12.

66. Tootal, *Danger Close*, 22.

67. Barno, 'Fighting "the Other War": Counterinsurgency Strategy in Afghanistan, 2003–5', 33.

68. Tootal, *Danger Close*, 21.

69. *Wanat: Combat Action in Afghanistan, 2008*, 12.

70. Fotini Christia and Michael Semple, 'Flipping the Taliban: How to Win in Afghanistan', *Foreign Affairs* (July/August 2009), 34.

71. William Maley, 'Afghanistan in 2011: Positioning for an Uncertain Future', *Asian Survey*, 52, 1 (2012): 91.

72. Antonio Giustozzi, *Koran, Kalashinokov and Laptop: The Neo-Taliban Insurgency in Afghanistan* (London: Foundation Books, 2007), 11, 13.

73. Mariam Safi, 'Afghanistan in 2011', in D. Suba Chandran and P.R. Chari (eds), *Armed Conflicts in South Asia 2012: Uneasy Stasis and Fragile Peace* (New Delhi/Oxon: Routledge, 2013), 40–1.

74. Giustozzi, *Koran, Kalashinokov and Laptop*, 12–13.

75. *Wanat: Combat Action in Afghanistan, 2008*, 8–9.

76. *Wanat: Combat Action in Afghanistan, 2008*, p. 8.

77. Colonel Thomas X. Hammes, *The Sling and the Stone: On War in the 21st Century* (St Paul, MN: Zenith Press, 2006), 168.

78. Warren Chin, 'Operation "Enduring Freedom": A Victory for a Conventional Force fighting an Unconventional War', *Small Wars & Insurgencies*, 14, 1 (2003): 61.

79. *Wanat: Combat Action in Afghanistan, 2008*, 9.

80. *Wanat: Combat Action in Afghanistan, 2008*, 9–10.

81. Jones, *Counterinsurgency in Afghanistan*, 38–9.

82. Giustozzi, *Koran, Kalashinokov and Laptop*, 33–4.

83. Jones, *Counterinsurgency in Afghanistan*, 40–1.

84. Giustozzi, *Koran, Kalashinokov and Laptop*, 35.

85. *Wanat: Combat Action in Afghanistan, 2008*, 10.

86. Kersti Larsdotter, 'Exploring the Utility of Armed Force in Peace Operations: German and British Approaches in Northern Afghanistan', *Small Wars & Insurgencies*, 19, 3 (2008): 352–73.

87. Rod Thornton, 'The British Army and the Origins of its Minimum Force Philosophy', *Small Wars & Insurgencies*, 15, 1 (2004): 83–106.

88. Tootal, *Danger Close*, 22–3.

89. Tootal, *Danger Close*, 23.

90. Tootal, *Danger Close*, 27.

91. Theo Farrell, 'Improving in War: Military Adaptation and the British in Helmand Province, Afghanistan, 2006–9', *JSS*, 33, 4 (2010): 574.

92. Leo Docherty, *Desert of Death: A Soldier's Journey from Iraq to Afghanistan* (London: Faber and Faber, 2007), 57–8.

93. Fariba Nawa, 'Women and the Drug Trade in Afghanistan', in Bashir and Crews (eds), *Under the Drones*, 237.

94. Tootal, *Danger Close*, 24–5.

95. Jones, *In the Graveyard of Empires*, 62.

96. Nawa, 'Women and the Drug Trade in Afghanistan', in Bashir and Crews (eds), *Under the Drones*, 238.

97. Jones, *In the Graveyard of Empires*, 63.

98. Tootal, *Danger Close*, 25.

99. Tootal, *Danger Close*, xiii.

100. Farrell, 'Improving in War: Military Adaptation and the British in Helmand Province, Afghanistan, 2006–9', 573.

101. Docherty, *Desert of Death*, 3–34, 44–5.

102. Docherty, *Desert of Death*, 55.

103. Docherty, *Desert of Death*, 56.

104. Docherty, *Desert of Death*, 56.

105. David Loyn, *In Afghanistan: Two Hundred Years of British, Russian and American Occupation* (New York: Palgrave Macmillan, 2009), 228.

106. Docherty, *Desert of Death*, 57; Tootal, *Danger Close*, 21.

107. Michael O'Hanlon, 'Toward Reconciliation in Afghanistan', *The Washington Quarterly*, 32, 2 (2009): 140.

108. Lewis, *The American Culture of War*, 406.

109. Docherty, *Desert of Death*, 65.

110. Anja Manuel and P.W. Singer, 'A New Model Afghan Army', *Foreign Affairs*, 81, 4 (2002): 47.

111. Antonio Giustozzi, 'Auxiliary Force or National Army? Afghanistan's "ANA" and the Counter-Insurgency Effort, 2002–6', *Small Wars & Insurgencies*, 18, 1 (2007): 48.

112. Manuel and Singer, 'A New Model Afghan Army', 57.

113. Docherty, *Desert of Death*, 74.

114. Giustozzi, 'Auxiliary Force or National Army? Afghanistan's "ANA" and the Counter-Insurgency Effort, 2002–6', 52–5.

115. Docherty, *Desert of Death*, 67, 71.

116. Docherty, *Desert of Death*, 73.

117. Maley, *Rescuing Afghanistan*, 34.

118. Giustozzi, *Koran, Kalashinokov and Laptop*, 16, 18–19.

119. Giustozzi, *Koran, Kalashinokov and Laptop*, 15.

120. Allan Orr, 'Recasting Afghan Strategy', *Small Wars & Insurgencies*, 20, 1 (2009): 87–8.

121. Loyn, *In Afghanistan*, 227.

122. O'Hanlon, 'Toward Reconciliation in Afghanistan', 140.

123. Safi, 'Afghanistan in 2011', in Chandran and Chari (eds), *Armed Conflicts in South Asia 2012*, 47.

124. Giustozzi, *Koran, Kalashinokov and Laptop*, 19, 163–64.

125. Lieutenant-Colonel John C. Mountcastle, 'Firefight above Gowardesh', in Donald P. Wright (General Editor), *Vanguards of Valour: Small Unit Actions in Afghanistan* (Fort Leavenworth, Kansas: Combat Studies Institute Press, 2012), 1–2.

126. Lewis, *The American Culture of War*, 413.

127. Nathaniel C. Fick, John A. Nagl and General David Petraeus, 'How to Win a Losing War', *Foreign Affairs*, 170 (2009): 43.

128. Fick, Nagl and Petraeus, 'How to Win a Losing War', 45.

129. Lewis, *The American Culture of War*, 416.

130. D. Suba Chandran, 'Armed Conflict in FATA and NWFP: Continuing Violence', in Chandran and Chari (eds), *Armed Conflicts in South Asia 2010*, 44; D. Suba Chandran, 'FATA & Khyber Pakhtunkhwa in 2011', in Chandran and Chari (eds), *Armed Conflicts in South Asia 2012*, 50–1.

131. D. Suba Chandran, 'FATA and NWFP: Spreading Anarchy', in Chandran and Chari (eds), *Armed Conflicts in South Asia 2009*, 63.

132. Farzana Shaikh, 'Will Sufi Islam Save Pakistan?', in Bashir and Crews (eds), *Under the Drones*, 174–85, 189.

133. Faisal Devji, 'Red Mosque', in Bashir and Crews (eds), *Under the Drones*, 153–61.

134. Ahmed Rashid, *Pakistan on the Brink: The Future of Pakistan, Afghanistan and the West* (London: Allen Lane, 2012), 140–42.

135. Chandran, 'Armed Conflict in FATA and NWFP: Continuing Violence', in Chandran and Chari (eds), *Armed Conflicts in South Asia 2010*, 44.

136. Chandran, 'FATA and NWFP: Spreading Anarchy', in Chandran and Chari (eds), *Armed Conflicts in South Asia 2009*, 64.

137. Rashid, *Pakistan on the Brink*, 139, 142–3.

138. Rashid, *Pakistan on the Brink*, 143–4, 146–7.

139. Ruttig, 'How Tribal Are the Taliban?', in Bashir and Crews (eds), *Under the Drones*, 115.

140. Lewis, *The American Culture of War*, 409.

141. Maley, 'Afghanistan in 2011: Positioning for an Uncertain Future', 89; Lewis, *The American Culture of War*, 391.

142. Lewis, *The American Culture of War*, 410.

143. Chandran, 'FATA & Khyber Pakhtunkhwa in 2011', in Chandran and Chari (eds), *Armed Conflicts in South Asia 2012*, 71–2.

144. Lieutenant-Colonel John J. Malevich and Daryl C. Youngman, 'The Afghan Balance of Power and the Culture of Jihad', *Military Review* (May–June 2011): 37–9.

145. Daniel Marston, 'Lessons in 21st Century Counterinsurgency: Afghanistan 2001–7', in Marston and Carter Malkasian (eds), *Counterinsurgency in Modern Warfare* (Oxford: Osprey, 2008), 220.

146. Mark Galeotti, *Afghanistan: The Soviet Union's Last War* (1995; reprint, London: Frank Cass, 2001), 3.

147. Ahmed S. Hashim, *Insurgency and Counter-Insurgency in Iraq* (London: Hurst & Company, 2006), 1–102.

5

AFGHANISTAN AND THE NATURE
OF FUTURE CONFLICTS

Historical examples clarify everything and also provide the best kind of
proof in the empirical sciences. This is particularly true of the art of war.
—Carl von Clausewitz[1]

FOR CLAUSEWITZ, THE NATURE OF war has an essential continuity and
even integrity, but the character of individual wars varies.[2] Discussion
about the nature of warfare in Afghanistan is related with several bigger interrelated debates in the field of military history. Firstly, is the
world witnessing a Military Revolution (MR), or a Military Technical
Revolution (MTR)/Revolution in Military Affairs (RMA) at the dawn
of the new millennium? A brief discussion about the evolution and
use of these concepts by the academic community and policy makers
is necessary. The concept of MR was first introduced by the historian of
Spanish empire, Geoffrey Parker. In his Lees Knowles Lecture delivered
in 1984, Parker asserted that between 1500 and 1800, the Western
World experienced an MR. Radical changes in weaponry, tactical concepts, and organizational infrastructure resulted in a quantum jump of
the Western military effectiveness. This in turn provided supremacy to
the West against the 'rest'. And the modern world, to a great extent, was

shaped by the new militaries spawned by the West.[3] MR is the product of not merely technology but substantial changes in society and politics.[4] Influenced by Parker, several other historians have identified MRs at different periods of Western history. Jonathan B.A. Bailey asserts that an MR occurred during the First World War. It was the product of fusion of industrial warfare and nationalist ideology. The military aspect of this MR, which especially developed during 1917–18 at the Western Front, witnessed the rise of mass indirect fire. This in turn gave birth to modern warfare, which is still relevant at the beginning of the twenty-first century.[5] Clifford J. Rogers attempts to synthesize the presence of several MRs in West European history by claiming that the history of warfare can be explained by the punctuated equilibrium thesis. It means that in the history of warfare long periods of slow and steady evolution are followed by sudden quantum jumps and the latter phenomenon could be categorized as MRs. Rogers asserts that West Europe, during the opening decades of the fourteenth century, witnessed an Infantry MR which replaced the paradigm of cavalry warfare. It was followed by an Artillery Revolution between the late fifteenth and early sixteenth centuries.[6] Rogers' focus on the technological aspects of the MR brings us to the concept of RMA.

Several historians claim that West Europe experienced successive RMAs. Dennis E. Showalter writes that in the 1860s, the Prussian army introduced an RMA. It involved radical changes in weapons (rifles), tactics (introduction of dispersed skirmishing formation), and organizational innovations (general staff system and universal short-term conscription). However, this RMA is very short lived.[7] Holger Herwig notes that the Royal Navy experienced an RMA just before the onset of the First World War. However, Herwig adds a rider that though advanced technology made this RMA possible, technology did not drive this RMA. Rather, the crucial integers were politics and strategy.[8] The US government initially became aware of an RMA through its analysis of Soviet military writings.[9] Marxist–Leninist theory made the Soviets receptive to the notion of major revolutionary change both in the social and military spheres. In the 1970s, the appearance of new weapons like precision-guided munitions (hereafter PGMs), cruise missiles, and stealth technology encouraged the Soviet thinkers to conceptualize that an MTR is in the offing.[10] For Colin Gray, RMA refers to a radical change in the character or conduct of war. A lower form of technological change (i.e., adoption of new weapon system by an army in a particular historical moment) is regarded as an MTR.[11]

Secondly, this chapter deals with the question whether conventional warfare is dead or not. Thirdly, are we witnessing a new form of insurgency? And, is the new form of insurgency part of the so-called Eastern way of warfare? Fourthly, does it mean that counter-insurgency (COIN) in Afghanistan is part of the West's ongoing Global War on Terror (GWOT and also dubbed as the Long War)? Taking the Prussian military philosopher Carl Von Clausewitz's statement quoted above at face value, we will try to generalize the future of warfare by making a case study of the recent conflict in Afghanistan. As two scholars note: '...we agreed that change and newness are not the same, and that change can be a reversal back to something which has existed before.'[12] Lastly, is the paradigm of war that can be culled from the Afghan experience the only possible paradigm of war for the future, or are other alternatives also possible? As regards the future of war, there is a slight contradiction. The wars that the USA has to fight could be different from the conflicts which might engulf the other states of the world. However, the USA as the world's sole superpower might have to fight most of the future wars. So, we will focus mainly on the USA.

CONTINUITY AND CONVENTIONAL WARFARE

Historians and political scientists are unclear about the nature of future warfare. One group (which includes Colin S. Gray and Stephen Biddle among others) claims that the near future will experience both conventional and unconventional warfare. Gray asserts that despite the presence of culture, warfare is always political in nature. Gray uses the term irregular warfare for unconventional conflicts. Terrorism is a mode of unconventional warfare. In his paradigm, post-modern terrorism is characterized by three features: religious motivation, its global reach, and use of lethal technologies for creating civilian casualties.[13] However, Gray observes, '...post-modern terrorism as exemplified by al Qaeda, for all its novelty, real and apparent, is still terrorism, irregular warfare, and warfare'.[14]

The US campaign in Afghanistan during 2001–2 against the Al-Qaeda and its host, the Taliban regime, was an air-ground theatre-level war with heavy fire support fought between the two land armies.

Stephen Biddle asserts that the Afghan conflict was very similar to the typical twentieth-century mid-intensity conflict.[15] Biddle writes: 'The key to success, whether in 1916 or 2002, is to team heavy, well-directed fires with skilled ground maneuver to exploit their effects and over-whelm the surviving enemy.'[16] Biddle derives from his thesis developed in another book that modern war first emerged in the Western Front during the First World War. And the early twentieth century wars are mere continuation of modern war. In *Military Power*, Biddle claims:

> I hold that a particular pattern of force employment—the *modern system*— has been pivotal in the twentieth century and is likely to remain so. I argue that since 1900, the dominant technological fact of the modern battlefield has been increasing lethality. Even by 1914, firepower had become so lethal that exposed mass movement in the open had become suicidal. Subsequent technological change has only increased the range over which exposure can be fatal. To perform meaningful military missions in the face of this storm of steel requires armies to reduce their exposure, and since 1918 the central means of doing so has been modern system force management.[17]

So, Biddle more or less argues like Bailey but does not use the term MR to signify the profound changes in warfare and the birth of modern war, which according to them occurred during the Great War. Moreover, Biddle, unlike Bailey, is not a technological determinist. The modern system, according to Biddle, is a tightly interrelated complex of cover, concealment, dispersion, suppression, small-unit independent manoeuvre, and combined arms techniques at the tactical level; and depth, reserves, and differential concentration, and so on, at the opera-tional level of war. These techniques in a holistic manner, writes Biddle, are designed to reduce vulnerabilities to even twenty-first-century weap-ons and sensors. The modern system of force deployment to a great extent insulates it from lethal technology of the hostile party. Biddle warns that numerical superiority in the absolute sense means noth-ing much. Without the modern system of exposure reduction, an army may not survive long to make its numerical superiority tell against the enemy. The real point is to concentrate greater number of combatants at the crucial points by taking advantage of the modern force employ-ment system. Rather than a battle of materials or mere technological supremacy, the art of force employment to a great extent has shaped and will shape land operations. The war against terrorism involves counterintelligence activities and police works against the terrorists. But it is also accompanied by conventional operations against those states which support the insurgents and the terrorists. This is one of the cardinal points of the Bush Doctrine.[18]

As far as the future war in Afghanistan is concerned, Biddle continues:

> Where our allies are good enough, they may provide the ground troops for us, but what Afghanistan really shows is that the wars of tomorrow—like those of yesterday—will continue to require skilled, motivated forces on the ground, in strength, if we are to exploit our technology's effects. Precision weapons are making the ground-air combination ever more capable, but against resolute opponents, neither air power nor conventional ground forces will be able to prevail without the other any time soon.[19]

As regards the future force structure of the USA in the light of the Afghan experience, Biddle warns that reduction of the ground forces would have a harmful effect on US capability in the near future. Airpower and special operations force by themselves cannot win a war. It would be erroneous to think that the PGMs have revolutionized warfare. Traditional ground forces are still required for conducting close quarter combat.[20] Biddle in an article notes: 'I argue below that skill is indeed essential: allies with inferior skills cannot exploit precision airpower even with US SOF. The Afghan model *will* sometimes work, but less often than Andres, Wills, and Griffith claim...'[21] Biddle writes that the Taliban strategy was to deploy the inferior troops forward and the better troops at the back as reserves. After the initial battles, the Taliban deployed the skilled warriors, especially the Al-Qaeda veterans. And they overwhelmingly used overhead cover and concealment. During the combat north of Kandahar and especially during December 2001, Al-Qaeda defences were well camouflaged, dispersed, and made skillful use of the natural terrain for expedient cover. This pattern was also evident during Operation Anaconda in March 2002 when the veterans utilized dummy fighting positions in order to draw fire and attention away from their real disposition. In such cases, PGMs became less useful and close quarter combat became necessary.[22] So, basically, Biddle is claiming that future wars are going to be medium-intensity conventional warfare on land which will require infantry armies backed by massive amount of firepower. However, Biddle has nothing much to say about the insurgency which engulfed Afghanistan after the collapse of the Taliban. And this brings us to the alternate view regarding future warfare.

DISCONTINUITY AND UNCONVENTIONAL WAR

Another view is that the future wars which the USA will have to fight will be mostly insurgencies. It seems that the dice is loaded in favour of this group. However, the proponents of this view differ substantially among themselves. One of the spokesmen of this school of thought is the American brigadier, Peter R. Mansoor, who served in Iraq in 2003–4. In his autobiography he writes that Somalia, Afghanistan, and Iraq are harbingers of conflicts to come. He says that it is easier for the opponents of the USA to challenge the capabilities of the American forces in an asymmetric manner. Precision weapons are decisive only if the intelligence, surveillance, and reconnaissance capabilities exist to target enemy forces. The insurgent groups like Al-Qaeda, and so on, cannot be checked by high-technology weapons.[23]

Mansoor offers the following critique of the RMA:

> In the 1990s various military officers, defence analysts, and commentators posited a coming revolution in military affairs based on information dominance coupled with precision weapons. Integral to concepts such as network centric warfare is near-perfect intelligence from manned and unmanned sensors, satellites, and other intelligence, surveillance, and reconnaissance assets…. What these commentators missed was that this revolution in military affairs had already been realized in the 1991 Gulf War. Inevitably America's enemies would either catch up or move on. The issue in the 1990s was not how to perfect the information-precision revolution but what would come next. The answer would come in New York City and at the Pentagon, in the mountains and deserts of Afghanistan, and in the cities and palm groves of Iraq.[24]

Unlike Biddle, who emphasizes evolution (continuity) of warfare, the proponents of MR, MTR, and RMA focus on discontinuity (radical break) in warfare. Most of the doctrinaires of MR/RMA like Bruce Berkowitz, Emily O. Goldman, Thomas G. Mahnken, and so on, focus on information technology. They argue that the rapid transition from firepower-intensive weapon system to an information-intensive military system is mainly the product of emergence of information technologies in the post-industrial society from the late 1980s onwards.

The characteristics of information-based RMA (also known as IT-RMA) are long-range precision weapons targeting enemy's command, tele-communications and information systems, and aggressive information warfare (computer network attack).[25] As one of its proponents, Berkowitz, a RAND Corporation analyst claims: 'The next wars will be fought not just on the battlefields but also in the world's computers and communication systems'.[26] Terrorists and international criminal cartels, Berkowitz tells us, will utilize the new information technologies. There will be no frontline in this war as the battles will be fought with fibre optic digital communications.[27] Martin Bayer claims:

> ...both movies and computer games will shape the future perception of historical and contemporary wars, especially as the distinction between reality and virtuality becomes increasingly blurred. Additionally, the convergence of commercial computer games and professional military simulations will increase, as the former offers low-cost alternatives to the military, while production costs can be shared.[28]

This development will continue, says Bayer, until the visualization matches the real world, and such a scenario will be achieved in the near future.[29] However, the battle for information dominance does not mean that killing would be absent in the information age warfare. Face-to-face and hand-to-hand encounters, notes Berkowitz, will continue along with the war fought along the information highways.[30] Goldman, unlike Berkowitz, is not concerned with intra-state wars but with inter-state wars. Goldman considers the importance of RMA for containing states geared for conventional warfare or to launch a pre-emptive strike against rogue states.[31]

Gray warns that the advocates of RMA focus mostly on techno-logical superiority and reflects the preferred American way of warfare, which is unwilling to absorb casualties. Gray, Williamson Murray, and MacGregor Knox, following Clausewitz, emphasize the non-linear, contingent, and complex nature of warfare.[32] However, Gray, unlike Murray and Knox, asserts: 'It may be that any trans historical grand theory of innovation, purporting to identify and explain a regular pattern in RMA, MR or MTR, must be fundamentally flawed.'[33] It must be admitted that Berkowitz despite harping on information warfare, like Mansoor but unlike Biddle and Gray, accepts that the wars in the twenty-first century will be asymmetric wars.[34]

Mansoor continues that the first requirement, however, is to jettison the mindset that all wars will be short and sharp, and will be fought at extended distances with stealth and precision, and without large numbers of troops or extended occupations. Insurgencies, by their very nature, are labour-intensive and long-term affairs, generational struggles that defy the domestic logic of opinion polls and election cycles. Mansoor and Biddle, despite their difference in views about the nature of future warfare, agree that in the near future, the USA will require large number of infantry. In the near future, asserts Mansoor, the USA will have to conduct mainly COIN operations which are characterized by 80 per cent political and 20 per cent military actions. Further, in COIN, the people are not the means to achieve the objective but are the objective.[35] Here, Mansoor is on similar ground with the retired British General Rupert Smith who has coined the term 'war amongst the people'.

Rupert Smith, somewhat like Mansoor, Martin Van Creveld, and others, asserts that the era of inter-state war is over. But Rupert Smith and others, whom we will discuss below, assert that the world is witnessing a new form of insurgency. The clear division between peace and war, as evident in inter-state war, is no more applicable.[36] This discourse is part of a wider debate among the military historians and the political scientists that the era of conventional warfare is over and twenty-first century heralds the beginning of a new form of unconventional warfare. The proponents of the death of conventional warfare are Herfried M. Munkler, Mary Kaldor, and Van Creveld. Munkler, Kaldor, Smith, and others call the new insurgencies as New Wars. Like the RMA proponents, the New War proponents accept radical break (i.e., discontinuity) in the evolution of warfare in the post–Cold War era. But, while the RMA theorists focus mainly on technology, the New Wars' advocates emphasize changing social and political conditions which has been functioning as an incubator to New Wars. Again, the RMA proponents accept that conventional warfare in future is a possibility. But, for the proponents of New Wars, conventional war is dead. Van Creveld writes that the advent of nuclear weapons resulted in the extinction of large-scale conventional warfare. Now, the field is open to the stateless and sub-state agents to conduct sub-conventional and unconventional warfare. He concentrates on the *Intifada* by the Palestinians to show the impotence of the Israeli Defence Force (IDF) equipped with conventional weapons in the face of such struggle.[37]

Kaldor opines on the basis of the breakdown of Yugoslavia in 1989 that the post–Cold War era is characterized by a new form of insurgency. Kaldor, however, says that the 1980s and the 1990s witnessed a new type of violence (which she terms as the 'New War') developed in Africa and East Europe. Kaldor accepts that an RMA has occurred. However, instead of harping on new sensor, information, and communication technologies like Berkowitz, Kaldor writes that the RMA centres around radical changes in social relations. Especially globalization (intensification of global interconnectedness) generated huge political, social, and cultural changes which underpin the new RMA.[38] She characterizes the New War in the following words: 'In the new wars, the monopoly of legitimate violence has broken down. And what is crucial is not the privatization of violence, as such, but the breakdown of legitimacy.... The strategy is political control on the basis of exclusion—in particular, population displacement—and the tactics for achieving this goal are terror and destabilizing.'[39] Kaldor notes that the fighting units of the stateless marginal groups finance themselves through pillage and plunder, black market, and through illegal trade in arms, drugs, and diamonds. Insurgents financing themselves through the diamond trade are applicable in the case of Liberia and Sierra Leone. Opium cultivation, narcotics trade, and its relationship with the Afghan warlords is also well known. And Kaldor's other point is that humanitarian interventions generally fail to stop these New Wars because humanitarian aid, to an extent, finances the warlords' activities and legitimizes the warring chieftains by bringing them in the negotiating table.[40] Kaldor's argument is that the warlords want the insurgency to continue because they make money and have power in such a scenario. The warlords, being total spoilers, do not have constructing a new state as their objective. To an extent, this assertion holds true for Afghanistan. The warlords, in order to maintain their private militia (source of power and income) and drug business, are not willing to engage in constructive activities in order to prepare the path for the evolution of a centralized government in Kabul.

The German scholar Herfried Munkler notes the following characteristics of the New Wars. Firstly, there is the ongoing privatization of war. States no longer enjoy monopoly in conducting warfare. Non-state and sub-state actors have increasingly seized the initiative from the polities. Secondly, there is the asymmetricalization of war. In other words, asymmetry has become the standard conditions of warfare.

Thirdly, demilitarization of war is another feature of the New Wars. Like the states, the armed forces have also lost control and monopoly over organized violence. Irregular armies dominate the battlefield and they target civilians and the non-military infrastructure. Munkler emphasizes that these characteristics might have been present in earlier conflicts. But what is new is that the three characteristics are present simultaneously in the present insurgencies. Hence, they are termed as New Wars.[41]

About the 'new' type of insurgency, Rupert Smith writes: '...the attackers depend on the people to be able to prosecute their attacks, whether they cooperate or not: they are carried out both on and amongst the people'.[42] Rupert Smith elucidates the central character-istics of the new form of war. The war is fought among the people and not on the battlefield. The conflicts tend to be timeless. And the oppo-nents are mostly non-state actors. Media plays an important role in shaping the will of the people during such conflicts.[43] Conducting a successful COIN requires large number of 'boots on the ground' and the USA lacks the capability to maintain many hundred thousands of soldiers for many years in the disturbed countries. Loyal troops, writes Mansoor, should be raised from the host societies.[44] For this aspect, the British experience of empire building might prove handy to the American policy makers.

Like Rupert Smith, Mansoor, and the US Special Forces Officer HY S. Rothstein, the United States Marine Corps Colonel Thomas X. Hammes, in his overview of modern conflicts, writes that Afghanistan, Iraq, Palestine, and so on, show that the principal threat for the USA, in the twenty-first century, will remain insurgency. However, he adds a new twist and calls that what we are witnessing is evolved insurgency. Hammes terms it as the Fourth Generation Warfare (4GW). The his-tory of warfare is divided into four generations by Hammes. The First Generation Warfare grew out of gunpowder. The Second Generation Warfare witnessed the rise of multi-million mass armies by the indus-trial states during the First World War. The Third Generation Warfare was initiated by the motorized *Wehrmacht's Blitzkrieg*. The end of twentieth century witnessed the emergence of 4GW. Hammes has been somewhat influenced by Tofflers' Wave Theory.

Though the Wave Theory is too general, still it has influenced at least some sections of the security community. Hence, a brief synopsis of the Wave Theory is required. According to Alvin and Heidi Toffler, the history of humanity could broadly be categorized as the product of three waves. The first wave was the product of agricultural revolution which started some 10,000 years ago. The second wave was triggered by the Industrial Revolution which began some 300 years ago. And the last wave which is still continuing is the product of Information Revolution.[45] It is to be noted that Tofflers' emphasis on information technologies initiating a revolution in human affairs to a great extent is similar to the proponents of RMAs, who also harp on information technologies initiating radical changes in the concept and conduct of present-day warfare.

Hammes offers the following definition of 4GW: 'It is an evolved form of insurgency. Still rooted in the fundamental precept that superior political will, when properly employed, can defeat greater economic and military power, 4GW makes use of society's networks to carry on its fight.'[46] Hammes tells us that Afghans are also practising this new form of insurgency. About the Afghan opposition to the Soviets, Hammes writes:

> The Afghans fell back on their traditional tribal tactics against the invaders, using ambushes, assassination, and sabotage to inflict casualties on the Soviets. But, for Afghans used to resolving their own fights, they added a new twist. They took their message to the world and sought assistance both from the Islamic nations and the West. In keeping with the networked nature of 4GW, they found allies with similar interests and made what were clearly temporary alliances.[47]

Hammes further warns the American analysts that if the Al-Qaeda or Taliban are seen as the only enemy, it oversimplifies the problem. For Hammes, a wide spectrum of people do not want to see an effective central government in Afghanistan. The AGF (anti-government forces) is a true networked, 4GW enemy, and will display all the resilience characteristic of such enemies.[48] Hammes describes the combat characteristics of the Afghan insurgents: 'Like previous 4GW conflicts, the insurgent is a networked, flexible force that avoids contact except on its own terms. It focuses on low-intensity activities—those one expects to find in phase I of a classic Maoist insurgency.'[49]

At times, the COIN forces might have to distinguish between insurgency and terrorism. Isabelle Duyvesteyn and Mario Fumerton differentiate between insurgency and terrorism. The difference between these two phenomenon in their mind is strategic. An organization can switch strategy and can initiate either of these two types of violence. In contrast to Kaldor, Duyvesteyn and Fumerton claim that global changes notwithstanding, the objectives of insurgency is to gain political and military control of a population and territory which involves establishment of some sort of governance, which may or may not include taking control of national government and state institutions. Terrorist actions aim at psychological results. But actual casualties resulting from terrorism are limited despite their symbolic value. Unlike the terrorist, for an insurgent organization, it is necessary that a decisive proportion of the populace, regardless of motives or sentiments, actively collaborates with the insurgents. The insurgents resort to population control either through persuasion or, mostly, through coercion.[50]

CULTURE AND INSURGENCIES

Think thou also of thy duty and do not waver. There is no greater good for a warrior than to fight in a righteous war.

There is a war that opens the door of heaven, Arjuna! Happy the warriors whose fate is to fight such war.

But to forgo this fight for righteousness is to forgo thy duty and honour: is to fall into transgression.

Men will tell of thy dishonour both now and in times to come. And to a man who is in honour, dishonour is more than death.

.... In death thy glory in heaven, in victory thy glory on earth.
—Lord Krishna's advice to Pandava Warrior Arjuna during the Mahabharata War (Bhagavad Gita, 500 BCE)[51]

An American military officer named Robert M. Cassidy, like Hammes, accepts that the twenty-first century is witnessing an evolving hybrid form of insurgency. However, unlike Hammes, Cassidy does not use the term 4GW. Cassidy writes that this new form of insurgency has two characteristics of the twentieth-century guerrilla war: first, it remains the weapons of the weak and, second, it involves 'hit and run' tactics. Cassidy asserts that most of the present-day insurgents are coming from the erstwhile Second and the Third Worlds.[52] Cassidy attempts to introduce a culturalist angle to explain the new insurgency:

Potential adversaries are from Asia and the East, from cultures that have generally espoused an Eastern tradition of war. The Eastern way of war stems from the philosophies of Sun Tzu and Mao Tse-Tung, and it is distinguishable from the Western way by its reliance on indirectness, perfidy, attrition, and protraction. In other words, the Eastern way of war is inherently more irregular, unorthodox, and asymmetric than our traditional conception of war.... John Keegan has posited that delay, evasion, and indirectness are three distinguishable behavioral traits of an Eastern way of war.[53]

Cassidy elaborates that the Al-Qaeda and other related terrorist networks in Afghanistan, Chechnya, Iraq, and elsewhere are following the Eastern way of warfare, which is attritional and emphasizes wearing down the enemy through prolonged struggle rather than defeating the enemy in a single trial of arms. Since the Islamic terrorists are weak in technology, they rely more on ideas in order to conduct asymmetric warfare.[54]

Christopher Coker, the British political scientist along with Cassidy and others constitute what can be termed as the Culturalist School. Rather than the immutable laws of Clausewitzian trinity, war for them is shaped by different cultures. Culture could be defined as mental structure that can change or control reality in order to fit a particular conception.[55] The assumption of this approach is that a nation's traditions, values, attitudes, patterns of behaviour, customs, specific ways of adapting to environment generate a particular type of martial culture.[56] Coker claims that the very industrialization of war during the two World Wars has transformed the meaning of warfare for the Western nations. Coker writes that the East and the West have different understandings of war and the role of the warriors. The mentalities of the Eastern and the Western people are remote psychologically and emotionally. The Americans in particular and the Western nations in general have a rigidly instrumental attitude towards warfare. In contrast, the Eastern societies possess existential warrior ethos. For them, violence is not instrumental but constitutes the moral essence of the warrior. To support this claim, Coker quotes from Lord Krishna's advice to the Pandava warrior Arjuna in the Bhagavad Gita. For the true warrior, violence is existential. In the existential dimension, war is a means of realizing one's humanity rather than merely the interests of the state. While from the mid-twentieth century, the existential dimension of war was dying in all the advanced industrial societies, the existential dimension of war survived in the non-Western backward societies.[57] The enormous casualties of the two World Wars had made the Western nations' casualty averse.

For Coker, the West is now disenchanted with war and warrior ethos.[58] Coker writes:

> But in a society in which soldiers are no longer encouraged to discover their self-worth through the esteem of other men—or...are not allowed to— western societies may only be able to engage in war not by emphasizing the cultural (the meme) over the biological (the gene) but by *emphasizing the biological at the expense of the cultural*-by re-engineering warriors through biotechnical means.[59]

Coker visualizes a near future when cyborg technologies and genetic engineering will enhance the power of the Western warriors. Technology will no more be an extension of the human body but in the near foreseeable future will be a part of the body. Soldiers' bodies and personalities will be reconfigured in order to enhance their physical and psychological capacity to withstand the stress and strain of war. The net result will be that human beings and machines will co-evolve equally.[60]

The disjuncture between the Eastern and Western views of warfare is a running thread in the format of the Culturalist School. Instead of relying on Clausewitz who argues about the universal nature of warfare, the Culturalist School focuses on Herodotus' bipolar division of the world. In fact, they look at insurgency at a systemic/global level. The same global lens which was used to analyse the Cold War between the East and the West with certain modifications is now used to analyse Islamic insurgency which is believed to be operating at a global level against the democratic Christian West. To an extent, it is also a throwback to the medieval West European idea of a Christian Crusade by the West against the Muslim empires of the East. One also finds some similarity with Samuel Huntington's 'clash of culture' thesis, where the twenty-first century is expected to experience a clash between the declining Western Christian civilization ranged against the Islamic, Confucius, and Hindu civilizations.[61] The 'civilizational' clash of Huntington is modified in the case of Culturalist School as the bipolar clash between Eastern Culture of Warfare with the Western Culture of Warfare.

However, a bipolar division of the culture of war, which is accepted by Cassidy and Coker at the global level, is problematic. The strategic culture approach marginalizes change in favour of continuity. Tensions and uncertainties between various subcultures within a culture are generally overlooked.[62] For instance, in India, from the ancient antiquity, there has been tension between two traditions of warfare, which evolved simultaneously. While the Mahabharata, Bhagavad Gita and *Manusamhita* emphasized *dharmayuddha* (as part of the existential dimension of war); Kautilya's *Arthasastra* and *Panchatantra*, among others, focus on *kutayuddha* (instrumental attitude towards warfare).[63]

Cassidy falls into the trap of bipolar division of global warfare, a flawed model which is pushed by a group of powerful American and British military historians like Geoffrey Parker, Victor Davis Hanson, and John Keegan. Deriving from Herodotus' division of the world into the Orient and the Occident, these military historians assert that from the dawn of civilization, two ways of warfare can be characterized. The Eastern way of warfare as practised by the Asians focus on hit-and-run tactics, and attritional warfare, emphasizing deceit, subterfuge, chicanery, and so on. Rituals, religious traditions, numerical superiority, and changing sides by the chieftains with their armed contingents during the conflict are important components of the Oriental war making. China, India, and Central Asia followed this model. In contrast, the Western way of warfare could be traced back to the Classical Civilization of Greece. The Greeks invented the concept of a single decisive battle in order to settle the issue in a single afternoon. The focus on battle and close quarter combat was carried forward by the Romans, and finally, culminated in the two World Wars of the twentieth century. The Western way of warfare is conducted by capital intensive technology-oriented military machines. The Western way of warfare emphasizes the role of discipline, standing army, qualitative superiority, leadership, managerial expertize, rationality, civic virtue, and application of scientific principles.[64]

This is not the place to debate about the historical evolution of warfare in Eurasia. But it should be noted that standing armies, scientific siege warfare, and disciplined infantry emerged first in Assyria, then in Egypt, and then these traits passed into Classical Greece, which was part of an Eastern Mediterranean Civilization rather than a unique 'Western' Civilization. It would be wrong to argue that China, India, and Persia did not maintain disciplined standing armies in the pre-modern era. Further, some of the pre-modern Asian battles like Chaldiran, Tu-Mu, First and Third Panipats, and so on, were greater in scope and lethality than contemporary West European battles.

Lastly, compared to the generalship of Attila, Chingiz Khan, Amir Timur, and so on, especially as regards to their capacity to conduct long-range manoeuvre warfare, practitioners of Western warfare like Alexander, Caesar, and Charlemagne appear as pygmies.[65]

NET ASSESSMENT

The Culturalist paradigm is ahistorical and attempts to explain Western triumphalism on the basis of cultural uniqueness of the West. The use of terms like '4GW', 'New War', and so on, in order to explain the twenty-first centuries' insurgencies does not advance our understanding of the latter phenomenon. The characteristics of New War which Munkler points out, to my mind, were present in Mao's conduct of war against Chiang Kai Shek till 1945. Hew Strachan notes that the current wars are being fought for traditional reasons like religious faith, political ideology, nationalism, and ethnic identity, especially in regions where political violence has been endemic for quite a long time.[66] At least from the beginning of the twentieth century and especially from the time of Communist insurgencies in the 1940s, gaining the 'hearts and minds' of the people was very important. So, Rupert Smith's concept of 'war amongst the people' denotes nothing new.

Ivan Arreguin-Toft says that in the near future, the USA would have to fight both conventional and unconventional wars. For the first type of war, the USA has a capital-intensive armed force at its disposal. However, for combating the insurgents, the USA requires a different type of army, which it yet does not possess. An army which excels in fighting conventional war, asserts Arreguin-Toft, just could not adapt successfully in combating the insurgents. In fact, an army with officers who have excelled in conventional warfare will obstruct the adaptability and flexibility of the fighting force trying to combat insurgencies. Arreguin-Toft continues that unconventional warfare is winnable if the regime follows a 'barbaric' strategy. Authoritarian regime could follow such a strategy much more easily than a democratic regime due to absence of public pressure in the home front. A great power which is not democratic could easily follow such a policy because international sanctions will not harm it. However, a minor power, even though it is powerful than the insurgents fighting against it, cannot follow such a policy for the fact that international public opinion and international economic sanctions will hurt it miserably.[67] Arreguin-Toft has a supporter in Gray. Gray opines that military and police terror is swifter and effective than the so-called 'hearts and mind' approach in crushing the irregulars.[68]

Arreguin-Toft has two strong points. In history for instance, Nazi Germany, being a totalitarian state, was quite effective in conducting barbaric COIN against the partisans in Russia[69] and against the *maquis* in France. The infamous 'Night and Fog' decree of December 1941 and the policy of 'reprisal shooting' enabled the Germans to contain the partisans with second-grade elderly troops and Russian auxiliaries. Further back in time, between 1905 and 1907, during the Maji–Maji uprising in German East Africa, more than 75,000 Africans were killed by the German troops. And, during Herero rebellion in 1904–7, 60,000 Herero died. Probably, winning the 'hearts and minds' of the populace in the guerrilla-infested region is not that important. If we believe T.E. Lawrence (1888–1935), then a successful rebellion could be accomplished with only 2 per cent active support among the population, provided the rest 98 per cent either sympathized with or acquiesced in guerrilla activity.[70] Whether present-day international opinion as well as the home societies in US and NATO countries will allow them to follow a 'barbaric' pacification policy in Afghanistan is debatable.

Again, the Russian army, which is the direct descendant of the Soviet army after being defeated in Afghanistan, failed to reorganize itself properly to conduct unconventional operations effectively against the insurgents. The lessons learnt from Afghanistan, as far as the Soviet/Russian army is concerned, is ambiguous at best and negative at worse. After the Soviet 40th Army withdrew from Afghanistan in 1989, the USSR/Russia was not merely thinking of how to win the next COIN campaign but how to deal with possible NATO incursions within its borders in the climate of political breakdown and economic decline. In the summer of 1991, the Chief of Airborne Forces, Colonel General V.A. Achalov introduced the idea of a mobile force in order to fulfil a wide range of missions. This proposal was officially accepted a year later by the Defence Minister General P.S. Grachev (who was a former deputy to Achalov) as the starting point for reorganization of the Russian armed forces. The Mobile Forces Directorate comprised five airborne divisions, eight independent airborne and air assault brigades, six motorized rifle brigades, six naval infantry battalions, two amphibious assault battalions, four military transport divisions, and one Spetsnaz brigade. The primary mission of the Immediate Response Force (IRF) is to provide peacekeeping forces for resolving regional conflicts adjacent to Russia or United Nations' mandated operations around the world. In case of a large-scale conventional war, the IRF would reinforce the border troops and provide the first echelon defence/counter-offence forces. After the parliamentary crisis of October 1993, internal peacekeeping also became part of the IRF's mission. To combat terrorism, organized crime, and paramilitary nationalist groups, the IRF was supposed to cooperate with MVD troops. If the mission becomes lengthy and the crisis escalates, then Rapid Deployment Force (RDF) is responsible to provide heavy ground support. The RDF comprised three army corps with a more responsive C2 network. The RDF in case of a large-scale conventional war is to become the second echelon ground force.[71]

The Russian army's performance in Chechnya and Georgia was not all that good. Probably, the capacity of a conventional army to prepare for unconventional warfare is limited. On 21 December 1994, the Russian Air Force started bombing Grozny. The advance of the Mobile Forces towards Grozny was slowed by harassing fire from the Chechen guerrillas. The Russian army was not prepared for isolated combat in the streets and in the rooftops amidst the concrete urban jungle. One Chechen guerrilla noted: 'The Russian infantry wouldn't get out of their armour to fight, so their vehicles had no cover. We just stood on the balconies and dropped grenades on them as they drove by underneath.'[72] It was an action replay of the Soviet experience along the narrow mountainous valleys of Afghanistan. The lightly armoured infantry and airborne units of the Mobile Forces proved unable to storm Grozny. Then, the Russian commanders created storm detachments which established strongholds and cleared the city, building by building. The storm detachments were inspired by the use of *bronegruppy* during the Afghan War and experiences in Stalingrad and Berlin during World War II. The storm detachments comprised BMPs, tanks, 122-mm and 152-mm self-propelled howitzers and helicopter gunships along with teams of assault infantry. After the Battle of Grozny, the Chechens defended various cities like Argun, Shali, and so on. In urban warfare, the Chechen tried to nullify superior Russian firepower from helicopters, aircraft, and tanks. The Chechen guerrillas blended with the local population in these urban centres. The use of indiscriminate force by the Russian army aided the Chechen guerrillas to recruit more people into their ranks. The Chechen guerrillas then withdrew to the forest in the mountains. Between December 1994 and March 1996, the Russian army suffered 6,000 killed.[73]

Like Arreguin-Toft, retired US Special Operations Officer HY S. Rothstein argues that the present US armed forces are geared for attritional conventional warfare. The US-armed forces focus on mass, manoeuvre, and concentrating firepower. Organizationally and doctrinally, the US force is incapable of fighting and winning unconventional warfare. Only the SOF could conduct unconventional warfare successfully. But they are marginalized and conventionalized by the dominant organizational culture of the Pentagon, which emphasizes Clausewitzian conventional warfare.[74] The role of technology is downplayed by Rothstein for fighting the insurgents. In his words: '...a focus on the acquisition of high technology for deployment against a sophisticated enemy may significantly limit a state's ability to deal with lesser threats from an unsophisticated foe'.[75] The importance of the special forces for conducting COIN is noted by Rothstein in the following words: 'These situations are characterized by a lack of defined enemy; the need for influence, negotiation, and even community leadership and by the ability to resort to deadly force if necessary. The component of the US military best prepared for these environments is the SOF.'[76]

Rothsetin's claim is supported by Mark Moyar. The latter writes:

> The problem was that many commanders in the regular army were deficient in flexibility, creativity, and other attributes of greater value in counterinsurgency than in conventional warfare. The importance of those attributes could be seen in the contrast between Special Forces officers, who often possessed them, and regular army officers, who often did not.[77]

The Special Forces officers are capable of winning the allegiance of the locals and thrive on rapid decentralized operations. In contrast, the regular officers of the US army regulars in Afghanistan kept their troops inside large bases and instituted lengthy bureaucratic procedures which caused delay or cancellation of numerous operations.[78] Rothstein warns that the SOF must never neglect training in civic affairs and psychological operations, and should never concentrate only on commando operations. This is necessary because like Rupert Smith, Rothsetin also believes that, after all, the principal objective of COIN is to fight amongst the people and win their allegiance.[79]

At the beginning of the new millennium, preparation for conventional warfare accounted for 75 per cent of USA's military budget.[80] Arguing that a state should have two types of armies for combating conventional and unconventional threats is asking for too much. Even the world's sole superpower, the USA probably cannot afford it. Then, SOF is not the silver bullet. Rune Henriksen writes: 'Special Operations Forces, on the other hand, tend to become caught in other missions, like nation-building, to which they are ill suited, and they tend to use airpower that plays into the hands of the terrorists and insurgents by alienating the local population.'[81]

If creating a new army is not possible, then at least modifying, if not completely changing, the operative philosophy of the conventionalized army, is possible at least up to an extent. The proponent of such a view can be categorized as Organizational Culture School. Unlike the Culturalist, they do not accept the unchangeable overdominance of cultural elements in human affairs. The spokesmen of this school believe that fusion of selective cultural elements and organizational precepts are possible in certain circumstances. Two examples of this school are Mark Moyar and David Kilcullen, who was the Senior Counterinsurgency Advisor to General David Petraeus in Iraq and later an Advisor to General Stanley McChrystal in Afghanistan. Kilcullen was an Advisor to NATO in 2010. As regards COIN in Afghanistan, Kilcullen writes: 'To end this insurgency and achieve peace, we may need more than extra troops, new resources, and a new campaign plan: as General Stanley McChrystal has emphasized, we need a new operational culture. *Organizations manage what they measure, and they measure what their leaders tell them to report on.*'[82] Kilcullen comes up with a cyclical model in order to explain continuation of insurgency. Corruption in the Afghan government, in the societal elites, and in the international assistance effort enables and encourages bad behaviour by the government officials and the power brokers. This in turn creates popular rage and disillusionment, which empowers the insurgency. Thus, the war against the insurgents creates further opportunities and incentives for corruption and criminality, driving the cycle forward. Kilcullen offers some organizational correctives to the US COIN force. Body counts are important for evaluating success during a conventional campaign but not during an unconventional campaign. One is reminded of the US army's infamous body count formula during the imbroglio in Vietnam. Kilcullen warns that body count data are notoriously corrupt and subjective, with differing interpretations of insurgent versus civilian casualties. An audit process should allow the units to redirect effort towards identified priority stabilization targets and rebuild local partnerships.[83] Kilcullen continues that the COIN forces must take into account the cultural differences that exist between them and the culture of the inhabitants of the disturbed regions. He writes: 'Unlike us, Afghans do not necessarily stop talking to the enemy when they start fighting: most conflicts end when one group switches sides or agrees to surrender. Thus, the mere fact that our local partners are in dialogue with the enemy is not an indicator in and of itself of disloyalty to the government.'[84] Moyar emphasizes that education of the COIN troops on foreign cultures demonstrates the real world value of empathy and illuminates the differences between cultures in how they view the world.[85]

Both Moyar and Kilcullen agree that population security must be the premium in COIN operations. Here they are on similar track with Mansoor and Rupert Smith. Lieutenant General David W. Barno, who took over command of the coalition forces in October 2003, emphasized on population security missions. Small American detachments were sent to various Afghan villages in order to live there and patrol relentlessly. Moyar believes that the constitution of 80-person-PRTs which the US army established in 2002 in order to reduce poor governance and unemployment, which are fuelling insurgency, is an innovative measure indeed. The PRTs comprised members of armed forces as well as civilian agencies. The PRTs tried to build up relationship with the local Afghan leaders which required good social skills and considerable patience.[86]

What could be the nature of future wars which other rising powers of Eurasia might fight in the near future? One example of an army of a hegemonic South Asian power which fought conventional and unconventional wars successfully during the second half of the twentieth century is the Indian army. Between 1947 and 2011, it fought four wars with Pakistan (1947–8, 1965, 1971, 1999), one with China (a minor defeat in 1962), and is combating Pakistani and Chinese-sponsored insurgencies in Kashmir and north-east India quite successfully. Being a democratic country and not being a superpower, India did not have the will or capability to follow a 'barbaric' strategy against the insurgents. In fact, without reading Kilcullen, Indian security establishment is following his policy long before he wrote them. Kilcullen's cyclical model is applicable to explain continuing insurgency in north-east India. Except Assam, economies of the six north-east Indian states are dependent on subsidies and grant from Indian central government. So, north-east India is a 'donor driven economy'. And corrupt government officials as well as the insurgents have an interest for continuation of the insurgency and COIN so that funds continue to flow into north-east which, in turn, gives them an opportunity to line their pockets. Again, the Indian state never stops talking with the insurgents. Rather, dialogue goes on during fighting. And, at times when dialogue is partly successful, then armistice/ceasefire occurs. And then again, COIN operations starts. Occasionally, dialogue is successful when the insurgents join the mainstream. Use of limited amount of force, and not using airpower and heavy artillery characterize India's COIN operation. For COIN, India maintains a labour-intensive army. The Indian army has 1.2 million men and is the fourth largest in the world. In addition, India has 1 million strong paramilitary forces. And some of the paramilitary forces like the Border Security Forces, Central Industrial Security Forces, and Assam Rifles have the same level of training as the Indian regular infantry, but lacks heavy weapons like artillery and tanks. The Indian commanders realize that COIN is a manpower-intensive attritional warfare and the Indian soldiers are only allowed to use light hand-held firearms while dealing with the insurgents. Limited coercion is followed by political cooption, decentralization and devolution of powers, and redrawing of the political boundaries.[87]

Another point worth looking into is that some advanced technologies, which are the products of RMA, might be useful both in cases of conventional and unconventional warfare. For instance, the UAVs can be used quite successfully for reconnaissance against both conventional enemies and the insurgents. A large number of British and American officers like Rupert Smith, Mansoor, and Rothstein argue that the current military training does not adequately emphasize unconventional warfare. It is a valid point, especially in the present context of rising importance of unconventional warfare.

This is because technology is no panacea for COIN operations in all terrains. The experience of the Indian army with super technology is not all that good. During General Shankar Roychowdhury's (Chief of Army Staff of India from November 1994 to September 1997) tenure, there was an attempt to induct US UAVs in the Indian army for checking unauthorized crossing across the Line of Control in Kashmir. The UAVs were taken to the Indian Air Force base at Awantipur near Srinagar for test overflights over actual terrain. The UAVs were not designed to operate at very high altitudes. But in Kashmir, the lower mountain peaks are at least 10,000 to 12,000 feet high. Again, limitations on the manoeuvrability of the UAVs prevented low-level search missions across the meandering valleys which were used by the insurgents.[88] However, the drone attacks by the US in FATA of Pakistan during 2011–12 have been quite successful.

Besides conducting COIN operations in Baluchistan and against the neo-Taliban in Waziristan and in FATA, Pakistan is also preparing for a conventional war under a nuclear umbrella with India over Kashmir. The two nuclear-equipped powers—India and Pakistan—actually fought a sub-conventional war at Kargil in 1999. The sub-conventional Kargil War was fought from May to July 1999 on a 200-km front. The war was fought on one of the world's most inhospitable battlefield. The harsh and cruel landscape is characterized by wind chill and knife-edged ridges. During the subzero temperature of winter, the Pakistani troops were able to move into the Kargil sector. In May 1999, when the Indian units reoccupied the posts vacated during winter, they found that infiltrators were commanding the heights above the strategic National Highway IA which climbs up from the Kahsmir Valley to Ladakh. The Indian troops had to ascend the cliffs with pitons and rope, laden with arms, ammunition, and essential supplies, under cover of darkness in the rarefied deoxygenated atmosphere in order to silence the *sangar*s. India used air power to contain the incursion. However, high-speed combat aircraft are not so useful in the narrow valleys with limited turning circles.[89]

To explain the future behaviour of the rising superpowers, concepts like RMA are of some help. Future war gaming for China might be different from the Afghanistan–Iraq paradigm of war. Beijing may have to fight small-scale insurgencies in Tibet or in the Muslim majority provinces (especially Xinjiang) in western China. However, Beijing's principal concerns are Taiwan Straits (against the US Navy). A pointer for the future is the 1995–96 Taiwan Strait Crisis. During July 1995, China fired half a dozen DF-15 missiles, 90 miles off the coast of north Taiwan, for demonstrative effect. And during March 1996, 40 naval vessels, 260 aircraft, and some 150,000 Chinese troops participated in live fire amphibious landing exercises and aerial bombing north and south of Taiwan Strait.[90] Moreover, security (if possible control) over eastern and central portions of the Indian Ocean is important in China's strategic calculus. This is because China's growing economy requires oil in larger quantities. And China imports most of it from the Middle East through the Indian Ocean. Beijing perceives threat from the Indian Navy (the largest in the Indian Ocean) with its two aircraft carriers. India's attempt to induct a nuclear submarine further unnerves Beijing. Further, China has border dispute with India along Arunachal Pradesh and Ladakh. Beijing claims both these provinces as part of China. Moreover, the Indus and the Brahmaputra are the life blood of Indian economy. Both these rivers flow from Tibet. In near future, growing water crisis will hit South Asia hard. China is already building a dam over the Brahmaputra in Tibet. So, struggle for water might generate war along the Himalayan frontier. In case of a limited conventional war under nuclear umbrella (as India and Pakistan fought in Kargil), Beijing perceives that the Indian Navy might cut China's sea lines of communication. In order to combat the two above-mentioned threat scenarios, China is preparing for high-technology conventional warfare. President Jiang Zemin's objective is that the People's Liberation Army (PLA), in the near future, might conduct high-technology regional wars at the periphery of China. China has neither the capability nor the intention the like the USA to acquire power projection capacity with nuclear war capabilities across the oceans and continents. This is despite the fact that China is developing tactical nuclear weapons from the 1980s. The regional wars, notes China, are to be won by applying superior scientific and technological skill rather than quantitative superiority in manpower, which was Mao's dictum. The PLA is transforming itself from being a manpower-intensive army to a capital-intensive army. Despite the reduction of the PLA's size (especially infantry) by some 500,000 men, the focus is on building up selective elite units called *quantou* (fist units). These units are designed to conduct limited war under high-technology conditions. The hostile forces are to be defeated near the border and the early battles are going to be decisive. So, the wars are designed to be short and sharp.[91] Lighting air and missile strikes, and then sustained air, missile, and electronic bombardment would characterize the conduct of future warfare.[92]

As part of preparation for conducting limited war in high-technology context, the Chinese armed forces are in the throes of an information technology (IT)-oriented RMA. Chinese Information Warfare (IW) capability comprises information acquisition, information protection, and information attack. One PLA researcher points out that about 80 per cent of the US military communications facilities rely on civilian networks. And this offers a window of opportunity for cyber attacks. China's development of a hard-kill IW capability focused on development of laser/particle beam weapon systems, anti-satellite weapon systems, cruise missiles, anti-radiation missiles, and laser-guided smart weapons. An attempt is made to develop ship-borne laser weapons for air defence. China is also interested in developing UAVs to serve as platforms for electronic warfare capability. The PLA probably also has developed electromagnetic pulse bombs in order to paralyse electronic and information systems of the hostile power. China is attempting to integrate Global Positioning System and the Russian Global Navigation Satellite System guidance technology in the fighters, helicopters, and cruise missiles. One of the crucial bottlenecks in integrating the information technology-oriented RMA within the Chinese armed forces are inadequate number of academically and technically qualified officers.[93]

THE OTHER SIDE OF THE HILL

In order to assess COIN policies in Afghanistan, the nature of war conducted by the Afghans in particular and the insurgents in general in the post Cold War era needs to be discussed. Brigadier General Itai Brun, an officer of the IDF turns the focus on the changing dynamics of warfare among the insurgents. He coins the term Other-RMA (O-RMA) to cover the changing character of warfare conducted by the insurgents from late twentieth century. The objective of the insurgents has been to create deterrence by preventing the stronger side from attacking them, and in case deterrence fails, then to win by not losing the war. Brun continues that the conceptual roots of the new war among the insurgents initially emerged in the Middle East during the late 1970s and then spread into Afghanistan in the 1980s. The point to be noted is that at that time, the armies of the big powers were developing the concepts of RMA from earlier concepts like Air–Land Battle and Follow-on Forces Attack, which initially emerged to fight conventional battles against the Soviets. To go back to the insurgents, O-RMA means making war against the stronger states in times of peace. The characteristics of O-RMA are as follows. The objective is to create large number of civilian casualties by using suicide bombers, improvised explosive devices, surface-to-surface missiles, and so on. The insurgents make use of fundamentalist Islam to strengthen the motivation of their active and passive supporters. Availability of a large number of volunteers and the impact it makes on the media encourage the insurgents to utilize suicide bombers. The insurgents are aware of the Western societies' sensitivity to human lives and their fragile home fronts. Similarly, the insurgents' focus on media and propaganda aims to challenge the legitimacy of Western military operations. Overall, the insurgents depend on attrition while the technologically superior states with their armies geared for high-intensity conventional warfare need a clear-cut victory in a quick war. Organizationally also, the insurgents radically restructured themselves. This is most evident in the case of Al-Qaeda. The latter with global aspirations is characterized by decentralized structure rather than a clear-cut chain of command.[94]

Credit is due to Brun for turning the limelight away from the governments and armies of the states to their opponents. Many of the characteristics which Brun cites about O-RMA, like attrition and the role of ideology, were present in the Maoist guerrilla warfare of mid-twentieth century, and civilian casualties are a feature of terrorism. The only radical change in insurgency in twenty-first century is that the ideology of class war has been replaced by the ideology of Islamic fundamentalism. And, instead of creating an egalitarian socialist society, the goal of the insurgents is now to establish a sort of Islamic Caliphate. Even then, there are exceptions to the global rule. For instance, in Nepal, the *Maobadi*s inspired by Mao Tse-Tungs' ideology between 1996 and 2006 had conducted a classic Maoist guerrilla war. The Maobadis of Nepal had some 30,000 fighters and the 10-year-long conflict against the Royal Nepal Army and the armed police resulted in 13,000 deaths.[95] Rather than using the term O-RMA, which suggests that an RMA has occurred in case of the technologically strong industrial states in the late 1990s, the changing dynamics of insurgency from the late 1980s till the present date could be covered better by the term evolution. While Brun's perspective is somewhat marred by looking at insurgency as a systemic global struggle, others have focused more on the regional and local dimension of insurgency in the new millennium.

Some scholars hint that there is a distinct Afghan way of warfare. According to this view, throughout history, the Afghan sirdars lacked any coherent national vision and operated according to local, tribal and religious interests. Moreover, they change sides in accordance with the changing balance of power.[96] For instance, Mark Galeotti in the context of Afghan opposition to the Soviet invaders writes: '…a people for whom blood feud and banditry were a way of life…and for whom civil war was as much a national sport as *buzkashi*, their distinctive form of polo…'.[97] David Loyn rightly states that the terrain of Afghanistan throughout history is ideal for the insurgents to conduct unconventional warfare. However, as regards the motivation of the Afghan insurgents across history, Loyn blames lack of opportunities for economic upliftment and the slow development of the Afghans in the scale of civilization.[98] The linear relationship between economic underdevelopment and evolution of insurgency is a catch phrase for Marxist scholars like E.J. Hosbawm. And Loyn and Galleotti's characterization of Afghan's cultural attachment with the conduct of irregular warfare could be challenged by the liberal postmodernist scholars as an example of 'Oriental' scholarship, that is, the product of Orientalism.

Rob Johnson rightly states that Islam has been used selectively by the Afghans to justify and legitimize war. Islam can motivate but does not determine how or why Afghans fight. Johnson goes on to say that the Afghans are not culturally determined in their actions but are reactive and adaptive. Their operations are shaped and influenced by the cultural 'lens' but they are also pragmatic. For instance *Pukhtunwali/Pushtunwali* code can be adapted as well as rejected in accordance with the changing circumstances. Pragmatism, adaptability, and opportunism throughout history have shaped Afghan behaviour. Johnson concludes that the key point is that there is no single Afghan way of warfare in history. Rather, the Afghan response has been contextual.[99]

* * *

Global warfare in general and warfare in Afghanistan in particular, at present, represents continuity and change. The new millennium does not represent *stunde null* as far as warfare is concerned. It would be too early to say that the era of conventional war is over. The frequency and intensity of conventional wars are decreasing but they remain in the background. Probably, warfare now has entered two stages. First weak states fight a conventional war and when the state structure collapses, non-state actors take over. However, the second stage only comes after the conclusion of the first stage. For instance, after the collapse of the Taliban and the Saddam regime due to Western victory in conventional warfare, insurgency came up like a hydra-headed monster in Afghanistan and Iraq. It would be wrong to argue that the Afghans, throughout history, have only waged unconventional warfare successfully. When the Afghans were united under a strong centralized state structure (i.e., under Ahmad Shah Abdali in the late eighteenth century), the Afghans were able to conduct conventional warfare effectively. When the Afghan state was not very strong as during the First and Second Anglo-Afghan Wars (1838–42, 1879–1881), then they first resorted to conventional warfare, and after being defeated, they turned to unconventional warfare. When the Afghans were disunited due to disintegration of the state structure (i.e., Mughal–Safavid era and during the Soviet occupation), the only option for them was to wage unconventional warfare. The great power rivalries in Afghanistan resulted in a sort of civil war among the Afghans. The Afghans fought on either side, that is, both for and against the great powers. And self-interest demanded that instead of fighting to death, the Afghan war bands should desert the sinking ship and side with the victorious side. Nevertheless, it must be admitted that due to terrain, clan, and tribal structure, as well as the traditional cultural ethos of jihad, the Afghans were able to conduct unconventional warfare effectively. In case of Afghanistan, the amalgam of patriotism with Islamic ethos continues to generate a lethal compound which motivates the insurgents to a great degree. However, it would again be wrong to argue that only Islam or the unique culture of Afghanistan encourages insurgency. To give an example from the Western world, the insurgency in Spain and Italy against the Napoleonic empire, to a great extent, was encouraged by Christianity. For instance, Catholicism fuelled insurgency in Calabria in the Kingdom of Naples between 1806 and 1811. While the monasteries (like mosques in Afghanistan) provided refuge to the guerrillas, clergy-men frequently led the guerrilla bands.[100] So, religious motivation for rebelling is not unique to the Asians in general or Afghans in particular. Probably, the end of the twenty-first century will witness 'Unisols' and 'Terminators' supported by drones instead of American GIs fighting the insurgents in the barren desert and mountain peaks. Who will win the next round is yet to be seen.

NOTES

1. Clausewitz, Carl Von, *On War*, ed. and tr. by Michael Howard and Peter Paret (1976; reprint, Princeton: Princeton University Press 1984), 170.

2. Hew Strachan and Sibylle Scheipers, 'Introduction: The Changing Character of War', in Strachan and Scheipers (eds), *The Changing Character of War* (Oxford: Oxford University Press, 2011), 11.

3. Geoffrey Parker, *The Military Revolution: Military Innovation and the Rise of the West, 1500–1800* (Cambridge: Cambridge University Press, 1988).

4. Williamson Murray and MacGregor Knox, 'The Future behind Us', in MacGregor Knox and Williamson Murray (eds), *The Dynamics of Military Revolution: 1300–2050* (2001; reprint, Cambridge: Cambridge University Press, 2003), 177.

5. Jonathan B.A. Bailey, 'The First World War and the Birth of Modern Warfare', in Knox and Murray (eds), *The Dynamics of Military Revolution: 1300–2050*, 132–53.

6. Clifford J. Rogers, 'The Military Revolutions of the Hundred Years War', in Clifford J. Rogers (ed.), *The Military Revolution Debate: Readings of the Military Transformation of Early Modern Europe* (Boulder, San Francisco, and Oxford: Westview, 1995), 55–93.

7. Dennis E. Showalter, 'The Prusso-German RMA, 1840–1871', in Knox and Murray (eds), *The Dynamics of Military Revolution: 1300–2050*, 92–113.

8. Holger H. Herwig, 'The Battlefleet Revolution, 1885–1914', in Knox and Murray (eds), *The Dynamics of Military Revolution: 1300–2050*, 114–31.

9. Thomas G. Mahnken, 'Conclusion: The Diffusion of the Emerging Revolution in Military Affairs in Asia, A Preliminary Assessment', in Emily O. Goldman and Mahnken (eds), *The Information Revolution in Military Affairs in Asia* (Houndmills, Basingstoke: Palgrave, 2004), 211.

10. Williamson Murray and MacGregor Knox, 'Thinking about Revolutions in Warfare', in Knox and Murray (eds), *The Dynamics of Military Revolution: 1300–2050*, 2–3.

11. Colin S. Gray, *Strategy for Chaos: Revolutions in Military Affairs and the Evidence of History* (London: Frank Cass, 2002), 4, 46.

12. Strachan and Scheipers, 'Introduction', in Strachan and Scheipers (eds), *The Changing Character of War*, 11.

13. Colin S. Gray, *Another Bloody Century: Future Warfare* (2005; reprint, London: Phoenix, 2006), 24, 59, 214

14. Gray, *Another Bloody Century*, 219.

15. Stephen Biddle, *Afghanistan and the Future of Warfare: Implications for Army and Defence Policy* (2002; reprint, Honolulu: University Press of the Pacific, 2004), iv, vii.

16. Biddle, *Afghanistan and the Future of Warfare*, viii.

17. Stephen Biddle, *Military Power: Explaining Victory and Defeat in Modern Battle* (Princeton: Princeton University Press, 2004), 2–3.

18. Biddle, *Military Power*, 3–5, 7.

19. Biddle, *Afghanistan and the Future of Warfare*, ix.

20. Biddle, *Afghanistan and the Future of Warfare*, 7.

21. Stephen D. Biddle, 'Allies, Airpower, and Modern Warfare: The Afghan Model in Afghanistan and Iraq', *International Security*, 30, 3 (2005/2006): 164.

22. Biddle, 'Allies, Airpower, and Modern Warfare: The Afghan Model in Afghanistan and Iraq', 168–69.

23. Peter R. Mansoor, *Baghdad at Sunrise: A Brigade Commander's War in Iraq* (New Haven/London: Yale University Press, 2008), 342.

24. Mansoor, *Baghdad at Sunrise*, 342.

25. Emily O. Goldman, 'Introduction: Military Diffusion and Transformation', and Mahnken, 'Conclusion: The Diffusion of the Emerging Revolution in Military Affairs in Asia, A Preliminary Assessment', in Goldman and Mahnken (eds), *The Information Revolution in Military Affairs in Asia*, 10–11, 216–17.

26. Bruce Berkowitz, *The New Face of War: How War Will Be Fought in the 21st Century* (New York: Free Press, 2003), 1.

27. Berkowitz, *The New Face of War*, 1–3.

28. Martin Bayer, 'Virtual Violence and Real War: Playing War in Computer Games: The Battle with Reality', in Edward Halpin, Philippa Trevorrow, David Webb, and Steve Wright (eds), *Cyberwar, Netwar and the Revolution in Military Affairs* (Houndmills, Basingstoke: Palgrave, 2006), 13.

29. Bayer, 'Virtual Violence and Real War: Playing War in Computer Games: The Battle with Reality', in Halpin, Trevorrow, Webb, and Wright (eds), *Cyberwar, Netwar and the Revolution in Military Affairs*, 13.

30. Berkowitz, *The New Face of War*, 4.

31. Goldman, 'Introduction: Military Diffusion and Transformation', in Goldman and Mahnken (eds), *The Information Revolution in Military Affairs in Asia*, 1–8.

32. Gray, *Strategy for Chaos*, 7, 34; Murray, and Knox, 'The Future behind Us', in Knox and Murray (eds), *The Dynamics of Military Revolution*, 178.

33. Gray, *Strategy for Chaos*, 50.

34. Berkowitz, *The New Face of War*, 7.

35. Mansoor, *Baghdad at Sunrise*, 342–3.

36. Rupert Smith, *The Utility of Force: The Art of War in the Modern World* (2005; reprint, London: Penguin, 2006), 17, 180.

37. Martin Van Creveld, 'Technology and War II: Postmodern War?', in Charles Townshend (ed.), *The Oxford Illustrated History of Modern War* (Oxford: Oxford University Press, 1997), 298–314.

38. Mary Kaldor, *New and Old Wars: Organized Violence in a Global Era* (1999, DehraDun: Natraj, 2005), 1, 3.

39. Kaldor, *New and Old Wars*, 115.

40. Kaldor, *New and Old Wars*, 9–10.

41. Herfried Munkler, 'What Is Really New about the New Wars? A Reply to the Critics', in John Andreas Olsen (ed.), *On New Wars* (Oslo: Norwegian Institute for Defence Studies, 2007), 68–9.

42. Smith, *The Utility of Force*, 279.

43. Smith, *The Utility of Force*, 17, 269.

44. Mansoor, *Baghdad at Sunrise*, 342.

45. Alvin Toffler and Heidi Toffler, *War and Anti-War: Survival at the Dawn of the 21st Century* (1993; reprint, London: Warner, 1994).

46. Colonel Thomas X Hammes, *The Sling and the Stone: On War in the 21st Century* (St. Paul, MN: Zenith Press, 2006), 2.

47. Hammes, *The Sling and the Stone*, 159.

48. Hammes, *The Sling and the Stone*, 166.

49. Hammes, *The Sling and the Stone*, 167.

50. Isabelle Duyvesteyn and Mario Fumerton, 'Insurgency and Terrorism: Is there a Difference?', in Caroline Holmqvist-Jonsater and Christopher Coker (eds), *The Character of War in the 21st Century* (2010; reprint, London/New York: Routledge, 2011), 27–41.

51. The Bhagavad Gita, tr. from the Sanskrit with an Introduction by Juan Mascaro (London: Penguin, 1962), 12.

52. Robert M. Cassidy, *Counterinsurgency and the Global War on Terror: Military Culture and Irregular War* (Westport, Connecticut: Praeger, 2006), vii, 1.

53. Cassidy, *Counterinsurgency and the Global War on Terror*, 3.

54. Cassidy, *Counterinsurgency and the Global War on Terror*, 10–11.

55. Gil-li Vardi, 'The Change from Within', in Strachan and Scheipers (eds), *The Changing Character of War*, 86.

56. Antulio J. Echevarria II, 'American Strategic Culture: Problems and Prospects', in Strachan and Scheipers (eds), *The Changing Character of War*, 432.

57. Christopher Coker, *Waging War without Warriors? The Changing Culture of Military Conflict* (Boulder: Lynne Rienner, 2002), 2–3, 6–7.

58. Christopher Coker, *The Future of War: The Re-Enchantment of War in the Twenty-First Century* (Oxford: Blackwell, 2004), 49.

59. Coker, *The Future of War*, 74.

60. Coker, *The Future of War*, xiii, 85–6, 96.

61. Samuel P. Huntington, *The Clash of Civilizations and the Remaking of World Order* (1996; reprint, London: Penguin, 1997).

62. Echevarria II, 'American Strategic Culture: Problems and Prospects', in Strachan and Scheipers (eds), *The Changing Character of War*, 433.

63. Kaushik Roy, 'Just and Unjust War in Hindu Philosophy', *Journal of Military Ethics*, 6, 3 (2007): 232–45.

64. Geoffrey Parker (ed.), *The Cambridge Illustrated History of Warfare: The Triumph of the West* (Cambridge: Cambridge University Press, 1995); John Keegan, *A History of Warfare* (New York: Vintage Books, 1993); Victor Davis Hanson, *Warfare and Agriculture in Classical Greece* (Berkeley/Los Angeles: University of California Press, 1998); Victor Davis Hanson, *Carnage and Culture: Landmark Battles in the Rise of Western Power* (New York: Doubleday, 2001).

65. Kaushik Roy, 'Military Transformation in Eurasia: Technology and Techniques of Warfare from 1000 CE to 1850 CE', *Journal of the Asiatic Society*, 2 (2008): 101–16.

66. Hew Strachan, 'War and Strategy', in John Andreas Olsen (ed.), *On New Wars* (Oslo: Norwegian Institute for Defence Studies, 2007), 24.

67. Ivan Arreguin-Toft, *How the Weak Win Wars: A Theory of Asymmetric Conflict* (Cambridge: Cambridge University Press, 2005), 219, 221–2, 226–7.

68. Gray, *Another Bloody Century*, 223.

69. Theo J. Schulte, *The German Army and Nazi Policies in Occupied Russia* (Oxford/New York: Berg, 1989).

70. Ian F.W. Beckett, *Modern Insurgencies and Counter-Insurgencies: Guerrillas and their Opponents since 1750* (2001; reprint, London/New York: Routledge, 2005), 19–20, 42, 61–3.

71. Carl Van Dyke, 'Kabul to Grozny: A Critique of Soviet (Russian) Counter-Insurgency Doctrine', in Ian Beckett (ed.), *Modern Counter-Insurgency* (Aldershot: Ashgate, 2007), 472–4.

72. Dyke, 'Kabul to Grozny: A Critique of Soviet (Russian) Counter-Insurgency Doctrine', in Beckett (ed.), *Modern Counter-Insurgency*, 478–9.

73. Cassidy, *Counterinsurgency and the Global War on Terror*, 59–69; Dyke, 'Kabul to Grozny: A Critique of Soviet (Russian) Counter-Insurgency Doctrine', in Beckett (ed.), *Modern Counter-Insurgency*, 478–9.

74. HY S. Rothstein, *Afghanistan and the Troubled Future of Unconventional Warfare* (Annapolis, Maryland: Naval Institute Press, 2006), xiii–xiv, xvi, 19, 33.

75. Rothstein, *Afghanistan and the Troubled Future of Unconventional Warfare*, xv.

76. Rothstein, *Afghanistan and the Troubled Future of Unconventional Warfare*, 17.

77. Mark Moyar, *A Question of Command: Counterinsurgency from the Civil War to Iraq* (New Haven/London: Yale University Press, 2009), 199.

78. Moyar, *A Question of Command*, 199.

79. Rothstein, *Afghanistan and the Troubled Future of Unconventional Warfare*, 20, 26.

80. Warren Chin, 'Operation "Enduring Freedom": A Victory for a Conventional Force Fighting an Unconventional War', *Small Wars & Insurgencies*, 14, 1 (2003): 61.

81. Rune Henriksen, 'The Character of War and the Nature of Combat', in Holmqvist-Jonsater and Coker (eds), *The Character of War in the 21st Century*, 26.

82. Italics in original. David Kilcullen, *Counterinsurgency* (Oxford: Oxford University Press, 2010), 51.

83. Kilcullen, *Counterinsurgency*, 53, 55, 57.

84. Kilcullen, *Counterinsurgency*, 58.

85. Moyar, *A Question of Command*, 260.

86. Moyar, *A Question of Command*, 198–200.

87. Kaushik Roy, *The Oxford Companion to Modern Warfare in India: From the Eighteenth Century to Present Times* (New Delhi: Oxford University Press, 2009), 222–52; Kaushik Roy, *The Armed Forces of Independent India: 1947–2006* (New Delhi: Manohar, 2010), 194–235.

88. General Shankar Roychowdhury, *Officially at Peace: Reflections on the Army and its Role in Troubled Times* (New Delhi: Viking, 2002), 62.

89. *From Surprise to Reckoning: The Kargil Review Committee Report, 1999* (New Delhi: SAGE, 2000), 16–20.

90. Andrew Scobell, *China's Use of Military Force: Beyond the Great Wall and the Long March* (Cambridge: Cambridge University Press, 2003), 171–91.

91. Swaran Singh, 'China's Doctrine of Limited Hi-Tech War', in Jasjit Singh (ed.), *Asian Strategic Review: 1998–1999* (New Delhi: Institute for Defence Studies and Analyses, 1999), 333–50.

92. You Ji, 'Learning and Catching Up: China's Revolution in Military Affairs Initiative', in Goldman and Mahnken (eds), *The Information Revolution in Military Affairs in Asia*, 101.

93. Ji, 'Learning and Catching Up: China's Revolution in Military Affairs Initiative', and Andrew Nien-Dzu Yang, 'China's Revolution in Military Affairs: Rattling Mao's Army', in Goldman and Mahnken (eds), *The Information Revolution in Military Affairs in Asia*, 113, 129–36.

94. Brigadier-General Itai Brun, '"While You're Busy Making Other Plans"– The "Other RMA"', *Journal of Strategic Studies*, 33, 4 (2010): 535–65.

95. Kaushik Roy, 'Insurgencies, Counter-Insurgencies and State-building in Asia: A Comparative Analysis', in Swarupa Gupta (ed.), *Nationhood and Identity Movements in Asia: Colonial and Post-colonial Times* (New Delhi: Manohar in association with MAKAIS, 2012), 112.

96. Fotini Christia and Michael Semple, 'Flipping the Taliban: How to Win in Afghanistan', *Foreign Affairs* (July/August 2009): 35–6.

97. Mark Galeotti, *Afghanistan: The Soviet Union's Last War* (1995; reprint, London: Frank Cass, 2001), 4.

98. David Loyn, *In Afghanistan: Two Hundred Years of British, Russian and American Occupation* (New York: Palgrave Macmillan, 2009), 231.

99. Rob Johnson, *The Afghan Way of War: Culture and Pragmatism, A Critical History* (London: C. Hurst & Co., 2011), 36, 301, 305.

100. Beckett, *Modern Insurgencies and Counter-Insurgencies*, 206.

CONCLUSION

THE EVOLUTION OF INSURGENCIES AND counter-insurgencies reflect both continuity and change. The globalization of insurgency after 1945 was due to development of communication technology and use of media by the insurgents in a way undreamt by Ho Chi Minh and Mao Tse-Tung. The period between the end of World War II and the end of the Cold War witnessed insurgencies mainly fuelled by Marxist doctrines of economic exploitation. After the collapse of the USSR and decline of Marxism, the world is experiencing a throwback to insurgencies fuelled by religious and ethnic animosities as was the case in the nineteenth century. Both the British officers of the late nineteenth and early twentieth centuries, and the American military officers as well as civilian intellectuals of the early twenty-first century believed that *jihad* and *mullah*s are crucial components of Afghan mentality. This volume acts as a corrective because we have shown that even the Mughals, Safavids, and the Uzbeks, despite being Muslim themselves, faced tough opposition from the Afghans. This is not to argue that Islam had played no role in Afghan insurgency. Rather, the point we are trying to make is that Islam in general and jihad in particular are not always crucial components of Afghan opposition to external invaders in their homelands.

From the medieval era, the control for Afghanistan represented a sort of 'Great Game' for controlling the heart of Eurasia. From nineteenth century onwards, extra-Asian powers (like Britain) also participated in the Great Game. The USSR's involvement in Afghanistan during the 1980s was part of the same tradition of a great Eurasian power trying to control the 'hell on earth'. The active involvement of the USA in the new millennium in the Afghan 'problem' represented a change in one aspect. Like Britain of the nineteenth and early twentieth centuries, the USA of the late twentieth and early twenty-first centuries is an extra-Asian power. But, unlike Britain, thanks to modern technology, the USA does not maintain a permanent power base (i.e., a formal empire) in southern Asia for conducting warfare in Afghanistan. The extra-Asian powers have been dependent on Asian military manpower for projecting power in Afghanistan. The British relied on Indian and Indus tribes for manning the Indian army which was the principal instrument for projecting power in Afghanistan. Further, it must be accepted that the Mughals were more successful than the British in maintaining a permanent presence in Afghanistan. Moreover, the Mughals, unlike the British, used Afghanistan as a springboard for projecting power in Central Asia. At present, a certain section of US policy makers seems to be interested in such a goal. One of the permanently operating factors in Afghanistan's history is that if this country remains disunited, then it becomes the playground of various great powers. On the other hand, if Afghanistan is united, then the Afghans collectively pose a threat to the neighbouring countries.

The Mughals and the British realized, and Pakistan and India are now realizing, that border management of the frontier tribes is inseparable from the related and greater Afghan problem. Despite the passage of time and changes in military hardware, certain COIN techniques remain operational during the last five centuries. Both the Mughals and the British used subsidies to placate the Afghan tribes. When the subsidy amount was cut, rebellions broke out which in turn cost the imperial power much more. So, reduction of tribal subsidies proved to be a false economy. Further, both the imperial powers through limited military recruitment tried to co-opt the potentially rebellious manpower of Afghanistan. Nevertheless, with time, certain innovative COIN techniques also evolved. For instance, the Mughals, unlike the British, did not possess police and paramilitary units geared especially for specialized COIN duties.

The British experience during the three Afghan Wars was that it was easier to defeat the Afghan regular army in conventional battles and sieges but almost impossible to permanently subjugate the militias and the armed tribesmen who conducted hit-and-run attacks. In other words, it was easier to win the conventional campaigns in Afghanistan but extremely difficult to maintain a lasting peace. Both the British and the Mughals found out that it was logistically difficult and financially expensive to maintain a large force in Afghanistan for a long period. But fighting the dispersed groupings of armed Pathans to secure peace required the maintenance of a large force. The Americans would certainly agree with such views in the beginning of the new millennium.

From the time of Mughal invasion till Barak Obama's US Marines, Afghanistan is a case of failed state. For our period (1500–2013), a commonality behind the motivation for insurgency has been Islam, and mobilization and recruitment of the insurgents on the basis of tribal structure. However, there is also a sense of Afghan (mostly Pashtun) patriotism. Despite the Mughal rulers being Islamic, the Afghans strongly resisted them. A conventional military operation in Afghanistan is a sure recipe for disaster. Afghanistan is an irony also. If one intervenes, the invading power burns its fingers. And, if Afghanistan is neglected, then troubles from the Afghan border could spill over into the surrounding areas and contaminate it. Quarantine or blockade is no solution. However, the porous north-west Pakistan–southern Afghanistan border inhabited by the Pashtuns needs to be demilitarized. US should pressurize Islamabad to demilitarize the Waziristan region so that the Afghan insurgents cannot derive logistical support from north Pakistan. Military and economic aid to Pakistan should be tailored to this demand. The USA should also request India to guard the Pakistan–India border along Kashmir to prevent the insurgents on the run to take shelter in this region. And the Indian government for the sake of its own Kashmir problem should accede to such a request. For maintaining stability in Asia, a stable Afghanistan is a necessity. However, the Afghan state throughout history (except for a short spell under the Ghaznavids, Ghurids between ninth and eleventh centuries, and the Durranis under Ahmad Shah Abdali) has always been weak. It is a shadow state and a multilayered loose structure. The centre has always been weak and the periphery strong. Moreover, due to the politics of *fitna* (rebellion), the power structure at the periphery is always experiencing kaleidoscopic changes. Since Afghanistan is an economically deficit area, for controlling the dynamic military labour market, subsidies are necessary. Instead of the drug trade, an alternative avenue should be opened for the Afghan power elites. They should have a stake in the natural gas pipeline from Iran or Central Asia. Local strongmen (*amirs*, maliks, clan leaders, warlords) were paid subsidies by both the Mughals and the British. Some of the Afghan warlords with their armed clan members could be absorbed in the revitalized ANA and the ANP. These two formations should be trained and equipped by US and NATO officers and during operations in the sensitive areas, US–NATO contingents should be attached to them both to strengthen the Afghan forces and to prevent desertion among them. And this policy should work.

Establishment of stable local networks in Afghanistan depends on strong indigenous leaders and not on Communist stooges (like Najibullah) or CIA-Pakistan 'manufactured' leaders. A mechanical *divide et impera* strategy further fragments the Afghan polity and in the long run will backfire on the protagonists (CIA's 'blow back' effect). The present US policy of putting the armed Shia tribesmen against the Sunni Al-Qaeda tribes may bring some tactical dividends in the short run but will not result in demilitarized stable Iraqi society in the long run. A nationwide loose federal structure needs to be set up in Afghanistan. One technique for ensuing local security is the establishment of Village Defence Militia. The local leaders should be given a stake in the economic developments, for instance, revenues from the projected pipeline of natural gas from Central Asia. If US and NATO treat Afghanistan as a pawn in the New Great Game with a declining Russia and a resurgent China, then the present chaos will be followed by catastrophe.

The recent debate in military and academic circles about the conventional versus unconventional warfare reminds one of a somewhat similar debate which occurred in the 1950s. Then, scholars and military officers argued whether the advent of nukes have made conventional armies irrelevant or not. It would be too early to say that the era of conventional warfare is passé. Probably, the dynamics between conventional and unconventional warfare is changing. Despite the assertion of some theorists and military analysts, the non-state actors require latent or active support of a state. The non-state actors are supported financially and morally by the state, or are grown inside a state. The relationship between the insurgents and the body politic which spawns the former varies between that of a parasite to a symbiotic one (i.e., in case of Al-Qaeda and the Taliban in Afghanistan). And conventional warfare (as Biddle visualizes) is required to destroy the host. Then, COIN/unconventional warfare is required to destroy the insurgents and rebuild the state. And the COIN operations by US–NATO in Afghanistan could be taken as a microcosm of COIN operations undertaken by the militaries in the new millennium in various parts of the globe. To conclude, these COIN operations in general and COIN in Afghanistan represents a complex amalgam of new and old elements rather than a sort of 'New War'.

GLOSSARY

ahadis	infantry and cavalry recruited and paid directly by the Mughal emperor from the revenue of *khalisa* land (crown land). The *ahadis* constituted the standing army of the Mughal emperor which was different from the quasi-feudal contingents of the *mansabdars*.
alims	religious scholars
Al-Qaeda	literal meaning, the base. It is the name of a transnational Islamic terrorist organization.
altamash	advance guard of the Mughal army.
amir	ruler of Afghanistan. The status is below the title of *shah*. At times, *amir* also meant Muslim nobles and rulers.
amir-ul-umara	a senior Mughal *mansabdar*
ashrafi	gold coin of pre-British rulers. In the fourth decade of the nineteenth century, *ashrafi* was equivalent to 1 pound and 18 shilling.
bait	pledge/oath
bakshi	a person in charge of administration of the Mughal army
Baluch	An ethnic group of south-west Afghanistan and present-day Pakistan's Baluchistan who speaks Baluchi/Brahui

bania	middle-caste Hindu businessman
banjaras	semi-nomadic tribes who from the pre-modern era supplied the indigenous armies as well as the British forces in South Asia till the nineteenth century. They were grain merchants and carried grain for the soldiers and fodder for the animals on the back of bullocks and travelled with the armies. They sold provisions to the highest bidder and supplied the *bazaars* from where the soldiers brought provisions.
bank-bashi	treasury officer
bans	rockets. Also known as *hawais*. Gunpowder was filled in an iron tube which was attached to a bamboo shaft. Big rockets also weighed thirty pounds per piece. Lighter rockets comprised darts thrown from a tube with the aid of gunpowder. The rocket technology came to India probably from China.
bazaar	market
beg	subordinate tribal chieftain who also functioned as a high-ranking officer of the army
Blitzkrieg	lightning warfare; rapid strike by armour and air elements
burqa	veil which covers the face of a Muslim woman
buzkashi	an Afghan game in which many men mounted on horses competed among each other to get hold of a goat. One who gets the goat becomes the winner.
caliph	spiritual and temporal head of the Islamic *qaum*
chaudhuri	high-caste hereditary Hindu village headman
cheriks	horse-mounted guerrillas
crore	one crore is 100 lakhs or 10 million in the Indian context. A crore in Persia means 5 million.
daks	posts
dam	a currency used in Akbar's time
deeni madaris	Islamic religious institutions/seminaries for guiding and educating the *talibs*
durbar	court of a Muslim ruler

Dur-i-Durrani	pearl of pearls
faqir	a holy man with spiritual power and capable of supernatural deeds
faujdar	a Mughal official in charge of criminal administration of a region
*feranghi*s	literal meaning, Franks and foreigners. South Asians used this term to refer to the British.
fitna	rebellion; when a particular component of a system rebels against the whole, the term *fitna* could be applied
furlough	paid leave for the soldiers so that they could go back to their villages, meet their families, and participate in harvest
ghazi	fanatic Islamic tribesman who volunteers to fight the infidel in order to gain martyrdom
hadith	tradition; a gist of Muhammad's teachings, sayings, and deeds
hakim bakshi	chief physician
harem	imperial/royal household
hathnal	light-field gun carried on the back of an elephant. This was somewhat equivalent to *shutarnal* or *zamburak*.
Hazaras	an ethnic group of the Mongolian race living in central Afghanistan. Their language is Hazaragi, a dialect of Persian Dari and they follow the Shia faith.
Hindustan	the medieval Muslim intellectuals meant 'Land of the Hindus'. It also meant land east of the River Indus. Geographically, the term referred to north India.
hircarah bakshi	head of intelligence department
imam	a person who leads the prayer
inams	special rewards
ishikagzi bakshi	royal doorkeeper, actually master of ceremonies
jagir	a piece of land was assigned to a Mughal *mansabdar* (imperial official) temporarily so that he could maintain himself and his cavalry contingent from the revenue of that area

jagirdar	one who holds a *jagir*
jemadar	rank below *subedar*
jang salar	warlord
jezails	long-barreled muskets used by the Afghan tribesmen
jihad	Islamic holy war against the infidels to convert *dar al-harb* (house of darkness inhabited by the heathens) to *dar al-Islam* (house of light, i.e., land of pure inhabited by the true Muslims)
jihadi	Islamic warriors who conduct *jihad*
jirga	tribal assembly where the tribal elders take decision collectively
kafir	infidel; unbeliever
kalantar	administrator
karoh/kos	also known as *cos*. Mughal unit of measuring distance. One *karoh* is roughly equivalent to 1.5 to 2 miles.
Kazak	an ethnic group in north Afghanistan and they speak Kazaki/Ghazaki, similar to Turkmani
khail	clan
Khalsa	literal meaning, Sikh brotherhood. The Sikh kingdom established by Ranjit Singh was known as the Khalsa kingdom.
khasadar	a tribesman who was an auxiliary of the GOI. In return for maintaining law and order, he received a subsidy from the government.
khutba	public preaching; religious sermon in Islam, especially on Fridays
kilogram	an Indian unit of measuring weight. 1 kg = 2.2 pounds
lakh	traditional Indian unit meaning 100,000. In 1940, Rs 100,000 = 7,500 sterling pounds.
lashkar	a tribal war band
loya jirga	grand tribal assembly called during emergencies
madrasa	Islamic religious seminary
mahal	subdivision of *suba*
maharaja	literal meaning, king of kings, that is, equivalent to *shahenshah*. The former title is taken by big Hindu rulers.

Many *maharaja*s became high-ranking *mansabdar*s under the Great Mughals.

majun   opium

malik   a tribal elder or, occasionally, representative of the tribe. Each Pashtun clan has a number of *malik*s.

mansabdar a Mughal imperial official. *Mansabdar* means holder of *mansab* (i.e., a rank, an office) with a *jagir* attached to it. Generally, a *mansabdar* had to maintain a cavalry contingent for service with the Mughal emperor. The size of the cavalry contingent depended on the rank held by the *mansabdar*.

maund   Indian system of measuring weight. One *maund* is equivalent to eighty pounds or 37.5 kg.

mehtar   a Muslim ruler whose status was below the *amir*

mir akhur master of horses

mir bakshi a high-ranking *mansabdar* who functioned as supervisor of all the paymasters of the Mughal troops

misl   Sikh territorial band organized around a particular leader or family

mistry   Indian artisan or a worker in the factory

morchas   artillery batteries

mufti   a scholar who interprets Islamic laws

mujahideen warrior of Islam ready to lay down his life while fighting the *kafir*s

mullah   Muslim priest/village-level religious leader

munshi bakshi chief secretary

murid   disciple of a mullah

murshid   teacher

naib   deputy

naik   a rank below *havildar*

nawab   Muslim ruler

nawabi   realm of the independent Muslim ruler

Pandies   high-caste (Brahmins and Rajputs) recruits from Awadh and Bihar who joined the Bengal army in the first half of the nineteenth century

Parcham	a faction within the PDPA who mostly speak Dari
pasha	commander
Pathan	now called Pashtuns/Pushtuns. This ethnic group is dominant in Afghanistan and they inhabit south and east Afghanistan and speak Pashtu or Pushto.
Peshwa	Prime minister of the Maratha confederacy
pir	Muslim holy man with spiritual power
postheen	rough sheepskin coat of the Afghans
pugri	traditional headdress. It comprises a cloth folded over and wrapped around the head.
qaum	Islamic community
qazi	Muslim judge
quantou	fist units (strike units)
Rabi	time of the year when spring crops were sowed
Raj	British Government in India
raja	Hindu ruler/king. Many of them accepted *mansab*s from the Mughals.
resaidar	a VCO rank in the cavalry below the *subedar*
risala	cavalry squadron
Roh	this region extended from the environs of Herat in the west up to Sarohi and Brahoi in Baluchistan in the east. The inhabitants of this region were known as Rohillas and many of them settled into western part of north India during medieval time.
rupee	basic currency of India from pre-British era. In the Mughal empire, 4 *tanka* was equivalent to 1 rupee. In early nineteenth century, Rs 100 = 15 sterling pounds. In 1855, Rs 10 = 1 sterling pound and in 1899, Rs 15 = 1 sterling pound. One rupee comprises 100 paise or 16 *annas*. In 2013, Rs 100 = 1 sterling pound.
sangar	Afghan technique of fortifying the hilltops with stones and boulders
*sarwan*s	camel drivers
shaakha	branch
shah	king of Persia

shahadah	martyrdom in the cause of Islam
shahenshah	literal meaning is king of kings. This was an Achaemenid title and used by the big Persian rulers till the eighteenth century.
shahruki	1 *shahruki* in early sixteenth century was equivalent to 11 pence. This silver coin with distinctive Timurid and Uzbek calligraphic style originally circulated in Central Asia and was introduced in Afghanistan and north India by Babur. This coin was replaced by Akbar.
shura	assembly
sirdar	chieftain
sowar	horseman
Spetsnaz	Soviet special-purpose troops under the General Staff's Chief Intelligence Directorate (GRU)
suba	Mughal province
subadar	Mughal governor of a province
subedar	Indian commissioned officer in the British-led Indian army. Above *subedar* in hierarchy was the '*subedar*-major'. The equivalent ranks in the cavalry were *resaldar* and '*resaldar*-major'. Such officers were also known as Viceroy's Commissioned Officers. However, the senior most *subedar* was below the junior most British ensign/officer.
sunduktur bakshi	keeper of the wardrobe or keeper of the jewels
tanzim	Islamic militant organization
thana	police station
thanadar	an Indian official who was in charge of policing and head of *thana*
tariqa	path to real knowledge of God
ulama/ulema	Islamic scholar well versed in *Sharia*
Uzbek	an ethnic group who lives in Uzbekistan, north of Afghanistan
vilayat	principality/realm
wakil	diplomatic agents
waliahd	heir apparent

wazir	also known as *vizier*, which means principal minister of a Muslim monarch
Wehrmacht	armed forces of the Third Reich
yabu	Afghan pony
yasawal	orderly officer
yatims	light cavalry
zamburak	also known as *shutarnal*. It is a camel swivel gun. Two barrels were attached either to the back or sides of a camel and when the gun was fired, the camel had to kneel down. It was the Asiatic equivalent of Western horse artillery.

BIBLIOGRAPHY

ARCHIVAL SOURCES

Army Department Miscellaneous Proceedings, vol. no. 141, NAI, New Delhi.

Army Despatches to the Court, 1914, NAI.

Charles Wood Collection, MSS.EUR.F.78, IOR, BL, London.

Eleventh Fortnightly Report submitted by the Secy. of State for India covering the period 1st–15th February 1940, 17 February 1940, WP(40)62, CP, NMML, New Delhi.

First Fortnightly Report submitted by the Secy. of State for India covering the period up to 11 September, 12 September 1939, WP(39)5, CP, NMML, New Delhi.

Foreign Secret Proceedings, NAI.

George White Collection, MSS.EUR.F.108/24, IOR, BL.

Home Department, GOI, Police Branch, 1943, NAI.

John Lawrence Collection, MSS.EUR.F.90/60, IOR, BL.

Memorandum by the Secretary of State for India, 21 September 1939, WP(39)55, CP.

Memorandum on the Different Systems adopted on the North-Western Frontier for the Employment of Local Levies (Simla: Government Central Branch Press, 1888), MSS.EUR.F.163/7, IOR, BL.

Memorandum on the Size, Composition and Organization of the Military Forces in India, General Staff April 1920, Enclosure to Despatch No. 2, 24 June 1920, Army Department Miscellaneous, vol. no. 141, NAI.

Military Collection, Confidential Reports of the Regiments, L/MIL/7/17008, IOR, BL.

Notes and Minutes by Lord Napier of Magdala, Commander-in-Chief of Bombay, 1866–9, MSS.EUR.F114, IOR, BL.

Papers regarding British Relations with the Neighbouring Tribes on the North-West Frontier of India and Punjab Frontier Administration (London: HMSO, 1901), MSS.EUR.F.163/15, IOR, BL.

Proceedings of the Government of India, Malakand, 1897–8, S.No. 13, MD, NAI.

Proceedings, Supply and Transport, December 1879, MD, NAI.

Report of the Expert Committee on the Defence of India 1938–39, CAB/24/287, PRO, Kew, Surrey, UK.

Reports for the Month of March 1940 for the Dominions, India, Burma and the Colonies, Protectorates and Mandated Territories, 2 April 1940, WP(40)107, CP, NMML.

Reports for the Month of April 1940 for the Dominions, India, Burma and the Colonies, Protectorates and Mandated Territories, 3 May 1940, WP(40)137, CP, NMML.

Reports for the Month of May 1940 for the Dominions, India, Burma and the Colonies, Protectorates and Mandated Territories, 6 June 1940, WP(40)164, CP, NMML.

Reports for the Month of June 1940 for the Dominions, India, Burma and the Colonies, Protectorates and Mandated Territories, 19 July 1940, WP(40)181, CP.

Reports for the Month of May 1944 for the Dominions, India, Burma and the Colonies and Mandated Territories, 29 June 1944, War Cabinet Papers, WP(44)352, CP, NMML.

Reports for the Month of December 1944 for the Dominions, India, Burma and the Colonies and Mandated Territories, 31 January 1945, War Cabinet Papers, WP(45)74, CP, NMML.

Reports for the Month of January 1945 for the Dominions, India, Burma and the Colonies and Mandated Territories, 22 February 1945, War Cabinet Papers, WP(45)108, CP, NMML.

Roberts, General Frederick. *Correspondence with England while Commander-in-Chief in Madras: 1881–5* (Simla: Government Central Printing Office, 1890), L/MIL/17/5/1615, PT 2, IOR, BL.

———. *Correspondence with India while Commander-in-Chief in Madras: 26 November 1888–2 April 1893* (Simla: Government Central Printing Office, 1893), L/MIL/17/5/1615, PT 3, IOR, BL.

———. *Correspondence with the Viceroy of India (The Marquess of Lansdowne): 1885–8* (Calcutta: Superintendent of Government Printing, 1890), L/MIL/17/5/1615, Part 4, IOR, BL.

Roberts, General Frederick. *Short Report on Important Questions Dealt with during the Tenure of Commander of the Army in India* (Simla: Government Central Printing Office, 1893), L/MIL/17/5/1613, IOR, BL.

Secret, Appreciation of the attached Eastern Report No. 1, 11 January 1917, Eastern Report No. 1, 10 January 1917, 31 January 1917, 1 February 1917, CAB/24/143, PRO.

The Military Situation in India and the Middle East, Memorandum by General E.G. Barrow, Military Secretary, India Office, Committee of Imperial Defence, 24 November 1915, CAB/24/1, PRO.

Twelfth Fortnightly Report submitted by the Secretary of State for India covering the period 16 to 29 Feb. 1940, 4 March 1940, WP(40)80, CP.

Waziris, Description of the Various Sections of the Three Great Divisions of Waziris, No. 4, MSS.EUR.F.163/3, IOR, BL.

ARTICLES, BOOKS AND CHAPTERS IN EDITED VOLUMES

Ali, M. Athar. 'Jahangir and the Uzbeks', *Mughal India: Studies in Polity, Ideas, Society, and Culture.* New Delhi: Oxford University Press, 2006.

———. 'The Objectives behind the Mughal Expedition into Balkh and Badakshan, 1646–7', *Mughal India: Studies in Polity, Ideas, Society, and Culture.* New Delhi: Oxford University Press, 2006.

———. 'The Passing of the Empire: The Mughal Case', *Mughal India: Studies in Polity, Ideas, Society, and Culture.* New Delhi: Oxford University Press, 2006.

———. 'Recent Theories of Eighteenth Century India', *Mughal India: Studies in Polity, Ideas, Society, and Culture.* New Delhi: Oxford University Press, 2006.

Allen, Charles. *Soldier Sahibs: The Men Who Made the North-West Frontier.* London: John Murray, 2000.

Andrabi, Tahir, Jishnu Das, and Asim Ijaz Khwaja. 'Madrasa Statistics Don't Support the Myth', Shahzad Bashir and Robert D. Crews (eds), *Under the Drones: Modern Lives in the Afghanistan-Pakistan Borderlands.* Cambridge, Massachusetts/London: Harvard University Press, 2012.

Arreguin-Toft, Ivan. *How the Weak Win Wars: A Theory of Asymmetric Conflict.* Cambridge: Cambridge University Press, 2005.

Baev, Pavel K. *The Russian Army in a Time of Troubles.* London: SAGE, 1996.

Bailey, Jonathan B.A. 'The First World War and the Birth of Modern Warfare', MacGregor Knox and Williamson Murray (eds), *The Dynamics of Military Revolution: 1300–2050.* Cambridge: Cambridge University Press, 2003.

Barfield, Thomas. *Afghanistan: A Cultural and Political History*. Princeton/Oxford: Princeton University Press, 2010.

Barno, Lieutenant-General David W. 'Fighting "the Other War": Counter-Insurgency Strategy in Afghanistan, 2003–5', *Military Review*, vol. 87, no. 5, 2007.

Bayer, Martin. 'Virtual Violence and Real War: Playing War in Computer Games: The Battle with Reality', Edward Halpin, Philippa Trevorrow, David Webb, and Steve Wright (eds), *Cyberwar, Netwar and the Revolution in Military Affairs*. Houndmills, Basingstoke: Palgrave, 2006.

Beckett, Ian F.W. *Modern Insurgencies and Counter-Insurgencies: Guerrillas and Their Opponents since 1750*. 2001, reprint, London/New York: Routledge, 2005.

Bellew, H.W. 'A New Afghan Question', *Journal of the United Service Institution of India*, vol. 47, 1881.

Berkowitz, Bruce. *The New Face of War: How War Will Be Fought in the 21st Century*. New York: Free Press, 2003.

Biddle, Stephen. *Afghanistan and the Future of Warfare: Implications for Army and Defence Policy*. 2002, reprint, Honolulu: University Press of the Pacific, 2004.

————. *Military Power: Explaining Victory and Defeat in Modern Battle*. Princeton: Princeton University Press, 2004.

————. 'Allies, Airpower, and Modern Warfare: The Afghan Model in Afghanistan and Iraq', *International Security*, vol. 30, no. 3, 2005/2006.

Bilgrami, Fatima Zehra. 'The Mughal Annexation of Sind—A Diplomatic and Military History', Irfan Habib (ed.), *Akbar and His India*. 1997, reprint, New Delhi: Oxford University Press, 2002.

Bird, Tim, and Alex Marshall. *Afghanistan: How the West Lost its Way*. 2011, reprint, New Delhi: Orient Blackswan, 2012.

Braithwaite, Rodric. *Afghantsy: The Russians in Afghanistan, 1979–89*. 2011, reprint, London: Profile Books, 2012.

Brun, Brigadier-General Itai. '"While You're Busy Making Other Plans"—The "Other RMA"', *Journal of Strategic Studies*, vol. 33, no. 4, 2010.

Butalia, Brigadier R.C. *The Evolution of the Artillery in India: From the Battle of Plassey (1757) to the Revolt of 1857*. New Delhi: Allied Publishers, 1998.

Caroe, Olaf. *The Pathans: 550 BC–AD 1957*. London: Macmillan, 1958.

Caron, James. 'Taliban, Real and Imagined', Shahzad Bashir and Robert D. Crews (eds), *Under the Drones: Modern Lives in the Afghanistan-Pakistan Borderlands*. Cambridge, Massachusetts/London: Harvard University Press, 2012.

Cassidy, Robert M. *Counterinsurgency and the Global War on Terror: Military Culture and Irregular War*. Westport, Connecticut: Praeger, 2006.

Chandra, Satish. *Parties and Politics at the Mughal Court: 1707–40*. 1959, reprint, New Delhi: People's Publishing House, 1979.

Chandran, D. Suba. 'FATA and NWFP: Spreading Anarchy', D. Suba Chandran and P.R. Chari (eds), *Armed Conflicts in South Asia 2009: Continuing Violence, Failing Peace Processes*. New Delhi/Oxon: Routledge, 2010.

———. 'Armed Conflict in FATA and NWFP: Continuing Violence', D. Suba Chandran and P.R. Chari (eds), *Armed Conflicts in South Asia 2010: Growing Left Wing Extremism and Religious Violence*. New Delhi/Oxon: Routledge, 2011.

———. 'FATA & Khyber Pakhtunkhwa in 2011', D. Suba Chandran and P.R. Chari (eds), *Armed Conflicts in South Asia 2012: Uneasy Stasis and Fragile Peace*. New Delhi/Oxon: Routledge, 2013.

Chiarelli, Peter W. and Stephen M. Smith. 'Learning from Our Modern Wars: The Imperatives of Preparing for a Dangerous Future.' *Military Review*, Sept–Oct 2007, p. 5.

Chin, Warren. 'Operation "Enduring Freedom": A Victory for a Conventional Force Fighting an Unconventional War', *Small Wars & Insurgencies*, vol. 14, no. 1, 2003.

Christia, Fotini and Michael Semple. 'Flipping the Taliban: How to Win in Afghanistan', *Foreign Affairs*, July/August 2009.

Coker, Christopher. *Waging War without Warriors? The Changing Culture of Military Conflict*. Boulder: Lynne Rienner, 2002.

———. *The Future of War: The Re-Enchantment of War in the Twenty-First Century*. Oxford: Blackwell, 2004.

Cordovez, Diego and Selig S. Harrison. *Out of Afghanistan: The Inside Story of the Soviet Withdrawal*. New York/Oxford: Oxford University Press, 1995.

Creveld, Martin Van. 'Technology and War II: Postmodern War?', Charles Townshend (ed.), *The Oxford Illustrated History of Modern War*. Oxford/New York: Oxford University Press, 1997.

Dale, Stephen Frederick. 'Indo-Russian Trade in the Eighteenth Century', Sugata Bose (ed.), *South Asia and World Capitalism*. New Delhi: Oxford University Press, 1990.

———. *The Garden of the Eight Paradises: Babur and the Culture of Empire in Central Asia, Afghanistan and India (1483–1530)*. Leiden: E.J. Brill, 2004.

Devji, Faisal. 'Red Mosque', Shahzad Bashir and Robert D. Crews (eds), *Under the Drones: Modern Lives in the Afghanistan-Pakistan Borderlands*. Cambridge, Massachusetts/London: Harvard University Press, 2012.

Docherty, Paddy. *The Khyber Pass: A History of Empire and Invasion*. 2007, reprint, London: Faber and Faber, 2008.

Dorronsoro, Gilles. 'The Transformation of the Afghanistan-Pakistan Border', Shahzad Bashir and Robert D. Crews (ed.), *Under the Drones: Modern Lives in the Afghanistan-Pakistan Borderlands*. Cambridge, Massachusetts/London: Harvard University Press, 2012.

D'Souza, Shanthie Mariet. 'Afghanistan: Tipping Point', D. Suba Chandran and P.R. Chari (eds), *Armed Conflicts in South Asia 2009: Continuing Violence, Failing Peace Processes*. New Delhi/Oxon: Routledge, 2010.

———. 'Afghanistan: Turning the Tide', D. Suba Chandran and P.R. Chari (eds), *Armed Conflicts in South Asia 2010: Growing Left-Wing Extremism and Religious Violence*. New Delhi/Oxon: Routledge, 2011.

Duyvesteyn, Isabelle and Mario Fumerton. 'Insurgency and Terrorism: Is there a Difference?', Caroline Holmqvist-Jonsater and Christopher Coker (eds), *The Character of War in the 21st Century*. 2010, reprint, London/New York: Routledge, 2011.

Dyke, Carl Van. 'Kabul to Grozny: A Critique of Soviet (Russian) Counter-Insurgency Doctrine', Ian Beckett (ed.), *Modern Counter-Insurgency*. Aldershot: Ashgate, 2007.

Echevarria II, Antulio, J. 'American Strategic Culture: Problems and Prospects', Hew Strachan and Sibylle Scheipers (eds), *The Changing Character of War*. Oxford: Oxford University Press, 2011.

Elphinstone, M. *An Account of the Kingdom of Caubul, and its Dependencies, in Persia, Tartary, and India Comprising a View of the Afghan Nation and a History of the Dooraunee Monarchy*, 2 vols. London: Richard Bentley, 1842.

Ewans, Martin, *Securing the Indian Frontier in Central Asia: Confrontation and Negotiation, 1865–95*. London/New York: Routledge, 2010.

Farrell, Theo. 'Improving in War: Military Adaptation and the British in Helmand Province, Afghanistan, 2006–9', *Journal of Strategic Studies*, vol. 33, no. 4, 2010.

Feifer, Gregory. *The Great Gamble: The Soviet War in Afghanistan*. 2009, reprint, New York: Harper Perennial, 2010.

Fick, Nathaniel, C. John, A. Nagl, and General David H. Petraeus. 'How to Win a Losing War', *Foreign Policy*, vol. 170, 2009.

Fredericks, Pierce G. *The Sepoy and the Cossack*. London: W.H. Allen, 1972.

Friedman, George. *America's Secret War inside the Hidden Worldwide Struggle between the United States and its Enemies*. London: Abacus, 2004.

Gabriel, Richard A. and Paul L. Savage. *Crisis in Command: Mismanagement in the Army*. 1981, reprint, New Delhi: Himalayan Books, 1986.

Galbraith, John S. 'The "Turbulent Frontier" as a Factor in British Expansion', *Comparative Studies in Society and History*, vol. 2, no. 2, 1960.

Galeotti, Mark. *Afghanistan: The Soviet Union's Last War*. 1995; reprint, London: Frank Cass, 2001.

Giustozzi, Antonio. 'The Demodernization of an Army: Northern Afghanistan, 1992–2001', *Small Wars & Insurgencies*, vol. 15, no. 1, 2004.

———. 'Auxiliary Force or National Army? Afghanistan's "ANA" and the Counter-Insurgency Effort, 2002–6', *Small Wars & Insurgencies*, vol. 18, no. 1, 2007.

Giustozzi, Antonio. *Koran, Kalashinokov and Laptop: The Neo-Taliban Insurgency in Afghanistan*. London: Foundation Books, 2007.

———. *Empires of Mud: Wars and Warlords in Afghanistan*. London: C. Hurst & Co., 2009.

Goldman, Emily O. 'Introduction: Military Diffusion and Transformation', Emily O. Goldman and Thomas G. Mahnken (eds), *The Information Revolution in Military Affairs in Asia*. Houndmills, Basingstoke: Palgrave, 2004.

Gommans, Jos J.L., *The Rise of the Indo-Afghan Empire, c. 1710–1780*. Leiden: E.J. Brill, 1995.

Goodson, Larry, P. *Afghanistan's Endless War: State Failure, Regional Politics and the Rise of the Taliban*. Seattle/London: University of Washington Press, 2001.

Grau, Lester W. 'The Battle for Hill 3234: Last Ditch Defence in the Mountains of Afghanistan', *Journal of Slavic Military Studies*, vol. 24, no. 2, 2011.

Grau, Lester W. and Ali Ahmad Jalali. 'The Campaign for the Caves: The Battles for Zhawar in the Soviet-Afghan War', *Journal of Slavic Military Studies*, vol. 14, no. 3, 2001.

Gray, Colin S. *Strategy for Chaos: Revolutions in Military Affairs and the Evidence of History*. London: Frank Cass, 2002.

———. *Another Bloody Century: Future Warfare*. 2005; reprint, London: Phoenix, 2006.

Gupta, Hari Ram. *History of the Sikhs*, vol. 4, *The Sikh Commonwealth or the Rise and Fall of Sikh Misls*. New Delhi: Mushiram Manoharlal, 1982.

Haidar, Mansura. *Medieval Central Asia: Polity, Economy and Military Organization (Fourteenth to Sixteenth Centuries)*. New Delhi: Manohar, 2004.

Hammes, Colonel Thomas X. *The Sling and the Stone: On War in the 21st Century*. St Paul, MN: Zenith Press, 2006.

Hanifi, Shah Mahmoud. 'Quandaries of the Afghan Nation', Shahzad Bashir and Robert D. Crews (eds), *Under the Drones: Modern Lives in the Afghanistan-Pakistan Borderlands*. Cambridge Massachusetts/London: Harvard University Press, 2012.

Hanson, Victor Davis. *Warfare and Agriculture in Classical Greece*. Berkeley/Los Angeles: University of California Press, 1998.

———. *Carnage and Culture: Landmark Battles in the Rise of Western Power*. New York: Doubleday, 2001.

Haroon, Sana. 'The Rise of Deobandi Islam in the North-West Frontier Province and its Implications in Colonial India and Pakistan 1914–1996', *Journal of Royal Asiatic Society*, Series 3, vol. 18, no. 1, 2008.

———. 'Religious Revivalism across the Durand Line', Shahzad Bashir and Robert D. Crews (ed.), *Under the Drones: Modern Lives in the Afghanistan-Pakistan Borderlands*. Cambridge, Massachusetts/London: Harvard University Press, 2012.

Hashim, Ahmed S., *Insurgency and Counter-Insurgency in Iraq*. London: Hurst & Company, 2006.

Hauner, Milan L. 'Afghanistan between the Great Powers, 1938–45', *International Journal of Middle East Studies*, vol. 14, no. 4, 1982.

———. *The Soviet War in Afghanistan: Patterns of Russian Imperialism*. Lanham, Maryland: University Press of America in association with Foreign Policy Research Institute, 1991.

Heathcote, T.A. *The Indian Army: The Garrison of British Imperial India, 1822–1922*. London: David and Charles, 1974.

———. *The Afghan Wars: 1839–1919*. 1980; reprint, Gloucestershire: Spellmount, 2007.

Henriksen, Rune. 'The Character of War and the Nature of Combat', Caroline Holmqvist-Jonsater and Christopher Coker (eds), *The Character of War in the 21st Century*. 2010; reprint, London/New York: Routledge, 2011.

Holcomb, Major James F. 'Developments in Soviet Helicopter Tactics', Air Commodore E.S. Williams (ed.), *Soviet Air Power: Prospects for the Future*. London: Tri-Service Press, 1990.

Huntington, Samuel P. *The Clash of Civilizations and the Remaking of World Order*. 1996; reprint, London: Penguin, 1997.

Irvine, William. *Later Mughals*, 2 vols. Reprint, New Delhi: Taj Publication, 1989.

Ji, You. 'Learning and Catching Up: China's Revolution in Military Affairs Initiative', Emily O. Goldman and Thomas G. Mahnken (eds), *The Information Revolution in Military Affairs in Asia*. Houndmills, Basingstoke: Palgrave, 2004.

Johnson, Rob. '"Russians at the Gates of India"? Planning the Defence of India, 1885–1903', *Journal of Military History*, vol. 67, no. 3, 2003.

———. *The Afghan Way of War: Culture and Pragmatism, A Critical History*. London: C. Hurst & Co., 2011.

Jones, Seth G. *In the Graveyard of Empires: America's War in Afghanistan*. New York/London: W.W. Norton & Co., 2010.

Kakar, M. Hassan, *A Political and Diplomatic History of Afghanistan: 1863–1901*. Leiden: Brill, 2006.

Kaldor, Mary. *New and Old Wars: Organized Violence in a Global Era*. 1999; reprint, DehraDun: Natraj, 2005.

Keegan, John. *A History of Warfare*. New York: Vintage Books, 1993.

Keppel, Arnold. *Gun-Running and the Indian North-West Frontier*. 1911; reprint, Lahore: Sang-e-Meel, 2004.

Khan, Iqtidar Alam. *The Political Biography of a Mughal Noble: Munim Khan-i-Khanan, 1497–1575*. New Delhi: Munshiram Manoharlal, 1991.

Kilcullen, David. *Counterinsurgency*. Oxford: Oxford University Press, 2010.

Larsdotter, Kersti. 'Exploring the Utility of Armed Force in Peace Operations: German and British Approaches in Northern Afghanistan', *Small Wars & Insurgencies*, vol. 19, no. 3, 2008.

Lewis, Adrian, R. *The American Culture of War: The History of US Military Force from World War II to Operation Enduring Freedom*. 2007; reprint, Oxon/ New York: Routledge, 2012.

Loyn, David, *In Afghanistan: Two Hundred Years of British, Russian and American Occupation*. New York: Palgrave Macmillan, 2009.

Macgregor, Douglas A. *Breaking the Phalanx: A New Design for Landpower in the 21st Century*. Westport, Connecticut/London: Praeger, 1997.

Macrory, Patrick. *Kabul Catastrophe: The Story of the Disastrous Retreat from Kabul, 1842*. Oxford: Oxford University Press, 1986.

Mahnken, Thomas G. 'Conclusion: The Diffusion of the Emerging Revolution in Military Affairs in Asia, A Preliminary Assessment', Emily O. Goldman and Mahnken (eds), *The Information Revolution in Military Affairs in Asia*. Houndmills, Basingstoke: Palgrave, 2004.

Malevich, Lieutenant-Colonel John J. and Daryl C. Youngman. 'The Afghan Balance of Power and the Culture of Jihad', *Military Review*, May–June 2011.

Maley, William. *The Afghanistan Wars*. 2002, reprint, London: Palgrave Macmillan, 2009.

——— 'Afghanistan in 2011: Positioning for an Uncertain Future', *Asian Survey*, vol. 52, no. 1, 2012.

Maloney, Sean M., 'Conceptualizing the War in Afghanistan: Perceptions from the Front, 2001–2006', *Small Wars & Insurgencies*, vol. 18, no. 1, 2007.

Manuel, Anja, and P.W. Singer. 'A New Model Afghan Army', *Foreign Affairs*, vol. 81, no. 4, 2002.

Marston, Daniel. 'Lessons in 21st Century Counterinsurgency: Afghanistan 2001–7', Daniel Marston and Carter Malkasian (eds), *Counterinsurgency in Modern Warfare*. Oxford: Osprey, 2008.

Matinuddin, Kamal. *The Taliban Phenomenon: Afghanistan 1994–1997, With an Afterword Covering the Major Events since 1997*. 1999; reprint, Karachi: Oxford University Press, 2001.

Moreman, T.R. 'The Arms Trade and the North-West Frontier Pathan Tribes, 1890–1914', *Journal of Imperial and Commonwealth History*, vol. 22, no. 2, 1994.

———. *The Army in India and the Development of Frontier Warfare: 1849–1947*. Houndmills, Basingstoke: Macmillan, 1998.

Morris, Mowbray. *The First Afghan War*. London: Sampson Low, 1878.

Moyar, Mark. *A Question of Command: Counterinsurgency from the Civil War to Iraq*. New Haven/London: Yale University Press, 2009.

Munkler, Herfried. 'What Is Really New about the New Wars? A Reply to the Critics', John Andreas Olsen (ed.), *On New Wars*. Oslo: Norwegian Institute for Defence Studies, 2007.

Murray, Williamson and MacGregor Knox. 'Thinking about Revolutions in Warfare', MacGregor Knox and Williamson Murray (eds), *The Dynamics of Military Revolution: 1300–2050*. 2001; reprint, Cambridge: Cambridge University Press, 2003.

———. 'The Future behind Us', MacGregor Knox and Williamson Murray (eds), *The Dynamics of Military Revolution: 1300–2050*. 2001; reprint, Cambridge: Cambridge University Press, 2003.

Nawa, Fariba. 'Women and the Drug Trade in Afghanistan', Shahzad Bashir and Robert D. Crews (eds), *Under the Drones: Modern Lives in the Afghanistan-Pakistan Borderlands*. Cambridge, Massachusetts/London: Harvard University Press, 2012.

Newell, Nancy Peabody and Richard S. Newell. *The Struggle for Afghanistan*. Ithaca/London: Cornell University Press, 1981.

Noelle, Christine. *State and Tribe in Nineteenth-Century Afghanistan: The Reign of Amir Dost Muhammad Khan (1826–1863)*. 1997; reprint, Oxon/New York: Routledge, 2008.

Nojumi, Neamatollah. *The Rise of the Taliban in Afghanistan: Mass Mobilization, Civil War, and the Future of the Region*. New York: Palgrave, 2002.

O' Ballance, Edgar. *Afghan Wars: Battles in a Hostile Land 1839 to the Present*. 2002; reprint, Karachi: Oxford University Press, 2003.

O'Hanlon, Michael. 'Toward Reconciliation in Afghanistan', *The Washington Quarterly*, vol. 32, no. 2, 2009.

O'Neill, Mark A. 'Air Combat of the Periphery: The Soviet Air Force in Action during the Cold War, 1945–89', Robin Higham, John T. Greenwood, and Von Hardesty (eds), *Russian Aviation and Air Power in the Twentieth Century*. London: Frank Cass, 1998.

Orr, Allan. 'Recasting Afghan Strategy', *Small Wars & Insurgencies*, vol. 20, no. 1, 2009.

Parker, Geoffrey. *The Military Revolution: Military Innovation and the Rise of the West, 1500–1800*. Cambridge: Cambridge University Press, 1998.

——— (ed.). *The Cambridge Illustrated History of Warfare: The Triumph of the West*. Cambridge: Cambridge University Press, 1995.

Pawloski, Richard A. 'Lanes, Trains and Technology', Air Commodore E.S. Williams (ed.), *Soviet Air Power: Prospects for the Future*. London: Tri-Service Press, 1990.

Rashid, Ahmed. *Pakistan on the Brink: The Future of Pakistan, Afghanistan and the West*. London: Allen Lane, 2012.

Richards, John F. *The Mughal Empire, The New Cambridge History of India*, vol 1, no.5, 1993; reprint, New Delhi: Foundation Books, 2002.

Robson, Brian. *Crisis on the Frontier: The Third Afghan War and the Campaign in Waziristan, 1919–20*. Staplehurst: Spellmount, 2004.

Roe, Andrew M. *Waging War in Waziristan: The British Struggle in the Land of Bin Laden, 1849–1947*. Lawrence, Kansas: University Press of Kansas, 2010.

Rogers, Clifford J. 'The Military Revolutions of the Hundred Years War', Clifford J. Rogers (ed.), *The Military Revolution Debate: Readings of the Military Transformation of Early Modern Europe*. Boulder, San Francisco/Oxford: Westview, 1995.

Rothstein, HY S. *Afghanistan and the Troubled Future of Unconventional Warfare*. Annapolis, Maryland: Naval Institute Press, 2006.

Roy, Kaushik. 'Just and Unjust War in Hindu Philosophy', *Journal of Military Ethics*, vol. 6, no. 3, 2007.

——. 'Military Transformation in Eurasia: Technology and Techniques of Warfare from 1000 CE to 1850 CE', *Journal of the Asiatic Society*, vol. 50, no. 2, 2008.

——. *The Oxford Companion to Modern Warfare in India: From the Eighteenth Century to Present Times*. New Delhi: Oxford University Press, 2009.

——. *The Armed Forces of Independent India: 1947–2006*. New Delhi: Manohar, 2010.

——. 'Insurgencies, Counter-Insurgencies and State-building in Asia: A Comparative Analysis', Swarupa Gupta (ed.), *Nationhood and Identity Movements in Asia: Colonial and Post-colonial Times*. New Delhi: Manohar in association with MAKAIS, 2012.

Rubin, Barnett R. 'Political Elites in Afghanistan: Rentier State Building, Rentier State Wrecking', *International Journal of Middle East Studies*, vol. 24, no. 1, 1992.

——. *The Fragmentation of Afghanistan: State Formation and Collapse in the International System*. 1995; reprint, New Haven/London: Yale University Press, 2002.

Ruttig, Thomas. 'How Tribal Are the Taliban', Shahzad Bashir and Robert D. Crews (eds), *Under the Drones: Modern Lives in the Afghanistan–Pakistan Borderlands*. Cambridge, Massachusetts/London: Harvard University Press, 2012.

Safi, Mariam. 'Afghanistan in 2011', D. Suba Chandran and P.R. Chari (eds), *Armed Conflicts in South Asia 2012: Uneasy Stasis and Fragile Peace*. New Delhi/Oxon: Routledge, 2013.

Saxena, K.M.L. *The Military System of India: 1850–1900*. New Delhi: Sterling, 1974.

Schofield, Victoria. *Afghan Frontier: At the Crossroads of Conflict*. 2003; reprint, London: I.B. Tauris, 2010.

Schulte, Theo J. *The German Army and Nazi Policies in Occupied Russia*. Oxford/New York: Berg, 1989.

Scobell, Andrew. *China's Use of Military Force: Beyond the Great Wall and the Long March*. Cambridge: Cambridge University Press, 2003.

Shaikh, Farzana, 'Will Sufi Islam Save Pakistan?', Shahzad Bashir and Robert D. Crews (eds), *Under the Drones: Modern Lives in the Afghanistan-Pakistan Borderlands*. Cambridge Massachusetts/London: Harvard University Press, 2012.

Sharma, Raghav. 'Sectarian Violence in Pakistan', D. Suba Chandran and P.R. Chari (eds), *Armed Conflicts in South Asia 2009: Continuing Violence, Failing Peace Processes*. New Delhi/Oxon: Routledge, 2010.

Showalter, Dennis E.. 'The Prusso-German RMA, 1840–1871', MacGregor Knox and Williamson Murray (eds), *The Dynamics of Military Revolution: 1300–2050*. 2001, reprint, Cambridge: Cambridge University Press, 2003.

Singh, Khushwant. *A History of the Sikhs*, vol. 1, *1469–1839*. 1963; reprint, New Delhi: Oxford University Press, 1989.

Singh, Swaran. 'China's Doctrine of Limited Hi-Tech War', Jasjit Singh (ed.), *Asian Strategic Review: 1998–1999*. New Delhi: Institute for Defence Studies and Analyses, 1999.

Sinno, Abdulkader H. *Organizations at War in Afghanistan and Beyond*. Ithaca/London: Cornell University Press, 2008.

Smith, Chris. *India's Ad Hoc Arsenal: Direction or Drift in Defence Policy?* New York: Oxford University Press in association with SIPRI, 1994.

Smith, Rupert. *The Utility of Force: The Art of War in the Modern World*. 2005; reprint, London: Penguin, 2006.

Spencer, Emily and Bernd Horn. 'Introduction', Emily Spencer (ed.), *The Difficult War: Perspectives on Insurgency and Special Operations Forces*. Toronto: Dundurn, 2009.

Steinbach, Henry. *The Country of the Sikhs*. N.d., reprint, New Delhi: KLM Book House, 1977.

Stewart, Jules. *Crimson Snow: Britain's First Disaster in Afghanistan*. 2008; reprint, Stroud, Gloucestershire: History Press, 2010.

Strachan, Hew. 'War and Strategy', John Andreas Olsen (ed.), *On New Wars*. Oslo: Norwegian Institute for Defence Studies, 2007.

Strachan, Hew and Sibylle Scheipers. 'Introduction: The Changing Character of War', Strachan and Scheipers (eds), *The Changing Character of War*. Oxford: Oxford University Press, 2011.

Strausz-Hupe, Robert. 'The Anglo-Afghan War of 1919', *Military Affairs*, vol. 7, no. 2, 1943.

Sykes, Percy. *A History of Afghanistan*, 2 vols. 1940; reprint, New Delhi: Munshiram Manoharlal, 2002.

Tanner, Stephen. *Afghanistan: A Military History from Alexander the Great to the Fall of the Taliban*. New York: Da Capo Press, 2002.

Tarzi, Amin. 'Political Struggles over the Afghanistan-Pakistan Borderlands', Shahzad Bashir and Robert D. Crews (eds), *Under the Drones: Modern Lives in the Afghanistan–Pakistan Borderlands*. Cambridge Massachusetts/London: Harvard University Press, 2012.

Thornton, Rod. 'The British Army and the Origins of its Minimum Force Philosophy', *Small Wars & Insurgencies*, vol. 15, no. 1, 2004.

Toffler, Alvin and Heidi Toffler. *War and Anti-War: Survival at the Dawn of the 21st Century*. 1993; reprint, London: Warner, 1994.

Towle, Philip. 'Air Power in Afghanistan', Air Commodore E.S. Williams (ed.), *Soviet Air Power: Prospects for the Future*. London: Tri-Service Press, 1990.

Trench, Charles Chenevix. *The Frontier Scouts*. London: Jonathan Cape, 1985.

Tripodi, Christian. *Edge of Empire: The British Political Officer and Tribal Administration on the North-West Frontier, 1877–1947*. Surrey: Ashgate, 2011.

Vardi, Gil-li. 'The Change from Within', Hew Strachan and Sibylle Scheipers (eds), *The Changing Character of War*. Oxford: Oxford University Press, 2011.

Vivekanandan, Jayashree. *Interrogating International Relations: India's Strategic Practice and the Return of History*. London/New York/New Delhi: Routledge, 2011.

Warren, Alan. 'Bullocks Treading down Wasps? The British Indian Army in Waziristan in the 1930s', *South Asia*, vol. 19, no. 2, 1996.

———. *Waziristan: The Faqir of Ipi and the Indian Army, The North West Frontier Revolt of 1936–7*. Karachi: Oxford University Press, 2000.

Williams, Brian Glyn. 'Report from the Field: General Dostum and the Mazar-i-Sharif Campaign: New Light on the Role of Northern Alliance Warlords in Operation Enduring Freedom', *Small Wars & Insurgencies*, vol. 21, no. 4, 2010.

Yang, Andrew Nien-Dzu. 'China's Revolution in Military Affairs: Rattling Mao's Army', Emily O. Goldman and Thomas G. Mahnken (eds), *The Information Revolution in Military Affairs in Asia*. Houndmills, Basingstoke: Palgrave, 2004.

Yapp, M.E. 'Disturbances in Eastern Afghanistan, 1839–42', *Bulletin of the School of Oriental and African Studies*, vol. 25, no. 1/3, 1962.

Zaidi, Sunita. 'Akbar's Annexation of Sind—An Interpretation', Irfan Habib (ed.), *Akbar and His India*. 1997; reprint, New Delhi: Oxford University Press, 2002.

AUTOBIOGRAPHIES, JOURNALS, AND MEMOIRS

Atkinson, James. *Afghan Expedition: Notes and Sketches from the First British Afghan War of 1839–1840*. 1842; reprint, The Long Riders' Guild Press, 2007.

Barr, Lieutenant William. *Journal of a March from Delhi to Peshawar and from Thence to Kabul with the Mission of Lieutenant-Colonel C.M. Wade, Including*

Travels in the Punjab, a Visit to the city of Lahore and a Narrative of Operations in the Khyber Pass undertaken in 1839. 1844; reprint, New Delhi: Munshiram Manoharlal, 2003.

Corwin, Phillip. *Doomed in Afghanistan: A UN Officer's Memoir of the Fall of Kabul and Najibullah's Failed Escape, 1992.* New Brunswick, New Jersey: Rutgers University Press, 2003.

Docherty, Leo. *Desert of Death: A Soldier's Journey from Iraq to Afghanistan.* London: Faber and Faber, 2007.

Eyre, Lieutenant Vincent. *The Military Operations at Kabul: The Retreat and Destruction of the British Army, 1832.* 1843; reprint, Stroud, Gloucestershire: Nonsuch, 2005.

Farivar, Masood. *Confessions of a Mullah Warrior.* London: Atlantic Books, 2009.

Henniker, Lieutenant-Colonel M.C.A. *Memoirs of a Junior Officer.* Edinburgh/London: William Blackwood & Sons, 1951.

Lawrence, Lieutenant-General George. *Reminiscences of Forty-Three Years in India.* 1874; reprint, Lahore: Sang-e-Meel Publications, 1999.

Mansoor, Peter R. *Baghdad at Sunrise: A Brigade Commander's War in Iraq.* New Haven/London: Yale University Press, 2008.

Mitford, Major R.C.W. *To Cabul with the Cavalry Brigade: A Narrative of Personal Experiences with the Force under Lieutenant-General F.S. Roberts with Maps and Illustrations from Sketches by the Author.* N.d.; reprint, New Delhi: Bhavna Books and Prints, 2000.

Musharraf, Pervez. *In the Line of Fire: A Memoir.* New York: Free Press, 2006.

Roberts, Field-Marshal Lord, *Forty-One Years in India: From Subaltern to Commander-in-Chief.* 1897; reprint, New Delhi: Asian Educational Services, 2005.

Roychowdhury, General Shankar. *Officially at Peace: Reflections on the Army and its Role in Troubled Times.* New Delhi: Viking, 2002.

Sale, Lady Florentina. *A Journal of the First Afghan War,* Patrick Macrory (ed.). 1969; reprint, Oxford: Oxford University Press, 2002.

Talbot, Strobe. *Engaging India: Diplomacy, Democracy and the Bomb.* New Delhi: Viking, 2004.

Tootal, Colonel Stuart. *Danger Close: Commanding 3rd PARA in Afghanistan.* London: John Murray, 2009.

Yousaf, Mohammed and Mark Adkin. *The Battle for Afghanistan: The Soviets versus the Mujahideen during the 1980s.* 1992; reprint, Barnsley: Pen & Sword, 2001.

BIOGRAPHIES

Axworthy, Michael. *The Sword of Persia: Nader Shah from Tribal Warrior to Conquering Tyrant.* London/New York: I.B. Tauris, 2006.

Lal, Mohan. *Life of the Amir Dost Mohammaed Khan of Kabul with His Political Proceedings towards the English, Russian, and Persian Governments including the Victory and Disasters of the British Army in Afghanistan*, 2 vols. 1846; reprint, New Delhi: Asian Educational Services, 2004.

Lane-Poole, Stanley. *The Emperor Babur*. New Delhi: Sunita Publications, 1988.

Sarkar, Jadunath. *A Short History of Aurangzeb*. 1930; reprint, New Delhi: Orient Longman, 1979.

Singh, Ganda. *Ahmad Shah Durrani: Father of Modern Afghanistan*. Bombay: Asia Publishing House, 1959.

Smith, Vincent A. *Akbar the Great Mogul: 1542–1605*. N.d.; reprint, New Delhi: S. Chand, 1962.

Wink, Andre. *Akbar*. Oxford: Oneworld, 2009.

OFFICIAL AND QUASI-OFFICIAL PUBLICATIONS

A Different Kind of War: The United States Army in OPERATION ENDURING FREEDOM October 2001-September 2005, Donald P. Wright with the Contemporary Operations Study Team. Fort Leavenworth, Kansas: Combat Studies Institute Press, 2010.

Baumann, Robert F. *Russian-Soviet Unconventional Wars in the Caucasus, Central Asia, and Afghanistan*, Leavenworth Papers, No. 20. Fort Leavenworth, Kansas: Combat Studies Institute, 1993.

Bullock, Brigadier Humphry. *History of the Army Service Corps*, vol. 1, *1760–1857*. 1952; reprint, New Delhi: Sterling, 1976.

Frontier and Overseas Expeditions from India, vol. 3, *Baluchistan and the First Afghan War*. 1910; reprint, Quetta: Nisa Traders, 1979.

Grau, Lester W (ed.). *The Bear Went over the Mountain: Soviet Combat Tactics in Afghanistan*. 1996; reprint, London: Frank Cass, 1998.

Hensman, Howard. *The Afghan War of 1879–80*. 1881; reprint, Lahore: Sang-e-Meel Publications, 1999.

Jones, Seth G. *Counterinsurgency in Afghanistan*. Santa Monica, CA: RAND Corporation, 2008.

MacMunn, George. *Vignettes from Indian War*. 1901; reprint, New Delhi: Low Price Publications, 1993.

———. *The Armies of India*. 1911; reprint, New Delhi: Heritage Publishers, 1991.

———. *Afghanistan from Darius to Amanullah*. 1929; reprint, Lahore: Sang-e-Meel Publications, 2002.

Majumdar, Lieutenant-Colonel B.N. *History of the Army Service Corps*, vol. 2, *1858–1913*. New Delhi: Sterling, 1976.

———. *History of the Army Service Corps*, vol. 3, *1914–39*. New Delhi: Sterling, 1976.

Matthews, Matt M. 'We Have Not Learned How to Wage War There': The Soviet Approach in Afghanistan, 1979–89. Occasional Paper, No. 36. Fort Leavenworth, Kansas: Combat Studies Institute Press, 2011.

Molesworth, Lieutenant-General G.N. Afghanistan 1919: An Account of Operations in the Third Afghan War. Bombay: Asia Publishing House, 1962.

Mountcastle, Lieutenant-Colonel John C. 'Firefight above Gowardesh', Donald P. Wright (General Editor), Vanguard of Valour: Small Unit Actions in Afghanistan. Fort Leavenworth, Kansas: Combat Studies Institute Press, 2012.

Official History of Operations on the N.W. Frontier of India 1936–7. N.d.; reprint, Uckfield, East Sussex: Naval and Military Press, n.d.

Riedel, Bruce. Deadly Embrace: Pakistan, America, and the Future of the Global Jihad. New Delhi: HarperCollins, 2011.

Shadbolt, Sydney H. The Afghan Campaigns of 1878–1880 Compiled from Official and Private Sources. London: Sampson Low, Marston, 1882.

Singh, Jaswant. Defending India. Chennai: Macmillan, 1999.

Skeen, General Andrew. Passing It On: Short Talks on Tribal Fighting on the North-West Frontier of India. 1932; reprint, New Delhi: English Book Store, 1965.

The Second Afghan War: 1878–80, Compiled by Major-General Charles MacGregor and Revised by F.G. Cardew. Reprint, Rawalpindi: Army Education Directorate, 1975.

The Soviet-Afghan War: How a Superpower Fought and Lost, The Russian General Staff, tr. and ed. by Lester W. Grau and Michael A. Gress. Lawrence, Kansas: University Press of Kansas, 2002.

The Third Afghan War 1919 Official Account Compiled in the General Staff Branch, Army Headquarters India. Calcutta: Government of India, 1926.

Thompson, H.C. The Chitral Campaign: A Narrative of Events in Chitral, Swat, and Bajour. London: William Heinemann, 1895.

Wanat: Combat Action in Afghanistan, 2008, The Staff of the US Army Combat Studies Institute. Fort Leavenworth, Kansas: Combat Studies Institute Press, 2010.

Wills, Lieutenant-Colonel Craig D. Airpower, Afghanistan, and the Future of Warfare: An Alternative View, Cadre Paper, No. 25. Alabama: Air University Press, 2006.

ONLINE SOURCES

Afghan Resistance, by Gordon Negus, 5 Nov. 1982, Directorate for Research, S-26553/DB-2C, George Washington University, online archives, http://www.gwu.edu/~nsarchiv/NSAEBB/NSAEBB57/us1.pdf, accessed 20 Aug. 2011.

Memorandum, The Soviets and the Tribes of South-West Asia, 23 September 1980, Georgetown University online documents, http://www.gwu.edu/~nsarchiv/NSAEBB/NSAEBB57/us1.pdf, accessed on 20 Aug. 2011.

REPORTS

From Surprise to Reckoning: The Kargil Review Committee Report, 1999. New Delhi: SAGE, 2000.

Proceedings of the Army in India Committee, 1912, vol. 1-A, *Minority Report,* vol. 3, *Minutes of Evidence.* Simla: Government Central Branch Press, 1913.

TRANSLATED PRIMARY SOURCES

Babur-Nama (Memoirs of Babur). Translated from the Original Turki Text of Zahiruddin Muhammad Babur by A.S. Beveridge, 2 vols. Reprint, New Delhi: Saeed International, 1989.

Clausewitz, Carl Von. *On War.* Edited and translated by Michael Howard and Peter Paret. 1976; reprint, Princeton: Princeton University Press, 1984.

Fazl, Abul. *The Akbar Nama.* Translated from the Persian by H. Beveridge, 3 vols, 1902–39. Reprint, New Delhi: Saeed International, 1989.

Khan, Inayat. *The Shah Jahan Nama.* An Abridged History of the Mughal Emperor Shah Jahan, compiled by his Royal Librarian. Edited and completed by W.E. Begley and Z.A. Desai. New Delhi: Oxford University Press, 1990.

Khan, Saqi Mustad. *Maasir-i-Alamgiri.* Translated into English and annotated by Jadunath Sarkar. 1947; reprint, Calcutta: The Asiatic Society, 1990.

Khan, Zain. *Tabaqat-i-Baburi.* Translated by S. Hasan Askari, and annotated by, B.P. Ambastha. New Delhi: Idarah-i-Adabiyat-i-Delli, 1982.

Nagar, Ishwardas. *Futuhat-i Alamgiri.* Translated and edited by Tasneem Ahmad. New Delhi: Idarah-i-Adabiyat-i-Delli, 1978.

Roy, Nirodbhusan. *Niamatullah's History of the Afghans.* N.d.; reprint, Lahore: Sang-e-Meel Publishers, 2002.

The Bhagavad Gita, tr. from the Sanskrit with an introduction by Juan Mascaro. London: Penguin, 1962.

The Empire of the Great Mogul, De Laet's Description of India and Fragment of Indian History. Translated by J.S. Hoyland and annotated by S.N. Banerjee. 1928; reprint, New Delhi: Munshiram Manoharlal, 1974.

The History of India as Told by Its Own Historians: The Muslim Period, The Posthumous Papers of the Late H.M. Elliot, ed. and continued by John Dawson. 8 vols, 1876–1877. Reprint, Delhi: Low Price Publications, 2001.

The Jahangirnama: Memoirs of Jahangir, Emperor of India. Translated, edited, and annotated by Wheeler M. Thackston. New York: Oxford University Press in association with the Smithsonian Institution, Washington DC, 1999.

The Tezkereh Al Vakiyat or Private Memoirs of the Mughal Emperor Humayun, Written in Persian Language by Jouher. Translated by Major Charles Stewart. London: Oriental Translation Fund, 1832.

INDEX

ABOUT THE AUTHOR

Kaushik Roy is Guru Nanak Professor at the Department of History, Jadavpur University, Kolkata, India, and Global Fellow at Peace Research Institute Oslo (PRIO), Norway. Roy has done his PhD from the Centre for Historical Studies, Jawaharlal Nehru University, New Delhi. He was a Junior Fellow at Nehru Memorial Museum and Library from 2001 to 2004. Thereafter he joined Presidency College, Kolkata, as Lecturer and later served at Visva Bharati, Santiniketan, as Reader. In 2009, he joined the Department of History, Jadavpur University. In 2012, he was ICCR Visiting Professor to Aarhus University, Denmark. Roy has edited and published 22 books and written about 54 articles in various edited volumes and peer-reviewed journals like *Modern Asian Studies, Journal of Global History, Studies in History, Indian Economic and Social History Review, Journal of Military Ethics, War in History,* and *Journal of Military History.*